The Politics of Prostitution

Women's Movements, Democratic States and the Globalisation of Sex Commerce

The most effective way to deal with prostitution has always been hotly debated by governments and women's movements alike. Feminists want it abolished or regulated as sex work; governments have to safeguard public health and order. This book shows how women's movements in Western Europe, North America and Australia have affected policies on prostitution and trafficking of women since the 1970s, asking what made them successful in some countries but a failure in others. It also assesses whether government institutions to advance the status of women – so-called women's policy agencies – have played a key role in achieving policy outcomes favourable to movement demands. Written by an international team of experts and based on original sources, all chapters follow the same framework to ensure comparability. The final chapter offers an overall comparison identifying what makes women's movements successful and women's agencies effective, presenting the case for 'state feminism'.

JOYCE OUTSHOORN is Professor of Women's Studies at Leiden University. She has been active in the Dutch women's movement since its re-emergence in the late sixties, was co-editor of the Socialist Feminist Texts from 1977 until 1989, and has published extensively on the movement, women's public policy and abortion politics in both Dutch and English.

The Politics of Prostitution

Women's Movements, Democratic States and the Globalisation of Sex Commerce

Edited by

Joyce Outshoorn

Leiden University

CAMBRIDGE
UNIVERSITY PRESS

PUBLISHED BY THE PRESS SYNDICATE OF THE UNIVERSITY OF CAMBRIDGE
The Pitt Building, Trumpington Street, Cambridge, United Kingdom

CAMBRIDGE UNIVERSITY PRESS
The Edinburgh Building, Cambridge, CB2 2RU, UK
40 West 20th Street, New York, NY 10011-4211, USA
477 Williamstown Road, Port Melbourne, VIC 3207, Australia
Ruiz de Alarcón 13, 28014 Madrid, Spain
Dock House, The Waterfront, Cape Town 8001, South Africa

http://www.cambridge.org

© Cambridge University Press 2004

First published 2004

Printed in the United Kingdom at the University Press, Cambridge

Typeface Plantin 10/12 pt   *System* LATEX 2ε   [TB]

A catalogue record for this book is available from the British Library

Library of Congress Cataloguing in Publication data
The politics of prostitution : women's movements, democratic states, and the
globalisation of sex commerce / edited by Joyce Outshoorn.
    p.   cm.
Includes bibliographical references and index.
ISBN 0 521 83319 1 – ISBN 0 521 54069 0 (pbk.)
1. Prostitution – Government policy.   2. Prostitution – Political aspects.
3. Feminism.   4. Women's rights.   5. Prostitutes – Legal status, laws, etc.
6. Prostitues – Civil rights.   I. Outshoorn, Joyce.
HQ117.P65   2004
306.74–dc21   2003053196

ISBN 0 521 83319 1 hardback
ISBN 0 521 54069 0 paperback

Contents

Figures

Tables

Notes on contributors

DELILA AMIR is a sociologist at the Department of Sociology and Anthropology at Tel Aviv University. She received her Ph.D. from Pittsburgh University, USA. Her publications include *The Politics of Abortion* (Tel Aviv University, 1989); 'Defining Encounters: Who are the Women Entitled to Join the Israeli Collective', in *Women's Studies International Forum* (1997); *Abortion in Israel, from an International and a Feminist Perspective* (Hakibutz Hameuhad Publishers, forthcoming).

MENACHEM AMIR is Professor of Criminology at the Institute of Criminology, Hebrew University in Jerusalem. Among his major publications are *Patterns of Forcible Rape* (Chicago University Press, 1971); *Violence in School* (Hebrew University Press, 1987); and *Police Security and Democracy* (OICJ Press, 2001).

DANIELA DANNA is a research fellow in the Department of Political Science, University of Milan. She received her Ph.D. in Sociology and Social Research from the University of Trento, Italy, and the title of her dissertation was 'Policies about Prostitution in the European Union in the Nineties' (2000). She has worked as a journalist and has published *Amiche, compagne, amanti. Storia dell'amore tra donne* (Mondadori, 1994); *Matrimonio omosessuale* (Erre Emme Edizioni, 1997); and edited *'Io ho una bella figlia . . . Le madrilesbiche raccontano'* (Zoe, 1998).

ANNE MARIA HOLLI is Lecturer in Political Science at the University of Helsinki, Finland, where she received her Licentiate. Her recent publications include 'On Equality and Trojan Horses: the Challenges of the Finnish Experience to Feminist Theory', in *European Journal of Women's Studies* (1997); *Equal Democracies? Gender and Politics in the Nordic Countries* (co-edited with Bergqvist et al.) (Scandinavian University Press, 1999); and the chapter on Finland in *State Feminism, Women's Movements and Job Training: Making Democracies Work in the Global Economy*, edited by A. Mazur (Routledge, 2001).

LESLIE ANN JEFFREY is Assistant Professor at the University of New Brunswick in Saint John. She received her Ph.D. in Political Science from York University, Toronto. Recent publications include her book on prostitution policy in Thailand, *Sex and Borders: Gender, National Identity and Prostitution Policy in Thailand* (University of British Columbia Press, 2002); and '"Because They Want Nice Things": Prostitution, Consumerism and Culture in Thailand', in *Atlantis: a Women's Studies Journal* 26, 2 (Spring 2002).

JOHANNA KANTOLA is a research student at the University of Bristol. She has a Politics degree from the University of Birmingham. She is currently working on her Ph.D. dissertation on feminist discourses of the state. Her publications include 'Gender and the Discursive Construction of the Access to the State: a Comparative Study on Britain and Finland', in *Gender Comparisons,* edited by W. Kolbe and I. Rittendorfer (forthcoming).

AMY G. MAZUR is Associate Professor at the Department of Political Science/Criminal Justice Program, Washington State University, Pullman, USA. She received a joint Ph.D. in Political Science and French Studies from New York University. Her publications include *Comparative State Feminism* (co-edited with Dorothy McBride Stetson) (Sage, 1995); *Gender Bias and the State: Symbolic Reform at Work in Fifth Republic France* (Pittsburgh University Press, 1995); *State Feminism, Women's Movements and Job Training: Making Democracies Work in the Global Economy* (as editor) (Routledge, 2001); and *Theorizing Feminist Policy* (Oxford University Press, 2002). She is co-director of the Research Network on Gender Politics and the State.

JOYCE OUTSHOORN is Professor of Women's Studies at the University of Leiden and head of the Joke Smit Research Centre in Women's Studies; she is also affiliated to the Department of Political Science. Among her recent publications are 'Prostitution as Sex Work: the Pioneer Case of the Netherlands', in *Acta Politica* (2001); the chapter on the Netherlands in *Abortion Politics, Women's Movements and the Democratic State: a Comparative Study of State Feminism,* edited by D. McBride Stetson (Oxford University Press, 2001); 'Debating Prostitution in Parliament: a Feminist Analysis', in *European Journal of Women's Studies* (2001). She is co-director of the Research Network on Gender Politics and the State.

BIRGIT SAUER is Associate Professor of Political Science at the University of Vienna since 1996; she has a Ph.D. in Political Science from the Free University of Berlin. Recent publications include 'Normalized

Masculinities: Constructing Gender in Theories of Political Transition and Democratic Consolidation', in *Gender in Transition in Eastern and Central Europe*, edited by Gabriele Jähnert et al. (Trafo Verlag, 2000); 'Conceptualizing the German State: Putting Women's Politics in its Place', in *Handbook of Global Social Policy*, edited by S. S. Nagel and A. Robb (Marcel Dekker, 2000); and *Die Asche des Souveräns. Staat und Demokratie in der Geschlechterdebatte* (Campus Verlag, 2001).

JUDITH SQUIRES is Senior Lecturer in Politics at the University of Bristol; she has a Ph.D. from the University of London. Her publications include 'Women in Parliament: a Comparative Analysis' (co-authored with Mark Wickham-Jones) (Equal Opportunities Commission, 2001); *Gender in Political Theory* (Polity, 1999); and *Feminisms* (co-edited with Sandra Kemp) (Oxford University Press, 1997). She is convenor of the European Consortium of Political Research Standing Group on Women and Politics.

DOROTHY MCBRIDE STETSON is Professor of Political Science at Florida Atlantic University where she is a member of the Women's Studies Faculty. She is author of numerous articles and three books: *Women's Rights in France* (Greenwood Press, 1987); *Women's Rights in the USA* (Garland, 1991, 1997); and *A Women's Issue: Family Law Reform in England* (Greenwood Press, 1982). She has edited *Abortion Politics, Women's Movements and the Democratic State: a Comparative Study of State Feminism* (Oxford University Press, 2001); (with Marianne Githens) *Abortion Politics: Public Policy in Cross Cultural Perspective* (Routledge, 1996) and; (with Amy G. Mazur) *Comparative State Feminism* (Sage, 1995). She is co-director of the Research Network on Gender Politics and the State.

BARBARA SULLIVAN is Senior Lecturer in the School of Political Science and International Relations, University of Queensland, Australia. She has written extensively on the sex industry in Australia including a monograph *The Politics of Sex: Prostitution and Pornography in Australia since 1945* (Cambridge University Press, 1997). Other recent publications have addressed feminist approaches to prostitution, notions of consent, contract, Australian feminism and women's mental health.

YVONNE SVANSTRÖM is Assistant Professor at the Department for Economic History, University of Stockholm, where she obtained her Ph.D. in Economic History. Her dissertation was published as *Policing Public Women: the Regulation of Prostitution in Stockholm 1812–1880* (Arena/Akademi, 2000). Recent publications in English include '"The Main Source of Syphilis is Prostitution". Fallen Women and Prostitutes in Medical Discourse 1812–1875: the Case of Stockholm', in *Sex, State and Society: Comparative Perspectives on the History of Sexuality*, edited by Lars-Göran Tedebrandt (Almqvist & Wiksell International, 2000).

CELIA VALIENTE is Visiting Professor at the Department of Political Science and Sociology of the Universidad Carlos III de Madrid Spain. She has a Ph.D. in Sociology from the Universidad Autónoma de Madrid. Her publications include 'Implementing Women's Rights in Spain', in *Globalization, Gender and Religion: the Politics of Women's Rights in Catholic and Muslim Contexts*, edited by Jane H. Bayes and Nayereh Tohidi (Palgrave, 2001); 'The Value of an Educational Emphasis: Child Care and Restructuring in Spain since 1975', in *Child Care Policy at the Crossroads: Gender and Welfare State Restructuring*, edited by Sonya Michel and Rianne Mahon (Routledge, 2002); and the chapters on Spain in *Abortion Politics, Women's Movements and the Democratic State: a Comparative Study of State Feminism*, edited by Dorothy McBride Stetson (Oxford University Press, 2001) and in *State Feminism, Women's Movements and Job Training: Making Democracies Work in the Global Economy*, edited by Amy G. Mazur (Routledge, 2001).

Preface

This study of the politics of prostitution has emerged from the co-operation of scholars within the Research Network on Gender Politics and the State (RNGS) which set out to answer the perennial questions of feminist politics and social movements: do feminist politics make a difference, and can democratic states, still dominated by men and often denoted as patriarchal, actually be feminist? Do women's policy offices work? And how do women's movements actually contribute to the improvement of women's status? To look into prostitution as a political issue to research these questions seemed both an obvious and an unlikely choice. On the one hand, prostitution is mostly about women selling sexual services to men, a long-time concern for feminism as it mainly occurs within unequal relationships of power. On the other hand, prostitution is usually neglected by the mainstream of political science and policy studies that tend to regard the matter as a social or public health problem. Both aspects made it a challenging topic for analysing the question about the impact of women's movements in democratic states and the role of women's policy agencies within government in improving women's status.

The Research Network on Gender Politics and the State was founded in 1995 at Leiden University, the Netherlands, by a group of political scientists, sociologists and women's studies experts from both sides of the North Atlantic. Previously many of them had collaborated on the book *Comparative State Feminism*, edited by Dorothy McBride Stetson and Amy Mazur (Thousand Oaks: Sage, 1995), which had explored the role of women's policy agencies in equal opportunity policies in a number of advanced industrial democracies. Its outcome called for more extensive, in-depth research into the policies designed since the 1970s in democratic states to meet the challenge and demands of the fast-growing women's movement. In Leiden the first steps were taken towards developing a common design to analyse the impact of the women's movement and 'state feminism' systematically. An analytical framework was set up, and the decision was taken to study the major research questions in several issue areas, in order to prevent generalisation on the basis of just one or two issues. Prostitution was one of the issues selected.

From then on the common research design was developed and adjusted in a truly collaborative spirit. Conferences were held at the Annual Meeting of the American Political Science Association (APSA) in San Francisco in 1996 in a two-day Short Course/Workshop session, a two-day meeting at CREDEP, Université de Paris IX in 1998, an APSA panel on Comparative Politics in Boston that same year, a three-day conference at the University of Southampton/Chilworth Centre in 1999, a five-day workshop on The Politics of Prostitution during the annual Joint Sessions of Workshops of the European Consortium for Political Research (ECPR) in Copenhagen in 2000, a Short Course/Workshop on Comparative Politics at APSA in San Francisco in 2001, and a final two-day meeting at Queen's University, Belfast, in 2001.

At these meetings, all members contributed to refining the framework. In a continual dialogue, care was taken to ensure comparability between different nation-states, guarding against conceptual stretching and the denial of important cultural differences between states. Researchers, coming from sixteen different countries and deeply familiar with their native political system and women's movements, could continually check the appropriateness of the framework for their particular country. At each meeting, Dorothy Stetson and Amy Mazur, co-convenors of the RNGS, kept track of the debates and reworked the research design, which they then distributed to all members. In this way the project has become a truly cross-national study, providing well-grounded theory based on thorough and qualitative research in each country.

After its inception RNGS organised itself into country teams, with a country director recruiting scholars from her country for each issue area. Around each issue a network of researchers developed, studying the issue in a particular country; in due course the work was co-ordinated by an issue area director. Research on the prostitution issue started in 1999 at the Southampton/Chilworth meeting; draft papers were presented and discussed at the 2000 Copenhagen ECPR sessions, the 2001 San Francisco APSA meeting and the conference in Belfast of that same year. I was the network director for the prostitution issue, and took on the responsibility of planning the book, monitoring the progress of the study of each country, making sure the deadlines were met and authors observed the requirements of the framework of the project. I have also written the introduction to the book and the final chapter, in which I make the cross-case analysis and test the hypotheses of the project framework. Without the commitment, enthusiasm and hard work of all the authors, this book would not have materialised, and I want to thank all of our prostitution network for their co-operation: Delila Amir, Menachem Amir, Daniella Danna, Anne Maria Holli, Leslie Ann Jeffrey, Johanna Kantola, Amy Mazur, Birgit Sauer, Judith Squires, Dorothy McBride Stetson, Barbara Sullivan, Yvonne Svanström and Celia Valiente.

This book is the third study completed in the RNGS project. The first issue studied, job training, resulted in a book, *State Feminism, Women's Movements and Job Training: Making Democracies Work in a Global Economy*, edited by Amy Mazur and published in 2001. That same year *Abortion Politics, Women's Movements and the Democratic State: a Comparative Study of State Feminism*, edited by Dorothy McBride Stetson, was published on the abortion issue. In the next two years the books on the remaining issues, political representation of women, edited by Joni Lovenduski, and the 'hot issue' (focusing on a major issue in each country), edited by Birgit Sauer and Melissa Haussman, will be published.

Many people have made this study possible. Thanks go to the various institutions that supported our work financially in the course of the years – the US National Science Foundation grant for the 1995 Leiden meeting, the European Science Foundation grant for the 1999 Chilworth meeting and the American Political Science Association travel grants for European RNGS members to attend APSA meetings – and to the universities that hosted our meetings: Leiden University, the University of Paris-Dauphiné, the University of Southampton and Queen's University, Belfast. My personal thanks also go to Australian National University, Canberra, where I was a visiting fellow at the Research School for the Social Sciences in 2000, enabling me to plan the book and present some of the first findings; to Barbara Sullivan of the University of Queensland, Brisbane, for her comments at these presentations; to Jantine Oldersma, my fellow researcher in the RNGS project on the Netherlands and colleague at the Joke Smit Centre for Research in Women's Studies at Leiden University; to Willemijn Jansen and Kathleen Asjes, also of the Joke Smit Centre, for helping to prepare the manuscript. I am also very grateful for the critical but very helpful comments on the original manuscript made by the two anonymous reviewers of Cambridge University Press. Thanks, too, go to Sarah Caro and Alison Powell at Cambridge University Press for their work, and Carol Fellingham Webb for her copy-editing of the manuscript. Above all, I want to thank Amy Mazur and Dorothy McBride Stetson, not only for all the hard work they have put into the RNGS, but also for their support and friendship over the years.

Joyce Outshoorn
Leiden/Amsterdam

1 Introduction: prostitution, women's movements and democratic politics

Joyce Outshoorn

How have women's movements challenged states over the past thirty years to deal with women's status and make them incorporate women as political actors? How have states responded to the challenge posed by the rise of the 'second wave' of feminism? Women's movement activists demanded state measures on a broad and diverse set of issues, ranging from equal representation in political decision-making and anti-discrimination measures on the labour market to the combat of sexual violence and the right to abortion. Governments responded by developing a varied set of 'women's policy machineries' (UN 1993), institutions to deal with such demands, ranging from temporary committees to full-fledged permanent departments within the national bureaucracy. The research described in this book addresses the role of these institutions in advancing the goals of women's movements in a number of post-industrial democracies. It focuses on one of the issues which re-emerged as a feminist concern, prostitution, and it sets out to answer the question of whether these institutions, here termed 'women's policy agencies', have been effective in dealing with the issue.

In this way the book raises the larger issue of whether governments have actually improved women's status, promoted women's rights and reduced gender-hierarchies that are at the basis of the inequalities between women and men. It has always been an issue hotly debated by feminist activists and scholars alike: can the state be 'feminist'? Does the government have the capacity to act on behalf of a feminist agenda and redress sex inequality? Or is the agenda of women's movement activists inevitably rendered innocuous or 'perverted' when they choose to collaborate with the state (Hernes 1987; Franzway et al. 1989; Eisenstein 1990, 1996; Watson 1990; Sawer 1990; Outshoorn 1994, 1998a; Sawer and Groves 1994)? Social movement scholars similarly debate the question of how far democratic states can be transformed by social movements (e.g. Kriesi et al. 1995; McAdam et al. 1996; Tarrow 1998; Della Porta and Diani 1999). Do women's movements make democratic states, often criticised for not being inclusive of women's interests and women's participation (e.g. Pateman 1988; Phillips 1991, 1995), more democratic? From an earlier study on women's policy agencies it emerged that these can be important vehicles to movement goals, making the case for state feminism (Stetson and Mazur 1995). This study hopes to contribute to comparative social movement theory, comparative public policy and theories of democratic citizenship by a systematic and cross-national empirical study of prostitution politics in twelve countries.

The research presented here grew out of a collaborative project of the Research Network on Gender Politics and the State (RNGS).[1] Using the analytical framework developed by the network, the book explores the politics of prostitution in Australia, Austria, Britain, Canada, Finland, France, Israel, Italy, the Netherlands, Spain, Sweden and the United States, all Western political democracies. It does so in a longitudinal way, covering the women's movements and the issue since the early 1970s. It is also a comparative study of the policy debates on prostitution in these states. In an in-depth analysis of these debates, the researchers determine whether the women's policy agencies bring the prostitution issue into the policy arena and promote feminist framing(s), as well as enable women's movement actors to gain access to the policy arenas of the state. With this information, it becomes possible to sort out why some governments and their women's policy agencies are more responsive to women's movement demands than others, and when women's movements are likely to have success or not.

Prostitution as a political issue was selected for study as it touches on one of the key areas of the prevalent gender order, i.e. the norms, principles and policies informing the allocation of tasks, rights and life chances to women and men (Ostner and Lewis 1995: 169, n7). The gender order underpins major social institutions, such as the division of labour in the home and workplace, the organisation of human reproduction and sexuality, and citizenship rights. All of these are crucial aspects of women's lives and potential areas for gender conflicts. A basic tenet of RNGS is that the activities of the women's policy agencies and women's movements should be analysed in each of these issue areas to be able to arrive at reliable statements about the impact of the women's movement and the effectiveness of women's policy agencies.[2] Issues were selected with an eye to cross-national comparability and the capability of being both gendered and not gendered. Since women's policy agency effectiveness is determined in this study by their ability to bring gender ideas into the policy definitions in debates, issues must not be inherently gendered. It must be possible to discuss them without explicit reference to gendered characteristics of people. Following the original distinction made by Harding (1986) and Scott (1986) between gender – social and cultural meanings attached to biological sexual differences – and sex – biological differences between women and men – this study uses gender to refer to meanings or ideas that people attach to biological and demographic differences between them. Its empirical referents are ideas and meanings, different from the referents for the concept of sex (biological differences) and women (demographic characteristics) (RNGS 2002: 10).

Prostitution touches on sexuality. In everyday parlance it is defined as the exchange of sex or sexual services for money or other material benefits; in more academic terms it can be defined as a social institution which 'allows certain powers of command over one person's body to be exercised by another' (O'Connell Davidson 1998: 9). More specifically it involves sexual commands, which involves a wide array of practices ranging from oral sex and sexual intercourse to s/m and urolagnia. Most prostitution involves heterosexual sexual exchanges, with men buying the sexual services of women, within a set of social relations implying unequal power relationships between the sexes. It is also an institution that states have tried to control in many historical periods; today most states have some kind of prostitution policy, even if it is not always actively enforced.

The unequal gender order has been politicised by women's movements at various points in time, giving rise to gender conflicts which found their expression in the political arena. As political issues these may become defined or framed as gendered issues. Although many issues are gendered in explicit ways, policy actors can address and handle issues as if they affect men and women in the same way. Women's movements try to gender issues, or to change their gender content by inserting their own definitions into the debate. The prostitution issue, although nearly always involving heterosexual men buying sexual services from women, has often been defined in gender-neutral ways, such as moral depravity or a threat to public health. Women involved in prostitution debates have usually stressed the gender content and have sought to insert new gender meanings of women, men and sexual practices into the debates.

Theoretical background

The process of gendering, whereby phenomena such as identities, observations, entities and processes acquire meanings based on gender, is central to this study. This study assumes that politics and policy-making are always about a conflict of meanings (Schattschneider 1960: 68); issues only make it to the political agenda when they are defined in such a way that they merit government attention and survive the competition between issues about which are the most important ones for governments to address (Bachrach and Baratz 1970; Cobb and Elder 1972).

Problem definition is about allotting blame and responsibility: who is to blame for a problem, who has the say over it, and who has to solve it? It also determines the direction for the solution of the problem and who will gain control over the issue. A social movement is faced by the challenge of framing the issue in such a way that it advances its goals (Snow and Benford 1992). Its strategy involves inserting its framing into the policy debate in order to influence policy content and to gain access to policy-makers. In gender conflicts, women's movements try to gender the dominant frames of the contested issues and to insert feminist meanings so as to improve the position of women and ensure their participation in the political arena. Questions to be studied here regard whether the issue is defined as threat, injustice or harm to women and whether women are identified as interested parties. Who do they think is to blame for the situation, and what should be done about it?

Critiques of post-industrialist democracies have put into question the extent to which these can be seen as truly democratic, in the sense of not being inclusive of societal interests, thus questioning their representativeness (e.g. Inglehart 1990; Przeworski 1991; Mény 1992). Much empirical research has demonstrated the conspicuous under-representation of women in political and government institutions, which has only gradually improved over the past three decades (e.g. Lovenduski 1986; Norris 1987; Lovenduski and Norris 1993; Bergqvist et al. 1999). Feminist critiques of Western welfare states have also criticised the consistent under-representation of women's interests in welfare state arrangements showing how these institutionalised a male breadwinner–female housewife model, limiting a woman's access to the labour market and often entitling her to welfare benefits only through her husband (Orloff 1993; Sainsbury 1994, 1996; Ostner and Lewis 1995; Daly 2000).

To analyse representation, Pitkin's (1967) distinction between various types of representation is the starting point. For our purposes here, the relevant distinction is between descriptive and substantive representation. Descriptive representation occurs when a person stands in for others and shares the basic characteristics with them; it is about the actual representation of women. Social movements attempt to access the policy arenas and have their spokespeople included. This holds for the women's movement in a double sense: not only do women's interest groups aim for access, but they have always been in favour in the inclusion of women as a demographic category, with parity – equal representation of the sexes – as the ultimate goal. For other social movements the sex of the representative or spokesperson does not matter; for the women's movement it is pivotal. Substantive representation occurs when policy preferences are incorporated into the policy process, here defined as the demands of women's movement groups. Movement groups have always been interested in gaining substantive representation by gendering policy debates in ways compatible to their demands and in achieving policy satisfaction. This study examines whether women's policy agencies contribute to bringing ideas from women's movement groups into the policy debates on prostitution as well as aiding access of women advancing women's movement ideas into the policy process.

The researchers in this volume are well aware of the controversies over the definition of the women's movement. Many contemporary authors, to avoid the deep divisions in present-day feminism, will speak of 'women's movements'; by being inclusive they bypass the debate on what distinguishes these from the 'feminist movement'. Others, acknowledging different types of feminism, do make the distinction: women's movements can be based on other ideals than feminism. Generally speaking, there is a consensus in the literature that feminist movements' *raison d'être* is to improve the position of women in relation to men. Feminist movements organise around eliminating inequality of women or redressing the gender-hierarchy that favours men. Moreover, as Stetson and Mazur (2002: 8) have noted, 'women's movements' is awkward to use when describing research findings. It has proved hard to develop a definition or description that is applicable to cross-national, longitudinal comparative research (Molyneux 1998; Beckwith 2000; Stetson and Mazur 2002). Social movement literature provides little solution as there is no overall consensus on what a social movement is (e.g. Tarrow 1998; Della Porta and Diani 1999).

This study employs a somewhat minimal working definition. It is based on the distinction made by Mansbridge (1996) and Jenson (1996) between the processes of establishing discourses about collective identities and their interests, and the actors that present these discourses in public life. The women's movement produces a set of discourses, beliefs, and opinions and identities around women, but these concepts are hard to define operationally to make for observations that apply across countries and time. Stetson and Mazur point out, however, that the activities of actors who stand for the interests of the movement – derived from ideas developed by women about their identity and on how to improve their status – can be observed (Stetson and Mazur 2002: 15). The resurgence of feminism since the late 1960s produced a whole series of movement actors, such as groups, organisations, movements in institutions, platforms, networks or grass-roots movements. These actors can then stand for the women's movement, an empirical approach that was employed *de facto* in the two earlier studies of RNGS, on job training (Mazur 2001b) and on abortion politics (Stetson 2001a). In this volume the women's movement will be defined operationally in a similar way. Feminist movements are then a subset of women's movements; not all women's movements are feminist ones.

While strong women's movements emerged in nearly all the selected countries of this study in the 1970s and addressed a huge range of issues, prostitution was never high on the agenda of the majority until the mid-1980s. Activities remained limited to specific groups. In the late 1980s and the 1990s new discourses and feminist groups formed around the issue; many of these had a service nature, offering advice and support to women in the sex industry. The profound differences among feminists on the issue led to widely different political demands, ranging from the criminalisation of clients in Sweden and in Finland, to regulating prostitution as labour in New South Wales and Australian Capital Territory, and legalising brothels in the Netherlands. This makes assessment of movement success challenging: many Swedish and Dutch feminists, for example, have hailed the diametrically opposed changes in the prostitution laws of their respective countries as feminist successes, while Australian feminists view the decriminalisation in some of their states either as a serious setback or as an important step to improve prostitutes' rights.

Prostitution regimes

The states under study have widely diverging 'prostitution regimes', sets of laws and practices governing prostitution that shape prostitution in their respective jurisdictions in distinctive ways, and make for more or less repression of the women selling sexual services and the possible prosecution of other involved parties, such as clients, entrepreneurs of sex work facilities or pimps. These regimes have in turn been shaped by the outcome of previous political debates. Governments, at all levels, have always attempted to control prostitution and, depending on the dominant definition of the issue, have done so in different ways. The definition determined the goal of state intervention: to maintain law and order, preserve morals, prevent the spread of STDs or protect women from exploitation. It also determined in which political arena and policy (sub)system the politics of prostitution were fought, which actors were able to get in or were excluded, and what interest groups formed around the issue.

Prostitution was often perceived by many authorities as a law-and-order problem, a phenomenon giving rise to rowdiness and drunken behaviour, generally causing public nuisance in the surrounding neighbourhood and threatening a breach of the peace. Authorities usually undertook measures to control and contain prostitution by limiting it to certain areas, registering the women providing sexual services as prostitutes, and clamping down on the taverns, pubs and brothels when affairs got out of hand.

In the morality view, prostitution was a sin or a vice. Campaigners would hold sit-ins at brothels and admonish the men who entered the premises. The prostitutes – 'fallen women' – would be approached to be saved and redeemed. In the late nineteenth century both women and men were involved in fighting prostitution, inspired by biblical teachings and the feminism of the time. The women's organisations involved fought against the double standard of sexual morality, which allowed men sexual freedom at the expense of women, a form of sexual domination to be ended by making men just as chaste as women. A target of contention was also state regulation; the state, by facilitating prostitution, was a 'pimp' in their eyes. Their overall aim was to abolish prostitution altogether.

Prostitution was also defined as a major health hazard, where women were seen as sources of contamination, passing on syphilis or gonorrhoea to unsuspecting men. Many European states tried to control the spread of STDs in the nineteenth century, especially in garrison towns and naval bases, fearing the infection of its fit and fighting young men. It led to the regulation of prostitution, limiting it to certain areas or houses, and the control of prostitutes, who were registered by local authorities and were often obliged to undergo medical testing. It was the indignity of these examinations and the double standard implied in the regulation that sparked off a strong feminist movement in several countries from the 1860s, with the major goal of abolishing regulation and eliminating prostitution altogether (Walkowitz 1980b; Rosen 1982; Hobson 1987; de Vries 1997).

Abolitionism, the movement to eliminate prostitution, grew into a major international movement when the British and Continental Federation for the Abolition of Government Regulation of Vice was founded in 1875, renamed the Fédération Abolitioniste Internationale (FAI) in 1898 (de Vries 1997: 81). It succeeded, in alliance with many Christian-inspired groups, in putting the issue of trafficking in women for the purposes of prostitution on the international agenda. By the first decade of the twentieth century, most European states and the USA had done away with regulation, shutting down the '*maisons closes*', the brothels of the time, so the state no longer was an accomplice to 'vice'. After these reforms, prostitution ceased to be a major political issue in most states.

The FAI and its allies also made headway in the international arena and the first international agreement was reached in 1904 – the International Agreement for the Suppression of the White Slave Traffic. It was followed by the International Convention for the Suppression of the White Slave Traffic in 1910 (Mensenhandel 2002: 18–19). After the First World War the League of Nations continued along this track, passing two more conventions aimed at the trafficking of women and children: the International Convention to Combat the Traffic in Women and Children (1921) and the International Convention for the Suppression of the Traffic in Women of Full Age (1933). The 1933 Convention represented a shift from earlier agreements, as it criminalised 'procurement' for prostitution even if this occurred with the consent of the woman (Wijers 2001: 212). When in 1949 the UN passed the International Convention for the Suppression of the Traffic in Women, this shift was also incorporated, calling on all states to suppress trafficking as well as prostitution, regardless of the consent of the woman involved. The convention superseded the earlier international agreements and set the standard for the next decades, although many states did not ratify it, partly because of its abolitionist intent. It was never monitored properly.

The variation in prostitution regimes has provoked an often confusing terminology in the literature. Terms to characterise policy as regulation, prohibition or abolition abound in the literature, as do (de)criminalisation and legalisation, not always distinguishing precisely what activities or persons in prostitution are criminalised, controlled or permitted. Here abolitionism is taken to refer to the position that prostitution should be banned and third parties criminalised, with the prostitute herself not liable to state penalties. Prohibitionism makes all prostitution illegal and all parties liable to penalties, including the prostitute. Regulation is an overall term denoting state intervention in the running of prostitution. This may take place in a variety of ways, allowing brothels or red light zones, leading to different degrees of control over prostitutes, especially when compulsory STD testing or registration are required. In this volume researchers have aimed at describing the prostitution regimes in their countries in more precise ways and explaining what certain generic terms mean in their specific national contexts.

The revival of prostitution as a political issue

With the increase in international tourism and migration (Truong 1990), growing affluence and important changes in the sexual mores in the West since the mid-1970s, prostitution and the trafficking in women returned to the political agenda of most post-industrial democracies by the end of the 1970s. The process was accelerated by the emergence of AIDS in the mid-1980s, which gave rise to renewed worry about the health hazards of sex. Groups within the women's movement mobilised around prostitution and trafficking and sought to develop new definitions of the issues. This produced a novel framing to the many already circulating: prostitution came to be defined as work, or sexual service, an activity that women can take on to earn a living and therefore should be regulated in the same way as other types of labour. Moreover, probably for the first time, women in prostitution started to articulate a new public voice and formed their own interest groups, giving rise to a prostitutes' movement in many countries (Delacoste and Alexander 1987; Phetersen 1989; Jenness 1993; Kempadoo and Doezema 1998).

Prostitution is a specially interesting case for studying the relationship between the women's movement and women's policy agencies, as women's movements are deeply divided over the issue. Although theoretically as many as four positions can be distinguished in feminist debates on prostitution (e.g. Shrage 1994; Zatz 1997), the major divide is between those feminists defining prostitution as sexual domination and the essence of women's oppression (e.g. Barry 1979, 1995; Jeffreys 1997; Hughes and Roche 1999) and those who maintain prostitution is work that women can opt for, the sex work position (Pheterson 1989, 1996; Bell 1994; Chapkis 1997). The first position calls for the abolition of prostitution by penalising those who profit from it, except the prostitute. The second aims at legalisation, usually entailing removal of prohibitive articles in criminal codes, as well as some kind of regulation in order to normalise sex trade and guarantee prostitutes' rights. Movement groups adhering to either of these positions raise very different demands in the policy process and can place women's policy agencies in a quandary about which strategy to follow.

Moreover, this divide influences the way migration of women in sex commerce is viewed. 'Trafficking of women' emerged as a political issue in the 1880s, and was then called 'white slavery'. As it was defined in criminal law as the forced transfer of women across (inter)national borders for the purposes of prostitution, it was intrinsically linked to prostitution. This basic definition characterised all international conventions and treaties after 1904, culminating in the 1949 UN Convention. In the sexual domination view, trafficking of migrant sex workers is always seen as against their will; they are by definition victims of trafficking. The best way to fight trafficking is to abolish prostitution. For those adhering to the sex work position, women can be victims of trafficking, but not all women sex workers migrating are victims of forced prostitution. Many women migrate across borders and increasingly across continents to work in the sex industry to make a living. In this view, trafficking women for prostitution is perceived as undesirable only when a woman is trafficked and forced into prostitution against her will.

In recent years some feminists have attacked the concept of trafficking itself, pointing out that since prostitution is sex work, it should be regarded as forced labour or slavery, and fought as such (Bindman 1998; Doezema 1998; Murray 1998; Wijers 2001; Sullivan 2003). In this way trafficking is disconnected from prostitution and disappears as a separate offence. It is a move that de-genders, as the link to prostitution reminds us who is usually being trafficked for whom and to what purposes, but at the same time the move would make for more effective strategies against the practice.

The opposing views have led to two different transnational alliances against trafficking: the abolitionist US-run Coalition Against Trafficking in Women (CATW) (of which Kathleen Barry is one of the leaders) and the Global Alliance against Traffic in Women (Global Alliance), based in Thailand, which holds on to the distinction between forced and voluntary prostitution – sex work. It calls for decriminalisation of prostitution and the combat of trafficking and forced prostitution.

The international arena

With the growth of the international sex industry in the late seventies, debate at the supranational level of the UN returned. The loose and fragmented nature of UN institutions allows for constant lobbying by NGOs within the arenas covering human rights, women's rights, children's rights and slavery/forced labour. A wide range of interest groups, including the two major feminist alliances against trafficking, have been struggling to get their framing of the issues into various UN conventions, which, when ratified by member states, set the standard for the legislation at the national level. In the 1990s, UN declarations and conventions triggered new policy debates in the post-industrial states studied in this volume, not only about their ratification, but also when interest groups actively started using them to promote their framing of the issue. Not only women's movement organisations, but also children's rights groups and more traditional and religiously inspired groups against prostitution on moral grounds seized the opportunity to forward their agenda.

The 1979 Convention on the Elimination of All Forms of Discrimination Against Women (CEDAW) contains an article on prostitution calling on states to take measures 'to suppress all forms of traffic in women and the exploitation of prostitution'. According to accompanying documents this was not to be taken that prostitution *per se* should be combated (Wijers and Lap-Chew 1997: 24), but no definition was provided of 'exploitation'. In the 1980s and 1990s, the lobby of NGOs forming the Global Alliance started to attack the abolitionist discourse and try to insert the possibility of voluntary prostitution into the UN treaties. Against this move CATW started to press for a Convention Against Sexual Exploitation (Barry 1995: Appendix) and later, in a new coalition, the International Human Rights Network, for a new UN protocol on trafficking (Sullivan 2003). Its major aim was to prevent a distinction between trafficking and prostitution in the trafficking protocol on which the UN was working in the late nineties.

The first shift away from abolitionism was the Vienna Declaration on the elimination of violence against women (1993) and the UN Beijing Conference's *Platform for Action* (1995). The declaration condemns only forced prostitution and trafficking, but not prostitution *per se*; the *Platform for Action* calls for fighting forced prostitution. NGOs started to invoke human rights to combat trafficking. CATW regards prostitution itself as a violation of human rights, equivalent to slavery, and recently has aimed at including prostitution in the anti-slavery and forced labour conventions the UN has been preparing. The Global Alliance has been moving to the position of treating trafficked women as migrant labourers and having them protected by international labour legislation. At the UN level it works with the pro-sex work international sex workers' rights movement, despite the fact that the latter argues that the distinction between forced and voluntary prostitution is untenable, a cornerstone of Global Alliance policy (Doezema 1998).

In 2000, the UN Protocol on Trafficking was finally agreed, a comprehensive international attempt to stop trafficking. It defined trafficking as the recruitment and transfer of persons by means of the threat or use of force or coercion, fraud, deception or abuse of power for the purpose of exploitation. Exploitation includes the prostitution of others, sexual exploitation, forced labour or services, slavery, servitude or the removal of organs (Mensenhandel 2002: 44). The protocol requires state parties to penalise trafficking and to protect victims of trafficking and grant them temporary or permanent residence in the countries of destination. However, the definition allows for several interpretations. Some maintain the protocol holds that any migration that involves sex work now falls under trafficking and that all migrating sex workers will be treated as victims of trafficking. Others, such as the Global Alliance, hold that the protocol intentionally does not define 'the exploitation of prostitution of others or other forms of sexual exploitation', as there was no consensus among states on its definition (Sullivan 2003). The protocol is then interpreted as a departure from the 1949 Convention as it permits states to focus only on forced prostitution and to deal with all adult prostitution in other ways than abolition. Given this controversy, it remains to be seen whether the protocol will be an effective instrument against trafficking and forced labour. It is now in the process of ratification; all European states studied in this volume have already ratified, while the USA has refused to do so owing to its strained relations with the UN. For similar reasons, Australia delayed ratifying until December 2002.

The countries in the European Union also have to take into account EU legislation, but to date the EU record on the issues has not been impressive. Here again the controversy between abolitionism and the sex work position influenced events and resolutions. At first the European Parliament took the lead, passing its first resolution on the issue in 1989, which condemned both prostitution and trafficking (Wijers and Lap-Chew 1997: 25). Lobbying by feminists in the Council of Europe led to the commissioning of pioneer research into trafficking (Brussa 1991) and a seminar where trafficking and prostitution were separated as issues, enabling recommendations against trafficking and forced prostitution in 1997. However, the Council of Europe can only give recommendations that have no binding effects on member states.

Some feminist members of the Greens in the European Parliament then started pressing the EU to adopt a similar position. The barrier here, along with the disagreement about abolition, was the new Schengen agreement with its strict rules about entry into the EU. Trafficking tends to be submerged in issues of illegal migration and human smuggling. The European Commission split trafficking from prostitution in a communication on trafficking in 1996; in 1997 the Council of Ministers brought out a joint action on trafficking.[3] It obliged member states to penalise trafficking of persons, to pass measures to prosecute those profiting from trafficking and to confiscate their profits, and to support and protect victims of trafficking. Only Belgium, the Netherlands and Italy have passed measures on this last point.

However, these activities had little effect, so the European Commission brought out a proposal for a Council Framework on combating trafficking in human beings in 2001. One of the problems was to establish a common definition of the offence; the final draft is in line with the UN protocol of 2000.[4] The framework calls for states to penalise trafficking, to protect victims of trafficking and to develop a common policy against illegal migration. Recent EU policy on trafficking does not concern itself with prostitution *per se*, indicating that the tie between trafficking and prostitution has become tenuous in this arena as well. Despite lobbies to the contrary, prostitution policy is left to the individual states, which is also in line with the principle of subsidiarity as formulated in the treaties of Maastricht and Amsterdam. States can decide to retain an abolitionist regime, legalise prostitution and/or regulate it, depending on their national policy preferences.

Studying prostitution politics: the RNGS model

To analyse the research question regarding the extent to which and under what circumstances different kinds of women's policy agencies provide necessary and effective linkages for women's movements in achieving substantive and procedural responses from the state, members of the RNGS developed a model. In this model the impact of the women's movement is taken as the dependent variable, the degree of effectiveness of the women's policy agency activities and its institutional capacities as the intervening variables, and the characteristics of the women's movement and the policy environment as the independent variables. The question is ultimately to determine not only the effectiveness of women's policy agencies in promoting women's movement goals in policy debates,

Unit of Analysis: Policy Debate

INDEPENDENT VARIABLES

Women's movement characteristics
Stage
Closeness to left
Counter-movement
Issue priority
Cohesion

Policy environment
Policy subsystem:
        Structure (open, moderately closed, closed)
        Dominant approach fit (matching, compatible, incompatible)
Party/coalition in power

INTERVENING VARIABLES

Women's policy agency characteristics
Scope; type; proximity; administrative capacity; leadership; policy orientation

Women's policy agency activities
Insider, marginal, non-feminist, symbolic

DEPENDENT VARIABLE

Women's movement impact/state response
Dual response, co-optation, pre-emption, no response

Figure 1.1   RNGS model

but also when women's policy agencies are necessary allies inside the state to gain state responses that are favourable to women.

The model does not proceed from the conventional approach that focuses on nation-states, but takes policy debates as the point of departure. The unit of analysis is a policy debate that has led to some type of state action. The effect of movement activities on problem definition, policy content and the policy process in that debate is then analysed. This permits the longitudinal study of women's movement groups and state interactions, as well as analysis across issues and policy arenas within states. Differences between states then become a matter of empirical study, rather than an assumption of the model (RNGS 2002: 7).

The approach to the study

The approach to the research problem is that of the comparative method (Lijphart 1971, 1975; Collier 1991), which employs in-depth analysis of a small number of cases to determine whether there are general patterns of variation and explanation cross-nationally, and to account for differences in patterns. This case-oriented method is usually classified as a qualitative approach, in contrast to quantitative comparative approaches which use large numbers of cases to test general hypotheses. It was chosen because the research questions are best understood through 'close analysis of relatively few observations' (Collier 1991: 7). The method allows one to go beyond national case studies and use cross-national comparison of multiple cases by increasing the number of cases as a means to sort out rival explanations. RNGS takes a 'most similar systems approach' by looking at Western political democracies with similar levels of economic and political development and certain common cultural attributes.

The comparative method allows for a rich and detailed analysis of complicated processes with sufficient attention to different cultural contexts, which yields valid and reliable results. Often the criticism is levelled that this stands in the way of more rigorous and quantitative approaches that are said to allow for the development of theory and scientific progress. However, with King, Keohane and Verba (1994) the RNGS holds that by careful attention to research design and increasing the number of observations, a more qualitative comparative approach is fruitful for theory-building. Ultimately, all findings of the RNGS studies will be transposed into numerical quantitative form to allow for statistical analysis.

To maintain reliability and to avoid the problems of conceptual stretching, i.e. the over-extension of concepts to different cultural settings that can undermine the validity of the comparative method (Sartori 1970; Collier and Mahon 1993), the RNGS decided on intensive collaboration of the researchers at each step of the project: developing the research questions, identifying the key concepts and operationalising these, elaborating the research design, the gathering of the data, the analysis of the cases and the final comparative analysis. Researchers all employed the same worksheets to conduct the research and discussed their application to the empirical material (see Appendix 2 for the worksheets).

Applying the RNGS framework

Each researcher started the research by identifying the women's policy agencies in a political system since their instalment and determining the decisional systems – institutions – that make the most important laws on prostitution. The next step was to identify the policy debates on prostitutes, the central *unit of analysis* in the comparative study. A policy debate is the active consideration of proposals for prostitution policy by the relevant decision-makers. Each researcher compiled a list of the 'universe' of policy debates on the issue, including only those debates that (1) took place in a public arena such as the legislature, bureaucracy, courts or political parties, (2) ended in some kind of official 'output' such as legislation, government proposal, bill or report, court ruling or party policy proposal, and (3) were held when a women's policy agency existed – given the fact that the focus is on the potential intervention of the agencies. Debates can differ in length; the time frame was not a criterion for selection. The researcher then decided which three debates would be analysed as cases, taking into account the representativeness of the debate in terms of (1) decisional system importance, (2) life cycle of the issue, so that the selected debates cover the time frame of the prostitution issue in their country, and (3) salience: the selected debates must include the most important decisions on the topic. This process has produced thirty-six policy debates on prostitution, cases that are at the heart of this study. The time range ensures that all stages of the life cycle of the women's movement are covered, not just its period of emergence or growth. The process also solves the problem of the more static approach within the political process approach in social movement theory, where the concept of 'political opportunity structure' is used to analyse the political context (Kriesi et al. 1995; Tarrow 1998).

For each debate it was determined how the debate reached the public agenda, what frame dominated at that time and whether the debate was gendered. Researchers then analysed whether new gender meanings were introduced into the debate and which actors did this, and then described the outcome of the debate: a law, or report, or other kind of decision. At that point, it was determined what the impact of the women's movement was on the outcome, in terms of coinciding with their demands and women's participation in the debate. The impact is classified on a typology drawn from the work of Gamson (1975). It is based on two dimensions: looking at substantive responses – whether or not the state changes the policy to meet movement demands – and procedural acceptance – whether or not women's movement actors are accepted as legitimate representatives for movement interests. This variable is expanded to include the presence of individual women and constituencies who may forward women's issues along with organised women's groups (RNGS 2002: 8). The impact of the movement is then classified in terms of the four-fold typology. When the state accepts individual women, groups and/or constituencies into the process and changes policy to coincide with feminist goals, it is the case of *dual response*. When the state accepts women and women's groups into the process but does not give policy satisfaction, it is classified as *co-optation*. *Pre-emption* occurs when the state gives policy satisfaction but does not allow women, as individuals, groups or constituencies, into the process. Finally, when the state neither responds to movement demands nor allows women or women's groups into the process, there is *no response*.

		Policy coincides with movement goals	
		yes	no
Women involved in	yes	Dual response	Co-optation
policy process	no	Pre-emption	No response

Figure 1.2   Typology for women's movement impact and state response

The next step in the research is to examine the women's policy agencies and their activities and possible interventions in the debate. The agency (or agencies in some cases) is then described in terms of a number of characteristics: scope, type, proximity, administrative capacity, individual leadership and policy mandate. The assumption here is that these dimensions have the potential to allow the agency to enhance movement ideas, promote demands and facilitate movement actors in the policy process. Scope refers to the policy mission of the agency; some have a cross-sectional approach and others are single-issue agencies. Type refers to the form the agency takes; there is a large variety of structures such as commissions, departments, advisory councils and even ministries. Proximity refers to its location within the executive and the closeness to the major locus of power there. Administrative capacity refers to budgets, staff and period of mandate, which can be temporary or unlimited. The professional and political background of the leadership can also determine the activities of the agency on the issue. Some heads are feminist and have close ties to the movement. Finally, policy mandate and orientation determine the priorities of the agency and whether the prostitution issue fits these.

The debate is then classified according to agency activities within a four-fold typology based on two variables: (1) whether or not the agency is an advocate of women's movement goals in the policy process on the issue and (2) whether or not the agency was effective in changing the frame of the debate to these terms. When the agency incorporates the goals of the movement and is successful in gendering, i.e. inserting these gendered policy definitions into the dominant frame of the debate, it is classified as *insider*. If the agency asserts movement goals, but is not successful in gendering the policy debate, it is classified as *marginal*. When the agency is not an advocate for movement goals but genders or de-genders the debate in some other way, it is classified as *non-feminist*. Finally, when the agency neither is an advocate for movement goals nor genders the policy debate, it is classified as *symbolic*.

		WPA advocates movement goals	
		yes	no
WPA genders frame	yes	Insider	Non-feminist
of policy debate	no	Marginal	Symbolic

Figure 1.3   Typology for women's policy agencies

After the analysis of the women's policy agency, the women's movement actors are more closely examined in terms of attributes during the debate considered to be important for mobilising. Characteristics such as stage of development, closeness to the left, priority of the prostitution issue on the movement agenda, cohesion of the movement on the issue and the strength of a possible counter-movement were used to assess this first independent variable. Four stages of development, a combined measure of size, support and mobilisation (Rosenfeld and Ward 1996) are employed: emerging/re-emerging, growth, consolidation and decline/abeyance. Closeness to the left refers to movement ideology and organisational closeness to the parties and trade unions of the left. Cohesion is present when movement groups active on the issue agree on the frame of the debate and the policy proposal. Priority refers to the priority of the prostitution issue to overall movement concerns.

Finally, researchers looked into the policy environment as the other independent variable. It is analytically split into three aspects. Firstly, the policy subsystem in which the debate takes place is examined on its degree of open- or closed-ness. When its organisation is amorphous, with no formal rules or conventions and broad participation of varying interest groups and individuals, and no fixed power balance or chain of command, it is classified as open. It is classified as moderately closed when it shows some degree of organisation and regular actors, with shifting balances of power, with some free agents around. It is classified as closed when it is codified by regular meeting and rules, with limited participation of interest groups and free agents, and one major actor controlling the policy space and area. Secondly, the dominant approach to policy is compared with that of the women's movement. It can match that of the women's movement, be partly compatible or incompatible if totally at odds. Thirdly, the party or coalition in power, which can control the policy environment, is scored in terms of strong left-wing control, when left parties have the majority in the legislature or the executive, or moderate left-wing control, sharing power as in the case of coalition government or *cohabitation* (the left either has a majority in the legislature or holds the executive), or when the left is out of power (for a summary of the indicators, see Appendix 1).

In analysing the debates, the researchers have supplied evidence for their assessment of the dependent variables: women's movement impact and women's policy agency activities. All classifications have been checked by the editor to ensure their consistent measurement. In each debate researchers provide answers to the following research questions:

a To what extent is the policy debate defined in gendered terms when it is under consideration in the public arena?

b Did the women's policy agency adopt a strategy to change the frame by inserting references to gender? Did any other participant adopt a strategy to insert gendered concepts?

c Did the terms of debate change to reflect the strategy?

d Did the gender terms increase the significance of groups of women and those who speak for them in the policy arena?

e To what extent did the women's policy agency's activities in the policy debates facilitate participation by individual women, women's organisations and constituencies? (RNGS 2002: 21)

To enable overall comparison and test for the case of state feminism, a set of hypotheses has been developed from the model for empirical analysis:

H.1 Women's movements in democratic states have tended to be successful in increasing both substantive representation, as demonstrated by policy content, and descriptive representation, as demonstrated by women's participation in policy-making process, that is, dual response.

H.2 Women's movements in democratic states have tended to be more successful where women's policy agencies have acted as insiders in the policy-making process, that is, have gendered policy debates in ways that coincide with women's movement goals.

H.3 Women's policy agencies with greater administrative capability and institutional capacity, as defined by type, proximity and mandate, have been more effective than agencies with lesser administrative capacity in providing linkages between women's movements and policy-makers.

H.4 Variations in women's movements characteristics and/or policy environments explain variations in both women's policy agency effectiveness and movement success in increasing women's representation.

H.5 If women's policy agencies are necessary and effective linkages between movements and state responses, then variations in movement resources and policy environments will have no independent relationship to state responses (RNGS 2002: 13).

These hypotheses are examined in the final comparative chapter.

Organisation of the book

All chapters, ordered alphabetically by country name, follow the same format in the presentation of the research. The order is similar to the one outlined above: after a description of the historical background of prostitution and prostitution regime and of the decision-making system, the researcher presents the universe of policy debates and justifies the selection of the three major debates. For all three the dominant frame, the gendering and the outcome of the debate are described. The researcher then classifies the debate in terms of the variables of the framework – impact of the women's movement, women's policy agency activities, women's movement characteristics and the policy environment – and comes to a conclusion on the major question guiding this research: how far have women's policy agencies been effective in furthering movement activists' demands and ideas on the issue of prostitution?

The concluding chapter of the book analyses the findings of all country chapters, comparatively examining the hypotheses and answering the larger questions of whether, how and under what conditions women's policy agencies are able to help women's movements in their attempts to change their status and come to terms with the substantive representation of interests and the descriptive representation of women.

NOTES

1. All authors in this volume are members of the Research Network on Gender Politics and the State (RNGS) studying the impact of women's policy agencies on a range of issues and countries. The research design used in this study has been developed in intense co-operation between the RNGS members, at present with forty-five scholars from fifteen post-industrial democratic countries. This introductory chapter draws heavily on the RNGS project outline (2002), developed co-operatively by the members.

2. This volume is one of a series of five, each comprising the research on one issue from each key area: for human reproduction – abortion; for work and family – job training; for sexuality – prostitution; and political representation. Studies of a major national issue from the past decade selected in each country, the so-called 'hot issue', will comprise the fifth study, its leading question being how far the women's movement and women's policy agencies were able to (re)gender the debate. To date, two RNGS studies have been published: Mazur (2001a) on job training and Stetson (2001a) on abortion.

3. Joint Action of 24 February 1997, 97/154/JHA concerning action to combat trafficking in human beings and sexual exploitation of women.

4. Council Framework decision on combating trafficking in human beings – proposal by European Commission 2001 COM (2000)854/2-2001/0024. It was to have passed in 2002, but to date there is no agreement on the height of the penalties for trafficking (Mensenhandel 2002: 45).

2 The women's movement and prostitution politics in Australia

Barbara Sullivan

Introduction

Prostitution has been legalised[1] in several Australian states and territories during the past twenty-five years. Street walking or public soliciting for the purposes of prostitution is legal in New South Wales (NSW). Brothels and/or escort agencies may operate openly in Victoria, NSW, Queensland, the Northern Territory and the Australian Capital Territory (ACT). In most cases, brothel premises and the owners and operators of brothels (not workers) are subject to licensing[2] and sex workers employed in legal prostitution businesses have many of the same rights as other Australian workers (Sullivan 1997).

This trend towards the legalisation of prostitution in Australia makes it similar to the Netherlands but puts it at clear odds with countries such as Britain, Canada, the USA and France. Like other former British colonies, Australia's legal system was inherited from Britain. Thus, while the act of prostitution has never been illegal, until recently most prostitution-related activities – for example, keeping a brothel, soliciting for the purposes of prostitution and living on the earnings of prostitution – attracted criminal penalties. This is still the situation in the three 'unreformed' states of Western Australia, South Australia and Tasmania. However, in other Australian jurisdictions, the 'British' model of prostitution law started to change in the late 1970s and 1980s. This occurred in the wake of a number of different developments including the rise of the women's movement and of feminist demands that prostitute women not be subject to unsafe and discriminatory laws; the election of reforming Labor Party governments in several states; the impact of a (sexually) libertarian political culture in cities like Sydney; the appearance of new public concerns about the proliferation of visible prostitution; the rise of neo-liberal public policy approaches positing new regulatory agendas for 'rational' management, including in prostitution; and the impact of Australia's pragmatic, harm-minimisation approach to the management of HIV/AIDS (Sullivan 1997).

The aim of this chapter is to look at the influence of feminist voices and, in particular, women's policy agencies on Australian debates about prostitution law reform. I examine three debates about prostitution that took place in Australia in the period 1979–99, analysing the framing of the debates and the role of women's movements and women's policy mechanisms in producing change.

Selection of debates

There are three levels of government in Australia – federal, state/territory and local government. Historically, prostitution has fallen under the rubric of criminal law (determined by statute and case law rather than a Napoleonic criminal code). As criminal law is a responsibility of states and territories, it is at this level of government that the vast majority of decisions about prostitution law and policy are made. There are, however, some exceptions to this general rule. Over the past ten years local government has also become an actor in the arena of prostitution; in those states where brothels are legal, local government – via its jurisdiction over town planning and land use – has started to assume a significant role in the regulation of brothels (Harcourt 1999). Under some circumstances, the federal government may also act in relation to prostitution – for example, where Australia has international obligations under a United Nations convention.

The key decisions about prostitution law in Australia are made in two main places: in parliament and within political parties that hold government. At both federal and state level, the political party that holds a majority of seats in the lower (directly elected) house of parliament constitutes the government. This means that political parties holding a parliamentary majority are usually able to enact policy changes, including in the arena of prostitution. Two main political parties have held government in Australia over the past fifty years – the (conservative) Liberal Party of Australia and the (left-leaning) Australian Labor Party (ALP). The latter has been particularly important in initiating prostitution law reform in a number of jurisdictions. It has also been the party most closely associated with organised feminism; since the 1970s Australian feminists have had an active presence within the ALP and ALP governments have led the way in the establishment of various feminist reforms (such as anti-discrimination laws) and in the development of women's policy mechanisms (Watson 1990; Sawer 1990).

There have been a large number of official actions in Australia pertaining to prostitution (bills and statutes, failed and lapsed bills, court decisions, government reports, etc.) over the past fifty years. For the purposes of this chapter, a subset of these official actions was considered: a list was made of all significant parliamentary debates (that is, all those which led to actual changes in the law) about prostitution in the period 1979–2000.[3] From this subset, three debates were selected for intensive scrutiny. The first debate selected began in NSW in the late 1960s and ended in 1979 with the repeal of laws that prohibited public soliciting for the purposes of prostitution. The second debate began in Victoria in the late 1970s and ended with the legalisation of brothels in that state in 1984. The third debate began in the mid-1990s with rising concerns about trafficking for the purposes of prostitution; it ended in 1999 with the passage of new federal laws addressing slavery and sexual servitude.

The main reasons for selecting these debates were as follows. Firstly, all three debates represent important turning points in Australian law addressing prostitution, and are thus the most salient. The first debate was selected because it was the first significant departure from traditional British-style prostitution law in Australia. The changes enacted in NSW in 1979 clearly took new directions by removing long-standing laws that penalised street soliciting for the purposes of prostitution – the only occasion that an Australian jurisdiction has legalised public soliciting. The second debate was selected because it too represents a major departure from traditional or British prostitution law. By putting in place a system for the establishment of legal brothels, the government in Victoria significantly changed the direction of law that had (previously) penalised all those who owned, managed or worked in brothels. This 'model' was also introduced in Queensland. The third debate also marks an important moment in which the limits of employment in the legal prostitution industry are established; slavery and sexual servitude are not to be permitted.

The second main criterion used for selection of debates is their representativeness over time. The first debate examines changes in the late 1970s, the second debate looks at the mid-1980s and the third debate is located in the late 1990s. So debates over a period of twenty years are examined.

The third criterion used for selection of debates is their representativeness in terms of different levels of government (and thus of the main decision-making arenas). The first and second debates are located at the state level of government, while the third debate is located at the federal level.

Debate 1: The legalisation of street soliciting in the state of NSW, 1968–1979

How issue came to the public agenda

From at least 1968, NSW's prostitution laws were problematised by civil libertarians in Sydney. They argued for an end to the legal harassment of poor and working-class men and women via laws against vagrancy and prostitution (Sullivan 1997: 110). In the early 1970s this group was joined by sexual libertarians and feminists who argued that prostitution was a private matter between consenting adults and that prostitution laws were an illegitimate interference in individual freedom. They also represented prostitution as a 'victimless crime' which – like abortion and vagrancy – was best dealt with by repealing punitive and discriminatory laws. In the 1970s some Australian feminists also began arguing that prostitution should be treated as 'work' and prostitutes as 'sex workers' (Aitkin 1978). From this perspective, laws that punished women sex workers – while their male clients remained immune from prosecution – were clearly unjust.

In the mid- to late 1970s, feminist groups in Australia began to lobby strongly on the issue of prostitution law reform. In 1974 the National Conference of Australia's largest and most influential feminist lobby group, the Women's Electoral Lobby (WEL), passed a motion calling for the repeal of all laws pertaining to prostitution. In NSW in 1976, a reforming ALP government was elected to power and feminists were influential in persuading it to act in relation to prostitution. The NSW branch of the ALP was already committed to various social justice issues including the need to combat sex discrimination and to reform laws in the area of victimless crimes, especially vagrancy and prostitution. In 1976 a general meeting of the NSW branch of WEL called on the government to keep its election promises in relation to the 'decriminalisation' of victimless crime. Members of WEL lobbied individual members of the government, branches of the ALP and the ALP Women's Conference. In 1976 the NSW Labor Women's Committee resolved that 'prostitution is not an offence and should not in any legislation be regarded as other than acts between consenting adults' (cited in Women's Advisory Council Report, NSWPD Vol. 141: 30). In 1977 the (federal) Royal Commission on Human Relationships added weight to the reform campaign in NSW by recommending the repeal of most prostitution laws, including those that pertained to public soliciting, brothels and living on the earnings of the prostitution of another. The commission suggested that prostitution laws were required only to protect minors, to protect prostitutes from exploitation and coercion and to prevent public nuisance.

In April 1979 the government presented a large set of bills to the NSW parliament – the Cognate Summary Offences Bills. These sought to repeal a number of 'repressive' statutes including those that prohibited street demonstrations, public drunkenness, vagrancy, begging, busking (street performances), being a 'suspected person' and fortune telling. In relation to prostitution, the cognate bills aimed to abolish two offences – public soliciting for the purposes of prostitution and being a reputed prostitute on premises habitually used for prostitution. The offence of living on the earnings of the prostitution of another was retained and new provisions were also addressed to 'offences in public places'. So any public soliciting that was 'truly offensive', that caused serious alarm and affront to reasonable persons, could still be penalised. However, the offence here was a general one – that is, it applied to all people in public places and not just to prostitutes.

Dominant frame of debate

In parliament the dominant frame of the debate around the Cognate Summary Offences Bill was set by arguments about the need to restore civil liberties and an appropriate relationship between the law and public behaviour. For example, prohibitions on street demonstrations were deemed illegitimate because of the 'inherent right' that people had to assemble in public places. (This right was said to have been trampled on by previous conservative governments who had used the law to arrest demonstrators opposed to the war in Vietnam.) Laws against begging and vagrancy were also deemed harsh and 'inappropriate' because they were used to penalise those who were destitute or indigenous; this was now said to be a 'a totally unacceptable way of dealing with what is basically a social problem' (NSWPD Vol. 146: 4919). In relation to the prostitution aspects of the bill, the existing law was seen to perpetrate a specific injustice on women. The Attorney-General argued that laws against public soliciting and being a reputed prostitute on premises habitually used for prostitution were 'discriminatory'. In both cases 'the prostitute is fined; the client is not' (NSWPD Vol. 146: 4923). Members of the ALP identified former conservative governments as the main source of blame for this situation. Repeal of the offending law was represented as the best way to counter the injustice. Members of parliament – both men and women – argued that the current prostitution laws were 'discriminatory' and an example of a male 'chauvinistic double standard'.

Within the dominant frame of the debate other issues were raised. Prostitution was represented as a (non-gendered) 'victimless crime' and as a private sexual arrangement in which the state had no business to interfere. However, the government also argued that the bill would 'in no way . . . condone prostitution' because 'to society as a whole prostitution is not acceptable'; in the modern world, 'moral condemnation should not be synonymous with legal condemnation and this legislation will, quite rightly, leave the matter squarely with the individual to decide for himself or herself' (NSWPD Vol. 146: 4945).

Gendering the debate

As suggested above, much of the debate in parliament was conducted from a gendered perspective. Male parliamentarians – particularly members of the ALP – were the main ones to advance this position in the lower house of parliament. In the upper house, however, there were also women members who advanced specifically feminist arguments. For example, the Hon. Dorothy Isaksen (ALP) argued that there was nothing inherently offensive about prostitutes soliciting on the street. She said she had visited Kings Cross (a centre of prostitution in Sydney) and found that:

most of the girls were standing quietly in doorways, or leaning against the wall; I saw only four girls speak to or approach prospective customers. Many more men approached the girls and conversed with them. They then went quietly into a nearby hotel or residential. I considered some of the spruikers[4] outside the blue movies or kinky sex shops to be much more offensive. (NSWPD Vol. 146: 4846–8)

From Isaksen's perspective then, street soliciting by prostitutes should not automatically be regarded as offensive and outside the law. As feminists outside parliament argued, soliciting laws selectively punished women – particularly women who were classed as 'bad' and who represented the antithesis of heterosexual marriage norms – while men were not punished for the same behaviour. Isaksen said that soliciting laws were 'discriminatory, unjust and inviting (police) corruption' (NSWPD Vol. 146: 4846–8).

Policy outcome

The bill was approved by the NSW parliament and passed into law in 1979. However, the changes proved to be very controversial. There were complaints from residents about increasing street prostitution and from police that the new laws gave them insufficient power to act against offensive street prostitution. In 1983 the government acted to prohibit soliciting for the purposes of prostitution that was 'near' dwellings, schools, churches and hospitals. This clearly still allowed some room for legal soliciting.

Women's movement impact

The outcome of this debate represents a positive state response to the demands of the women's movement. The state accepted individual women and women's groups into the law reform process and changed the law to coincide with feminist goals. Thus, the impact of the women's movement on the state can be termed 'dual response' on this issue.

Women's policy agency activities

In 1977, under pressure from WEL, the new Labor government in NSW appointed a bureaucrat (and WEL member) as women's advisor to the Premier. This position later became the basis of the (bureaucratic) NSW Women's Co-ordination Unit. Following the Australian model for 'femocrat' reform of government (Sawer 1990: xvi), the NSW Women's Co-ordination Unit focused not on program implementation but on the development and co-ordination of mechanisms to integrate gender equity into all government activities and in all government departments. Thus, its scope should be seen as cross-sectional. The Women's Co-ordination Unit was located within the Premier's Department and thus had close proximity to at least one major centre of power. In 1978 this unit had six policy staff which suggests a moderate administrative capacity. As indicated above, leadership of the unit was feminist. Sawer (1990: 141) says that the influence of WEL was so strong that some saw the Women's Co-ordination Unit in its early days as 'more or less an extension of the WEL office'.

In 1976 the new Labor government also appointed a Women's Advisory Council to undertake public consultation with women in the broader community. The Women's Advisory Council was designed to assist and complement the work of the women's advisor and the Women's Co-ordination Unit. It was composed of non-bureaucrats, women appointed by the government and who had strong community links. Sawer (1990: 153) reports that the head of the Women's Co-ordination Unit, Carmel Niland, 'was able to use the newly appointed Women's Advisory Council to say things to government which she could not say in her bureaucratic position'.

It is certainly not clear what the views of Niland or the Women's Co-ordination Unit were on the prostitution issue. However, in its first report to the NSW parliament in 1978, the NSW Women's Advisory Council presented a position paper on prostitution. It called for the removal of laws against soliciting or loitering for the purposes of prostitution (as cited in NSWPD Vol. 146: 4847).

Taken together, the Women's Co-ordination Unit and the Women's Advisory Council acted as 'insider' agencies. The Women's Co-ordination Unit maintained strong links with WEL. The Women's Advisory Council visibly incorporated WEL and women's movement goals into its own position paper on prostitution law reform. This position paper was cited by politicians during the debate in parliament. Thus, to a significant degree, women's policy agencies were able to gender the dominant frame of the debate about prostitution law reform.

Women's movement characteristics

In the late 1970s the Australian women's movement was in a stage of significant growth (Watson 1990). It was divided into two main streams: the more radically oriented 'women's liberation' and a pragmatic/reformist stream represented by groups such as WEL. The latter orientation came to have a particularly significant impact on state policies and processes (Watson 1990). By the mid-1970s feminists in Australia were also forging strong links with the left-leaning political party, the ALP. Moreover, prostitution had started to become a moderate priority on feminist agendas (see above). The campaign for prostitution law reform was largely run by WEL (that is, there was no specific prostitution lobby group within the women's movement) and there was little in the way of a counter-movement.

Policy environment

The key turning point in the drive for prostitution law reform came in 1976 when a reforming ALP government was elected under the leadership of Neville Wran. This government had only a one-seat majority in the lower house of the NSW parliament and, in 1979, was probably concerned to move cautiously on the issue of prostitution law reform. It is clear that embedding prostitution law reform within a set of bills oriented around 'civil liberties' mobilised maximum support (both within the ALP and within the community more generally).

In general, the policy environment can be described as moderately closed; outsiders are not directly participating in the debate. However, the party in power (ALP) is left leaning and clearly sympathetic to women's movement demands. The dominant approach in parliament matches the positions adopted outside parliament by WEL and by the Women's Advisory Council.

Debate 2: The legalisation of brothels in the state of Victoria, 1984

How issue came to the public agenda

The debate about legal brothels in Victoria began in the late 1970s and centred around rising public concerns about the visible growth of street prostitution and (in particular) about the growing number of 'massage parlours', often in residential areas. Some argued that legalising brothels would help reduce street prostitution and allow better control of prostitution businesses. As in NSW, a significant feminist lobby for prostitution law reform also appeared in Victoria in the mid- to late 1970s. According to Gorganicyn (1998: 182), there were two leading figures in the initiation of the debate about prostitution law reform – a crusading male member of the Liberal Party and Joan Coxsedge, a feminist who was a member of the ALP and chaired the ALP Status of Women's Policy Committee. Coxsedge worked with a newly formed prostitute rights group – the Prostitutes Collective of Victoria[5] – and was 'the key figure in getting a policy of decriminalisation onto the ALP's agenda' (Gorganicyn 1998: 182). This ALP policy looked to a thoroughgoing withdrawal of the criminal law from prostitution, to a legalisation of brothels and (as in NSW) to a legalisation of public/street soliciting for the purposes of prostitution.

At the 1982 state election an ALP government, under the leadership of John Cain, took office. In 1984 the government presented the Planning (Massage Parlours) Bill to the Victorian parliament. In the upper house, members of the opposition forced the government to remove the 'euphemism' from the title of the bill which was then re-formulated as the Planning (Brothels) Bill. This bill proposed that brothels should be treated like other businesses. So, for brothels with a valid town-planning permit, issued by local government, most prostitution-related activities (such as managing a brothel or soliciting within a brothel) would be legal. However, the penalties on illegal brothels and on public/street soliciting for the purposes of prostitution were to be significantly increased. Clearly, the bill did not represent a thoroughgoing withdrawal of the criminal law from the realm of prostitution (as the ALP Status of Women's Policy Committee had recommended). Gorganicyn reports (1998: 182) that neither Joan Coxsedge nor the Women's Policy Co-ordination Unit in

Victoria was involved in the planning or drafting of this legislation. She says that the task of designing prostitution policy was given to the Minister of the Department of Planning and Environment and then passed on to the Attorney-General, 'marking the beginning of the end of direct feminist involvement in the design of prostitution policy within the Victorian ALP' (Gorjanicyn 1998: 182).

Dominant frame of debate

In parliament, the dominant frame of the debate around the Planning (Brothels) Bill was set by arguments about the inevitability of prostitution and the need for more rational and effective management of prostitution businesses. ALP members of parliament argued that the previous conservative government had evaded its leadership responsibilities by allowing prostitution, in particular massage parlours, to get out of control. The Cain government said it was now determined to face up to its responsibilities and bring some measure of order into the prostitution arena. The 'solution' was to design more modern and 'rational' prostitution laws (VPD Vol. 374: 4415–16).

The government argued that prostitution was an inevitable feature of human society and could not be eliminated. The Minister for Local Government, for example, said that 'The Government accepts that prostitution is a reality in our society and that brothels exist and will continue to exist in some form or another' (VPD Vol. 374: 4415–16).

From this perspective it was important 'to face up to the reality of things as they are in the real world'; legalisation was represented as a 'sensible, rational and reasonable' way to do this and to address a number of the problems associated with prostitution including drugs, the involvement of organised crime, HIV/AIDS and the proliferation of visible prostitution in residential areas (VPD Vol. 374: 4415–16). However, the government also contended that legalisation did not mean that parliament approved of prostitution; it was simply an acknowledgement that the prostitution industry needed to be 'controlled in more efficient ways' (VPD Vol. 374: 4422).

Gendering the debate

As will be apparent from the above, the dominant frame of the debate paid little attention to issues of gender. There was no acknowledgement that most workers in prostitution are female or that clients are mostly male. So the prostitution industry was not seen as a fundamentally gendered industry. Consequently, the impact of the proposed new laws on gender power relations was not considered. The bill clearly *did* offer the possibility to some sex workers of safer and better working conditions in legal brothels. However, the bill also threatened to undermine the position of the most marginal and vulnerable group of women in prostitution, those who worked on the streets and in illegal brothels and massage parlours. This group faced larger criminal penalties and a lack of other work options.

The only attention to gender during the debate was by members of the ultra-conservative National Party who argued that prostitution was about the exploitation of women (and men) and that the legalisation of brothels probably contravened the United Nations Declaration on the Elimination of Discrimination Against Women to which Australia was a signatory (VPD Vol. 374: 4425).

Policy outcome

The Planning (Brothels) Bill was supported in parliament by the ALP and the Liberal Party and passed into law in 1984. When the bill was being debated in parliament, the government announced its intention to hold a full inquiry into prostitution and to review the new legislation. This inquiry was conducted by a feminist law professor, Marcia Neave. The final report of this inquiry was presented to the Victorian parliament in 1985. Neave recommended measures to reduce the demand for prostitution (for example, by restricting advertising). But she also recommended a model for the better management of existing prostitution – a licensing scheme for the owners and managers of legal brothels and a limited legalisation of street prostitution (Victoria 1985). A licensing scheme was introduced in 1986 (the legalisation of street prostitution was rejected) and significantly strengthened in 1995. To date, it cannot be said that these measures have offered better and safer working conditions for most workers in the prostitution industry (Neave 1994; Sullivan 1999).

Women's movement impact

Taken as a whole, the Planning (Brothels) Act does not represent a positive state response to the demands of the women's movement. While offering some policy satisfaction (the legalisation of brothel prostitution), it did not address street prostitution and so did not coincide with feminist goals. Moreover, the state did not allow individual women or women's groups to participate in the law reform process. Thus, the impact of the women's movement on the state can be termed 'pre-emption' on this issue.

Women's policy agency activities

Women's policy agencies were originally appointed by Liberal Party governments in the mid-1970s. An Advisory Council was established in 1975. In 1976 the consultative and advisory role of this committee was supplemented by the appointment of a (bureaucratic) women's advisor and, later, a Women's Advisory Bureau within the Premier's Department (Sawer 1990: 162). This later became the Office of Women's Affairs. When the ALP came to power in Victoria in 1982, it was slow to review and establish new women's policy machinery. A permanent (and feminist) head for the Office of Women's Affairs was appointed in 1983. Her first priority was to build up staff and resources and, very shortly, there was a staff of up to eighteen people working on a range of projects (Sawer 1990: 163–4); thus it had a significant administrative capacity. In 1984 the office was renamed the Women's Policy Co-ordination Unit. It was cross-sectional in its operation and maintained a close proximity to the centre of power within the government.

Sawer (1990: 163–6) argues that the Women's Policy Co-ordination Unit had a range of problems in its early days. Though a reform government had been elected, 'its women's policy was very thin – the only concrete commitment was to the decriminalisation of prostitution'. So the Women's Co-ordination Unit had to adopt a significant role in the development of new policy and then, retrospectively, have this approved by the ALP Status of Women Policy Committee and the ALP party conference. Clearly, this was a convoluted and tricky process. Sawer also reports 'bureaucratic hostility to the idea of the Unit initiating projects and raising community awareness of issues' (Sawer 1990: 165). In the debate about prostitution, for example, the Premier's Department vetoed the unit speaking publicly on this issue (Sawer 1990: 165). Thus the unit had little opportunity to gender the debate about the legalisation of brothels in 1984. As suggested above, the unit was not consulted in the drafting of the 1984 bill. Consequently, the Women's Co-ordination Unit should be regarded as having only a symbolic role in this debate; it was not an obvious advocate for women's movement goals and did not play any part in gendering the debate about prostitution law reform.

Women's movement characteristics

In 1984 the women's movement in Victoria was in a stage of growth with a moderate number of organisations and growing public support. As in NSW there were important differences in approach between revolutionary/radical feminists and feminists engaged in reform via WEL or membership of the ALP. However, these differences were diminishing in importance as, elsewhere in Australia, reformists and 'femocrats' were becoming involved in the funding of radical feminist projects such as women's refuges (McFerran 1990). In Victoria, individual feminists and feminist groups such as WEL were strongly allied to the left-leaning ALP; and feminist ideas were beginning to have some impact on ALP policy. While there is little evidence that prostitution law reform was a high-priority issue within the Victorian women's movement in the mid-1980s, there were clearly individual feminists and activists (such as Joan Coxsedge) working for reform. There was little opposition to the legalisation of prostitution within the Victorian women's movement at this time.

Policy environment

The election of a reforming ALP government in Victoria in 1982 was clearly the key turning point for the introduction of prostitution law reform. The Cain government had an absolute majority in the lower house of the Victorian parliament, but did not have a majority in the upper house, the Legislative Council, where the National Party held the balance of power (Shamsullah 1992). This meant that the Cain government was frequently stymied in its plans for social reform (Gorjanicyn 1992). However, in 1984 the Planning (Brothels) Bill was supported by the Liberal Party opposition and so was not vulnerable to a National Party veto.

In general, the policy environment can be regarded as closed; outsiders were excluded from both participation in the development of the law reform proposal and its debate in parliament. Although a left-leaning (ALP) government was in power, the dominant approach during the debate was largely incompatible with the position taken outside parliament by the women's movement. It was not gendered and there was little concern to see prostitution as a gendered activity.

Debate 3: Debate about slavery and sexual servitude, 1995–1999

How issue came to the public agenda

In the 1990s a significant debate took place in Australia about sex tourism, child prostitution and trafficking for the purposes of prostitution. Feminists were particularly active in these debates and lobbied for new laws to outlaw both trafficking and sex tourism that involved children.

In 1994 the Australian government enacted the Crimes (Child Sex Tourism) Act and provided criminal penalties for Australian citizens or Australian residents who had sexual relations with children while travelling overseas. The Australian branch of an international non-government organisation, ECPAT (End Child Prostitution and Trafficking), was particularly active in lobbying for this legislation and for raising public awareness about the whole issue. This was assisted in the mid-1990s by several high-profile prosecutions under the Crimes (Child Sex Tourism) Act of Australian diplomats who had been stationed in Asian countries.

In 1995, the authors of a report titled *A Modern Form of Slavery: Trafficking of Burmese Women and Girls into Brothels in Thailand* (Asia Watch and the Women's Rights Project 1993) toured Australia as guests of the International Women's Development Agency (IWDA), an Australian non-government organisation founded in 1985 to work with women in developing countries. The Asia Watch authors spoke to many feminist groups around the country and were widely reported in the mainstream press. This clearly raised feminist and public awareness about forced prostitution and trafficking. In December 1997 the federal Minister of Justice, Senator Amanda Vanstone (a member of the Liberal Party), said that Australia had insufficient laws to stop women being trafficked and forced into 'sex slavery' (*Courier Mail* 13 December 1997). She announced her intention to address this problem and, as a result, the issue was referred to Australia's Standing Committee of Attorney-Generals (a group consisting of all state attorney-generals plus their federal counterpart). An expert team appointed by this group investigated the options, produced a discussion paper in April 1998, conducted widespread public consultation and published a final report in November 1998 (MCCOC 1998). The report recommended new legislation and reported overwhelming public support for this.

Almost immediately, the federal government (a coalition government dominated by the Liberal Party but including the National Party) introduced a bill to this effect, although the bill lapsed when a federal election was called. The coalition government was re-elected and a new bill was introduced into the Australian parliament in 1999. This bill proposed to outlaw slavery and 'sexual servitude'. The provisions against slavery addressed situations where 'ownership powers are exercised over a person'; this included any bondage that arose as a result of debt or contract. The maximum penalty for slavery offences was to be twenty years imprisonment. The lesser offence of 'sexual servitude' was designed to address situations where a person 'provides sexual services and, because of force or threats (or debt bondage), is not free to cease providing the services or leave the place where they provide those services'. The maximum penalty

for forcing another into sexual servitude was to be seven years imprisonment or nine years if committed against a person under the age of eighteen
(C. of A. *Hansard* 21 March 1999).

Dominant frame of debate

In the Australian parliament debate about this bill was dominated by
three main concerns: the exploitation of women and children by traffickers, the role of international organised crime in the elaboration of
trafficking and the impact on the Australian economy of these activities.
Some of these concerns were evident in the Attorney-General's speech
to the parliament. He said that the need for a new law had arisen as there
was 'a growing and highly lucrative international trade in people for the
purposes of sexual exploitation. Essentially, the trade involves recruiting
persons from one country and relocating them to another to work as prostitutes in servile or slave like conditions for little, if any, reward. Young
women are the primary target' (C. of A. *Hansard* 21 March 1999). The
Attorney-General reported that the National Crime Authority had investigated a number of cases and the young women caught up in this trade
were often 'desperate to escape poverty' and were lured to Australia with
the promise of legitimate jobs. On arrival they were forced into prostitution. Alternatively, they knew they would be employed as sex workers
but were unaware of the conditions under which they would be required
to work. In many cases, these women were kept under strict security
and were unable to leave their working or living premises. The Attorney-
General said that many recruits had little control over how many clients
they saw in a day and unsafe sexual practices were regularly imposed on
them. Their passports were frequently taken from them and there could
be violence and threats to harm them or their families or to report them
to the immigration authorities. In many cases, the women were also in-
debted to their sponsors for the costs of airfares, arranging false travel
documents and for ongoing costs such as accommodation and board.
The debt was usually far in excess of the actual costs and was commonly
as high as A$50,000. Thus, 'they would have to service up to 500 clients
before they could discharge their debt. In many cases recruits receive little
or nothing for their work by the time they are detected by the authorities
and deported back home' (C.of A. *Hansard* 21 March 1999).

The Attorney-General said that an Australian Federal Police report indicated that there were numerous individuals and syndicates engaged in
sex trafficking into Australia, that they used sophisticated methods and
appeared to have links with international crime syndicates and major drug
traffickers. Large untaxed profits were said to be made by the traffickers

with significant sums of money transferred overseas. Investigations suggested that the gross cash flow to organisers of the trade could be in the region of A$1 million per week.

It is notable that a similar range of arguments structured the contributions to the debate of most other members of parliament (regardless of their political party affiliation). The main problem to be addressed was the exploitation of young Asian women in Australia by organised criminals. These criminals were regarded as the main ones to blame for the current situation, although some members of parliament did point to the role of globalisation and poverty in generating a pool of potential trafficking victims. The solution to this problem was seen largely in terms of ensuring that individual perpetrators of trafficking crimes could be punished under Australian laws.

Gendering the debate

As suggested above, the dominant frame of the debate about this legislation was gendered and both male and female parliamentarians raised gender issues in their speeches. However, it is notable that two women members of parliament – Senator Dee Margetts (of the West Australian Greens) and Tanya Plibersek of the ALP – saw the need for more extensive action than the bill implied. They both spoke in favour of increasing aid programmes as a way to combat trafficking, thus clearly identifying poverty, rather than the criminal behaviour of traffickers, as the main problem. Plibersek's contribution is particularly interesting as it locates trafficking for the purposes of prostitution in the broader context of an Australian history of forced labour.[6] She sought to have the ambit of the bill expanded to include all cases of forced labour and argued that the Migration Act needed to be amended so women who suffered slavery or sexual servitude could remain in Australia and thus need not fear deportation if they reported their situation. These were all issues raised outside parliament by other feminist speakers (most notably during the community consultations that occurred around the 1998 discussion paper) (MCCOC 1998: 30–2). However, none of Plibersek's suggestions was taken up by the government or by other/male speakers in the parliament.

Policy outcome

The Criminal Code Amendment (Slavery and Sexual Servitude) Bill attracted broad-based support, from all political parties, in the Australian parliament. It passed quickly through both houses of parliament and became law in 1999. It is notable, however, that there have been no prosecutions under this statute since its inauguration in 1999; clearly a great deal of time and money may be required to pursue charges against international traffickers (and, at present, there is no devoted police group or team in Australia that has this role). In December 2002 Australia signed the UN Protocol against Trafficking that supplements the Convention against Transnational Crime.

Women's movement impact

Taken as a whole, this measure should be seen as a positive state response to the demands of the women's movement. While the final measure did not wholly coincide with feminist goals, it went a significant way towards this. Moreover, the state conducted widespread consultations with women's groups on this issue and individual women (parliamentarians) participated directly in the debate. Thus, the impact of the women's movement on the state can be termed 'dual response' on this issue.

Women's policy agency activities

The main women's policy agency at federal level is the Office of the Status of Women (Sawer 1995). This bureaucratic agency was established by a reforming ALP government in 1974. It was maintained, although often with a more marginal relationship to centres of power, by later conservative governments. Its scope has always been cross-sectional and its administrative capacity quite significant. In 1999 the Office of the Status of Women was centrally located within the Department of the Prime Minister and Cabinet and headed by a feminist handpicked by the prime minister. The office did not play any obvious or public role in the debate around the bill. It did, however, organise extensive consultations with women's groups after the discussion paper on slavery and sexual servitude, commissioned by the Standing Committee of Attorney-Generals, was released in 1998 (MCCOC 1998). The Office of the Status of Women should probably be classified as having played a symbolic role in the debate on trafficking in 1999. It was neither an advocate for women's movement goals nor a key player in gendering the policy debate.

Women's movement characteristics

The women's movement at this time in Australia was diverse and in a stage of consolidation. While it retained close ties to the left-leaning ALP, feminists were now also visible members of the other major political party – the Liberal Party (holding government in 1999) – and of minor parties like the Australian Democrats and the Greens.

In the 1990s a significant disagreement became apparent between feminists in Australia about the legalisation of prostitution. Radical feminists – such as Sheila Jeffreys (1997) at the University of Melbourne – oppose the legalisation of brothels and escort agencies. Other Australian feminists, including this author, argue for an approach which allows prostitution to be regarded as 'sex work' and for sex workers to receive the same rights as other citizens and workers. Thus, while critical of some details of the prostitution legalisation enacted in Australia, feminists from this camp basically support the legalisation approach (Sullivan 1995, 1997, 1999, 2001).

Despite these differences on the issue of prostitution legalisation, there *was* a broad-based feminist consensus in Australia about the need to combat forced prostitution and (forced) trafficking. For example, in January 1996 the National Conference of WEL called on the Australian government to conduct an investigation into the nature and extent of trafficking in women and children to Australia; to develop strategies to prevent trafficking; and to enact legislation to make trafficking illegal (*In Kwell* (WEL National Newsletter) 1996/1–2.1). By 1999, the issue of trafficking was a high priority for the Australian women's movement.

There was some important opposition to feminist approaches to trafficking in the late 1990s particularly from sex worker rights groups (see Murray 1998). However, the mainstream feminist position was fairly straightforward: that – despite its weaknesses – the 1999 bill should be supported.

Policy environment

In 1999 the Liberal coalition government of John Howard had just won its second term in office. While this meant it had a majority in the lower house of parliament, it did not hold a clear majority in the upper house (where the Australian Democrats held the balance of power). However, as already indicated, the Slavery and Sexual Servitude Bill attracted broad cross-party support. Members of the government, ALP opposition and minor parties all wanted to see stronger sanctions against forced prostitution.

In general, the policy environment should be regarded as moderately closed. While the government maintained control over the passage of the bill, women from all political parties participated in the debate in parliament and there was extensive consultation with women's groups outside the parliament. Although the left was *not* in power, the dominant approach in parliament was compatible with the positions being adopted by the women's movement.

Conclusion

To what extent do women's movement characteristics, women's policy agencies and policy environment variables explain these variations in state responses? It would seem from the evidence in this case study that women's policy agency characteristics/activities and women's movement characteristics are not significant indicators of state response. In all three debates examined here, women's policy agencies (perhaps apart from the NSW Women's Advisory Council in the 1970s) played no public role in gendering debates about prostitution law reform. It mattered little whether these agencies were 'insiders' or were largely symbolic in their function; they may have been active behind the scenes but there is little evidence of this on the public record. In relation to women's movement characteristics – including factors such as the stage of development, closeness to the left, cohesiveness and presence of counter-movements – there is little that appears to be a clear indicator of state response. As long as some activists within the movement are prioritising the issue of prostitution or trafficking, the *possibility* of a feminist impact on state processes emerges. In all three debates examined here, the women's movement was an important actor in getting prostitution law reform on to state agendas. In the NSW and Australian (federal) parliaments this led to changes that matched or were largely compatible with feminist demands. In Victoria, however, the policy outcome was only partly what the women's movement sought; important feminist demands (for example, in relation to the legalisation of street prostitution) remained unaddressed and the debate about prostitution law reform was almost wholly conducted in non-gendered terms. This suggests that a key variable in predicting the impact of women's movements on the direction of policy debate is the openness of the policy environment to feminist participation, if only because a gendering of policy debates is more likely to occur when feminists have the opportunity to participate in the debate from the beginning, thus influencing the dominant framing. Thus, in both the NSW and federal debates – where the policy environment was more open to feminist demands – the terms of the debate were substantially gendered. As suggested above, this did not occur in the Victorian debate.

NOTES

1. Throughout this chapter I use the term 'legalisation' to indicate law reform proposals that expand the space of legal prostitution in any way.
2. In Victoria and Queensland brothel owners and operators are subject to significant bureaucratic and police scrutiny in a licensing process; brothel premises also need a planning permit from local government. In the ACT brothel owners are not subject to licensing but must record their names and addresses on a brothel register and conduct their businesses in commercial zones of the city. In NSW, brothel owners and operators are not subject to licensing or registration but their business must have a valid planning permit from local council (Sullivan 1997).
3. The subset consists of the following debates:
   - NSW in 1968–79 and 1982–3: leading to the legalisation of public soliciting for the purposes of prostitution;
   - NSW in 1988: leading to increased legal penalties for all existing public prostitution offences (including soliciting);
   - NSW in 1995: leading to the establishment of procedures for legal brothels and the repeal of laws for 'living on the earnings of prostitution' (except where this involved force or deception);
   - Victoria in 1984: leading to the legalisation of brothels;
   - Victoria in 1985–6: leading to a new regulatory framework for legal brothels;
   - Victoria in 1995: leading to a strengthening of the regulatory framework for legal brothels;
   - Queensland in 1987–92: leading to new prostitution laws, expanded legal penalties for prostitution offences and a rejection of legalisation;
   - Queensland in 1999: leading to the legalisation of brothels;
   - Northern Territory in 1992: leading to the legalisation of escort agencies;
   - Australian Capital Territory in 1992: leading to the legalisation of brothels;
   - federal level in 1999: a debate about 'sexual servitude' (trafficking);
   - Western Australia in 2000: a debate that led to increased penalties on a range of prostitution-related offences, but particularly public soliciting.
4. A 'spruiker' is a man who stands outside a shop or entertainment premises, calling to people on the street about the delights to be found within.
5. The Prostitutes Collective of Victoria was clearly a significant actor in this process; see http://www.arts.unimelb.edu.au/amu/ucr/student/1996/ m.dwyer/pcvhome.html. For an overview of sex worker activism in Australia see Sullivan (1997:202).
6. In the nineteenth century south sea islanders were 'blackbirded' or forcibly removed from their homes to work on cane farms in Queensland. Indigenous people were also often forced to work without pay – for example, as domestics or on cattle stations (Saunders 1982; Saunders and Evans 1992).

3 Taxes, rights and regimentation: discourses on prostitution in Austria

Birgit Sauer

Introduction

Prostitution was an important part of Viennese culture during the *fin de siècle*. Both Felix Salden's famous novel *Josefine Mutzenbacher* and Karl Krauss's essays on 'morality' reflect the public presence of prostitution during the Habsburg Empire. In post-war Austria, prostitution did not become a public issue until the mid-1980s, although the city centre of Vienna remained a famous red light district. Prostitution was seen as 'immoral', dangerous and criminal, and was therefore taboo at the lofty heights of the policy-makers.

Today sex work in Austria is mostly performed by migrant women. In October 2000, 513 prostitutes were registered as working in Vienna, 20 per cent of whom were without Austrian citizenship. It is estimated that fewer than 10 per cent of all Viennese sex workers are registered, meaning that 5,000 to 7,000 prostitutes work in the city and that 85 per cent of them are migrant women, most of whom come from the former socialist countries (Stockinger 2001: 10).

Prostitution first appeared on the political agenda in the 1970s through the comprehensive reform of the authoritarian Penal Code (1975). The new Penal Code no longer considered prostitution criminal; only 'illicit sexual acts in public' (§ 218), soliciting (§ 219) and pimping to exploit (§ 216) were still included in the Penal Code. Since then prostitution policy has evolved 'by chance', as by-product of other policies, such as health or taxation policies. More often than not, it was the courts, not the legislature, that initiated the most important decisions regarding prostitution.

Other major impulses to change prostitution policy came from contradictory rulings by the federal and provincial (*Länder*) or municipal legislature. National legislation rules over matters concerning the Penal Code, HIV/AIDS laws, tax and social insurance laws. Article 118.3 of the federal constitutional law of 1962 states that prostitution is to be regulated by provincial or municipal law.

The legislation and policy-making on prostitution therefore are complex and bewildering processes, and prostitution policy is often caught up in conflicts between the legislature and executive about who is responsible for such policies. There is no legal evidence – except historic tradition – as to why certain aspects of sex work are regulated on a federal level and others on a provincial level.

Laws and policies in the nine Austrian provinces do not comply with general guidelines and differ from province to province and even from one city to another. The provincial laws or decrees prohibit prostitution at certain places and certain times of the day. Street prostitution is prohibited by police laws in seven provinces, the exceptions being Vienna and Lower Austria. Six provinces implemented a 'brothel-solution' in the 1980s (Upper Austria, Salzburg, Carinthia, Tyrol, Vorarlberg and Burgenland). Styria's prostitution law, which allows brothels, has only been in existence since 1998. In provinces with laws allowing brothels, the brothel owner is required to apply for a permit from the city authorities. Yet most of the municipalities still prohibit brothels.

From 1970 to 2000 the Social Democratic Party (Sozialdemokratische Partei Österreich, SPÖ) was the leading party in government. Throughout this entire era of thirty years, a Social Democratic chancellor was the head of the government. Although the SPÖ has had a strong women's organisation since the nineteenth century, prostitution policy failed to reflect any feminist ideas until the late 1980s. This was indicative of the party-centred and corporatist policy process, which privileged the monopoly-like interest groups surrounding the two '*Lager*' parties of the SPÖ and the conservative Austrian People's Party (Österreichische Volkspartei, ÖVP). But also the Austrian feminist movement only occasionally took part in the debates on sex work.

Selection of debates

A patchwork of policy debates on prostitution at federal, provincial and municipal levels resulted from the country's federal state structure. For this reason, the universe of the debate must include all three levels. Since the early 1970s, when prostitution became an issue debated in the national parliament, eleven policy debates and decisions have been made on the *national level* and four debates have occurred on the *municipal level* in *Vienna*, the nation's capital, which is also a province.[1]

For my purposes here I have selected two federal debates – the amendment of the Penal Code in 1984 and the amendment of the law on social insurance for private enterprise (GSVG-Novelle) in 1998 – and one provincial debate, the Viennese prostitution law of 1991. These are the most salient decisions on prostitution, because they changed the working conditions for prostitutes and caused most of the public debate.

The selected debates also represent the importance of the decision-making systems which have been involved in the process. These include the national parliament, the national ministries, the municipal Council of Vienna and the local administrative agencies. In addition, courts and – if professional (or worker's) rights are concerned – the social partners, and the social insurance agencies have been decisive during the procedure.

This selection of debates reflects the life cycle of the issue beginning in the early 1970s, and also demonstrates the acceleration of policy-making on prostitution during the 1990s. This acceleration is due to both internal and external developments. Firstly, the Greens and the Liberal Party (Liberales Forum, LIF) arose as new players on the political field, both of them including demands on human and women's rights in their political programmes. Furthermore, the increasing globalisation of migration and trafficking in women transformed Austria into a prostitution hotspot within Europe.

Debate 1: The amendment of the Penal Code, 1984

How issue came to the public agenda

Until the beginning of the 1970s, the 'law against vagrancy' from 1885 not only prohibited prostitution but also defined it as a criminal act (§ 5.1). In 1973, the Constitutional Court ruled § 5.1 of the 'vagrancy law' to be unconstitutional as the paragraph left the punishment of prostitutes, pimps and johns at the discretion of the local police and the vice squad. Yet article 18.1 of the Austrian constitutional law states that the national executive must take action on the grounds of these same laws. As a consequence, the Penal Code then had to be altered (Toth 1997).

The revised Penal Code of 1974 (effective 1975) did not prohibit prostitution but only pimping with the intent to exploit. The 'decree concerning the health supervision of professional sex offenders' by the Federal Ministry for Health and Education (BGB1. 314/1974), which also came into effect in 1975, forced prostitutes to comply with strict health supervision, usually performed by state authorities. Three western provinces, which had a more prohibitive approach to prostitution, all opposed the revisions of the Penal Code. They claimed that pimps could not be fined, because it would be extremely difficult to prove 'exploitation'. Salzburg finally enacted a provincial decree on the punishment of pimps, which was then ruled unconstitutional. These *Länder* governments, with conservative governors, put pressure on the Federal Minister of Justice,

Christian Broda (SPÖ), to consider more restrictive measures on pimping. Between late 1981 and early 1982, parliamentarians from the opposition parties ÖVP and pre-Haider Austrian Freedom Party (Freiheitliche Partei Österreich, FPÖ) proposed a more restrictive bill (§ 216) to the national parliament.[2] Both parties linked criminal offences, such as murder, to prostitution and pimping, all of which pose a threat to society and disturb public order. The newspapers were full of 'sex and crime' stories, increasing the pressure on lawmakers to put an end to this 'lawless' situation introduced by the new Penal Code. But the SPÖ Minister of Justice seriously delayed the proposition of a new bill.[3]

In early 1982, the Austrian High Court ruled that pimps should be prosecuted not only if they 'exploit' prostitutes, but also if they employ prostitutes' money for their own purposes. This decision spurred the legislature into action. On 18 October 1982, the Federal Ministry of Justice organised a conference on prostitution and pimping in Vienna (Bundesministerium für Justiz 1983), which was attended by administrative workers, police, health and medical officers as well as public prosecutors, governors from the provinces and academic experts. The conference paved the way for the debate on a new Penal Code, increasing publicity for the issue.

In 1983, eight of the nine provinces supported the new paragraphs in the Penal Code concerning pimping. When the SPÖ formed a coalition with the pre-Haider FPÖ (who were also the 'law and order' faction) in 1983, the way opened for a new definition of pimping in the Penal Code. Harald Ofner, the new FPÖ Minister of Justice, provided the legislative backing. On 29 November 1983, the governing parties presented the bill to the parliament, which passed the restrictive law that very day.[4] The new Penal Code came into effect in 1984.

Dominant frame of debate

Within this debate, law-makers mainly focused on pimping and prostitution as threats to public health and safety. For the ÖVP the liberalisation of the Penal Code was viewed as posing a 'just cause for the rise in secret prostitution, police problems [and the] increase of sexually transmitted diseases' (Pernthaler 1975: 288). The parliamentary debate on the new law centred on a 'law and order' discourse. Neighbourhood safety and 'keeping the streets clean' were the main objectives of the restrictions by ÖVP and conservative Social Democrats. A group of leftist Social Democrats presented prostitution as a class problem.[5] The logic of their arguments also included the punishment of pimps.

The relationship between pimps and prostitutes was not framed as a business affiliation subject to regulation; it was not seen in terms of work contracts or as a matter involving women's rights. Although the policy debate focused on pimping, prostitution was the 'secret background' of the discussion. It was judged 'immoral' and as a 'vice'. Parliament member Hilmar Kabas (FPÖ) said that prostitution was a 'social evil' that must be 'contained'.[6] Both pimps and prostitutes were perceived as 'problem groups' within society that should be banished from the public eye.

Gendering the debate

The bulk of the debates on the amendment of the Penal Code were not gendered (e.g. Bundesministerium für Justiz 1983). One gendered issue was the criminal actions of pimps, who were primarily perceived as *men* who make a living from exploiting prostitutes. Yet within this whole discourse, prostitutes were not addressed specifically as being *women*. Maria Hosp (ÖVP) was the only woman who was vocal throughout this debate. She raised the issue of violence between male pimps and female prostitutes, painting a picture of prostitutes as victims. Her gendered approach reduced pimps to 'criminal' individuals. Yet she neglected to contextualise the issue within a gendered power structure in which male violence is a reality.[7]

Another dominant gendered frame was the polarisation between 'normal women' and prostitutes. An ÖVP member of parliament even went as far as claiming to protect 'innocent women' against johns, pimps and prostitutes by clamping down on the legal situation of prostitutes and pimps. Leftist Social Democrats considered prostitution a problem of 'exploitation' and 'intimidation' of women through pimps.[8] Prostitutes' rights remained absent from both the political and public agendas.

Policy outcome

In November 1983, the federal parliament enacted the new Penal Code.[9] The new version of § 216 defined 'exploitation' – which remained a difficult term to interpret, even for the courts – and earning a living from sex workers' money as punishable criminal acts. The new law distinguished four categories of criminal pimping. 'Simple pimping' describes any relationship in which a person utilises prostitutes' earnings for their own purpose. This paragraph turned out to be more of a demand for compulsory celibacy for sex workers. The second category was pimping with the intent of 'exploitation' and 'intimidation'; the third prohibited 'gangs' of pimps; and the fourth 'intimidation' with the intent to discourage women from quitting prostitution.

Women's movement impact

The policy process was entirely a male affair. The dominant actors were the Minister of Justice and the male governors of the nine provinces. Only two women participated in the policy debate: a representative of the ÖVP in the parliamentary debate and the representative from Salzburg in the hearing on prostitution and pimping. The SPÖ women's organisation did not participate in the parliamentary debate. The Women's State Secretary in the Federal Chancellery was not invited to take part in the debate. The state did not respond to the demands made by the women's movement. Women's movement activists were not represented in the policy process nor was the topic discussed in gendered frames.

Women's policy agency activities

Until the late 1970s, women's policy was included in social or family policies and thus remained limited to questions of waged labour or family and children. The social partnership, Austria's 'corporate corporatism' (Neyer 1996: 88ff.), which is the particularly intense co-operation between parties, unions and industry organisations in parliament, committees, commissions and the ministries' administrative departments, was literally 'manned'. This androcentric structure contributed to excluding women's issues, except abortion – a traditional part of the Social Democratic agenda (Köpl 2001) – from the political system. At the end of the 1970s, dissent among the interest organisations and conflicts within the social partnership increased the influence of the parties in political processes (Tálos 1997: 436). This formed an opportunity structure in which women's questions could be discussed. By the end of the 1970s, after some pressure from the women's movement, the SPÖ managed to institutionalise women's policies, in the 'Austrian way' of modernisation 'from above' (Gottweis 1997).

The year 1979 was a milestone for women's politics in Austria. Not only was the equal opportunity law passed, but the first women's policy agencies were also established. The secure position of the SPÖ's parliamentary majority in 1979 gave the SPÖ women the possibility to lobby in favour of more women's policy agencies, despite the social partnership's defence mechanisms that had previously hindered this development. Moreover, they were able to strengthen their position in the government by securing two State Secretaries in charge of women's concerns. At the time, the proportion of women in the National Assembly was 9.8 per cent.

The State Secretary responsible for 'issues of working women' was located in the Ministry of Social Welfare. The State Secretary's office for 'general women's issues' was installed in the Federal Chancellery. Johanna Dohnal, a well-known SPÖ feminist with strong backing from the party's women's organisation and the women's movement, was appointed to head this office. State Secretaries are not members of cabinet, yet are still subordinates of the heads of the department. The Women's State Secretary was allotted a minimal number of staff and received no independent budget.

Consolidation of the women's policy agency of the 1980s was hampered when the transition to a 'minor coalition' between the SPÖ and FPÖ in 1983 resulted in the dissolution of the State Secretary's Office in the Ministry of Social Welfare. The resources of the remaining Women's State Secretary's office were scarce, although Johanna Dohnal held a cross-sectional mandate, and the office was still situated high in the national political hierarchy as part of the Federal Chancellery.

In the early 1980s, the State Secretary's main issues were abortion (Köpl 2001), equal pay and discrimination in the workplace. However, it had a purely advisory function and had to be consulted for governmental issues related to policies on women. The agency served as a catalyst for many growing women's projects in Austria. However, it still failed to contribute to the policy debate on pimps and prostitutes in connection with the Penal Code amendment. The agency did not gender the debate nor did it advance women's movement goals in the policy process. At the beginning of the 1980s, the office proved to play a merely symbolic role in the prostitution debate.

Women's movement characteristics

Feminism as a social movement arrived late in Austria, as did other social movements, due to the uninviting political opportunity structure which suppressed conflict by intricate decision-making processes. Until the end of the 1970s, the SPÖ was adept in 'bundling together the hope for change, participation, and reform' and in 'channelling political protest' (Gottweis 1997: 345, 357). At the time, the women's movement worked in close co-operation with the SPÖ women's organisation.

In 1972, the first so-called autonomous women's group was founded in Vienna, the 'Platform of Autonomous Women' (Aktion unabhängiger Frauen, AUF), a small group of women activists with a socialist background (Dick 1991: 38–51). The Austrian movement mobilised only slowly, mainly around the issue of abortion. In the 1980s, it expanded and became more of a project-oriented movement. The projects, mostly state-subsidised, co-operated with the Women's State Secretary's office and with the Social Democratic administration to gain funding for their work. The movement was critical of the socialists in power, remaining sympathetic but distanced toward the left (Dick 1991: 214–15). The societal hegemony of the ruling left was one reason for the general absence of a counter-movement.

The SPÖ women were mainly concerned with abortion and equal opportunity, while the autonomous women's movement primarily stressed issues of sexuality and violence against women. Neither included prostitution on its political agenda until the mid-1980s.

Policy environment

The SPÖ had been the leading party in government since 1970. The Ministry of Justice, its authorities and experts, as well as the Parliamentary Committee on Justice formed the policy system, which regulated the Penal Code. The Ministry of Justice bureaucracy was traditionally male-dominated and belonged to the 'law and order' fraction. Ofner, the FPÖ Minister of Justice since 1983, assumed responsibility only for fining pimps while refusing to deal with social and health issues.[10]

Participation in the policy environment was limited to the actors from the ministry, the Parliamentary Committee on Justice, the provincial governments and some experts. Free agents had no chance to enter the policy debate. The gender culture of the policy environment was male and the policy environment did not develop any responsibility and sensitivity for women and gender issues. The dominant approach of the policy sub-system was incompatible with the women's movement's view. As a whole, this policy environment was closed.

Debate 2: Vienna's prostitution law, 1991

How issue came to the public agenda

The Viennese Police Decree on Prostitution in 1975[11] was a reaction to the liberalisation of the Penal Code. Street prostitution had increased and the city tried to ban it from the city centre. In 1984 the first Viennese Prostitution Law restricted street prostitution to areas outside the city centre. Prostitution in private flats and by married women became illegal. According to the 'Viennese Government's Decree' on prostitution (1968) it was mandatory that sex workers register with the vice squad, a division of the Federal Police Department. They were fingerprinted and photographed and had to appear at weekly health check-ups performed by the municipal health department (*MA* 12) – not by a gynaecologist of their own choice. Then they received an 'inspection or control card'. When leaving the city, prostitutes had to notify the vice squad of their departure.

In 1987, members of the opposition party ÖVP in the Council of Vienna proposed a bill that aimed to put restraints on Vienna's prostitution law of 1984. The main objective was to limit street and bar prostitution, both of which were perceived as 'secret prostitution'. The council did not vote on the bill. It was only in 1988, during the new legislative period, that a parliamentary commission on the matter was formed with members from the SPÖ, ÖVP and FPÖ. After the fall of the 'Iron Curtain', street prostitution was on the rise and numerous sex bars and clubs were established. Prostitution received public attention as the media jumped at the chance to report on the topic. Now the commission proposed a new bill, and on 19 April 1991, the Council of Vienna passed the law. It became effective on 1 January 1992.

Dominant frame of debate

The debates on AIDS represented a major shift in the prostitution debate in the 1980s. This was actually 'progress' in the sense that, before AIDS, there was basically no attention to prostitution (Prostituiertengewerkschaft in Österreich 1987). Prostitutes were marked not only as immoral women, but also as a 'high risk group'. Consequently, 'secret prostitution' was perceived as a public health issue. The ÖVP, fractions of the SPÖ and the chief of the Viennese Health Department, Wolfgang Kopp, all supported the main, yet non-controversial political objective of 'containing' secret prostitution in Vienna (*Profil* 20 June 1988).

The policy solution circulating in the media and parliamentary debates aimed to reduce the number of prostitutes on the streets, encourage registration with the police and urge prostitutes to go to the weekly health checks. Also counselling and assistance in finding another profession dominated the content of the debate (*Profil* 20 June 1988).

Gendering the debate

Gender sensitive ideas were still rare in the debate on Vienna's prostitution law. The 'Austrian Organisation of Prostitutes' (Verband der Prostituierten Österreichs, VPÖ), founded on 8 March 1986, International Women's Day, moved public discourse in Vienna towards gender-specific themes. The organisation was founded in Linz by a prostitute, 'Frau Eva', along with 200 founding members (*Oberösterreichisches Tagblatt*, 10 March 1986). It became defunct in 1992. The VPÖ demanded the recognition of prostitution as a legal trade, allowing advertising and working in one's own flat. A further demand was a non-discriminatory registration that would not be based with the police, but in the Health Department (Brezany 1987: 22–23).

The Vienna AIDS organisation (AIDS-Hilfe Wien) focused its political energy on HIV-infected female sex workers and on the sex work market, where safe sex minimised profits. As a result of the AIDS discussion and the concentration on health issues, the conservative parties gendered the issue insofar as they separated the 'good' registered prostitutes from the 'bad' non-registered (and therefore illegal) prostitutes.

Policy outcome

Vienna's prostitution law's § 2 no longer defined prostitution in moral terms as a 'sex offence' but as 'professional sex acts'. Aside from some exceptions, such as the prostitution of minors, prostitution was permitted. Zoning laws were set up. Street prostitution within 150 metres of schools, youth centres, playgrounds, hospitals, churches and stations was prohibited (§ 4). Prostitution in bars and private apartments remained illegal, whereas sex work in clients' apartments became legal (§ 5). The law permitted brothels or 'houses where only prostitutes live' (§ 5).

Prostitutes were still obliged to register and notify the police when leaving the city (§§ 6 and 7). In an effort to encourage registration, 'secret prostitutes' were generally not fined for their first offence (*Die Presse* 8 May 1990). The new law guaranteed more privacy rights for prostitutes. A new requirement was that prostitution records must be destroyed within six months of cancellation of registration with the police (this period had previously been five years).

Women's movement impact

At the beginning of the 1990s, the Viennese women's movement showed no strong interest in the prostitution issue. Women had participated neither in the debates nor in the decision process leading to the prostitution law. The Viennese Department of Women's Affairs was not involved in the policy debate. At the end of the 1980s and the beginning of the 1990s, the Federal Minister of Women's Affairs, Johanna Dohnal, became interested in the prostitution issue along with the VPÖ. However, she made only a limited impact on the policy process in Vienna. Despite the lack of interest and participation of women and women's groups throughout the policy process, the outcome did reflect some feminist ideas. However, this outcome should be considered as pre-emptive: the state gave policy satisfaction but women were not included in the policy process.

Women's policy agency activities

During the 1980s, women's politics in Austria stagnated at the provincial and communal government levels (Rosenberger 1986: 266). In Vienna, the agendas on women's issues were added to the already existing departments responsible for family and social welfare, youth, sports and health. In the 1980s and early 1990s, the ministers responsible for women's affairs in Vienna (*Stadträtin für Frauenangelegenheiten*), Christine Schirmer and Ingrid Smejkal, were SPÖ members. By 1987, only the province of Vienna had established an independent municipal office for the support of women, called the Women's Service Office, initiated by Christine Schirmer. This counselling agency concentrated on matters of violence.

The tasks of Vienna's *Stadträtin* of Women's Affairs were designed in a cross-sectional manner. Its main issues were equal opportunity employment and violence against women, which included the establishment of a crisis hotline. Although the policy mandate did not exclude it, prostitution did not reach the minister's agenda until the late 1980s and early 1990s. The department had very limited administrative capacity, having no personnel and finances at its disposal. In addition, it lacked the administrative infrastructure necessary to become involved in all policy topics. Both the *Stadträtin* and the Women's Service Office therefore had a marginal role in the policy debate. They did not forward women's movement demands and did not gender the debate.

Women's movement characteristics

In the late 1980s and early 1990s, the Vienna women's movement had reached its zenith and was a bustling project-oriented movement that focused on issues such as violence against women, education, gender equality in the workplace and the right to equal political representation (Dick 1991). Many women's projects in Vienna were state-subsidised, mainly by the municipality, for instance the mayor's office, and the Department of Women's Affairs. The women's groups were close to the left-wing politicians in power at the time.

Nevertheless, the movement continued to neglect the prostitution issue. In the mid-1980s, the first self-help groups for prostitutes came about. Besides the VPÖ, LEFÖ (Lateinamerikanische emigrierte Frauen in Österreich/Latin American Women Migrants in Austria), a feminist group counselling migrant women from Latin America, was founded in 1985. LEFÖ became involved in the issue of sex work only after the Viennese prostitution law had come into effect. Even though some women's groups included prostitution in their political agendas, the priority of the issue was moderately low and the movement was not cohesive on the topic. No counter-movement developed within the arena.

Policy environment

In the 1970s and 1980s, the 'proportional government' (SPÖ, ÖVP and FPÖ) of Vienna was led by the Social Democrat Helmut Zilk (1984–94). In the early 1990s the SPÖ and ÖVP had the majority in Vienna's governing body and the FPÖ formed the opposition. In 1987, the proportion of women in the Council of Vienna was 24 per cent; in 1991 it had risen to 34 per cent (Frauen in Wien 1996: 58).

The legislation was developed within the local government of the city of Vienna. The municipal department for 'elections and various legal matters' was responsible for the proposition of a new prostitution law. A commission composed of members from the SPÖ, ÖVP and FPÖ met in 1988 to draw up an amendment of the law. The commission consulted the AIDS organisation, social workers and gynaecologists from the Health Department of the city of Vienna, as well as the vice squad. The subsystem's approach was at least compatible with the movement's aims. In the late 1980s and early 1990s, the policy-making sub-system remained moderately closed.

Debate 3: Amendment of the social insurance law for private enterprise, 1998

How issue came to the public agenda

In 1983, the federal Administrative Court classified prostitution as a 'commercial enterprise'.[12] A prostitute then sued a car driver for compensation due to her loss of income resulting from injuries in a car accident and won the case. This induced the finance authority to tax prostitutes and, some months later, pimps as well. This decision set off an ongoing debate about prostitution as a profession. The FPÖ Minister of Justice, Ofner, completely opposed the taxation of sex workers. However, ÖVP parliamentary members pleaded for levying taxes based on a 'just taxation'. The taxation law, initiated by the Minister of Finance, Herbert Salcher (SPÖ), came into effect in 1985.

Although sex workers were forced to pay taxes, they were still not eligible for a 'business licence', nor were they granted access to the state social security system, as stated in the *self-employment laws*. Moreover, prostitution was not recognised as a form of labour which ought to be included in the mandatory public insurance payment and benefits; sex workers were denied the right to participation in the social insurance system's division responsible for *employees*. Since the 1980s, sex workers have had limited access to state health care, and have had the option of insurance only as 'housewives' or at very high insurance rates. Unemployment and pension insurance remained unavailable to sex workers, even after discussions in the late 1980s on expanding the retirement insurance for self-employed workers to include them.

In the debate on secret prostitution, the 'prostitutes' union' – as the VPÖ defined itself – stressed the urgency of permitting sex workers the right to enrol in the state social security system. It concluded that all prostitutes should register and pay taxes at equitable rates. The VPÖ was supported by such well-known politicians as Helmut Zilk (at that time head of Vienna's Department of the Arts) (*Wochenpresse* 26 April 1983: 20) and Friederike Seidl (Social Democratic chief of Vienna's Department of Health and Social Welfare) (*Profil* 20 June 1988).

The legislature and the Ministry of Labour and Social Welfare refused to amend the social insurance law for private enterprise (*Profil* 24 November 1997). This was partly due to the strong resistance put up by the state insurance agency responsible for businesses during negotiations on the issue. Institutions in charge of commerce and social insurance collectively refused to accept prostitutes as members or beneficiaries within the Chamber of Commerce or insurance agencies up until the early 1990s.

By the end of the 1980s, the VPÖ had contacted the Women's State Secretary Johanna Dohnal. From that point on, she picked up the issue of the discriminatory practice of taxing prostitutes, legal inequality and the unequal treatment of sex workers (Dohnal 1992). Together with several feminist groups she succeeded in moving prostitutes' social situation on to the political agenda. The State Secretary co-operated with the Ministers of Labour and Social Welfare (all members of the SPÖ) and with the tax authorities (Brezany 1987: 22). Dohnal claimed that taxation should be fair and that prostitution should be recognised as a profession with full rights of access to the social insurance system. She promoted the issue of social insurance for sex workers in the media. The newspapers were full of vicious articles on the double standard of taxation, describing the state as the 'ultimate pimp'.

At the beginning of the 1990s, lesbian feminists in the AIDS self-help movement in Vienna took on and encouraged the Green Party to include the prostitution issue in its agenda (interview with Gudrun Hauer, 27 July 2001). Towards the end of the 1990s, the Green Party and the LIF publicised the issue more broadly. Still, the SPÖ Ministry of Labour and Social Welfare remained inactive on the issue until 1997. On 11 July 1997, LIF and Green Party members of parliament petitioned the Minister of Labour, Health and Social Welfare, Eleonore Hostasch (SPÖ), to act on the issue of social insurance for prostitutes. In late 1997, the Forum for the Rights of Prostitutes (Plattform für die Rechte von Prostituierten) was founded by members of the Green and Liberal parties in collaboration with other organisations offering counselling to prostitutes. The initial impetus for establishing the Forum was the conservative government members' attempts to pose further restrictions on the Viennese prostitution law. It organised public events with prostitutes, members of parliament and women's groups in Vienna's city centre. They publicly demanded government action, raising the issues of social security and recognition of prostitution as an enterprise or as regular employed work. In December 1997, the national parliament amended the social insurance law for private enterprise (GSVG-Novelle, effective January 1998), which allowed sex workers to enrol in the state insurance system.

Dominant frame of debate

There was little opposition to the frame that prostitution must be included in the self-employed workers social security system. Still, sex work was framed as coercive work by most of the policy-makers. The policy discourse within the governing SPÖ framed sex work as a 'social problem'. Within this 'social work discourse' female prostitutes were seen as victims of social conditions, exploited by pimps and organised crime. The SPÖ discussed prostitution as work, coerced labour, but not voluntarily chosen work. The main task was to assist women in getting out of sex work.

More technocratic debates concentrated on the health threat posed by 'secret prostitution', caused by the refusal of professional rights. The ÖVP perceived prostitutes as a social burden, especially in terms of a state-funded retirement plan for prostitutes. This fiscal argument was in support of allowing sex workers entrance into the pension system.

The LIF, the Green Party and the Forum framed the issue in terms of the normalisation of sex work and as a human rights issue, demanding the destruction of police files on prostitutes. All moral laws should be abolished and prostitution further regulated in terms of labour, contract, social security and trade laws. Both the reduction of discriminatory practices pertaining to prostitutes' work as a trade and the insurance agency's efforts were able to redefine discussions on social insurance as a right of social citizenship.

Gendering the debate

From the late 1980s, the social security issue concerning sex work was discussed in terms of gender by the VPÖ. At the very beginning of the 1990s, the process of redefining the issue in non-moral terms had begun. Feminists in the Green Party as well as the well-established Federal Ministry of Women's Affairs enabled the gendering of policy issues at a government level.

In the 1990s, the Social Democrats criticised the state's regulation of prostitution. This was mainly the work of a strong group of Social Democratic feminists engaged in and around the Ministry of Women's Affairs. Johanna Dohnal framed the issue in terms of the discrimination of women's work and of the right to work. She was Federal Minister of Women's Affairs from 1990 until 1995, and was succeeded by Helga Konrad (1995–7) – not a committed feminist but more a Social Democrat from the party apparatus – and Barbara Prammer (1997–2000). Along with Renate Brauner, head of the Department of Women's Affairs, and the Vienna Office for Women, they connected the subject of prostitution to the issue of poor working conditions and focused on the social injustice of paying taxes while simultaneously being excluded from the social insurance system. They claimed that social insurance and counselling were political means for achieving social security benefits and equality for sex workers.

Members of the Green Party framed sex work as a matter of female inequality based on unequal gender relations and regimes. In the parliamentary debate on the AIDS law in 1992, Christine Heindl, a Green MP, attacked the moral double standard of claiming to be committed to preventing HIV infection, while putting the blame on the prostitutes alone, leaving out their clients from the discussion. Together with the LIF they took on prostitution in terms of demanding rights for prostitutes. Some feminist activists claimed that prostitutes are not simply victims of patriarchal structures and men, but that they voluntarily choose the work (Hauer 1987). Lesbian feminists within the AIDS self-help movement discussed the issue in terms of prostitution as a profession and of the rights of prostitutes to improved working conditions, health care and social insurance.

Policy outcome

The amended social insurance law for private enterprise did not take sex workers explicitly into consideration, but regulated 'precarious' self-employed workers. The new law expanded the previously limited definition of private enterprise to include sex workers. The new legislation on social insurance recognised prostitution as a form of work, even though it was regarded as coercive and immoral work. Prostitutes are now eligible for enrolment in the social insurance system.

Women's movement impact

The new insurance law coincided in part with feminist demands. Major civil rights issues around sex work, such as police repression, coerced health control and full economic citizenship rights, remained unsolved however.

Activists from the movement, particularly from the LEFÖ, were invited to participate in the policy process as expert advisors. They negotiated with the Ministry of Women's Affairs, the Minister of Labour and Social Welfare, with parliamentarians responsible for the issue and with members of the parliamentary commission.

The successful amendment of the law on social insurance can, therefore, partly be attributed to women's policy agencies and to feminist groups who affected the policy content and created access to the procedures and debates on prostitution. Women parliamentarians from the Green Party acted as 'policy entrepreneurs' (Mazur 2001b: 312). They served as an interface between women's groups, the Ministry of Women's Affairs and the government. The movement's impact on this debate can be classified as a dual response: its demands were met, the debate was gendered and the women's minister and feminist experts were included in the policy process.

Women's policy agency activities

The 1990s were the period of growth and consolidation of women's politics in Austria (Siegmund-Ulrich 1994). In 1990, the State Secretary for General Women's Issues was restructured to become the Federal Ministry of Women's Affairs as part of the deal by the new coalition in government. For the first time, the ministry was allotted its own, though low, budget. It was able to expand its staff and to design three new sub-departments. The minister's status also expanded beyond the previously limited advisory function, gaining a veto right in the Cabinet of Ministers as well as the power to initiate further political women's initiatives. The ministry still maintained its cross-sectional manner of work. The office of the Minister of Women's Affairs remained in SPÖ hands. During the course of restructuring the federal government in 1997, the Ministry of Women's Affairs also took on the field of consumer protection. A re-evaluation resulted in the establishment of a woman's section within the ministry in 1998.

The Ministry of Women's Affairs actively introduced into the public agenda topics such as social insurance, health care, workers' rights and counselling for prostitutes. These issues were also placed on the agendas of the other ministries concerned with the issue (Labour and Social Welfare) as well as on provincial governments' agendas (Dohnal 1992). From the late 1980s, the women's minister, not part of the policy environment, sought to convince ministers to take action and open up the social insurance system to sex workers. In 1985, the first 'Report on the Situation of Women in Austria' was published by the State Secretary for General Women's Issues (Frauenbericht 1985). In 1995, the second 'Report' was published by the Ministry of Women's Affairs (Frauenbericht 1995). Both were compiled by feminist researchers. One chapter dealt with prostitution (Hausegger 1995). Helga Konrad was exceptionally committed to the sex work issue. She funded research on the social situation of prostitutes, and experts developed model projects for counselling and health care. In 1996, a report on the 'Social Aspects of the Situation of Prostitutes' (Soziale Aspekte 1996) and a report on 'Social Security of Prostitutes' (Soziale Absicherung 1996) were published. In the same year, the Federal Ministry for Women's Affairs released a report on trafficking in women (Frauenhandel 1996). The Ministry of Women's Affairs had an insider role, as it advanced movement goals and was successful in gendering the debate.

Women's movement characteristics

By the mid-1990s, the autonomous women's movement was consolidated and it changed strategy and focus. It became more and more difficult to secure state funding for feminist projects during an era of neo-liberal retrenchment. Despite this, feminists continued to do agency outreach work with prostitutes and worked within the health administration. The SPÖ and Green Party had already adopted activists from the women's movement who also did lobby work on the prostitution issue. Movement activists were invited as experts to speak at hearings and conferences.

In the second half of the 1990s, women's organisations offering counselling for sex workers were founded in several Austrian cities.

'Lilith', an organisation for 'communication between prostitutes and non-prostitutes', was founded in 1997 and dissolved in 2001. MAIZ (Autonomous Integration Centre by and for Migrant Women) started in Linz in 1996. LENA (Linz), an 'international counselling centre for female sex workers and their friends', was founded in 1997. Women's Service (Frauenservice) in Graz is a counselling project run by the city government.

These women's organisations and prostitutes' groups remained distant from the Social Democratic left in government, which can partly be attributed to the SPÖ coalition with the ÖVP over the years. On the other hand, most of the organisations were in close contact with the Green Party. Despite their cautious stance with regard to the SPÖ, however, most of the groups were funded by state money and thus co-operated with certain members of the SPÖ.

Prostitution, as an issue, was not able to unite the movement, but it did take priority for some activists and women's organisations. These groups did agree on the prostitution issue, whereas other parts of the women's movement stressed domestic violence and violence against women, rather than addressing the sex work issue. The movement also co-operated with the 'Forum'. During this period there was no counter-movement that opposed the framing of the issue or the new legislation.

Policy environment

From 1987 to 2000, the 'grand coalition' between SPÖ and ÖVP once again created a comparatively good climate for women's politics. The growing influence of the political parties within the social partnership (Tálos 1997: 449) and the newly formed parties, the Greens and LIF, were able to facilitate a greater quantitative representation of women in parliament.

The legislature, the executive and the social partnership formed the policy sub-system. The policy sub-systems concerned with work and social security traditionally are highly codified and closed for free agents. They are dominated by the main actors of the social partnership. Up to the mid-1990s, the claims of the women's policy agency were ignored, particularly by the organisations of the social partnership and the insurance system. The Federal Social Insurance Agency argued against opening the pension system to sex workers (*Wochenpresse* 12 November 1985). The Chamber of Commerce as well as the trade section of the Ministry of Commerce refused to recognise sex work as a trade. The Union of Arts, Media and Free Enterprise also denied sex workers the representation of their interests (*Wochenpresse* 12 November 1985).

Although eager to avoid publicity, the Ministers of Social Welfare were open to the demands from the early 1990s. The Minister of Labour, Health and Social Welfare, Eleonore Hostasch (SPÖ), was responsible for the amendment of the social insurance law for private enterprise in 1997. This ministry traditionally has been in the hands of the SPÖ. The sub-system's dominant approach to sex work was compatible with the movement's views. At the end of the 1990s, the policy environment was moderately closed.

Conclusion

Most of Austria's provinces upheld their regulatory and prohibitive approaches to prostitution, although the Penal Code did not explicitly prohibit sex work. The provinces and municipalities continue to treat prostitutes like criminals, attempting to make them invisible by restrictive zoning regulations. On the federal level, in the 1970s and early 1980s, the Austrian prostitution discourse oscillated between prohibition, regulation and moralisation. The federal legislature legalised prostitution during the 1970s, a 'modernisation' period in Austrian history, yet it simultaneously gendered 'immoral behaviour'. While the old 'vagrancy law' punished both the prostitute and the client, the 'decree concerning the health supervision of 'professional sexual offenders' (1975) made the prostitute solely responsible for the 'immoral act' of selling sex. The state neglected to respond to the demands of the women's movement in the policy debate on the amendment of the Penal Code in 1984. The Women's State Secretary held a weak position, having merely a symbolic role. In addition, the policy debates on prostitution were, for the most part, 'gender-blind'. In general, the policy environment as a whole was closed towards the issue.

A 'law and order discourse' de-gendered the policy process even up until the late 1980s. Sex work was depicted as a moral threat and health problem. Prostitutes' rights, especially their economic rights, were totally ignored. Prostitution policy faced a cultural environment and a policy system that were extremely discouraging.

In the period from the late 1980s to the early 1990s, women's policy agencies and women's groups made great headway in 'making a difference' in Austrian women's policy. Together they were increasingly successful at gendering the prostitution debate in a feminist manner. The amendment of the Viennese prostitution law in 1991 also took some gender aspects into account and the debate on social insurance for sex workers was placed within the gendered discourse of economic citizenship for sex workers. Both laws decriminalised selling sex and improved prostitutes' access to social security, undoing the previous moral framing.

The women's movement's impact on the prostitution issue was minimal in the 1970s and 1980s, because prostitution policy was not a vital issue to the movement. In that context, prostitutes were perceived not as sisters, but as collaborators with 'patriarchy'. From the late 1980s, the women's movement and some women's projects became more educated on the topic and the project-oriented movement grew increasingly aware of migrant women's role in sex work.

In the late 1990s, some women's groups and lesbian activists from the AIDS self-help movement were able to influence women's policy agencies and the policy process at large. Party feminists from the SPÖ and Green members also made reference to gender throughout the debate and framed the policy discourse in terms of legal and professional rights for prostitutes. In turn, the Federal Women's Ministry embraced the issue. It was also influenced by international debates, transporting it to the public and bringing it into the policy environment. Women's policy agencies in the 1990s were necessary catalysts in bringing prostitution on to the political agenda and discussing the matter in feminist contexts. Women's policy agencies helped the feminist movement to reach its procedural and substantive goals on the prostitution issue. The Federal Ministry of Women's Affairs was also a chief organiser and impetus and catalyst for many women's groups concerned with sex work.

The willingness of feminists in the government to co-operate with feminist experts led to a gender-differentiated policy outcome in the 1990s. Women's policy offices were necessary and effective mediators between the movement, feminist groups, and the state's substantive and procedural responses. Yet, in 2003 selling sex is still an 'immoral' contract and prostitution is not considered a legal form of work. An amendment of the Vienna prostitution law, which is now under non-public evaluation, again has a prohibitive approach and suggests fining clients.

NOTES

Special thanks to Claudia Brunner, Erika Doucette, Eva Kreisky and Ulrike Plichta.

1. These debates were:
   • Penal Code of 1974
   • Decree concerning the health supervision of prostitutes, 1974
   • Viennese Police Decree on Prostitution 1975
   • Decision of the Austrian High Court in 1982
   • Decision of the Administrative Court in 1983
   • Amendment of the Penal Code in 1984

- First Viennese prostitution law 1984
- Amendment of the taxation law 1985
- Federal law on measures against the transmission of AIDS 1986
- Amendment of the Viennese prostitution law 1991
- Amendment of the AIDS law 1993
- Amendment of the Viennese law on taxation of advertising 1995
- Amended law on social insurance for free enterprise 1998
- Debate on the amendment of the Viennese prostitution law 1998
- Decree of the Ministry of Interior concerning 'female dancers' 2001.

2. Parliamentary Correspondence no. II-2464 of the appendix to the National Council's stenographic protocols, during the XV legislative period, on 25 May 1981.

3. See e.g. the Minister of Justice's response on 7 July 1981, Parliamentary Correspondence no. II-2665 of the appendix to the National Council's stenographic protocols, no. 7094/1-Pr 1/81.

4. BGBl. 295/1984, National Parliament, GP XVI IA 29/A and 66/A AB 326, p. 55.

5. See Dietrich, parliamentary debate, GP XVI, Sitzung 55, 28.6, 1984.

6. See parliamentary debate, GP XVI, Sitzung 55, 28.6, 1984.

7. See parliamentary debate, GP XVI, Sitzung 55, 28.6, 1984.

8. See Dietrich, parliamentary debate, GP XVI, Sitzung 55, 28.6, 1984.

9. BGBl. 295/1984, National Parliament, GP XVI IA 29/A and 66/A AB 326, p. 55.

10. See parliamentary debate, GP XVI, Sitzung 55, 28.6, 1984.

11. Wiener Prostitutionsverordnung, Ortspolizeiliche Verordnung vom 13.2.1975; Amtsblatt der Stadt Wien 1975, H. 20, 17.

12. Decision of the Administrative Court, 16 February 1983, Zahlen 82/13/0208, 0215.

4   Prostitution policies in Britain, 1982–2002

Johanna Kantola and Judith Squires

Introduction

Within Britain's current legal framework prostitution is conceived of as a public nuisance. The position of the prostitute is ambiguous in relation to the law: the sale of sex is not an offence but many of the activities connected with it are. This framework was created by the Report on Homosexual Offences and Prostitution (Wolfenden et al. 1957). The Wolfenden Report aimed to apply a more rigid distinction between law and morality, claiming that however immoral prostitution may be, it was not the law's business. It also aimed to rationalise resources directed towards the control of prostitution while increasing the certainty of convictions. Finally, it encouraged a more systematic policing of the public sphere in order to remove the visible manifestations of prostitution in urban centres (Matthews 1986: 188–9). Within this legal framework two key pieces of legislation were swiftly introduced: the Sexual Offences Act 1956 and Street Offences Act 1959. While the Sexual Offences Act deals with the various activities, relationships and behaviours that might aid, manage, exploit or encourage prostitutes, the Street Offences Act deals directly with prostitutes and prostitution and regulates the manner and means by which prostitutes and their clients can contact each other (Phoenix 1999: 19–20). These two pieces of legislation proved successful in removing prostitution from view and encouraging the growth of more clandestine and commercialised operations (Matthews 1986: 189). However, since the 1970s there has been increasing dissatisfaction with the liberalism associated with Wolfenden. This dissatisfaction led to the legislative changes that we explore in this chapter: the abolition of imprisonment of prostitutes and kerb-crawling legislation.

Selection of debates

Legislation covering prostitution in the United Kingdom (passed at Westminster, pertaining to England and Wales, but not Scotland or

Northern Ireland) is made at a national level by government. There has been relatively little legislation passed on this issue during the past few decades. The three debates selected are the most significant in the UK in that they alone have been high profile. The cases are all representative with regard to the decisional arena. As there were no debates resulting in any official output in the 1970s, all cases selected fall into the decades of the 1980s and 1990s.

The first debate culminated in the Criminal Justice Act 1982, which abolished the use of imprisonment as a punishment for women convicted of soliciting. Kerb crawling, our second debate, has been the dominant focus of public and parliamentary attention regarding prostitution during the past fifteen years. Persistent kerb crawling was made an offence in the Sexual Offences Act 1985 and an arrestable offence in the Criminal Justice and Police Act 2001. The third debate, on the trafficking in women, is a newly emerging debate about prostitution in the UK. In 2000 the Home Office published a recommendation that a new offence of maintaining a person in sexual servitude be created.

This selection omits only two significant developments in relation to prostitution within the specified time period: the placing of advertisements relating to prostitution in public telephone kiosks (which was made an offence in the Criminal Justice and Police Act 2001) and new government guidelines for bodies dealing with children involved in prostitution. The Children Act 1989 had placed specific duties on agencies to co-operate in the interests of children involved in prostitution. The new guidelines reinforce and expand upon this, emphasising that children should be treated primarily as victims of abuse (Home Office 2000a: 5). We have chosen not to focus on the advertising debate because this policy change came at the same time as the kerb-crawling legislative change, and public debate was framed by the same set of issues. Similarly public debate leading up to the child prostitution guidelines was framed by the same set of issues as the trafficking debates.

Debate 1: Abolition of imprisonment for prostitutes, 1979–1982

How issue came to the public agenda

There were three private members' bills in the House of Lords between 1967 and 1969 concerned with deleting reference to 'common prostitutes' in the law and suggestions that the law against the client should be initiated. None of the bills achieved a second reading. However, they reflect a growing concern with women's rights and legal inequalities. Two further private members' bills in 1979 and 1981 did not receive a second reading either. Nevertheless, the latter, introduced by Clive Soley (Labour MP for Hammersmith North), on 'The Imprisonment of Prostitutes Abolition Bill' was influential in ultimately achieving the abolition of imprisonment for prostitutes convicted of soliciting (Matthews 1986: 190). In December 1982, the Criminal Law Revision Committee (the parliamentary committee handling this legislative change) published a working paper on 'Offences Relating to Prostitution and Allied Offences'. From 31 January 1983, imprisonment for loitering and soliciting was abolished.

There were women's movement organisations that campaigned for the abolition of imprisonment of prostitutes. Campaigning for the new legislation were organisations such as PUSSI (Prostitutes United for Social and Sexual Integration), PLAN (Prostitution Laws are Nonsense) and PROS (Programme for Reform of the Laws on Soliciting). Their common aim was to draw attention to the inequities and inconsistencies within the legislation (McLeod 1982: 119–47). However, the legislative change was, ultimately, motivated by other concerns.

Dominant frame of debate

The dominant frame of the parliamentary debate in the early 1980s focused on the perceived need for penal reform. This was motivated by general humanitarian concerns and also a growing concern with a crisis in the prison system. As Susan Edwards suggests, 'Though many claimed that this was a humanitarian move, it was more likely to have been a politically expedient measure, calculated to deal with the problem of prison overcrowding' (Edwards 1987: 46). The pragmatic desire to deal with prison overcrowding was high on the agenda of parliamentarians.

The parliamentary debates on the Criminal Justice Bill, held during 1981 and 1982, were conducted entirely in terms of the 'dangerous crisis in the prisons' as a result of overcrowding and poor conditions (*Hansard* 20 March 1981). The bill gave legislative effect to an important section of the Conservative Party Manifesto and was defended mainly by (male) Conservative MPs. The one female MP who spoke in these debates was Jo Richardson (Labour MP for Barking). She stated that: 'In general there is much that is wrong with the Bill and there is relatively little in it that is welcome.' (*Hansard* 20 January 1982: 313) Yet even she mentioned prostitution only once in passing.

Gendering the debate

There was no explicit focus on gender or gender relations in this debate. The dominant frame focused largely on humanitarian and pragmatic concerns. The legislative change in relation to the imprisonment of prostitutes was a very small element of the wide-reaching Criminal Justice Bill, which primarily sought to address youth crime and the criminalisation of 'petty and persistent offenders'. The debate was situated within the more general Thatcherite concern with law and order.

Outside of parliamentary debate, there were attempts to provide a more explicit gendering of debate. The most notable attempt emerged with the contribution of the English Collective of Prostitutes (ECP), which focused attention on female sex workers. This collective highlighted the economic and legal consequences of Thatcherite policies for women. They stressed the dramatic increase in the number of prosecutions for offences relating to prostitution since the coming to power of the Thatcher government in 1979, itself a reflection of the increase in the number of prostitutes as a consequence of the deterioration of women's economic position (Edwards 1987: 50–3). However, the ECP had a marginal status, even within the women's movement.

Policy outcome

The outcome of these parliamentary debates was the publication of a working paper by the Criminal Law Revision Committee (December 1982) and new legislation, which abolished imprisonment for loitering and soliciting (February 1983). However, despite the desire to reduce prison overcrowding, the legislation appeared to have precisely the opposite impact in relation to prostitutes. The number of prostitutes being arrested and prosecuted actually increased following the legislation. In 1979, prosecutions totalled 3,167, in 1981, 4,323, and in 1983, 10,674 (Edwards 1987: 43). Also the rate of incarceration substantially increased through the non-payment of fines; in 1982, 83 women were incarcerated for the non-payment of fines; in 1983, the figure rose to 172.

Women's movement impact

During the early 1980s the broader political climate in Britain was shaped by Thatcherism, which represented a weakening of the women's movement. The most successful response of the women's movement to the Thatcher era was in the area of anti-militarism. The Greenham Common peace camp, for example, was the focus of the women's movement agenda during this period (Pugh 2000: 337). The ECP was one of the few women's organisations to issue any direct statements or to campaign in relation to prostitution debates. Whilst it has a somewhat marginal relation to the women's movement generally, we here take it to represent the women's movement on this issue. In an attempt to influence the policy outcome of this debate, the ECP engaged in various forms of non-governmental civil protest. It was not engaged in the parliamentary process. Other organisations, such as PUSSI and PROS, also engaged with the debate, but were similarly marginal.

In April 1982, the ECP initiated Legal Action for Women (LAW), a grass-roots legal service for all women. It also launched a movement of women pleading not guilty to prostitution offences in court (ECP 1997: 86). The ECP also went on strike on 17 November 1982 to protest against widespread police harassment. Its demands included an end to illegal arrests of prostitutes, and immediate protection, welfare and housing for women who want to leave prostitution (ECP 1997: 88).

The legislative change did not positively address their demands. It was introduced as part of a law and order agenda that worked to socially ostracise prostitutes rather than address their concerns. The ECP felt let down by the legislation and argued that their contribution to the policy process was marginalised: 'Making us invisible was not an oversight' (ECP 1997: 89). It notes that politicians and the police are still calling for more policing to clean the streets of prostitute women (ECP 1997: 89). However, despite the fact that the reform was motivated by concerns other than demands from the women's movement, and notwithstanding the fact that the effect of the legal change was counter-productive for prostitutes, the outcome did coincide with movement demands and so the state response can be categorised as one of pre-emption.

Women's policy agency activities

Since the 1970s a women's policy machinery has been created within the UK, yet these agencies played no discernible role in the debate and policy changes relating to prostitution in the past three decades. The Women's National Commission (WNC) was established in 1969 and the Equal Opportunities Commissions (EOC) in 1975. The WNC was founded to bring 'the informed opinion of women to bear on government policy' (Stokes 2002). The EOC was established to oversee the implementation of the Sex Discrimination Act of 1975. Prostitution policy was not part of the mandate of either agency. Moreover both the WNC and the EOC were relatively autonomous from government. Lovenduski notes that, possibly as a result of these factors, 'the early work of the EOC proved disappointing to many observers' (Lovenduski 1995: 121). Stokes concurs with this judgement, concluding that – despite producing valuable research – the EOC 'is not a campaigning body and lacks both the authority and the resources to initiate action' (Stokes 2002: 193). She also argues that the WNC was generally regarded as 'a conservative, somewhat marginal body', which failed to engage with important issues.

We suggest that both the WNC and EOC took a symbolic role in relation to prostitution debates. The WNC had a very low profile generally and made no attempt to gender policy on this issue. The EOC did have a significant role in developing sex equality policy debates (Lovenduski 1995: 115) and was therefore potentially an 'insider' policy agency. However, it failed to make any contribution to the gendering of this particular debate.

Women's movement characteristics

By the 1980s the women's movement in the UK was losing momentum: it was at a stage of decline and increasingly fragmented. Many feminists, increasingly alienated from the parliamentary political process in a period of right-wing government, focused on pre-figurative, separatist political projects. Others focused their energies on developing links with trade unions and the Labour Party (Pugh 2000: 334).

Within the former camp, the ECP proved to be the most significant group campaigning in relation to this policy debate. Yet, given its roots in Wages for Housework (the early 1970s campaign which based itself on a marxist analysis claiming that women's oppression was rooted in the exploitation of the surplus value women produced), which has always had a tense relationship with other more mainstream groupings in the women's movement, the ECP is not representative of the women's movement as a whole. Its focus on sex work is at odds with other feminist perspectives, which focus on sexual domination (see for example Rape Crisis Federation and Campaign to End Rape; Kelly 1988).

Amongst those who did prioritise institutional politics, the discipline of British party politics meant that attention was focused within parties and trade unions rather than across government departments (Lovenduski 1995: 115). The women's movement was, at this time, close to the left. Many women pursued their agendas within unions and the Labour Party, where they had some institutional support, but little power. Those feminists who campaigned outside of the party system were also broadly left-aligned. However, the left itself was relatively weak. The issue of the abolition of imprisonment for prostitution was a moderate priority for the women's movement. It was not a uniting issue: it was simply not a priority for women working within the parliamentary system, but it was important for organisations such as the ECP. However, their voice was so marginal to mainstream debates that no counter-movement emerged.

Policy environment

The UK has a first-past-the-post electoral system, which usually guarantees governments in which a single party has a clear majority. In addition the UK operates with a closed policy sub-system, where participation in policy formation is limited to the executive, and the political party in government controls policy space and the parameters of policy debate.

The barriers to active feminist engagement in the policy-making process created by the closed policy sub-system were magnified by the political climate during the 1980s. This first policy debate occurred in the context of a profound shift towards a new right political agenda, and the successive defeats of the Labour Party throughout the 1980s until Labour's return to office in 1997. The relationships between the various strands of the increasingly fragmented women's movement and the Thatcher governments were almost entirely hostile. Feminist demands were articulated via numerous small non-governmental organisations within civil society, which lacked institutional avenues into the policy-making process (notwithstanding the existence of the WNC, or the presence of women within the Labour Party, which was itself relatively powerless during this period). The sex work discourse deployed by the ECP was incompatible with the public nuisance approach adopted within the policy circuit.

Debate 2: Kerb crawling as an offence (1985) and an arrestable offence (2001)

How issue came to the public agenda

This debate came on to the public agenda primarily via local constituency concerns about the moral and environmental 'pollution' caused by kerb crawling (Matthews 1986; Hubbard 1998a). Residents formed *ad hoc* associations and 'spokesmen' arranged public meetings to discuss the subject, so that the local community could be mobilised against it. Local residents and police, in co-operation, patrolled streets in small groups trying to dissuade prostitutes from frequenting the area. Most large metropolitan areas in Britain, including Birmingham, Bradford and Manchester, experienced such activism. These activities gained both local and then national media coverage. The debate entered parliament via the MPs of constituencies particularly affected by kerb crawling, and legislation resulted from private members' bills.

There have been several major parliamentary debates on kerb crawling to date: in 1984 parliamentary debate led to the Sexual Offences Act (1985); in 1990 a private members' bill was proposed, with the aim of removing 'persistently' from the Act, to no avail; in 1993 and 1994, as a response to community activism, further debates were introduced, which questioned whether existing legislation was sufficient to deal adequately with kerb crawling, but did not result in policy change; in 1999, debate again reviewed the law on kerb crawling in response to concerns of MPs with constituency-related problems; finally in 2001 these debates resulted in legislative change whereby the Criminal Justice and Police Act (2001) made kerb crawling an arrestable offence. In each of these debates, MPs spoke of the concern expressed by their constituents about the problem of street prostitution.

In 1984 the parliamentary debate on street prostitution was introduced by Tom Cox (Labour MP for Tooting). He stressed the experience of 'local residents', the threats and nuisance they endure, and the positive action they had taken to work with local police to deal with the problem. In 1994 Lynne Jones (Labour MP for Birmingham, Selly Oak) opened the kerb-crawling debate by stating: 'I have sought this debate on behalf of my constituents who live in what should be a pleasant residential area, but which for decades has been blighted and unjustifiably stigmatised as a result of the nuisance and disturbance associated with street prostitution and, latterly, window prostitution' (*Hansard* 19 July 1994: 292). Jones went on to argue that 'from a resident's perspective prostitution creates a poor environmental image . . . An atmosphere of fear is created for female residents and children.' In 1999 Diane Abbott (Labour MP for Hackney, North and Stoke Newington) asked: 'Is the Minister aware of the great concern about this matter in my constituency, expressed by among others, the Amhurst Park action group – a long-standing activist organisation that has campaigned on this issue . . . ?' (*Hansard* 15 March 1999: 701). In other words, both legislative changes resulted from private members' bills, introduced as a result of local community pressure. The problem of kerb crawling, as experienced by local communities, is still discussed within the media on a regular basis (see *The Times* 9 May 2001; *Guardian* 29 January 2001).

Dominant frame of debate

In this debate the emphasis on prostitution as a public nuisance was absolutely dominant. As the Conservative MP David Mellor (Parliamentary Under-Secretary of State for the Home Office) stated: 'We are under no illusions about the nuisance caused by prostitutes soliciting in the streets, and the genuine distress experienced by respectable and law abiding residents who live in the vicinity of red light areas' (*Hansard* 20 February 1984: 675).

For the local communities (including the Muslim communities active in this debate), prostitution was a moral vice. The harassment of local female residents by the kerb crawlers was one of the main complaints. A conservative distinction was drawn between the 'good' and the 'bad' women. Local and national media played a significant role in supporting these campaigns, reproducing stereotyped ideas of the prostitute as polluting. These ideas were echoed in the attitudes expressed by residents and pickets: that selling sex is immoral and dangerous. These local discourses produced a seemingly commonsense view that commercial sex work is unnatural and deviant. Local apprehensions about drugs, environmental degradation and crime were projected on to the stigmatised figure of the street prostitute. Importantly, commercial sex work was identified as a cause, rather than a symptom, of the problems that afflicted these marginal inner-city areas (Hubbard 1998a: 283).

Gendering the debate

Much of the public and parliamentary debate on kerb crawling was conducted in terms of 'communities'. In this way, the gendered nature of the debates was downplayed. Within these communities two groupings were especially significant: mothers concerned to protect the safety and freedom of movement of their children and themselves in their local communities, and Muslim communities concerned with the moral threat that street-based prostitution posed to their religious and cultural values. The public debate was therefore articulated not by 'women' as a group, but by mothers and Muslim men.

However, the dominant frame of debate was itself gendered in that it focused on women's sexuality. Although the link between prostitution and crime was the most persistent theme in the local newspapers (Gwinnett 1998: 90; Hubbard 1998b: 68–9), another strong theme was that innocent women were to be protected from the manifestations of conspicuous sexuality (Phoenix 1999: 25). Moreover, prostitutes were understood as a source of disease, constructing them as a risk group likely to spread ill health to the rest of the community. Women, via local community groups, were active in shaping and articulating these debates. In one sense then, women were successful in gendering the debate, in that they – along with male members of the community – emphasised the importance of the safety of women and their right to freedom of movement. Moreover, it was largely female Labour MPs who took up their cause and represented their case in parliamentary debates. Yet, other concerns expressed by women were marginalised. In particular, the issues surrounding the causes behind prostitution were not on the agenda. The unequal treatment of the prostitutes by the law and the problems they experience in their everyday lives were hardly addressed in the public debates.

The voice of the ECP was highly marginal in shaping the 1985, 1994 and 2001 debates on kerb crawling. The collective argued strongly against kerb-crawling legislation: 'It has equalised women down by taking away some of the rights men had which women were fighting to get: instead of prostitute women not being arrested for soliciting men, men are being arrested for soliciting women' (ECP 1997: 90). In 1984, the ECP initiated the Campaign Against Kerb Crawling Legislation (CAKCL) – a coalition of anti-rape, Black and civil rights organisations, AIDS prevention groups, lawyers, probation officers and Labour Party activists. However, it has been the local protest against street prostitution which has counted the most. Tighter controls for kerb crawling remain a core policing issue (West 2000: 107). Prostitutes' organisations have had very little influence in the UK, partly – as West suggests – because of 'moral majority' hegemony and preoccupations with disorder and abuse (West 2000: 115).

Policy outcome

The debates surrounding prostitution in the mid-1980s and 1990s led to two legislative changes, in 1985 and 2001. In 1984 parliamentary debate led to the Sexual Offences Act (1985), which introduced the offence of 'persistent kerb crawling'. The 1985 Act soon became unworkable because police had to prove 'persistent' solicitation rather than solicitation *per se*. By direct comparison, the evidential requirement for solicitation by women (under the Street Offences Act 1959) does not require persistence. Alongside this evidential obstacle to effective prosecution was the unwillingness of police to prosecute men (Edwards 1997: 66). Although kerb-crawling legislation is about men, it has resulted in large numbers of prostitute women being arrested. In 1993, for example, 7,912 females were prosecuted for loitering and soliciting compared with the prosecution of 857 males for the offence of kerb crawling (Edwards 1996: 49).

In 1999 further parliamentary debate, again reviewing the law on kerb crawling in response to concerns of MPs with constituency-related problems, resulted in legislative change whereby the Criminal Justice and Police Act (2001) made kerb crawling an arrestable offence. Making the offence arrestable enables the police to take offenders into custody and question them rather than having to summon them to appear at a magistrates' court to answer the charge.

Women's movement impact

The fragmentation of the women's movement, indicated in relation to the first debate, is clearly manifest in relation to this second debate. Those women's organisations that were campaigning around issues of prostitution were effectively silenced in relation to the kerb-crawling debates. On the other hand, those women who had focused their energies within the party political system found that they were able to exercise their power to gain a strong public profile for a debate of particular concern to many of their female constituents. The parliamentary debates on kerb crawling were mainly introduced by female MPs, speaking on behalf of their constituents. This implies that an institutionalised party political form of women's political activity gained priority over a more radical movement-based form of political activism.

The ECP did secure representation among the witnesses called by the UK parliamentary groups, and the oral evidence of working prostitutes was heard in closed session. However, MPs took more written and verbal evidence from other constituencies with a stake in law reform, particularly the police and local authorities, as well as health professionals and residents' groups. It was the concerns of these more established groups that played a more prominent role than those of sex workers in the MPs' final recommendations (West 2000: 109). From this it is clear that the state accepted certain groupings of women into the policy-making process, but excluded others.

Women campaigning as local community mothers, fighting to secure their own safety and that of their children, received wide public attention and access, via their local MPs, to the policy-making process. Their concerns coincided with the dominant frame of debate. By contrast, women working within radical NGOs and feminist academics were marginalised from the policy-making process (O'Neill 1997; O'Connell Davidson 1998). Although women used local residents' organisations to put the issue of kerb crawling firmly on the political agenda, they did not organise as part of the women's movement. Therefore the ECP may be more representative of the women's movement in this case. We conclude that the movement's impact on the state was no response.

Women's policy agency activities

During the period in which kerb crawling was debated within the public sphere and parliament, a third women's policy agency was created, in addition to the WNC and EOC. The EOC continued to be relatively autonomous from government and kept its focus on equality in the labour market. The issue of prostitution was not close to its mandate. The WNC maintained its autonomous position in relation to government and its non-feminist leadership. The issue of prostitution was not close to its mandate either.

Following the 1997 general election, the Labour government established a Minister for Women at cabinet level, supported by a more junior Minister for Women and a Women's Unit (WU). The WU was a cross-cutting unit, whose central aim was to support ministers across Whitehall in their efforts to promote women's interests. It aimed to provide 'a two-way voice between Government and the women of the UK', ensuring that 'the concerns of women in the UK are fed directly into policy making across Government' (Women's Unit 1998). The unit was staffed by thirty-six civil servants seconded from other departments. Areas of expertise included women's incomes and financial security; work/life policies and practices; women in enterprise and ICT; communicating with and for women, including EU and UN representation; teenage girls and education and training; women's safety in and outside the home; women's health; and women and the environment. It had ultimate responsibility for international and European women's affairs (particularly Beijing +5). All other policy areas were the responsibility of particular government departments. There was also an educative and monitoring role, raising gender awareness amongst policy-makers and auditing the development and implementation of policies and programmes. The WU's agenda did not include any reference to the kerb-crawling debate or prostitution more generally. It certainly did not take any part in shaping the kerb-crawling legislation. In addition, as with the first debate, both the EOC and the WNC failed to make a significant contribution to this second debate. So, all three acted as symbolic women's policy agencies in relation to kerb crawling.

Women's movement characteristics

The debate on kerb crawling spanned two decades (from the early 1980s to 2001). During this period certain characteristics of the women's movement shifted profoundly. Specifically those women who had focused their energies on developing links with trade unions and the Labour Party in the 1980s gained, following the Labour Party victory in the 1997 election, new-found access to the policy-making process. This marked a period of resurgence for the groupings within the women's movement that had taken a parliamentary route (the Women's Budget Group, a think tank on the relationship between women, men and economics, became influential, for example). This element of the women's movement was very close to the left, having institutional power within the government. None the less, kerb crawling remained a low priority issue. It did not unify women across the movement. The only significant counter-movement to the lobby calling for kerb-crawling legislation was found in the alternative women's movement groups such as the ECP.

Policy environment

Notwithstanding the change in government and the coming to power of 'New Labour', with its rhetoric of inclusiveness and openness, the policy sub-system was still closed during this debate. Indeed there is widespread concern that the Blair governments have shifted the balance of power away from parliament towards the executive. The sex work discourse deployed by the ECP was incompatible with the public nuisance approach adopted within this closed policy circuit.

Debate 3: Maintaining a person in sexual servitude, 2000

How issue came to the public agenda

This debate entered into the UK public sphere via the international and European legislative frameworks. International actors have played a significant role in presenting many of the ideas surrounding the trafficking in women debate. In the case of Britain, the European Union and the United Nations have shaped the debate (EU actions include STOP and DAPHNE programmes, which aim at improving the position of the victims of trafficking). The Human Rights Act (1998) incorporates the European Convention on Human Rights into UK law. The Select Committee on European Scrutiny considered the draft framework decision on combating trafficking in human beings and combating the sexual exploitation of children and child pornography in the spring of 2001. In addition to signing the Trafficking Protocol to the United Nations Convention on Transnational Organised Crime, the government recognised the need for a specific offence of trafficking in human beings. It also considered it desirable to harmonise offences and penalties in this area on an EU basis (Home Office, 2001b).

In 1999 the United Nations stressed the role of criminal networks in trafficking in women and children and argued for a change in state policies, away from punishing the victims to punishing the criminals. The UN suggested that government policies and the practices of border control, immigration, police and justice agencies often concentrate on the illegal aspects of migration leaving aside the involvement of organised criminal groups in the smuggling of human beings. As a consequence, the primary targets of state interventions are the illegal migrants, not the criminal organisations involved in the smuggling and exploitation of human beings (UN 1999: 7). The UN notes that those who have become victims of trafficking may often lose more than they gain when co-operating with the justice system. In many countries, such persons are considered perpetrators of illegal acts rather than victims of crime and are persecuted for violations of immigration laws, prostitution or criminal or statutory offences (UN 1999: 7).

The General Assembly of the United Nations adopted the UN Convention against Transnational Organised Crime in November 2000 (the first legally binding UN instrument in the field of crime), which has to be signed and ratified by forty countries before it comes into force. The UK signed the convention along with 120 other countries in December 2000 in Palermo, Italy. The convention includes two optional protocols. These require the countries to undertake in-depth measures to combat smuggling of migrants and the buying and selling of women and children for sexual exploitation or sweat-shop labour (Protocol to Prevent, Suppress and Punish Trafficking in Persons, Especially Women and Children). The UK signed both the optional protocols as well as the convention.

Dominant frame of debate

The debates on trafficking have been conducted within parliament, the House of Lords and government, in terms of international human rights discourses and European human rights legislation. The Home Office report *Setting the Boundaries: Reforming the Law on Sex Offences* (2000) states: 'individuals are often held in circumstances which effectively restrict their freedom: passports and identification papers are removed; there may be limits on their ability to refuse clients or certain sexual practices and violence may be used to control them' (Home Office 2000b: 111). There is frequent appeal to a humanitarian, and particularly a Christian, frame of debate. For example, Baroness Cox (Conservative Party) refers to trafficking as entailing 'some of the most brutal forms of man's inhumanity to man' (Lords *Hansard* 19 January 2000: Column 1182). Lord Cocks (Conservative Party) states that: 'there is not just the question of humanity towards other people. Christians have a very great vested interest' (Lords *Hansard* 19 January 2000: 1186).

Trafficking has also been debated in the media, where there has been clear outrage about the difficulty in gaining convictions and the low penalties for trafficking in people (see *Guardian* 19 March 1999, 9 March 2001; *The Times* 26 April 2001, 13 June 2001). Judge Peter Singer, calling for new laws to crack down on the human traffickers, wrote in a letter to *The Times* that those found guilty of controlling prostitutes face a maximum of seven years in prison, or only two years if they caused or encouraged the prostitution of girls under the age of 16 years. Even these penalties were 'rarely imposed' (*The Times* 2 January 2002).

The discussion of trafficking is framed by a concern with child welfare. *The Times* reports: 'Martin Malone, who ran a ring of under-age prostitutes recruited from children's homes, was sent to prison for four years by Southwark Crown Court yesterday' (5 February 2000). The quote captures effectively the frame of the debate on trafficking in Britain. The debate, both within the press and within parliament, has focused on children rather than women. 'Refugee girls forced to work as prostitutes' claims *The Times* (26 April 2001). The debate is being framed in terms of the moral and physical welfare of children rather than women and women's rights. Significantly, the most outspoken actors in this debate are Barnardo's and children's charities rather than British women's movements (see Home Office 2000b: 114).

There is also a perception that trafficking is a particularly 'Metropolitan problem' (Kelly and Regan 2000: 35). The 'environmental pollution' frame that was important in the kerb-crawling debate focused on the 'public nuisance' element of prostitution. This works to sideline any concern with more 'private' forms of prostitution, and the phenomenon of trafficking (in which women are frequently kept out of the public sphere entirely) is not apparent within this context. For this reason, the issues of kerb crawling and of trafficking have been viewed as quite distinct within public debates: kerb crawling was a community-level concern, whereas the actors in the trafficking debate are found at the international or national level. There is little interest or commitment locally to allocating scarce resources to such 'marginal areas, or to re-enter the contested arena of prostitution generally' (Kelly and Regan

2000: 35). In the absence of willingness to countenance that trafficking may be happening locally, it is extremely unlikely that cases will be
identified, which will serve as justification for inaction (Kelly and Regan
2000: 35).

Gendering the debate

The debate about trafficking in women was brought to the UK public
agenda partly as a result of the campaigning work of international feminist organisations. Within the UK it has been child welfare groups and
those women's groups that have focused on child sexual abuse that have
determined the focus of debate.

The government consultation paper on sex offences was a product
of an open and inclusive review process. Members of the review included staff from the Women's Unit and WNC, representatives of feminist NGOs such as Rape Crisis Federation (RCF) and Campaign to End
Rape (CER), and feminist academics such as Liz Kelly. Kelly has been a
central figure in promoting a women's movement perspective on sexual
offences in UK policy-making. She has been a member of various governmental and police consultation groups on this issue. However, the review
also included a large number of representatives from children's charities
(such as Action for Children, The Children's Society and Barnardo's) and
religious representatives, from Christian and Muslim denominations. It
also included various government and police representatives. This composition indicates that various groups, broadly aligned with the women's
movement, were included in the policy-making process.

Women's movement groups and activists have been included in the policy debates on trafficking. Their perspective on abuse (which draws on a
sexual domination perspective) is sufficiently close to the dominant moral
order concern that frames public debate to be integrated into this (see
Kelly et al. 1995). However, the general humanitarian concern for child
welfare has tended to eclipse any focus on female prostitution in particular. They have not drawn on a sex work frame, as adopted by the ECP. In
this debate the sex work discourse was also articulated by Europap-UK,
a network which provides HIV and STD prevention services to sex workers (Europap-UK 1999a). Hilary Kinnell of Europap-UK was invited to
submit written comments to the Home Office on trafficking and sexual
exploitation (Europap-UK 1999b).

The distinction between forced and voluntary prostitution, emphasised
by both these organisations, has little significance in the context of policies
aiming to protect vulnerable children and women. This child welfare approach downplays the moral agency and legal rights of prostitute women

and instead emphasises trafficking in women as a contemporary form of slavery (Kelly and Regan 2000: 37).

The policy shift away from the traditional law-enforcement practice in Britain of prosecuting children for prostitution offences rather than their clients for child sexual abuse has been welcomed by some feminist commentators. Yet it is noted that this reflects the greater influence of well-organised 'moral constituencies' such as Barnardo's and The Children's Society than of groups promoting sex workers' occupational rights (West 2000: 109). Currently, trafficking and child prostitution are on the agenda while other dimensions of prostitution are excluded from review. Issues of abuse and coercion are beginning to dominate the UK debate, both in the media and at official levels, encouraged by a Labour government with a programme of moral renewal (West 2000: 109). Given this, Liz Kelly and her colleagues have been able to make a substantial contribution to the debate on trafficking and shape government policy. They have been able to gender the debate because their sexual domination frame is in sufficient ideological alignment with the moral order frame of the government.

Policy outcome

In the Home Office report of February 2002, David Blunkett, the Labour Home Secretary, announced that the government will strengthen the law, including a fourteen-year penalty for facilitating illegal entry and trafficking for the purposes of sexual exploitation (Home Office 2002:7).

The White Paper incorporates the recommendation of a previous Home Office report that there should be a specific trafficking offence, which would involve 'bringing or enabling a person to move from one place to another for the purposes of commercial sexual exploitation or to work as a prostitute, for reward'(Home Office 2000b: xvi). This is one of sixty-two recommendations within the report, placing trafficking within a new sex offences legal framework. The White Paper details six specific measures that the government will be taking to deal with trafficking: it will combat illegal working through improved enforcement action; strengthen the law; deal appropriately and compassionately with victims of trafficking; target the criminals through intelligence and enforcement operations; co-operate with the EU and other international partners; and tackle organised crime through prevention strategies (Home Office 2002:17).

Women's movement impact

There is no dedicated NGO, within the UK, providing support and advocacy for trafficked women. However, certain groups within the women's movement, such as the RCF and CER, have had an impact on the policy process. They have been consulted directly by the Home Office and the women's policy agencies regarding the drafting of the government report on trafficking. Significantly, Kelly and Regan produced a Home Office paper on trafficking in women for sexual exploitation in the UK (Kelly and Regan 2000). In this they recommend 'the creation of a crime of "sexual exploitation" where proving the offence would require showing that a sexual act took place and that someone else benefited from it in monetary terms or in kind' (Kelly and Regan 2000: v–vi). They call for basic and regular monitoring of off-street prostitution and reform to en-sure that the legal framework, including sentencing, acts as an effective tool to prosecute traffickers and exploiters (Kelly and Regan 2000: vi). These recommendations are very closely aligned to the policy proposals made in the Home Office report.

By contrast, the impact of the ECP has been much weaker. Police raids in Soho, London, illustrate this. In the name of protecting women from trafficking, about forty women were arrested, detained and in some cases summarily removed from Britain. The ECP protested against the raids, arguing that most of the immigrant women prostituting in Soho were doing it voluntarily. Nina Lopez-Jones from the ECP argued in the *Guardian*:

The Soho raid to 'liberate' victims of trafficking was an abuse of power. Women were led to believe that they could expect protection, only to find themselves arrested and deported. This raid lays the basis for trafficking legislation which would give the police greater power of arrest, while the women on whose behalf they are supposedly acting would no longer need to give evidence – the police, not the victim, would testify about the truth of her situation. (*Guardian* 22 February 2001)

The deep scepticism that this view expresses has not received much atten-tion in the public debates on trafficking in women and children. Europap-UK also felt its perspective to be marginalised in the debate (Europap-UK 2002).

The approach of the international feminist groups and the RCF and CER is often at odds with that of the ECP. Unlike the ECP, the Coalition Against Trafficking in Women (CATW) does not find the consent of the victim important. The CATW argues that it played a pivotal role in the evolution of the optional UN trafficking protocol, Article 3b of which states that the consent of a victim of trafficking is irrelevant (Raymond 2001: 3).

So, whilst the impact of the ECP and Europap has been marginal in this debate, the RCF and CER, along with particularly influential feminists such as Kelly and Regan, have had a significant role in gendering the debate and shaping policy proposals. They have been included in the policy process, and the resulting government proposals on trafficking in women are very much in keeping with their recommendations. We therefore suggest that there was a dual response to a women's movement agenda in this debate.

Women's policy agency activities

Following the 2001 General Election, the Women's Unit was re-launched as the Women and Equality Unit, based in the Cabinet Office. This unit continues as a cross-cutting unit, but with an enlarged staff of fifty. It now has responsibility for co-ordinating policy on women and gender equality issues, including all issues relating to the Sex Discrimination Act and equal pay legislation. This gives the unit a much more significant role than was previously the case. In addition, it now sponsors the EOC and the WNC, giving it a pivotal role in the co-ordination of these bodies and overall responsibility for equality issues. Any evaluation of the impact of women's policy agency activities in relation to trafficking should therefore now focus on the WEU.

In 2001 the WEU issued a document, 'Living Without Fear', which develops an integrated approach to tackling violence against women. In relation to the trafficking in and exploitation of women, the WEU states that: 'We are fully committed to opposing trafficking in women and its associated activities' (2001). In addition it also states that it is continuing to work on the problem with other EU member states. This signals that the central UK women's policy agency does have a stance on the issue of trafficking, and is working to influence policy in this area. There is now an 'insider' women's policy agency, with a feminist leadership, that has both influence within government and links with grass-roots women's movement organisations, via the WNC.

Women's movement characteristics

Since the late 1990s, when trafficking emerged on the UK political agenda, we have witnessed a re-emergence of particular groups within the women's movement. For instance, the Fawcett Society has campaigned prominently and successfully on the issue of women's representation in parliament (Stephenson 1998). The emerging links between women's movement groups and government, made possible by a new left agenda, allowed long-established women's movement actors to influence the policy-making process. Specifically, the increased role and profile given to the women's policy agencies by the government allowed the RCF to become more integrated in the policy process regarding trafficking in women. Well-established political agendas within the women's movement, concerning sexual violence and abuse, found a voice in a left government. This agenda is a high-priority issue for the women's movement. Violence against women has long been one of the central concerns of the UK women's movement: campaigns around this issue unite many diverse groups within the women's movement and also foster collaboration with other groups, such as child welfare organisations.

Policy environment

Since 1997 the UK has had a new Labour government. In 1998 the UK ratified the European Convention on Human Rights. These factors ensure that the policy environment is more open to international initiatives than was previously the case. The government has shown itself to be reasonably willing to ratify international and European conventions.

The policy sub-system is now moderately closed: the institutional organisation remains largely unaltered, but the ethos of the current government is more benign in relation to women's movement goals. The government has made substantial efforts to increase the participation of women in parliament and government, and to widen the avenues of access and accountability. In addition it is relatively open to international interventions within a civil rights frame and yet also maintains a strong concern with moral order. This combination of agendas has proved to be relatively open to that women's movement agenda which focuses on sexual violence and abuse. The sexual domination discourse deployed by these organisations within the women's movement was compatible with the public nuisance approach adopted within the policy circuit.

Conclusion

Prostitution has been a low-priority issue for both the women's movement and the various women's policy agencies in the UK throughout the period that prostitution legislation has been debated and introduced until the late 1990s. For much of this period the women's movement has been in decline; only recently have we witnessed some resurgence. Women's activism has fragmented into numerous discrete, often antagonistic single-issue campaigns. The public debate around gender issues in the UK has focused primarily on labour market inclusion and equality of employment terms and conditions. Prostitution was not on the agenda of the EOC or WNC at all during the first and second debates. These agencies played a symbolic role in relation to prostitution policies up until the establishment of the Women's Unit. In the third debate a newly strengthened WEU did have a policy on trafficking, but this was not articulated in relation to prostitution issues more generally. More recently still, the WEU has acted as an insider policy agency in relation to the debate about trafficking. This development is a product of two central factors: the election of a new Labour government, combined with the appeal to a high-priority women's movement issue. The debate on trafficking has invoked a core women's movement concern of violence against women, in a way that other debates on prostitution have not. The issue of violence against women has always been a high-priority issue for the UK women's movement, whilst prostitution has not. The greater political alignment between government and the women's movement since 1997 has allowed this agenda to impact on the policy formation process.

NOTE

We would like to thank Joni Lovenduski and Jackie West who provided invaluable information and comments in the writing of this chapter.

5 Prostitution as public nuisance: prostitution policy in Canada

Leslie Ann Jeffrey

Introduction

Since 1972 prostitution law in Canada has had the dubious distinction of making it legal to 'be' a prostitute but next to impossible to actually engage in prostitution-related activity. While many Western countries have moved away from stricter criminal laws against prostitution, Canada has moved in quite the opposite direction with the maintenance of anti-brothel laws and the introduction of laws aimed at the street-level trade, a small percentage of prostitution-related activities (Davis and Schaffer 1994: I). Until the late 1970s, street prostitution was dealt with under the vagrancy provisions of the Criminal Code, which allowed for the arrest of 'common prostitutes' found in public places. Following changes in the interpretation of the law in the late 1970s that made it more difficult to arrest prostitutes, police forces and residents' groups began to campaign for tougher laws to control street solicitation. Feminist attempts to lobby for decriminalisation of prostitution (i.e. its complete or near complete removal from the Criminal Code) have continued to meet strong resistance from these groups. The current 'anti-communications' law, which makes communication for the purpose of prostitution illegal, is technically more gender equitable than in the past – in that it addresses both prostitutes and clients and includes both male and female prostitutes. However, it fails to address the underlying gender inequity that results from the criminalisation (i.e. using criminal sanctions against activities associated with prostitution) of prostitute women. Women in prostitution continue to be disproportionately charged by police (Shaver 1993: 154–5). They also face a disproportionately high risk of violence (including murder) compared with women in general (Robertson 1999). Since the 1985 law, adult prostitution has nearly disappeared from the national political agenda, although there are some recent stirrings from within the federal bureaucracy to address the issue of international trafficking in women and continued action at the local and provincial levels to deal with the 'nuisance' of street prostitution. Most recently, the government has become concerned over youth in prostitution. This led to a number of bills that address this specific aspect of the problem being introduced during the course of the 1990s.

Selection of debates

There have been a number of attempts to change the law governing prostitution since the 1970s at the federal, provincial and municipal levels. Generally, prostitution is dealt with by the federal government under the Criminal Code. Thus, the key players in establishing this law are the Federal House of Commons and the Ministry of Justice. As Canada has a parliamentary system with a tradition of large majorities and strong party discipline, the real power over such changes lies with the federal cabinet. However, because the central issue in debates over prostitution in recent years has been the nuisance aspect of street solicitation, municipal and provincial governments have been regularly involved in attempting to regulate prostitution and in pushing the federal government to amend its laws. The Supreme Court of Canada and the various provincial Supreme Courts have also played a central role in interpreting prostitution laws, often in ways that have forced the government back to the table to redesign prostitution law. Finally, the federal and provincial governments have often used the popular Canadian technique of establishing bureaucratic task forces and extra-parliamentary royal commissions to conduct background research on prostitution issues and 'feel out' public opinion.

Several debates leading to policy decisions have occurred since the mid-1970s when a women's policy agency was created.[1] The key issues have been how to deal with street-level prostitution and with youth in prostitution. For this discussion I have chosen first the debate over prostitution policy in the Fraser Committee, which held hearings and made recommendations on the issue in 1984–5. The second debate, coming on the heels of the first, is the debate over the anti-communications law (Bill C-49), which is now the key law on prostitution. The third debate that will be considered is the debate during the Federal/Provincial/Territorial Working Group on Prostitution and the resulting bill on child prostitution introduced under the Liberals in the mid-1990s. These three debates cover the key issue areas concerning prostitution that have dominated the public agenda since the 1970s. Two take place at the federal level, which has been the most important policy-making arena, while the Federal/Territorial/Provincial Working Group represents a joint initiative of both levels. Finally, while the first two debates occurred within a relatively short space of time and there is no debate from the 1970s, this selection reflects the relative absence of important policy decisions in the 1970s. Also the Fraser Committee debates in many ways mark a culmination of debates begun in the late 1970s.

Debate 1: Fraser Committee, 1983–1985

How issue came to the public agenda

Prior to 1972, prostitution in Canada was governed under the British derived Vagrancy Laws in the Criminal Code. Known as 'Vag. C', the law specifically pertaining to prostitution stated that 'Every one commits vagrancy who, being a common prostitute or night-walker is found in a public place and does not, when required, give a good account of herself' (S.164.1 of the Criminal Code) (Brock 1998: 27). The law was obviously enormously discriminatory in that it targeted women only and gave police extensive discretionary powers to arrest and detain women who could not 'give a good account' of themselves. In 1972, all vagrancy laws were repealed on the grounds that they contravened the 1960 Bill of Rights (Larsen 1991: 110). Prostitution was immediately re-incorporated into the Criminal Code under a new provision that prohibited public solicitation for the purposes of prostitution (S.195.1) (Larsen 1991: 111). This new law, however, quickly ran into interpretative difficulties in the courts and enforcement difficulties on the streets. In particular, the degree of communication and interaction that constituted 'soliciting', what could be considered a 'public nuisance', whether men could be considered prostitutes and whether clients could be convicted of soliciting were issues of continuing debate. Finally, in 1978, the Supreme Court of Canada in R. vs. Hutt rendered the judgment that solicitation must be 'pressing and persistent' in order to invoke S.195.1. This judgment came at a time, however, when a number of municipalities were up in arms over the sex industry and police forces and municipal governments were trying to crack down on the 'sin strips' that had appeared to mushroom during the 1970s recession (Brock 1998: 32–9).

Thus, in the aftermath of the Hutt decision, public panic over police incapacity in the face of an apparently 'thriving' sex industry reached new heights. Growing pressure from the mayors of the major cities, police associations, residents' associations, media coverage and court decisions overturning municipal by-laws prohibiting solicitation forced the government to seek a solution to the solicitation problem. The Minister of Justice, however, argued there was a 'wide divergence of opinion as to solutions', and he therefore announced the formation of a Special

Committee on Prostitution and Pornography (the Fraser Committee), with the aim of 'considering prostitution and the exploitation of prostitutes; and looking at the experience of other countries in their attempts to deal with pornography and prostitution' (Minister of Justice 1983: 1–2).

Dominant frame of the debate

Throughout the late 1970s and early 1980s the prostitution debate was essentially between public order and private freedom. Residents' associations, police chiefs and local mayors presented evidence of the public nuisance created by street solicitation, such as the decline in property values, an increase in traffic problems, harassment of residents and harm to 'legitimate' businesses in the area (Brock 1998: 47). They viewed prostitution as a public nuisance that required stricter criminal measures in response. The Liberal government itself, however, had expressed discomfort with increasing the purview of the state in what could be considered moral issues. As Prime Minister Pierre Trudeau had famously expressed it (in discussing homosexuality in Canadian society) 'the state has no place in the bedrooms of the nation'. This discomfort with moral regulation extended to issues of prostitution as the government rejected parliamentary and public pressure for harsh anti-prostitution measures as 'unacceptable in a liberal-democratic society' (Larson 1991: 181).

Gendering the debate

The debate on prostitution was, for the most part, ungendered in that it did not overtly address gender differences. The problem, according to one view, was the public nuisance created by unscrupulous men and women looking to buy and sell sex. In the other view, the problem was state intrusion into the private affairs of undifferentiated individuals (it was ambiguous as to whether this referred to women as prostitutes or men as clients). A gendered sub-text was apparent in the first case however, in that the threat posed to residents by prostitution was gendered – 'good' women walking on the streets were exposed to danger and harassment because of the possibility of their being mistaken for prostitutes. In this sense the discourse was a paternalistic one towards women, who required protection (by the police, most significantly) and who were properly sexually innocent or monogamous.

Feminists were very active in contributing to this debate from a variety of positions. One feminist contribution to this debate was not to challenge the paternalist view of women as such, but to introduce an understanding of prostitute women as victims of gender inequality (both social and economic) that drove them into prostitution and who therefore did not deserve to be treated harshly by the law. Groups espousing this position emphasised the barriers to women caused by sexism that resulted in their turning to prostitution. Feminists allied with civil libertarians, gay rights organisations and prostitute organisations viewed the prostitute as much more of an independent actor and were able to insert a gendered understanding of the impact of state intervention. They emphasised the unfairness of prostitution law that in its application relied on a double sexual standard by targeting prostitutes and not clients. They therefore supported decriminalisation as the only practical way to avoid this discrimination. A more radical approach by one feminist group argued that addressing prostitution required addressing male demand, clearly targeting men and male sexual behaviour as the problem (women are presumably less sexually aggressive). Therefore, the law should in fact penalise clients but not the women themselves (Fraser 1985: 520).

Policy outcome

The Fraser Committee recommendations combined both criminalisation and decriminalisation in an innovative effort to address both the gender inequities inherent in the prostitution issue and the complaints of residents over the nuisance issue. The committee clearly took a feminist line in starting its recommendations by emphasising the need to eradicate the economic inequality that underlay prostitution (through adequate funding to social programmes for women and children) as well as the need to address the 'distorted notions of sexuality' that motivated clients (through education programmes). In their legal recommendations, the committee also followed the recommendations of the feminist groups in removing both prostitutes and clients from the Criminal Code. However, this was with the rider: except where nuisance provisions of the Criminal Code were contravened (Fraser 1985: 539). In effect, according to Brock, this was a limited criminalisation approach that continued to identify the problem as prostitution rather than the associated nuisances of noise, littering, etc. (Brock 1998: 69). One committee member, Andrée Ruffo, a feminist lawyer, dissented from these recommendations on the grounds that sex workers should be treated as responsible adults and should not be singled out by the criminal law (Fraser 1985: 535). However, the committee did put forward some surprising recommendations that would significantly loosen the bawdy house and pimping/procuring provisions despite the Liberal Minister of Justice's expressed opposition to legalised brothels (MacLaren 1986: 46). The committee recommended a revision to the bawdy house laws that would allow one or two prostitutes to work out of their own home (as regulated by the provinces) and a revision to procuring and pimping laws so that only the use of force in pimping or procuring would be considered an offence (Fraser 1985: 545–53). Feminists and prostitute organisations in the future would continue to refer to these recommendations as the most amenable yet put forward.

Women's movement impact

Clearly the feminist organisations had substantial impact on the Fraser Committee report. While prostitution was not particularly high on the feminist agenda, it had been brought up in policy discussions of the largest organisation, the National Action Committee on the Status of Women (NAC) at least since 1978, and NAC was well prepared to discuss the issue at some length at the Fraser Committee (Vickers et al. 1993: 212). Other organisations, such as the National Association of Women and the Law (NAWL), were also active in preparing briefs and reports. However, much more energy and interest was 'drained off' in a sense into the issue of pornography, which was being dealt with simultaneously at the Fraser Committee hearings.

None the less, this division of organised feminist attention was more than offset by the positioning of high-profile feminists on the Fraser Committee itself. Indeed, the committee included a number of feminists such as a former executive of the women's policy agency (the Canadian Advisory Council on the Status of Women), Joan Wallace, who had spoken out against harsher penalties during earlier debates (Vickers et al. 1993: 211). Altogether the four female members of the seven-member committee were committed feminists (Larsen 1991: 254, n41). Generally the Fraser Committee report reflected feminist demands as far as it could in recommending social and economic measures, while in legal measures it took a cautious approach that partially decriminalised prostitution in brothels (in keeping with women's movement demands), but also forcefully addressed street solicitation (to address the issues of the anti-solicitation groups). The women's movement received a dual response in that women were incorporated into the policy process and the demands of the movement were met.

Women's policy agency activities

In 1973, an arm's-length advisory body (funded and supported by the government but not directly controlled by it), the Canadian Advisory

Council of the Status of Women (CACSW), was created to be an independent source of research and policy advice. The twenty-seven part-time and three full-time members were to be appointed by the government (Geller-Schwarz 1995: 44). The extent of this independence, however, was almost immediately a point of contention and an issue that haunted the CACSW until 1995 when it was disbanded and its functions were folded into the government department Status of Women Canada. In this period the CACSW can be classified as cross-sectional in scope and as political in type as well as distant in proximity to centres of power. Its administrative capacity was moderate (a small full-time staff and an independent budget) and its leadership feminist. Its policy mandate was interpreted in this period to be one of providing research on current issues to advise government while networking with women's groups (Burt 1998: 123). Burt views the CACSW as most active and independent in seeking to push a feminist agenda within government in the late 1970s and early 1980s. However, 'with stronger ties to women's groups, the CACSW had greater difficulty in establishing its credibility as an advisory rather than a lobby group' (Burt 1998: 121). The CACSW and the government found themselves on opposite sides during the debate over the Constitution in 1982. After this point new CACSW presidents sought to emphasise the CACSW's advisory rather than activist role (Burt 1998: 123). None the less, the CACSW was active in the debate over prostitution, particularly in producing research on prostitution issues, and it was also active in lobbying against harsher criminal measures along with feminist groups; it had the insiders' role. The CACSW brief to the Fraser Committee emphasised the gender discrimination inherent in prostitution and prostitution legislation. It argued for measures that addressed 'the relative poverty of women, the advantageous socio-economic position of men, and the sex role socialisation of both sexes' (Canadian Advisory Council 1984: 69). At the same time it proposed a compromise with residents' groups in order to address the concerns of female residents and therefore supported a limited criminalisation for the nuisance aspects of prostitution (Fraser 1985: 516).

Women's movement characteristics

The most important and largest of the feminist groups, the National Action Committee on the Status of Women (NAC), was formed in 1972. NAC continues to operate today as an umbrella group representing hundreds of smaller women's organisations. Throughout the 1970s the group maintained close connections with the government, adopting a 'lobby and brief' style of politics (Vickers et al. 1993: 216). There was often movement between NAC executive and government positions either in the bureaucracy or political parties, giving NAC insider status at an informal level as well. Such inside connections were clear in the placement of high-profile NAC-connected feminists on the Fraser Committee itself. Indeed, in 1984 NAC was dubbed the 'most powerful lobby in Canada' (Vickers et al. 1993: 192; Geller-Schwarz 1995: 54). During the time of the Fraser Committee therefore the women's movement was in a period of growth and was close to the (Liberal) left. The prostitution issue was of moderate priority and enjoyed a fairly cohesive approach within the movement. The strength of the counter-movement was increasing during this period but was only moderate.

Policy environment

The policy environment during this debate was quite open, especially given the role of the Fraser Committee – a politically appointed royal commission designed to gather and process public opinion in order to make recommendations to parliament. The party in power (up until the end of 1984) was the Liberal Party, which enjoyed majority status within the House and therefore had strong control in both the executive and the legislature. The party was fairly attuned to feminist demands and feminist insiders. Also, the Liberals were not comfortable with the demands for greater criminalisation coming from residents, police and mayors and in establishing the Fraser Committee wanted to ensure greater representation of more sympathetic views. Thus the dominant approach was at least compatible with feminist demands.

Debate 2: The Anti-Communications Law (C-49), 1985

How issue came to the public agenda

The appointment of the Fraser Committee was widely viewed by anti-prostitution forces as a stalling tactic on the part of the Liberal government. The Conservative government, elected in late 1984 with a nearly unprecedented majority, continued to face strong pressure from local and provincial politicians (particularly from those areas with large urban centres) and residents' groups to deal with the problem of street solicitation. The government faced internal pressure as well. Pat Carney, a senior female Conservative MP from Vancouver, BC, which had a strong anti-prostitution lobby, and a member of the new Conservative cabinet, was vocal in her support for stronger measures against street prostitution. The new Conservative Justice Minister, John Crosbie, very early into his position, announced that the Ministry of Justice was already working on new legislation to control street prostitution and hinted that he might not wait for the Fraser Committee report in order to introduce new legislation, given the need to respond immediately to the problem (Larsen 1991: 196). The Conservatives introduced Bill C-49 to deal with prostitution exactly six working days after the Fraser report was released, suggesting that the bill had indeed been prepared in-house long before the committee's input was available (Larsen 1991: 233). Bill C-49 criminalised 'communication' for the purposes of prostitution for both clients and prostitutes, thereby greatly expanding the scope of the criminal law.

Dominant frame of debate

The problem at hand had been established as one of 'public nuisance' and the disruption of the lives of good citizens by pimps and prostitutes who were 'taking over' certain neighbourhoods and threatening the safety and morality of the residents who lived there. There were many personal stories at the hearings on Bill C-49 from residents' groups, repeated by sympathetic mayors and police, of people being unable to leave their homes without being threatened and intimidated by either the prostitutes or their pimps – making it difficult to 'go to the store for a jug of milk' or 'get to church on Sundays' (emphasising the wholesome way of life that was under threat.) Prostitution was described by government members and residents' groups as a 'plague' and a 'blight' on neighbourhoods in Vancouver, Montreal, Halifax, Winnipeg and Calgary (House of Commons 1985). A certain moralistic stance against prostitution in general was apparent. Many saw the massive Conservative victory as a reaction against the liberalism of the Trudeau era, and 'family values' became a new watch-word in Canadian society.

Gendering the debate

Gender played out in different ways in this debate. In the predominant anti-soliciting view, gender differences do not appear to be immediately at issue. The problem was soliciting and public nuisance and the answer was increased police strength. However, these groups, and the government in introducing Bill C-49, did emphasise that both prostitutes and their clients would be subject to arrest (although the government could not guarantee enforcement would be equitable and refused to amend the bill to name clients specifically as targets). The government argued that by using the term 'anyone who communicates' it was responding to the concerns of women's groups and adhering to the legal gender equity newly enshrined in the Canadian Charter of Rights (Larsen 1991: 234). Thus the government endorsed a limited, legal notion of gender equality in that the bill did not in its wording actively discriminate against women. Secondly, the government, some residents' groups and a few women's groups that supported the bill, drew on a paternalistic gender discourse that posed the nuisance of street solicitation as a threat to 'good' women who lived in those neighbourhoods and may be subject to harassment. In this discourse then, only 'good' women who lived up to the code of decent female behaviour deserved protection by the state from sexual threats. That these threats came from many other places (most importantly husbands and boyfriends) was not raised by these groups – nor was the underlying sexism that threatened the socio-economic status of all women.

A number of women's organisations, however, actively campaigned against increased criminalisation on the grounds that it was discriminatory against women in the sex trade who would only face increased exploitation under such a legal regime. Women's groups, and the Canadian Organization for the Rights of Prostitutes, that appeared at the parliamentary hearings on Bill C-49 argued, as they had at the Fraser Committee hearings, that prosecution of solicitation reflected a moral agenda that failed to address the underlying social and economic problems that lead to prostitution. Further, increased criminalisation would disproportionately affect women despite the gender-neutral language of the legislation.

Policy outcome

In the end, Bill C-49 passed rather quickly through the House. Despite the opposition's resistance to the bill both parties promised to 'not unduly delay' the legislation (indeed, the Liberal Justice Critic urged its speedy passage). Bill C-49 made it an offence for 'every person' 'in a public place or in any place open to public view' to 'communicate or attempt to communicate with any person for the purpose of engaging in prostitution or of obtaining the sexual services of a prostitute' (S.213 Criminal Code).

Women's movement impact

As Louise Dulude, then president of NAC, expressed it, in C-49, the Mulroney government had 'passed a new prostitution law . . . that severely increases the police harassment of prostitutes' (Dulude 1988: 263). Thus, while women were accepted into the policy process the state did not give policy satisfaction. The second debate can therefore be classified as a case of co-optation.

Women's policy agency activities

The election of a new Conservative government at the end of 1984 marked the beginning of the decline for the CACSW. While the CACSW had been fairly active in lobbying the Fraser Committee it was much less visible once Bill C-49 was introduced. It continued to have the same characteristics as listed in the first debate: cross-sectional in scope, political in type, distant from the centres of power, moderate in administrative capacity and feminist in leadership. Sylvia Gold, the new president of CACSW in 1985, understood the CACSW's mandate as providing 'research and advice' to women's groups to use in their own lobbying efforts (Burt 1998: 123). According to Burt, Gold's presidency marked a more cautious approach to change, an agenda 'more firmly contained by Council members and staff' and a much more 'conciliatory' approach to government (Burt 1998: 123). This came just at a time when women's groups such as NAC were taking a much more critical and 'outsider' stance towards the government, so the distance between the CACSW and feminist groups began to grow. Thus the agency's role in this debate can be characterised as marginal in that it advocated women's goals but did not succeed in gendering policy.

Women's movement characteristics

The mid-1980s were a watershed for the feminist movement in Canada. With the new Conservative government the women's movement became increasingly radicalised (Geller-Schwarz 1995: 55). In particular, the government's plans for a Free Trade Agreement with the USA announced in mid-1985 catalysed many leftist feminists within NAC. At the same time, conservative women's groups were increasing their access to cabinet (Geller-Schwarz 1995: 55). Indeed, NAC's higher profile following what some consider the height of its visibility during the 1984 election also attracted the attention of conservative groups who began to attack NAC in the press (Vickers et al. 1993: 146). Prostitution, however, had slipped down the list of priorities of a women's movement that was now rapidly expanding on the policy front. Thus the movement can be characterised as in a stage of growth. It can also be seen as close to the left (particularly in its Liberal guise but also moving closer to the social-democratic New Democratic Party). The issue of prostitution was of low priority, the cohesion of the movement on prostitution issues was moderate and the counter-movement was strong.

Policy environment

The election of the Conservative government in late 1984 was also a key factor in feminists' declining access to government. The Progressive Conservatives under Prime Minister Mulroney lost much of their old 'red-Tory' leanings and adopted an aggressively neo-liberal stance – as evidenced by the Free Trade Agreement with the United States. Feminist emphasis on the social and economic inequalities in prostitution fell on deaf ears in this context. A certain moral conservatism, the 'family values' approach, also marked some members of the Mulroney government, making prostitution a problematic issue (Bashevkin 1998: 190).

While the location of debates over C-49 in the House allowed for a certain amount of public input, with a powerful cabinet system within a massive majority government, there was little real access to the power centres. The preparation of the draft within the Ministry of Justice while feminist activists were busy elsewhere in appearing before the Fraser Committee meant that there was little access to the internal machinations of the Justice Department. The policy structure therefore was closed. The dominant approach of prostitution as a blight on communities was also incompatible with feminist demands. The Liberal left was in opposition and without real policy influence.

Debate 3: Youth in prostitution, 1992–1996

How issue came to the public agenda

Concern over the issue of youth in prostitution began to build in the late 1980s. A new law aimed at attacking the role of pimps in youth prostitution was passed in 1988, but police complained that it was unenforceable because of the difficulty of forcing youth to testify against their pimps (Lowman 1998). Media stories about 'runaway youths' who entered the sex trade grew throughout the late 1980s. These stories tended to emphasise the role of pimps. The term 'white slavery', with all its racial overtones, re-entered the public lexicon, reaching new heights in the early 1990s with the media attention generated by a 'pimping ring' out of Nova Scotia into Toronto dominated by young black men acting as pimps and young white women as prostitutes (Brock 1998:118–26). These fears and police complaints were backed up by evidence of the weakness of prostitution laws generally. Reviews of Bill C-49 (now S.213 of the Criminal Code) conducted in the late 1980s had concluded that 'street prostitution was as prevalent as it was before the new law' (Lowman 1998). A parliamentary standing committee reviewing S.213 similarly concluded that the law on prostitution needed to be strengthened to make it more enforceable. (The government declined its recommendations.) The standing committee also noted the growing number of youth (a slippery term, sometimes referring to those under eighteen and sometimes to those under twenty-six) in prostitution over the 1980s (Standing Committee 1990: 18). The provinces also put pressure on the federal government to address youth prostitution. Some provinces – particularly British Columbia, where Vancouver's mild climate attracted large numbers of runaways – had begun to investigate the youth prostitution problem. Frustrated with the progress on prostitution laws generally, the British Columbia government pushed to establish a joint working group of federal and provincial Ministries of Justice. The Federal/Provincial/Territorial Working Group on Prostitution (hereinafter the Working Group) was set up in 1992 to review legislation and make recommendations on prostitution policy and, additionally, to focus on youth in prostitution (Federal/Provincial/Territorial Working Group 1998: 15). Concern over youth in prostitution increased in the mid-1990s with the lead-up to the 1996 World Congress against Commercial Sexual Exploitation of Children organised by international children's rights NGOs and UNICEF. The approach of the World Congress not only stimulated the federal government to start taking action but generated a great deal of new media interest in the child prostitution issue. The media began to focus not only on child prostitution in Canada but on the exploitation of children overseas.

Dominant frame of debate

While during the 1970s and 1980s there had been some contention over whether youth in prostitution were victims or criminals, by the 1990s the victim view had won out. There was a great deal of agreement among all participants in the debate on the need to protect children from predatory adults – pimps and johns – and to prevent children from becoming vulnerable to such abuse. It was clear to most participants and to the Working Group that youth prostitution was the result of family dysfunction and child abuse and that the appropriate response to youth in prostitution was through social welfare measures as well as stricter punishment of their abusers. The major barrier to combating child prostitution, it was generally felt, was the inadequacy of police power to enforce the law against pimps and those who procured the services of a minor (Federal/Provincial/Territorial Working Group 1998: 24–5).

In this context, decriminalisation of prostitution nearly disappeared from the agenda. Even those who supported decriminalisation, women's groups in particular, limited their demands to adult prostitution. However, actual youth in prostitution who appeared before the Working Group sometimes argued that complete decriminalisation (including for youth) was the only effective defence against violence against prostitutes, which had increased since the 1985 law. These youth pointed out that with decriminalisation prostitutes would be able to reduce reliance on pimps (a problem for youth in particular) and work in less dangerous and remote areas (Federal/Provincial/Territorial Working Group 1998: 75). This position reflected a different understanding of youth in prostitution, in which they were viewed as economically vulnerable workers rather than as victims of sexual abuse. None the less, the recommendations of the Working Group and the policy changes put forward by government all reflected a concern to make anti-child prostitution laws stricter and more easily enforceable.

Gendering the debate

The debate over youth in prostitution in the 1990s was surprisingly ungendered. Women's groups seem to have been uninterested in the issue of youth in prostitution. The few prostitutes' rights groups were also quiet on the issue of youth. In the Working Group hearings, there was some mention of gender in discussions of youth but it was extremely limited. 'Youth' were generally thought to be an age group undifferentiated by gender. Indeed there was some effort to ensure that it was clear that youth in prostitution did not refer only to girls. The only factor distinguishing the involvement of girls from that of boys that was mentioned in the report was the tendency for 'sex for survival' to be 'more of a factor for females than males'. However, this fact, which problematises a strict 'youth prostitution as sexual abuse' interpretation, was not brought up again in the report (Federal/Provincial/Territorial Working Group 1998: 20). Having made this one gendered observation, the report then went on to stress that the proportion of males may be higher than generally thought and then continued to refer throughout the report only to 'youth' of unspecified gender (Federal/Provincial/Territorial Working Group 1998: 21).

Furthermore, while youth in prostitution were understood to be the product of abuse within the family there was no discussion of the gendered differentiation of power within families. Despite the government's own statistics indicating that girls are the majority of child abuse victims (both sexual and physical) (Alliance 1999), this fact was not addressed in the debate, aside from one brief mention during House of Commons debate, nor was the predominant role of men as abusers (House of Commons 1996: 3573). Thus, there was no discussion of girls as particular victims of child prostitution and none of men as particular problems. The imbalance of power was understood to be between 'adults' generally and 'children'. That is, age, rather than gender, was the axis of power.

Policy outcome

In October 1995 the Working Group released its interim report recommending that the anti-child prostitution laws be made more easily enforceable. In November Justice Minister Rock, still faced with demands by some municipalities for changes to prostitution legislation that would allow them to regulate the trade, announced 'tougher penalties – not legalisation of the sex trade – to tackle problems associated with street prostitution' (Bastow 1995). These tougher penalties, it turned out, had only to do with child prostitution. Despite the ongoing discussion on adult prostitution the government chose to address only the issue of youth. In December the government introduced bill C-115, which addressed the problem of enforceability of anti-child prostitution laws. After the bill died on the order paper in the spring, it was re-introduced in the summer of 1996 in a bundle of Criminal Code changes that addressed child prostitution, child sex tourism, criminal harassment and female genital mutilation (Bill C-27). With the passage of this bill a new offence of 'aggravated procuring' was created that carried a minimum penalty of five years and a maximum of fourteen. The use of a minimum sentence was intended to signal the government's seriousness in dealing with the crime. The bill made it an offence to 'seek the services of a person *believed to be* under 18', as well as those actually under 18, in order to facilitate sting operations by the police. Finally, the bill created procedural safeguards to facilitate the testimony of youth against pimps and customers. Bill C-27 also extended the reach of Canadian law on child prostitution outside the country with its provision on child sex tourism, clearly in response to the Stockholm Conference (Robertson 1999). Thus, the government's response focused very narrowly on increasing the strength of anti-prostitution laws.

Women's movement impact

While there were women sitting on legislative committees and the Working Group, as well as women at the Working Group hearings, very few advocated women's or girls' particular interests. Nor did the policy coincide with these weakly expressed interests. Thus the policy outcome was no response.

Women's policy agency activities

Women's policy agencies at the federal level were 'compressed significantly' during the 1990s according to Rankin and Vickers (2001: 9). The arm's-length CACSW and its research and public relations functions were 'folded' into the government department, Status of Women Canada (SWC), in 1995. The SWC had very different characteristics from those of the CACSW as we shall see below. The research function of the CACSW was taken over by the Policy Research Fund within SWC. The funding programme for women's organisations was also moved out of the Citizenship Branch of the Secretary of State and into the SWC. This move only emphasised a trend towards increasing insularity of the policy agencies from public input and communication (Burt 1998: 124–5). According to Rankin and Vickers 'the restructuring has not strengthened the consultative process between women's movements and the state' and indeed the feminist movement has complained of a growing distance between it and the bureaucracy (Rankin and Vickers 2001: 9). Women's groups complained that the reorganisation came out of a less than fully consultative process, resulted in the reduction of core funding to women's organisations, and would mean increased centralised control by the SWC over research direction (Coulter 1997). Indeed after the introduction of Bill C-27 in 1996, SWC claimed it had a mandate from women's groups to target child prostitution and violence against the girl-child as important areas of research; however, many feminist organisations again complained that this consultation process was based on a pre-set agenda (Status of Women Canada 2000; Coulter 1997).

Not only was the SWC becoming increasingly distant from women's organisations, it was also in a weaker position within government. Under the Liberals (re-elected in 1993) the ministers appointed to the Status of Women were given the lesser title of 'Secretary of State', which meant they were not part of cabinet meetings unless specifically invited to participate. Thus the access of SWC to the cabinet process – the most important policy-making arena – was severely curtailed. None the less the SWC can be classified as near to the centres of power (as compared with the CACSW). Its scope was cross-sectional, it was bureaucratic in type and had considerable administrative capacity (with full-time staff, inner administrative divisions and subsidies for women's groups), although this capacity was being eroded. The leadership, however, was reluctant to recognise feminist connections. The mandate of the SWC clearly reflected the concerns of government, rather than women's groups, particularly the issue of youth.

Thus, in the debate over youth in prostitution the SWC acted more as an *ex-post facto* champion of the government's intention to strengthen anti-child prostitution laws rather than an advocate of women's groups' interest in decriminalisation. However, SWC did respond to the Working Group's initial consultation paper by putting forward its concern that legislative changes should not further marginalise or make vulnerable those working in the sex trade and advocating a social interventionist approach (rather than a criminal one). The SWC also continued to promote the issue of child prostitution and to provide funding to groups willing to take up research on the issue *after* C-27 was passed. Its role, therefore, was symbolic in that it did not advocate women's movement goals and was unsuccessful in gendering policy.

Women's movement characteristics

The Canadian women's movement was on the decline in the 1990s. It had been greatly affected by deep budget cuts in the early 1990s as the government cut back funding (by 50 per cent for the national organisation, NAC). Some women's centres and smaller organisations were forced to close because of the loss of funding (Petten and Jefferson 1995; Coulter 1997). The government refused to attend NAC's annual lobby days on Parliament Hill until 1998 (indeed these had become less important to NAC itself). Throughout the 1990s the movement, especially as embodied in NAC, moved closer to the social-democratic left as it focused more and more on issues of economic inequality, globalisation and trade. Thus in an age of neo-conservatism (marked by the growth of the right-wing Reform Party) NAC took on a 'leftist' image (Vickers et al. 1993: 294; Petten and Jefferson 1995). The counter-movement generally, at this time, was very strong. Neo-conservative parties had entrenched themselves at both the provincial and federal levels.

The issue of prostitution generally, however, had dropped off the feminist agenda following the battles of the late 1980s when prostitutes' rights groups put forward a motion that NAC explicitly recognise prostitution as a form of work. The resulting debate left permanent scars on the organisation. The issue of prostitution was rarely addressed thereafter. Despite a number of high-profile Supreme Court cases on prostitution law in the early 1990s, the premier feminist legal organisation, LEAF (Legal Education and Action Fund), did not intervene (McGinnis 1994: 106). While NAC made an appearance at the hearings on C-27 it did not address prostitution. The few specialised women's groups that did address the issue throughout the debate were divided between prostitutes' rights organisations and anti-john, anti-prostitution organisations. Thus not only was the issue a low priority but the movement was divided on the issue. The feminist movement can be characterised as in decline and close to the left and the counter-movement as strong.

Policy environment

The Liberal Party had returned to power in 1993 and remained in power with a strong majority in the legislature throughout the 1990s. Thus we can classify the policy environment as one in which the left were in strong control – with the understanding that the Liberals had moved away from their Trudeau heritage and become a much more fiscally (neo-) conservative party than in the past. The policy sub-system in this issue was centred on the Department of Justice and the cabinet, but also involved legislative committees and instruments such as the Working Group that encourage wider participation but are staffed by bureaucrats (unlike the politically appointed Fraser Committee). The sub-system can therefore be classified as moderately closed. The dominant approach was, however, at least compatible with the women's movement. The focus on child prostitution, and on children as victims of sexual exploitation, was not incompatible with mainstream women's movements' goals, but it was not an explicit demand of theirs either.

Conclusion

In two of these three major debates over prostitution policy in Canada the women's movement and women's state agencies have had very little impact on the state response. Only in the first case, when the policy environment was quite open, do we see a positive state response to pressures from the women's movement. While in the second case, with Bill C-49 the government does make a claim to be responding to pressure for more gender-equitable prostitution law, they do this in precisely the way the women's movement had been hoping to avoid – by punishing both the clients and the prostitutes. In the final case, the women's movement and the agency were much less involved and the government moved ahead with a de-gendered policy on prostitution. Indeed, the pattern appears to be one in which the government's policy direction is predetermined within cabinet and there is very little that either women's groups or women's state agencies can do to alter that direction.

None the less, during the 1980s the CACSW, at least, did play a very active role in the debate on prostitution policy; both its research and lobbying efforts as well as its 'connections' within parliament were clearly very important in putting forward a gendered critique of greater criminalisation of prostitution. If the Liberals had stayed in power into 1985 it is anyone's guess whether they would have followed through on the Fraser Committee's recommendations to at least partially decriminalise. The strength of the feminist movement in the mid-1980s indicates that policy environment may have played a key role in determining the failure of a feminist approach. Under the Liberals and in the open environment of the Fraser Committee hearings, the feminist movement had a good deal of influence. With the election of the Conservatives, the introduction of stronger criminal measures was almost a foregone conclusion. Most importantly, the strength of the cabinet system and the influence of senior cabinet ministers from the electoral districts affected by street prostitution gave the criminalisation approach the upper hand. Without direct access to cabinet the CACSW had little chance of influencing policy, although their research continued to be used both by women in the Liberal opposition and by the women's movement to criticise C-49.

Policy environment in terms of party in power also appears to be important in determining the success of women's groups in the Fraser case versus the C-49 case, where women's movement characteristics are held nearly constant. With the Liberals, who appointed strong feminists to the Fraser Committee, in power, feminists at the hearings had a sympathetic audience. Once the Conservatives took power in 1985, women's groups were shut out as the dominant discourse moved from compatible to incompatible. None the less, it should be noted that the Liberals' return to power in the 1990s did not necessarily improve the fortunes of the women's movement. So other factors are clearly also at work. Here it appears that the policy environment, which may have been conducive to women's interests, was not taken advantage of by the women's movement itself, which was at a low point in its organisational strength.

As for the role of women's policy agencies, it appears that where the political environment is conducive they may provide a supportive role for the women's movements. For example, in the first case, the CACSW was able to offer a solution that bridged the gap between pro- and anti-criminalisation forces, a solution which did not fall on deaf ears because of the internal connections of the CACSW. It is also important to note, however, that this particular women's policy agency was an arm's-length, feminist-led organisation that felt itself responsible to the women's movement. In the 1990s, the government department of the SWC did not take the opportunity to fill the policy gap between the women's movement and the government despite the potential to do so through the Federal/Provincial/Territorial Working Group. The SWC in the 1990s was much more clearly an instrument of government rather than of the women's movement. Thus the characteristics of the policy agency may be an important factor in determining its effectiveness in gendering policy.

NOTE

1. The following is a list of the policy debates of the period:
    1 In 1978 the Supreme Court decided, in its interpretation of the 1972 anti-solicitation law (S.195), that solicitation must be 'pressing and persistent' in order to merit charges. The following uproar over the growing 'nuisance' of street solicitation led the Liberal government, in 1983, to refer the matter of prostitution (and pornography) to an extra-parliamentary committee (the Fraser Committee) for investigation. Their 1985 report was the most liberal policy recommendation on prostitution produced to date.
    2 In 1990 the Ministry of Justice and the House of Commons investigated the effects of Bill C-49 (now S.213 of the Criminal Code) on prostitution. Hearings were held by the Parliamentary Committee on Justice. Their report, which recommended harsher laws on prostitution as well as funding to community-based agencies for preventative and rehabilitation programmes, was rejected by the Conservative government in 1991.
    3 In 1992, provincial and federal Deputy Ministers of Justice formed a Federal/Provincial/Territorial Working Group on Prostitution to review legislation and make recommendations concerning prostitution-related activities. Following extensive public consultations the Working Group presented its interim report in 1995. The following year the government acted on the Working Group's recommendations concerning youth in prostitution by introducing Bill C-27 which introduced a new offence of 'aggravated procuring' concerning youth prostitution and made Canadian law extra-territorial in child sex tourism cases.
    4 In 1998 the provincial government of Manitoba introduced legislation enabling police to impound vehicles used in a prostitution offence unless the accused agrees to participate in a 'john school'.
    5 Also in 1998, the provincial Alberta government passed the 'Protection of Children Involved in Prostitution Act' to increase the power of police to apprehend and to hold for up to seventy-two hours youth 'in need of protection' because 'the child is engaging in prostitution or attempting to engage in prostitution'.

6 Towards a new prohibitionism? State feminism, women's movements and prostitution policies in Finland

Anne Maria Holli

Introduction

By the 1980s, most Finns had begun sincerely to believe that there was no 'prostitution problem' at all in the country. This belief was supported by the exceptionally low number of prostitutes nationally (Häkkinen 1995) as well as by the 'hidden' forms prostitution had taken in the society (e.g. Varsa 1986). At the turn of the 1990s, however, both day tourism from nearby Russia and Estonia and a domestic recession brought prostitutes back to the streets. The sex industry started to expand in the country, acquiring novel forms (e.g. Näre 1994, 1998; Näre and Lähteenmaa 1995). The prostitution issue made its way back to the political agenda after decades of silence.

By then, Finnish society had tried out many of the most common methods of controlling prostitution. Until 1907, authorities regulated it: prostitutes were licensed and the police were in charge. From 1907 to 1943, the main form of surveillance was medical and aimed at the prevention of venereal diseases (Häkkinen 1995). From 1936 onwards, the Vagrant Act became the major instrument of the newly adopted prohibitionist regime for the next fifty years. This law defined prostitutes as a fourth category of vagrants, i.e. 'those pursuing a lewd life-style professionally', who were 'in the habit of earning their income in indecent and morally deplorable ways'. Prostitutes were put under the control of social workers and, in the last instance, according to a hardening grid of sanctions, sent to institutions of labour. It was not until 1987 that Finland adopted a purely abolitionist regime with prostitutes no longer penalised and sanctions against pimping only (Järvinen 1990; Häkkinen 1995).

This chapter on Finland explores the role of state feminism and women's movements in three policy debates on prostitution from the mid-1980s to the present. During the past decade, abolitionist prostitution policies have become subject to strong pressures for change, resulting in an incremental turn towards a new prohibitionism, outlawing prostitutes, pimps and clients. State feminism and women's movements

103

have played an extremely ambiguous role in this process. They have on the one hand been central in gendering the discourse and bringing sex clients into focus in an unprecedented manner. On the other hand, the women's movements have taken diffuse and divided standpoints on the position of prostitutes and policy recommendations. This, in turn, has contributed to the establishment and success of the prohibitionist policy line.

Selection of debates

Historically, in Finland, prostitution as a political issue has been understood as a moral, health, social, law and order, youth or a gender-equality problem (Järvinen 1987: 30–9; 1990: 81–9). In the 1990s the list can, perhaps, be expanded by including the notion that prostitution is a 'foreigner' problem. This issue, however, has been more visible in the media debates than in the 'politically correct' debates taking place in formal decision-making arenas, namely the government and the parliament.

These ideas of the nature of the problem often overlap in any given debate, but they also tend to structure the attitudes and discourse of the policy actors in their respective fields. The 'classical' area of prostitution-related problems has traditionally been divided between three ministry-led policy preparation sub-systems, each of which represents a different viewpoint on prostitution. The Ministry of Justice prepares matters concerning criminal law and, thus, has the final responsibility for determining whether prostitution is a crime or not. The Ministry of the Interior deals with matters concerning public order and the authorisation of police activity to combat prostitution, as well as issues concerning the local authorities, a decision-making arena that has lately become more prominent with regard to prostitution. Against the conceptualisation of prostitution as a law and order problem stands the third major actor, the Ministry of Social Affairs and Health, representing a social policy view with abolitionist overtones and a responsibility for the service aspect of prostitution.

The disintegration and decentralisation of prostitution-related policies is further demonstrated by the fact that the 'new problems' emerging in the 1990s were a concern of still other policy actors. For example, the issue of phone sex services falls under the Ministry of Transport and Communications, the prevention of sex tourism under the Ministry of Trade and Commerce, and the questions concerning sex workers' labour-related rights under the Ministry of Labour in co-operation with organised labour and management.

The era of Finnish state feminism spans a period from the establishment of a permanent advisory council for gender equality in 1972 until the present. The only major reform concerning prostitution during the 1970s and 1980s was the repeal of the Vagrant Act. This first case in my selection of debates also represents prostitution as a social policy issue, which was dealt with by the institutional arena headed by the Ministry of Social Affairs and Health.

As prostitution became re-politicised in the early 1990s, Finnish society found itself quite unprepared to deal with it. Several committees and working groups were established to investigate the issue. The problems were also dealt with more directly, as the responsible executive bodies started to amend lower-level statutes, regulations and instructions. There were no policy outcomes in the form of national laws until the end of 1990s when the Penal Code was reformed to include the limited criminalisation of sex clients (1998) and a prohibition for known prostitutes to enter the country was added to the Foreign Nationals Act (1999).

I have selected one of the two available national-level laws, the Sex Crime Act of 1998 (representing the youth protection issue and the policy sub-system under the Ministry of Justice), as my second case. This reform caused heated debate, whereas the restrictive paragraph in the Foreign Nationals Act was passed without notice. The third debate to be studied in detail is the 1999 reform of Helsinki municipal ordinance with its ban on public prostitution (representing the law and order issue). The latter was also one of the few open and democratic processes found in lower-level decision-making. The selection of debates thus includes three of the four salient Finnish debates on prostitution during the 1980s and 1990s;[1] it also represents a sample of three different decision-making sub-systems.

The research material consists of all the relevant documents produced in the course of the Finnish policy-making deliberations, from initial committee reports and subsequent hearings statements to the minutiae of parliamentary plenary sessions. These data have been supplemented with information gathered from some key policy-makers when necessary. In the case of the Helsinki municipal ordinance, six key persons were interviewed during the decision-making process. I also was fortunate enough to be able to observe the city council meetings and to follow the ongoing press debate on the issue.

Debate 1: The repeal of the Vagrant Act, 1984–1986

How issue came to the public agenda

As early as the 1960s and 1970s several state committees had regarded the Vagrant Act as anachronistic and suggested repealing it. However, this did not occur until the mid-1980s when a last-minute proposal to repeal the Vagrant Act was included in the intoxicant abuse bill under preparation (Gov. prop. 246/1984).

According to Tapani Sarvanti, the secretary general of the Delegation for the Prevention of Intoxicant Abuse at the time, this occurred because of a change of ministers in the government: Marjatta Väänänen of the Centre Party, who had opposed the repeal of the Vagrant Act, was replaced by the Social Democrat Vappu Taipale. The Social Democratic bureaucrats within the Ministry of Social Affairs and Health saw this as an opportunity to carry out the needed reform (interview, 16 March 2000).

The new minister was hardly a political puppet for the ministerial bureaucrats in this matter, though. A self-professed feminist and the leader of the Social Democratic Women (1984–90) with a long career in social policy administration, Taipale also had close connections to the November Movement, a 1960s protest movement speaking for the human rights of social outcasts and the abolition of outdated vagrancy laws.

In the government, the Minister of the Interior, Matti Luttinen (Social Democratic Party), actively opposed a total repeal of the Vagrant Act, defending his own ministry's opinion that the Act should be kept in force because of its deterrence value (Council of State 1984). In contrast to the quarrel within the government, during the reading of the bill prostitution was hardly mentioned.

Dominant frame of debate

In the dominant social policy frame, prostitution was regarded as neither an independent nor a gendered problem but was predominantly subsumed under 'the vagrant question'. The problems of vagrants – including the category of prostitutes – were considered to be caused by a disadvantaged social situation, e.g. the abuse of alcohol, the lack of housing, criminal behaviour and mental illness. The key to solving the problems was to be found in developing social policies and services for intoxicant abusers – not in introducing measures of control that would marginalise these groups further.

Consequently, the dominant frame of the debate was open to an implicit understanding of prostitutes as 'a socially disadvantaged group', in line with other vagrant groups. The Social Democratic view also had a strong tendency to treat the causes of social problems as structural and to consider public policies as remedies. Although non-gendered in character, the predominance of the social policy frame, with its willingness to see prostitutes as 'victims', nevertheless prepared the way for a more gendered analysis.

Gendering the debate

There were early indications in the preparation process of the Intoxicant Abuse Act that the ongoing debate on gender equality had had some impact on the views of the policy actors. For example, the Ministry of Justice (1984) pointed out how the Vagrant Act outrageously discriminated against women. At one phase of the preparation process, sanctions on both the selling and *buying* of sexual services were under consideration (e.g. Delegation for the Prevention of Intoxicant Abuse 1984).

The Committee for Investigating the Consequences of the Repeal of the Vagrant Act, however, can be regarded as the key actor in gendering the policy debate, as it added its understanding of prostitution as a gendered problem to the dominant social policy view. The Ministry of Social Affairs and Health had created this committee in the spring of 1985, at least partly to accommodate the wishes of the opponents of the repeal who expected a substitute control law would be proposed. In contrast to the early stages of the process, this committee, consisting of civil servants and a professor of law, had a gender balance and even included a representative of the women's policy agency. In its proceedings it also asked for the opinions of outside experts. The committee's task of investigating the need for policy measures was accomplished with a report that was very much based on the most recent feminist research on prostitution.

The committee stressed the connections between prostitution and the gender system, seeing the prevalent sexual culture and the uneven power balance between the sexes along with social and economic factors as causes of prostitution. At the individual level, prostitution was regarded as a symptom of accumulated social problems: low social status, intoxicant abuse, physical or mental problems or criminal activities. Female prostitutes were basically defined as victims of a patriarchal culture and other social structures, and they needed help in the form of social policies. Insisting that prostitution must always be regarded as a relation between at least two parties, the buyer and the seller, the committee consistently brought up the male clients as part of the problem (Committee Report 1986: 109).

In the final analysis, the committee did not consider prostitution acceptable. Nor did supporting the repeal of the Vagrant Act signify its approval of either the buying or the selling of sexual services. Instead of enacting new control laws, the prevention of prostitution was to be accomplished through the prevailing legislation, a change of attitudes, information and co-operation between the authorities as well as outreach social work. In addition, gender equality policies should be strengthened to provide for a more equal society, and thus put an end to the sexual exploitation implicit in prostitution (Committee Report 1986: 110).

Policy outcome

The Intoxicant Abuse Act, including the repeal of the Vagrant Act, was passed by parliament in November 1985 (Law 41/1986). After the repeal came into force in 1987, prostitutes were no longer liable to prosecution in Finland, with penalties for pimping only. In addition, the Committee for Investigating the Consequences of the Repeal submitted its report in late 1986. To the disappointment of the opponents of the repeal, the committee did not propose a new law to control prostitution.

Women's movement impact

There were feminist women involved in various stages of the policy process, most notably the minister in charge and two femocrats participating in the work of the Committee for Investigating the Consequences of the Repeal of the Vagrant Act. Both the committee report and the final policy outcome very much reflected the standpoints of academic women's studies and the feminist movements of the day. The debate resulted in a dual response by the state to the joint demands of both feminist and left-wing activists.

Women's policy agency activities

The Council for Equality between Men and Women was established in 1972 as a permanent, advisory committee charged with the task of proposing reforms for gender equality. It was a national, cross-sectional, politico-administrative body with limited administrative capacity and having a small budget and a secretariat as its main resources. Both of the secretaries general of the 1980s (Leila Räsänen and Eeva-Liisa Tuominen) had feminist backgrounds. Although the composition of the council reflected that of the non-socialist parliamentary majority, the secretariat was relatively close to the left.

The council reported to the Prime Minister's Office until the autumn of 1986, when it was transferred to the Ministry of Social Affairs and Health. It nevertheless had close personal relations with the top of the ministry, as the minister in charge (Eeva Kuuskoski-Vikatmaa, of the Centre Party) also functioned as the chair of the politically nominated council. The second Minister of Social Affairs and Health, also responsible for the intoxicant abuse affairs, Vappu Taipale of the SDP, had at least two easily discernible personal links to the council: her husband had been a vice-member and her political secretary, Marianne Laxén, a former femocrat, was the vice-chair of the Council for Equality at the time.

These close personal relations may also explain why the Council for Equality did not need to participate formally in the preparatory or decision-making stages of the policy process. The government's proposal already coincided with its ideas. On the other hand, the council was directly involved in the work of the Committee for Investigating the Consequences of the Repeal, as it was represented both in the membership (Pirkko Kiviaho) and the pool of experts (Hannele Varsa), and worked to translate feminist ideas into practical policy proposals in that context. Thus the council can be classified as having played an insider role. It both pleaded the case for women's movement demands and effectively gendered the debate.

Women's movement characteristics

During the debate, the women's movement was growing, and above all feminist studies were mobilising women in academia. Women's party organisations have traditionally been the most stable part of the Finnish women's movements; all of them, but especially those on the left, had started drawing on feminist ideas. The prostitution issue was certainly discussed in theoretical terms within the women's studies part of the movement, but it had a low priority on the political agenda of the movement. The issue did not cause any discernible internal divisions within the movement either. The moderate counter-movement was concentrated around the parallel policy sub-system headed by the Ministry of the Interior and some of the more conservative parties in terms of sexual morals.

Policy environment

The socialist parties had 42 per cent of the seats in parliament during 1983–7. The Social Democrats and the Centre Party made up the core of the governmental coalition, with both the right wing and the extreme left wing in opposition. Traditionally, the two ministerial posts within the Ministry of Social Affairs and Health were divided between the major coalition partners, at least one of them usually being a 'female post'. The repeal of the Vagrant Act was initiated by a Social Democratic woman minister and guided to final passage by a male party colleague.

In general terms, the domain of social policy-making can be described as moderately closed, involving mainly governmental bodies, political parties, municipal organisations, social partners and voluntary organisations, but also offering a relatively free and responsive space for additional pressure groups to participate (Mattila 2000). Apart from the other two ministries concerned with the prostitution issue, there was in practice no established policy network in the sub-field of prostitution policy in the 1980s, which made it relatively easy for the Council for Equality and feminist researchers to gain access and recognition as experts on prostitution. The process was facilitated by the compatibility of the approaches of the relevant policy sub-system and the women's representatives.

Debate 2: The new Sex Crime Act, 1993–1998

How issue came to the public agenda

From the very beginning in the 1970s, the work for reforming the Sex Crime Act (from 1889) aimed at protecting individual rights to sexual self-determination and integrity in a neutral manner with regard to gender, sexual orientation and marital status. A second purpose of the new law was to protect children more effectively from sexual abuse, e.g. by criminalising new aspects of child pornography and molestation (Ministry of Justice 1993; Gov. prop. 6/1997).

Initially, the aim of the policy-makers was to reform pimping laws only. However, during the 1990s other issues concerning prostitution also gained a prominent place in the policy debate.

Dominant frame of debate

With regard to the prostitution issue, three different frames interacted in the lengthy political process and dominated it: the social policy frame (1972–93), the youth and child protection frame (1994–8) and the law and order frame (1997–8). The evolution of the bill's prostitution paragraphs and the specifics of the policy process are closely connected to this change of frames.

The expert committees under the Ministry of Justice during 1972–93 were initially in favour of an abolitionist reform of pimping laws only, demonstrating concern for the self-determination of female and male prostitutes in the face of sexual exploitation. Prostitutes were defined very much from the by-now-familiar social policy frame as victims unable to make decisions freely. Prostitution was also seen as connected to violence, criminal activities and disturbance of public order, and as a threat to gender equality. However, from a social policy and judicial point of view, the criminalisation of prostitution was not considered feasible (e.g. Ministry of Justice 1993; Gov. prop. 6/1997).

When the proposal for a new Sex Crime Act was sent to a hearing in 1993, many participants (including the two women's policy offices, many women's organisations and children's affairs NGOs, as well as the Ministry of Social Affairs and Health and the Ministry of Labour) wanted additional protection for children and the young. They demanded, firstly, that the purchase of sexual services from those under the age of eighteen should be criminalised, and, secondly, that extra-territorial child molestation (including sex tourism for the purposes of child prostitution) should be prosecutable in Finland. Young people were seen as too immature to decide upon the career of a prostitute; some were driven to selling themselves by a drug addiction. The responsibility for the consequences of prostitution for the life of the young person was firmly placed upon the exploiter/molester, the adult client. Many of these policy interest groups also demanded tougher penalties for pimping and tougher measures of indirect pimping, to include sex clubs and sex ads (Ministry of Justice 1994; Parliamentary Law Committee minutiae 1998).

The law and order perspective entered the scene in full during parliamentary debates. The idea of regarding prostitution basically as a public nuisance had already developed in municipal-level debates in Helsinki city and spread to the parliamentary discussions. The perspective tended to concentrate on the effects of prostitution on outsiders, 'ordinary people', and their rights to privacy and non-disturbance by prostitution activities. Consequently, the recommended policies designated different measures for prohibiting prostitution or submerging it from the public view.

As early as 1996, Paula Kokkonen, a National Coalition Party MP from Helsinki, had submitted a private member's bill (Parliamentary law initiative 31/1996 Diet) that proposed penalising offers to buy sex in public places. The initiative was a compromise solution worked out in the Network of Women MPs in Parliament. According to the proposed law, such a broad social problem as prostitution could not be solved via the Penal Code; instead, the code should be used to reduce the problems that prostitution caused for outsiders. The main problem was the harassment of ordinary women in Helsinki city streets by men looking for sexual services. Hence a spatially limited criminalisation of clients was justified.

During the plenaries, the 'realism' of Kokkonen's initiative was subject to heated debates, and male MPs were often highly sceptical of its arguments. Proposals for some forms of client criminalisation were also submitted by Annika Lapintie (the Left-Wing Alliance) and Toimi Kankaanniemi (a male MP of the Christian League). In the final stage of the parliamentary process, the executive committee of the Network of Women MPs formulated a policy recommendation that aimed at a Swedish-style total criminalisation of clients, presented in the plenary by its vice-member Annika Lapintie.

Some male MPs from the centre and right-wing parties saw a re-introduction of the Vagrant Act – and thus basically a re-criminalisation of the prostitutes – as the proper solution to the problem. They also criti-cised the idea of criminalising only the clients and blamed the prostitutes for enticing innocent young men.

The Greens, on their part, offered milder solutions: they preferred to prohibit only those activities that constituted a public nuisance in order to ensure public peace for both women and men in a gender-neutral manner. The Greens had also become increasingly convinced during the parliamentary process that prostitution-related problems were best solved at the local level.

Gendering the debate

It was quite common during the debate to regard prostitution as a conse-quence of the uneven balance of power between the sexes and as a threat to the continued development towards a gender equal society. Many of the feminist slogans introduced by the 1986 committee's report on prosti-tution were industriously recycled in the debate by both the female ac-tivists and the state authorities. To this extent the government's proposal included these viewpoints. Thus, a gendered analysis had successfully permeated policy-making on prostitution.

Both feminists and other representatives of women's constituencies were quite visibly present and instrumental in influencing the shift of frames that occurred during the policy-making processes of the 1990s. It was very much the women's forums that introduced the topic of child protection to the public agenda. However, as long as the 'exploitation of children' was in focus, the debate tended to be non-gendered. The only exception was the concern shown towards young boys by some MPs, who considered that boys mature later than girls and therefore are especially susceptible to male paedophiles.

In addition, it was primarily the women MPs who adopted and pro-moted the law and order frame in the final stage of the process, even though they combined it with elements from other frames, thus mak-ing the debate even more gendered. For example, the idea of the guilt of male sex clients bears a clear resemblance to the arguments against child molesters in the child protection frame. The social policy frame on the other hand had traditionally turned against pimps – now the idea of 'exploitation' was extended to include sex clients as well.

What stands out in the later debates is the almost invariable identification of prostitutes as women and customers as men. In the law and order frame adopted by the women MPs during the parliamentary process, 'ordinary women' – and in the case of the Green women MPs, 'ordinary men' too – were also unambiguously identified as the suffering parties. One can perhaps discern a process of radicalisation in the evolution of the women MPs' proposals. The final proposal, which was modelled on Swedish legislation, was more explicit in identifying prostitute women as victims and their male clients as exploiters than the preceding ones had been.

There were many indications in the discourse that prostitution was overall regarded as an 'abnormal' activity, foreign to Finnish people and their conception of consensual sexual relations. A 'normal woman' did not sell herself; nor did a 'normal man' buy sexual services. The latter can for instance be seen in Annika Lapintie's defence of total client criminalisation: 'a prohibition (to buy sexual services) would be effective in the case of a normal, sensible Finnish male, and he surely would leave these services unbought' (Gov. prop. 6/1997; Parliamentary documents 90/1998 Diet, MP Annika Lapintie). The argumentation implied that only abnormal men – in line with paedophiles, rapists and pimps – would engage in an unethical and exploitative activity unambiguously forbidden in the Penal Code.

Policy outcome

The new Sex Crime Act retained the criminalisation of pimping in the form proposed by the government, which was motivated by considerations for the sexual self-determination of prostitutes. The final law also included a limited criminalisation of sex clients: henceforth, it was prohibited to buy sexual services from persons under the age of eighteen years (the general age limit for sexual consent was retained at sixteen years) under threat of a fine or a maximum of six months' imprisonment. The government's supplementary bill prohibiting extra-territorial child molestation, including sex tourism for the purposes of child prostitution, was passed simultaneously in parliament. Together, these two additions to the law started a new era of sanctioning clients, and made it possible to press charges against sex clients who bought sexual services from teenage prostitutes in Russia and Estonia.

Women's movement impact

Various women's organisations and women MPs were active in the debate during the 1990s, participating in both the hearing process and the legislative preparation of the reform. They were also successful in that the final law embodied two of their main demands: a limited criminalisation of sex clients and a prohibition of extra-territorial child molestation.

The more radical demands for broader client criminalisation were formulated by individual women MPs or their network within the parliament, acting in this instance as representatives of women's interests against the government and the party line. However, these demands failed to have any impact on the policy outcome, despite support from a majority of women MPs over party lines.

With evidence of both success and failure in different stages of the policy process, I will, however, in this instance evaluate the former as more significant in terms of the model. Thus, the state gave a satisfactory response to the demands of the women's movements (dual response).

Women's policy agency activities

From 1986, the Council for Equality was located under the Ministry of Social Affairs and Health, one of the main actors in prostitution policy-making. During 1992–5, the chair was MP Tuula Kuittinen (Centre Party), and from 1995 on, MP Tuula Haatainen (SDP). The council had been among the first to mobilise around the prostitution issue early in the 1990s by starting an internal working group, headed by Tuula Haatainen. The council had also successfully carved out a niche as an expert institution on prostitution-related issues. In the 1990s, the secretariat, with diminishing administrative capacity and a more non-partisan profile than before, was still headed by the same two feminist women.

From 1987, the authority over equality policy was shared with the Equality Ombudsman, a cross-sectional, judicial, formally independent official charged with supervising the equality act. The ombudsman also has a role in the political deliberations in her/his role as the expert on the scope and implications of equality legislation. Until 2001, the women's policy agencies shared an office and most of the personnel resources under the formal leadership of the ombudsman. From 1991 to 1994, the ombudsman was Tuulikki Petäjäniemi, a former National Coalition Party MP; from 1995, it was Pirkko Mäkinen, a non-partisan femocrat who had functioned as the second-in-command in the Equality Ombudsman's Office since its establishment.

Both the Council for Equality and the Equality Ombudsman occupied an insider position in the policy deliberations leading to the passage of the new Sex Crime Act. Both were consulted in the initial hearing round and proposed a limited client criminalisation in the case of young prostitutes. The former also was heard in the parliamentary committee hearings, and the chair of the council, MP Tuula Haatainen (SDP), participated actively in the parliamentary debate by bringing in the supportive standpoints of the council in favour of client criminalisation. Therefore both of the women's policy agencies can be classified as insiders in terms of the model: they advanced the demands of the women's movement and effectively gendered the debate.

Women's movement characteristics

Women's movements had entered into a stage of consolidation in the 1990s. Women's networks became a more common form of organising: the most important fora were the Network of Women MPs in Parliament (from 1991) and NYTKIS (Naiset Yhteistyössä – Kvinno-organisationerna I Samarbete, the Coalition for Joint Action of Finnish Women's Organisations (founded in 1988)), both working for gender equality and women's rights from within established structures. Involving women from both ends of the political spectrum, a consensus concerning the women's political agenda was the prerequisite for co-operation. Sex business was high on the list of the joint concerns of Finnish women's organisations, although they interpreted this concern in different ways. There was no counter-movement to the demands for additional child protection, whereas in regard to general client criminalisation, the counter-forces, most of the involved ministries, the parties in government and the majority of male MPs, were strong.

Policy environment

The socialists had regained 43 per cent of the seats in parliament in 1995 after the defeat of 1991. The Social Democrats formed a rainbow coalition government with the National Coalition Party as the major partner, with the Greens, the Left-Wing Alliance and the Swedish Party thrown in, and the Centre Party and the Christian League in opposition.

The policy sub-system headed by the Ministry of Justice was more closed in the 1970s than in later years, consisting mainly of legal and social policy experts but with the participation of the Council for Equality. In the late 1990s, the policy sub-system can be described as moderately closed, with a stronger participation of NGOs. In the late 1990s, the male Ministers of Justice were recruited from the right-wing National Coalition Party. The dominant approach of the Ministry of Justice partly matched the women's movement ideas as both motivated their ideas with gender equality concerns and with extra protection for children. However, they partly clashed, as the ministry pursued a strictly legalistic, abolitionist prostitution policy line throughout the whole process, with a negative attitude towards proposals to criminalise either prostitutes or clients.

Debate 3: The municipal ordinance of Helsinki, 1995–1999

How issue came to the public agenda

Helsinki, the capital of Finland, was one of the first municipalities to suffer from open street prostitution at the beginning of the 1990s. Soon, there were vehement demands by the inhabitants that the state and the city put a stop to street prostitution by a law or a municipal ordinance. However, during the 1990s, the city of Helsinki responded to these demands only by traffic regulations, e.g. by prohibiting night traffic in some streets and by increasing police control in the concerned areas. Nor did the first proposal for a new municipal ordinance in 1998 include any references to prostitution (Helsinki City Council 1998).

A neighbourhood association of Kallio (Kallio-Seura) had been the main local pressure group in the prostitution issue since the end of the 1980s. In spring 1996 some of its activists had organised a movement called 'Prostitution off the Streets' that consisted of about thirty active members (interview, Saara Tolonen, 22 October 1999). In spring 1998, both of these pressure groups again called for a ban on prostitution by municipal ordinance, i.e. the prohibition of both the selling and buying of sexual services in public and private places (Helsinki City Council 1999a: Appendix 16; 1999b: Appendix 14). The organisations had obtained a couple of hundred signatures in support of a petition and had organised a letter campaign to be conducted by the neighbourhood.

Two of the Green councillors, Sari Näre and Inka Kanerva, had submitted over the years a series of initiatives for restricting prostitution by municipal ordinance. Some of the municipal boards, i.e. the Board for Urban Planning and the Real Estate Board, also joined the forces in favour of a prostitution ban in 1998.

The campaigns were successful in that the modified proposal for a new municipal ordinance submitted in autumn 1999 included a prohibition of public prostitution (Helsinki City Council 1999b: Appendix 40).

Dominant frame of debate

The law and order issue set the dominant frame. The problem was defined in terms of the increasing visibility of prostitution and the disturbances it caused for 'ordinary citizens'. They were the victims of prostitutes, clients and pimps, as well as of the 'criminal activities' (for example, drug abuse and organised crime) prostitution was seen to be connected with. The general agreement was that something had to be done. A ban on prostitution in the municipal ordinance was a compromise solution to immediate problems that would also give the police the needed authorisation to interfere.

The more ideal solutions to the problem proffered by the councillors varied considerably, however. For example, two male representatives in the city council supported the legalisation of brothels or, at least, tolerance zones reserved for prostitution. Many participants argued in favour of measures for the prevention of prostitution as well as for social services for those presently engaged in it.

Gendering the debate

Gendering and egalitarian viewpoints played a central role in women's conceptions of prostitution in the policy debate. From the perspective of the law and order frame, prostitution and the increase of sex business were seen as threats both to 'public peace' and to 'women's peace' (*naisrauha* – referring to a medieval statute that prohibited the harassment of women under threat of punishment), i.e. every woman's right to move and act freely and without threat of harassment in the city. The sex trade was seen to reflect and partly strengthen the prevalent sexual culture and its tendency to oppress women and to undermine the progress made by Finnish women in achieving gender equality. Men were blamed too: especially the clients of prostitution, but also other men in so far as they behaved in a similar manner, assuming that all women were available to satisfy their desires.

For example, city councillor Sari Näre of the Greens described the recent shift in the urban scene as one from a geography of sexual peace to a geography of sexual harassment. The victims of the situation were ordinary women who were compelled to continuously evaluate their risk of being harassed or violated when moving around in the city (Helsinki City Council 1999c; *Iltasanomat* 10 September 1999). Näre, a feminist sociologist who had studied, among other things, the sex business, also proposed an additional clause to the prostitution ban that would have strengthened it in regard to clients. According to Näre, 'using sexual epithets and offering to buy sex in public places' should also be prohibited. Näre's proposal was, however, not taken up to vote in the city council.

Typically, it was assumed in the debate that prostitution was heterosexual, with women offering sexual services and men buying them. This hetero-normative view was challenged in the city council by councillor Jorma Hentilä of the Left-Wing Alliance, a gay activist who gendered the debate in a reverse manner by bringing up the issue of male prostitutes and reminding the council of the fact that they had both male and female clients (Helsinki City Council 1999c).

Women participants in the policy debate almost invariably agreed on the need to prohibit the activity of both the sellers and buyers of sex. Many of them justified their standpoint more or less explicitly with a kind of a liberal feminist view that was partly inherited from the Greens' parliamentary debate a year earlier. The liberal feminist standpoint saw the sex trade as a threat to women's status and demanded penalties for sex clients. However, they also challenged the idea of prostitutes as just victims who had to be protected from sanctions. As prostitution was seen as a relationship between two parties, both of whom should be considered as equally responsible for the problems they created for others, they were also to be punished equally.

The liberal feminist interpretation of prostitution went practically un-challenged in the debate, save by the Support Centre for Prostitutes (Pro-Tuki Piste). It had provided outreach social services for sex workers since 1990 and spoken for their human rights and dignity. Its critique of the municipal prostitution ban was met with almost total incomprehension.

So were the viewpoints of Eevamaria (pen name), a prostitute. In a letter to the editor of *Helsingin Sanomat*, she pointed out that the prosti-tutes' own perspective tended to be overlooked in the debate. Eevamaria opposed criminalisation of the selling and buying of sexual services – both would just cause more problems for prostitutes, for whom prostitution was a last resort to make money. Punishment and restrictions would not help the prostitute's position; neither would they help her get out of the business (*Helsingin Sanomat* 24 August 1999). Eevamaria's letter pro-duced an angry response from a proponent of the prostitution ban: 'You can't accuse others if you yourself demean your human rights by being a piece of merchandise. In today's Finland, you should not talk about "a last resort for earning money", either' (*Helsingin Sanomat* 4 September 1999). This opinion was very popular in the debate.

Policy outcome

The total ban on public prostitution proposed by the city board won in the city council over other proposals (no prostitution ban, a ban on nuisance only), as it was supported by the large political groups in the council. The debates in the city council had quite clearly indicated that the ban was meant to include both the selling and the buying of sex. The expectations about this end by both the city councillors and the citizen activists nevertheless fell flat when the ban went into effect at the beginning of December 1999. The police and the city authorities interpreted the prohibition to concern only the sellers, i.e. the prostitutes. (The English language version actually stated that soliciting in public places is prohibited.) Many of the women activists denounced both the gender bias and the watering-down of the ban in press interviews and demanded punishment of the customers as well (*Iltasanomat* 1 December 1999).

Women's movement impact

Women played a prominent part in the debate in two ways: they brought the issue of prostitution to the local agenda and they very much set the frame of the debate. However, as far as the policy outcome was concerned, in practice they succeeded in criminalising only the prostitutes, not the clients. Thus, in the final analysis, the outcome did not correspond with the women's demands and the local response was rather that of co-optation.

Women's policy agency activities

The city of Helsinki has had a municipal Equality Board since 1986, with a cross-sectional preparatory role in gender equality matters within the city government. Its members are politically nominated from the parties represented in the city council with a non-socialist majority profile. In 1999, the chair was a male non-councillor from the National Coalition Party. None of the members at the time belonged to the city council, a fact that clearly reveals the marginalised status of the board in spite of its formal closeness to the local decision-making arenas. It had a limited administrative capacity: its main resource was the use of a part-time secretary employed by the city administration.

In this debate, the Council of Equality displayed the same characteristics as in the second one. The main difference was that in this debate its proximity to the policy-making process was distant, because it was mainly concerned with national policy-making.

Neither of these women's policy offices was consulted and neither offered its opinion voluntarily in the debate. Both the municipal Equality Board and the national Council for Equality had earlier on taken social policy standpoints on prostitution with some demands for client criminalisation only. At this earlier stage, however, they were not yet required to define a standpoint on concrete penalties. The feminist chair of the council, Tuula Haatainen (SDP), also functioned as the vice-chair of Helsinki City Council, a position that could have offered a direct channel of access to the agency. There is no indication, however, that Haatainen actively participated in the debate, or presented council viewpoints, or deviated from the party line on the subject. In conclusion, the role of the women's policy agencies can be assessed as symbolic; they were not active in the process and did not articulate women's movements demands.

Women's movement characteristics

During the third debate, the women's movement was in a stage of consolidation. In addition to the anti-prostitution movement, the Kallio Society and many female citizens mobilised on the debate, especially some of the Green Party women and the conservative National Coalition Party women joined the forces for a prostitution ban at the local level. For many of them, the campaign was a continuation of the failed parliamentary effort of 1998. In comparison, left-wing women's local organisations remained remarkably silent on the issue. Also the Unioni, a national-level feminist organisation, participated as early as 1996 in the local policy process and proposed that restrictions to pimping and other exploitative practices should be added to the municipal ordinance. In hindsight, this abolitionist view stands out in stark contrast to the prohibitionist outcome of the debate.

The prostitution issue had a high priority on the local scene too, considering, for instance, the concern shown towards the reform of the Sex Crime Act by some local-level organisations. The counter-movement was moderate as the local authorities resisted taking up the prostitution issue for a long time.

Policy environment

The local policy-making sub-system was moderately closed, with the city administration playing a central role, along with the police and the Organisation of Finnish Municipalities; in the prostitution issue a variety of other actors were also involved. The proportion of the socialist parties in the city council was 31 per cent. The National Coalition Party was the largest group, followed by the SDP and the Greens. The high female representation must not be forgotten either: 47 per cent of the city councillors were women. Moreover, the top troika in the city hierarchy (the mayor, the chair of the city council and the chair of the city board) consisted solely of women. The policy-making system displayed a relatively non-gendered law and order approach to prostitution, whereas the women's movements utilised a gendered variation of the same frame, making for a compatible fit.

Conclusion

In this case study, I have analysed the role and impact of state feminism and the women's movements in Finnish prostitution policy of the 1980s and the 1990s. In the first two debates, the insider activity of the women's policy agencies led to full policy satisfaction. In contrast, in the third debate the women's policy agencies played a purely symbolic role and the outcome was that of co-optation.

The results show the pronounced impact of women's movements on policy outcomes in the area of prostitution, with women's policy agencies providing effective linkages between women's movements and the state. In the Finnish case, all of the studied policy sub-systems showed similar, moderately closed characteristics, thus excluding policy sub-system variations from the explanation. Instead, left-wing control seems to have played a role.

In the first debate, a positive state response was achieved by a convergence of leftist and women's movement ideas. Although the Council for Equality was given access to the policy process only at the very end, it was successful in gendering the dominant frame in a manner that has affected all Finnish debates on the issue ever since. Indeed, as Järvinen (1990) also argues, a new frame that regarded prostitution from the standpoint of gender equality entered the scene. The new conception of the problem was never absent in the following debates but intertwined with other dominant frames, often with quite ambiguous results.

By the second debate, the Council for Equality and the Equality Ombudsman and women's organisations had achieved access and voice in policy-making in prostitution. The resulting policy success included the limited criminalisation of sex clients, with an aim to protect children. In contrast, women's demands for a broader client criminalisation went unheeded.

In 1999 in Helsinki, pressure politics by women activists led to the introduction of a local prostitution ban. However, women's central demand – that of criminalising clients, too – was not implemented by the ambiguously worded ban. In this local-level debate, the women's movements lacked strategic alliances with women's policy agencies. Also, in contrast to the successful policy outcomes where there was considerable left-wing control, it was the right wing that was in power in Helsinki (Norris 1987, 1997; Caul 1999; see also Holli 2001).

The partial or divided successes in the last two debates also suggest that Finnish state feminism and women's movements have obtained access and voice in policy-making, so long as they do not challenge the prevalent conceptions of prostitution and sexuality. Demands for client criminalisation did challenge these: they were either rejected outright or co-opted even when the women thought that they had achieved their goals.

A challenge for the future lies in the question of how deep the vested interests in defining prostitution in a patriarchal manner are embedded in the Finnish political structures. A continuing trend towards the development of prohibitionist policies is well underway, as a new bill on public order, including sanctions on both prostitutes and clients, is currently (January 2003) being discussed in parliament. In contrast, three political parties (the Swedish People's Party, the Left-Wing Alliance and the Christian Democrats) and the Social Democratic Women's party organisation have adopted Swedish-style total client criminalisation as their agenda.

The demands for client criminalisation have become the uniting platform for Finnish women's movements, in spite of their disagreement regarding the treatment of prostitutes. Accordingly, the policy recommendations vacillate between two solutions. The first one, favoured by the Greens and the right-wing women, advocates penalties for prostitutes and clients equally. The second solution, with support coming principally from left-wing women and the Swedish women's party section, advocates measures for client criminalisation only, regarding prostitutes as victims of male exploitation. Both standpoints are convincingly being defended with gender equality arguments – illustrating once again (Holli 1999) the span, flexibility and power of the concept in the Finnish social context.

NOTE

1. The universe of debates consists of the following:
   1 modification of the Vagrant Act (1974, 1976, 1980 and 1982) and the repeal of the law (1986);
   2 the Sex Crime Act (1998);
   3 the Foreign Nationals Act (1999);
   4 municipal decision-making on prostitution (Helsinki municipal ordinance 1999, followed by other municipalities later on);
   5 administrative decisions concerning sex business from 1994 onward by ministries and other authorities.

Amy G. Mazur

Introduction

Prostitution policy experts in France identify three different regimes
of prostitution policy: regulatory, prohibitionist and abolitionist (e.g.
LeGardinier 1989, 1997; Louis 1991). Since 1960, France has followed
an abolitionist approach to prostitution. For most French policy experts
and practitioners, this approach includes policies that seek to eliminate
any official regulation of prostitution, to punish the organisation of prostitution including public solicitation and pimping, to prevent the social
conditions that lead to prostitution, and to help prostitutes leave prostitution. Individual prostitution itself is not illegal. There is disagreement,
however, over whether an abolitionist regime should eliminate prostitution or its regulation (e.g. Cabiria 1999: 23–5).

Up until 1960, France took a regulatory approach to prostitution. In
1946, the law Richard closed state-run bordellos or *maisons closes*, but
maintained the monitoring of prostitutes. In 1960, France signed the
1949 UN Treaty on the 'Elimination of the Traffic in Persons and of the
Exploitation of the Prostitution of Others'. From 1960 to 1965, twenty-
five policy statements were adopted to establish the framework for the
abolitionist regime (*Femmes et Monde* 1987: 77). Individual policy-makers
and politicians have periodically argued to reopen state-run bordellos in
the interest of public health and order. The last major public debate on re-
opening the *maisons closes* took place in 1990. In 2000, the variety of policy
actors involved with prostitution policy considered neither regulatory nor
prohibition regimes a viable alternative. Recent public opinion polls echo
the elite consensus. In a 1996 survey, 74 per cent of those polled were
against the prohibition of prostitution and 84 per cent felt that public
authorities should develop prevention and rehabilitation measures over
law enforcement (IPSOS in *Le Monde* 22 November 1996).

Since the late 1980s, successive French governments have actively
defended the abolitionist position in international arenas. Feminists,
femocrats, non-feminist ministers, politicians from the right and the left,

prostitutes' rights groups, and Catholic and secular prostitution aid organisations work together, often in uneasy coalitions, to advance the French position in international policy discussions. For many, defending the abolitionist position outside France is just as important as, if not more so than, dealing with prostitution issues at home.

Selection of debates

As French observers point out, there are many contradictions between the official position that prostitution is legal and the realities of law enforcement. For example, the Penal Code stipulates that prostitutes cannot be arrested, but solicitation when it disturbs public order is penalised quite severely, up to 20,000 francs (3,359 euros). Many assert that the use of the ambiguous term solicitation – *racollage* – gives latitude to police and judges to fine prostitutes rather than clients. Prostitutes are also required to pay into social security like other liberal professions. These contradictions in domestic policy are indicative of a wider government apathy towards developing a coherent approach to prostitution (e.g. *Prostitution et Société* July–August 1988; Falco 1991).

The intricacies of the abolitionist system implicate a broad range of actors, often with conflicting approaches. Although governments of both the right and the left have called inter-ministerial meetings on specific aspects of the policy issue, there is no centralised office, department or bureau that co-ordinates policies on prostitution. Jurisdiction was not decentralised to the regions in the major reform of 1983, but the highly urban nature of prostitution gives municipal governments important roles in enforcement and rehabilitation. Field services of the central administrative offices at both regional and departmental levels implement different aspects of policy as well, often in a highly piecemeal manner. At the national level, there are two permanent, but small, agencies with statutory authority over prostitution. The Human Trafficking Enforcement Agency, located in the Central Directorate of the Judicial Police under the authority of the Ministry of the Interior, is supposed to work in partnership with 'all ministries, international agencies, non-governmental organisations and prevention and rehabilitation groups' (*Prostitution et Société* July–August 1997). It primarily collects information on enforcement for the national police and works with other law enforcement agencies outside France to police worldwide prostitution.

A single position in the Department of Social Services oversees rehabilitation and prevention. Anny Roucolle worked in this position until her retirement in the mid-1990s. According to the femocrat responsible for the prostitution portfolio in 1998, Roucolle kept this portfolio alive on her own when the larger Social Services administration ignored it. The person in this position distributes government funds to prostitution aid groups – in the 1990s around 30 million francs (4.6 million euros). A 1960 ordinance established the Services de Prévention et de Réadaptation (SPR) to focus on prevention and rehabilitation at the departmental level. The SPR has been largely inoperative given the lack of financial or institutional support from the government (Falco 1991; Legardinier 1997). A handful of local services are kept alive by local prostitution aid groups and individuals working for social services, often with the help of the women's rights administration's field services. For instance, the SPR of the Alpes-Maritimes department was listed as a non-state group in a 1998 guide of prostitute aid organisations (Fondation Scelle 1998).

The women's rights administration – periodic cabinet-level offices, the permanent Women's Rights Services and its regional and departmental field offices – has also been periodically given formal responsibility over co-ordinating prostitution policy. Prostitution issues are not usually raised in policy discussions on women's rights policy by the administration unless the ministry is formally given the portfolio. The Ministry of the Rights of Woman, under the leadership of Yvette Roudy (Parti Socialiste, PS) from 1981 to 1987, co-ordinated prostitution policy to a limited degree. It held one session of an Inter-ministerial Committee of Prostitution (*Libération* 10 June 1981) and hosted several inter-ministerial cabinet meetings on Penal Code reform on prostitution. From 1986 to 1997 the government basically ignored rehabilitation and prevention, except for Anny Roucolle in the Department of Social Services. In 1997, the right-wing government transferred the prostitution portfolio back to the Women's Rights Services without any new resources. The budgetary responsibility for funding prostitution aid groups remained in the Social Services Department. The femocrat in charge of prostitution organised several day-long meetings to revitalise the implementation of policy and inter-ministerial meetings.

The unprecedented co-ordination of prostitution issues came to a close in 1998 when the femocrat in charge of the dossier left her position. In 2000, the portfolio remained inactive. The service was trying to transfer formal responsibility for the portfolio back to the Department of Social Services. One femocrat explained that the women's rights administration was not equipped to deal with prostitution issues and found it difficult to develop a feminist position.

In addition to these permanent offices, the Ministry of Health, the Ministry of Finance, the Ministry of Justice, the policing division in the Ministry of the Interior, the Ministry of Foreign Affairs and the Ministry of Education participate periodically in the elaboration of prostitution policy. The parliament and the Council of Ministers, therefore, can be arenas in which prostitution policy issues are discussed.

About sixteen prostitution aid associations, kept active by state subsidies, fill in the gaps of prostitution policy implementation, particularly with regards to prevention and rehabilitation (Fondation Scelle 1998). Although many groups may pursue action that can be seen as feminist, most do not identify with organised feminism in France.

There have been eight major debates on prostitution policy issues from the mid-1970s to 2000 that have ended in formal government policy statements.[1] The three debates selected for analysis represent the life cycle of prostitution policy issues: prostitution rights issues prominent on the public agenda in the early 1970s, a virtual policy silence on the question from the mid-1970s to the end of the 1980s, and prostitution re-appearing on the government's agenda in the context of broader Penal Code reform in the early 1990s. The first debate on prostitute rights took place at the local level, in Lyons, and hence captures one of the major arenas for prostitution policy. The government report that closed this debate is also typical of the 'symbolic' policy statements made on prostitution that propose or adopt reforms with virtually no concrete government action (Edelman 1964). The 1990 controversy over a former Health Minister's call to re-open state-run bordellos was selected as the second debate because it was one of the highest profile debates on protection and because the debate was closed by elites from government, political parties and interest groups agreeing that re-opening state-run bordellos was not an acceptable option. The debate also involved health issues and the health policy actors that periodically become involved with prostitution policy. The third debate on major Penal Code reform in 1992 and 1994 represents debates over law enforcement. It also involved the Ministries of Justice and the Interior.

Debate 1: Prostitute rights and law enforcement, 1972–1975

How issue came to the public agenda

In 1972, a Ministry of the Interior decision to crack down on prostitution, in the context of a nationwide campaign against police corruption, thrust the issue on to the national agenda. A part of this effort was firing the head of the city of Lyons' vice squad, who was subsequently tried for corruption and pimping. As a result, the Lyons police force was re-organised (*Le Figaro* 12 June 1975). In 1972 the police fined 6,290 prostitutes for soliciting, imprisoned 43 pimps and closed down 41 prostitute hotels (*Le*

Figaro 12 June 1975). Women prostitutes organised an initial demonstration in the city centre to protest what they saw as unfair police harassment (*Le Monde* 29–30 June 1974). City judges, also following the orders of the Ministry of the Interior, began sentencing repeat offenders. The murder of two prostitutes in Lyons and a state crackdown on tax fraud mobilised Lyons prostitutes to organise a 'collectif des femmes prostitutées' under the leadership of prostitute Marie-Claude Masson, alias Ulla.

Ulla remained the major spokesperson for the amorphous *'collectif'* until 1975. The *collectif* occupied two Catholic churches in Lyons, went to visit President Valéry Giscard d'Estaing (Union pour la Défense de la Republique, UDF) in his home district, and sought to meet with a range of government officials, including the Deputy Secretary of Women's Status, Françoise Giroud (*Valeurs Actuelles* 24 November 1975). The *collectif* also organised an 'Etats Généraux de la Prostitution' in Lyons and participated in the first 'Assises Nationales de la Prostitution' in Paris (Mathieu 1999).

Dominant frame of debate

Prior to the women's prostitutes' movement, there was little discussion of women prostitutes' rights. The major frame of policy debates on prostitution was gender neutral. Prostitutes were seldom identified as women or clients as men. Prostitution was not discussed in the context of sex discrimination and violence against women. The gender-neutral approach was also contained in the original United Nations 1949 convention signed by France. Formal government texts on prostitution barely mentioned individual prostitutes, usually referring to prostitution, pimping (*proxénétisme*) and solicitation (*racollage*). The definition of prostitution in the Penal Code embodied this approach: '[prostitutes include] those for whom the attitude on the public streets is to provoke debauchery, those whose gestures, spoken and written words, or by other means would pursue publicly the solicitation of persons of either sex with the intent of provoking debauchery' (cited in Falco 1991: 49).[2]

The major focus of government policy and private prostitute aid associations was either to keep women out of prostitution or to help women leave prostitution. When prostitutes' rights were raised by the social services actors it was in the context of the legal and fiscal impediments that kept women in prostitution. Prostitute aid associations did talk about women as prostitutes in the context of the abolition of prostitution and trafficking. They saw prostitution as a form of oppression and slavery not just against women by men but against all 'human beings' by gender-neutral institutions. Some prostitution aid associations talked about abolishing the traffic of women and children, defining women as minors (Cauly 1974). Thus, the gender-neutral approach to prostitution was also underpinned by a certain level of gender-bias towards women defining them as the inferior sex.

Gendering the debate

The women prostitutes' movement entered the gender-neutral/biased debate with a new perspective: women prostitutes' rights should be respected as those of working women with 'normal' (*sic*) lives. They demanded equal treatment from government, the police and society at large. They asserted that police should focus their attention on individual prostitutes and their partners rather than clients and avoid assuming that the partners of women prostitutes were pimps. A Lyons court, for example, had given Ulla's husband a thirteen-month prison sentence with eleven months probation (*Valeurs Actuelles* 24 November 1975). The movement, however, was firmly against the state regulation of prostitution. Women prostitutes stated in press interviews that they did not want to be '*fonctionnaires de sexe*' (sexocrats) and that the *maisons closes* were 'the best example of women's slavery' (*Le Figaro* 12 June 1975). While the *collectif* did point out that there was little interest in denouncing clients who were male and that '*le milieu*' was male oriented, there was little discussion of sexism, of the need for gender equality as a solution or of prostitution as a form of sexual violence against women.

Policy outcome

In July 1975, the Minister of Health, Simone Veil, appointed Guy Pinot, president of the Court of Appeals of Orleans, to 'try to understand the phenomenon in its entirety and to see if certain aspects necessitate judicial or administrative solutions' (cited in *Le Monde* 25 July 1975). The Pinot report, presented to President Valéry Giscard d'Estaing in January 1976, was a symbolic government response to the two months of direct action and protest by the women prostitutes' movement. No new policies were adopted as a direct result of this report and the pro-women prostitutes' rights policy statement was quickly forgotten in ensuing years.

Women's movement impact

Here we see a dual response; women were important players in the policy process and the Pinot report incorporated certain demands of the prostitutes' rights movement. Women as individuals and as collectives were the

major actors of the prostitutes' rights movement and of the debate that
unfolded. The Lyons *collectif*, however, did not seek government subsidies and disappeared soon after the Pinot report was issued in 1976.[3]
Although two feminist groups from the new women's movement in Paris
supported the prostitutes' rights movement – the Mouvement du Planning Familial (Family Planning Movement) provided financial support
for the prostitutes' rally in Paris (Falco 1991) and the Ligue du Droits
des Femmes came out in defence of prostitute rights – the major force behind the campaign was women prostitutes. Indeed, the philosophy of the
prostitutes' rights movement was at odds with the Paris-based women's
movements. Press coverage of the Assises Nationales in Paris, for example, discussed the clash between the entrepreneurial/ '*petit-bourgeois*' views
of the women in the prostitutes' movement and the more revolutionary
views of the liberation feminists and extreme left-wing intellectuals who
came out to support the prostitutes' movement (*Le Monde* 29–30 July
1975, 30 November 1975; *Le Nouvel Observateur* 24 November 1975).

The Pinot report reflected the demands for equal rights forwarded by
the women prostitutes' movement more than the analyses of the new
women's movements. In addition to interviewing established policy actors, Pinot talked with women prostitutes to prepare his report (*Le Monde*
25 July 1975). In the report, he discussed the dignity of 'women prostitutes' and their right to professional status and recognition (Pinot 1976:
1, 19, 39). In a separate section entitled 'Real equality for women', Pinot
urged public authorities to 'guarantee effectively to women equal opportunities compared with men with regards to job training, salaries, social
mobility, etc.' (Pinot 1976: 33). The report also called for law enforcement to penalise male clients rather than only women prostitutes and to
lighten penalties for individual pimps.

Women's policy agency activities

The prostitutes' rights movements introduced women's rights into the
debate on prostitution policy and the Pinot report vocalised their positions without any support from the women's policy agency. The Deputy
Minister of Women's Status, Françoise Giroud, consistently refused to
get involved with any debates on prostitution, stating that it was a man's
problem (*Le Monde* 6 June 1975). She also refused to meet a group of
women prostitutes from Lyons who came to see her in Paris. The women's
policy agency activities therefore were symbolic.

Giroud, the editor of one of the major weekly news magazines, was
named by centre-right president Valéry Giscard d'Estaing to the first
ministerial-level women's policy office as a political appointee. She was

not a feminist activist. Although she had relatively easy access to the president, the administrative capacity of her office was limited, having a small budget, a tiny staff and no field offices. Furthermore, she could attend Council of Ministers meetings only when women's rights issues were discussed. Her appointment was seen, none the less, as an unprecedented response to the women's movement and shifting public opinion on women's rights (Mazur 1995). She was identified with Giscard's liberal approach to social issues. Her ministry had a cross-sectoral mandate to promote women's status in all domains. In her policy recommendations and actions she primarily focused on issues that allowed women better to reconcile work and family responsibilities without challenging established gender-hierarchies; there was no mention of women's sexual violence issues or prostitution (e.g. Giroud 1976).

Women's movement characteristics

The French women's movements were in a period of growth in the mid-1970s. The otherwise fragmented and amorphous movement unified around the campaign to legalise abortion, which ended in 1979. The more organised parts of the movement – the Ligue des Droits des Femmes (LDF) and the Mouvement du Planning Familial – were very close to the established left, particularly the Socialist Party. The fluid and radical parts of the movement, the Mouvement de Libération des Femmes, came out of the radical left student movement of 1968 (Duchen 1986; Jenson 1989; Picq 1993). Established women's groups connected to the political parties, such as the Union des Femmes Françaises and Union Féminin Civique et Sociale, also were re-energised during the 1970s. While sexual violence issues were important to the women's movement, prostitution reform was a low priority. For example, the platforms of the new LDF and a coalition of established women's groups did not include any points about prostitution (*Le Monde* 8 March 1974, 22 May 1975, 30 September 1975). There were no counter-movements mobilising against either the prostitutes' rights groups or the other new women's movements during this period.

Policy environment

The prostitution policy sub-system during this period was moderately closed. Gender-neutrality underpinned by predominant gender stereotypes about men and women was the norm in official positions taken by the various prostitution actors. The law enforcement actors in the sub-system were more prominent and powerful than the social actors as well, particularly in the early 1970s. The dominant approach of the policy sub-system was for the most part incompatible with the approach of the womens' prostitutes' movement. At the same time, the liberal approach of Giscard and the Pinot report were quite compatible with the prostitutes' rights movement. The debate opened just as Giscard was elected in May 1974. Giscard had been elected on a liberal-oriented platform of individual rights and improving women's rights specifically (Mazur 1995). At the time, the centre-right UDF shared power with the more right-wing Gaullist party; thus the coalition in power was under moderate right-wing control.

Debate 2: Public health/AIDS and closing the debate on regulatory regime, 1989–1990

How issue came to the public agenda

On 8 June 1990, Michèle Barzach (Rassemblement Pour la République, RPR), former Minister of Health and Vice-Mayor of Paris, made the following statement in an interview with *Le Monde*: 'At the risk of shocking many, I think that we must raise the question of re-opening state-run bordellos. And to this question I answer clearly Yes . . . We need to establish a real public health system and required public health checks. But enough of this hypocrisy and collective irresponsibility' (*Le Monde* 8 June 1990).

During the following two months a host of government decision-makers, interest groups' representatives and public personalities responded to what they saw as an unacceptable proposal in the national and regional media (Legardinier 1991).

Dominant frame of debate

Michèle Barzach's statement was made from a purely public health perspective without mentioning gender issues, in terms of the health of women prostitutes, the larger causes of prostitution or the gendered relations of power between prostitutes and clients. Prior to the Barzach affair, periodic proposals had been made to re-open state-run bordellos in the interest of public health, the last one in 1986. These proposals usually emanated from the health administration or individual members of parliament in private members' bills. The argument for re-opening went as follows: prostitutes run a high risk of spreading disease – sexually transmitted diseases and beginning in the late 1980s AIDS; government-run bordellos would allow more systematic supervision of prostitutes in order to reduce the public health risk. Prostitutes, not male clients, were the object of government action. The term *prostituées* in the feminine form was used in advancing this position, suggesting that women were to be the primary objects of the health checks.

An article published in October 1989 in a Ministry of Health newsletter on epidemics contributed to the rising public concern about the role of prostitutes in the spread of AIDS at the end of the 1980s (De Vincenzi 1989). De Vincenzi summarised studies of the incidence of AIDS amongst prostitutes, indicating that they were mostly inconclusive as to whether prostitutes actually spread AIDS. There was no discussion of the health of male prostitutes. Still, the article identified that male clients were also possibly responsible for public health problems that came out of prostitution and that future studies should focus on male clients. It was cited in the press and underpinned Barzach's public remarks (e.g. *Le Monde* 27 October 1989). A Louis Harris/VSD poll taken in May 1990 reflected public concern about AIDS and a certain level of support for Barzach's proposal. The wording of the questions took a gender-biased health approach. Eighty per cent of those surveyed felt that 're-opening the state-run bordellos would reduce the risk of spreading AIDS through better medical supervisions' of *prostituées*' (feminine form). Also, 61 per cent felt that closing the state-run bordellos had been a bad move and 64 per cent stated that they were in favour of re-opening (*Hebdomadaire de Louis Harris/VSD* 12–19 May 1990).

Gendering the debate

The day following Michèle Barzach's statement, *Le Monde* published the official reactions of different members of the Socialist government – the Ministers of Health (Claude Evin) and Humanitarian Action (Bernard Kouchner) and the Deputy Minister of Women's Rights (Michèle Andrée); the Socialist Party – Ségolène Royale, a Socialist deputy; Charles Millon – the president of the centre-right parliamentary group, the UDF; and mayor of Paris, Jacques Chirac, who was also head of the right-wing Gaullist RPR. One day later public statements by the Mouvement du Planning Familial, the Ligue des Droits de l'Homme and the Mouvement du Nid were published (*Le Monde* 12 June 1990). The Mouvement du Nid is an official association affiliated with the Catholic church that aims to abolish prostitution. It works with individual prostitutes to help them leave prostitution and participates in most public discussions on prostitution issues, but is neither formally associated with the French feminist movement nor recognised as a women-oriented group.

Two public officials supported Barzach's proposal. The Minister of Health in an initial statement indicated that he was ready to examine any positions that would prevent the spread of AIDS (*Le Monde* 10–11 June 1990). The next day, in the context of the vocal opposition to re-opening state-run bordellos, Evin opposed the proposal. Bernard Kouchner also supported consideration of a proposal that would help the situation of prostitutes (in the feminine form) and not just deal with the AIDS epidemic. Right-wing and left-wing politicians and ministers opposed the proposal.

For the most part, opponents of the proposal argued that it would weaken women's rights or status. The head of the UDF group, for example, stated that re-opening the state-run bordellos would be bad for women's status – '*la condition féminine*'. The spokesperson for the Mouvement du Nid, its founder Père Talvas, reflecting the overall frame of the association, did not take a feminist stance in his criticism of Barzach's statements. Instead, he cited studies that showed there was no link between AIDS and prostitution and, in this light, argued that re-opening the *maisons closes* would do nothing to end the AIDS epidemic (*La Vie* 14 June 1990).

Statements made by the Deputy Minister of Women's Rights, the Socialist Party, the Socialist member of parliament Charles Millon and the Mouvement du Planning Familial all opposed the re-opening of the *maisons closes* from an overtly gendered perceptive. They all mentioned the way in which prostitution was a form of sexual slavery of women or sexual oppression of women, and not as the Mouvement du Nid would argue, of all people. One PS deputy deplored the use of women as scapegoats for a complex problem. The Deputy Minister of Women's Rights in her statement asserted that 'Women are not commodities.'

Policy outcome

The debate ended when the former Minister of Health publicly admitted that she had made a major 'communication error' and had taken a purely health perspective (interview, *Gai Pied Hebdo* 6 December 1990). From a broader purview, Barzach's provocative statement allowed a broad coalition of state and society actors to renounce decisively in a highly public manner the re-opening of state-run bordellos and in doing so stopped any further consideration of a regulatory regime in France.

Women's movement impact

Given the prominence of the feminist gendered positions in the public debate, this final rejection of a regulatory approach to prostitution in France was clearly grounded in women's movement positions that had developed on prostitution. Moreover, none of the women's movement advocates supported a regulatory regime on prostitution by 1990. Elite women were important actors in this debate. Positions easily identified with the women's movements were advanced by women speakers as representatives of their organisations/ministries and as independent actors. Moreover, women's groups were involved with the debate. Thus, the impact of the women's movement in the second debate was dual response once again.

The extent to which the feminist outcome of the 1990 debate determined the frame of future health debates is unclear. On one hand, the Health Ministry funded an in-depth feminist study of health issues among a collective of Parisian prostitutes (Coppel et al. 1990) that was carried out following a request from women prostitutes. On the other hand, a 1991 statement made by two professors in the name of the Academy of Medicine on the ineffectiveness of state-run bordellos in reducing the incidence of HIV/AIDS was not gendered at all (*Le Monde* 21 March 1991).

Women's policy agency activities

The national-level reaction of elites against re-opening state-run bordellos was gendered from a women's movement perspective, with the participation of the Deputy Minister of Women's Rights, in other words insider women's policy agency activities. Although the work of the national-level women's policy administration under Andrée's leadership had not included prostitutions' issues in its campaigns against domestic violence and battery of women in 1989 and in 1990, Andrée advanced her feminist position in the debate and presented a clearly feminist analysis of prostitution (*Prostitution et Société* April/May/June 1990). Andrée took a similar position on the issue to Socialist Party feminists and the Mouvement du Planning Familial. That is, prostitution must be placed in a larger context of sexual discrimination and violence against women.

The Deputy Ministry of the Rights of Woman had a cross-sectoral approach to women's rights issues at the time. Since the mid-1970s, the women's rights administration had grown significantly. At its high point, under the Ministry of the Rights of Woman in 1986 the agency had seven divisions at the national level and permanent offices at the regional and departmental levels (Mazur 1995). The administration was maintained under Andrée's care with a smaller budget and more problems with maintaining staff in its field offices; thus its administrative capacity was at a moderate level. Many feminist observers saw the lower status of the ministry and the political appointment of Andrée as a step backward.

Prime Minister Michel Rocard (PS) had originally omitted a separate ministerial portfolio for women's rights. When he did give in to feminist criticism he appointed Andrée who was a supporter of his faction of the PS and not an active participant in the feminist action of the PS.

Still, Andrée's ministry focused a significant amount of its limited resources on sexual violence: the creation of Departmental Councils on Violence Towards Women, public information campaigns on conjugal violence and battery of women, and sensitivity training for police regarding violent crimes against women. The deputy minister's support of sexual violence policy underpinned clearly her vocal position in the debate on *maisons closes*. Moreover, given that the prostitution portfolio was not formally under the control of the women's rights administration, as it had been in the 1980s and would be later after 1997, the absence of any treatment of prostitution issues in these programmes may have been a result of the formal mandate of the deputy ministry.

Women's movement characteristics

The women's movements from the 1970s had virtually disappeared by 1990 with a very small number of new groups emerging. The Association Européene des Violences Faites Contre les Femmes au Travail (AVFT) was founded in 1989 and the movement to promote women's representation – *parité* – was beginning to gain public support. The existing women's movement groups were also quite divided. While the parity movement did not treat sexual violence issues, the AVFT in its first years was focused primarily on sexual harassment in the workplace. Thus, prostitution issues were given a low priority by the women's groups. Unlike the clear links between autonomous feminist groups and the left in the 1970s, the new feminist groups were not close to the left during this period. There was no significant counter-movement that mobilised against the pro-women's movements' consensus on prostitution.

Policy environment

The policy sub-system involved with the 1990 debate was moderately closed with an emphasis on Health Ministry actors and an absence of any law enforcement or social services actors. The gender-neutral and gender-biased approaches of the health policy actors were important in the way the debate unfolded. Ministers like Barzach and Evin close to the health administration were far less critical of considering state regulation of prostitution. The dominant approach here, therefore, was incompatible with women's movement ideas. There was strong left-wing control of the government, with the Socialist Party controlling both the presidency and the government.

Debate 3: Penal Code reform of pimping and solicitation, 1991–1992

How issue came to the public agenda

Public positions on reforming the criminalised aspects of prostitution can be traced back to the prostitute rights movements and the Pinot report discussed in the first debate. The Mouvement du Nid also supported increased penalties for pimps and lightening criminal laws that were potentially damaging to prostitutes themselves. These dispersed calls for Penal Code reform on prostitution were ignored until the Socialist government began the lengthy process of overhauling the entire Penal Code in 1981. The Ministry of the Rights of Woman, through the first and only Comité Interministeriel sur la Prostitution, had formally asked for increased penalties for pimps as early as 1981 (*Libération* 6 October 1981). In 1986, the powerful Roudy ministry formulated official recommendations on the Penal Code reform proposal being drafted by the Socialist Fabius government; however, they appeared to have little impact in the parliamentary debate on the Penal Code reform (Henniquau 1986). The recommendations included re-establishing penalties against clients who threatened or raped prostitutes, and increasing penalties for pimping and international trafficking by organised crime. These proposals used gender-neutral language, e.g. 're-establishment of serious circumstances in the area of threats, constraints or rape' (p. 7). Although the language was gender-neutral, the proposals were in line with feminist positions on prostitution of the prostitute rights groups and feminist organisations at the time.

The Fabius government formally submitted the first sections of draft Penal Code legislation to parliament for commission scrutiny in 1986 (Louis 1994: 40). The intended magnitude of the reforms was articulated by the Minister of Justice in 1989: 'to redefine the values of our society, or, more precisely, those for the society of the third millennium' (cited in Louis 1994: 41). Penal Code reform had been on the agenda since 1981, but now the reforms were discussed in parliamentary session beginning in April 1992 and adopted in July 1992.

Dominant frame of debate

The dominant frame of the debate on prostitution Penal Code reform was determined by the purposefully gender-neutral approach of the Penal

Code and the policy actors in the justice and interior administration who contributed to its content and implementation through law enforcement and court decisions. For instance, in 1989, the Minister of Justice used the universal male in identifying the principal aim of the Penal Code reform of 1991: 'to protect for the first time in a law that supreme value of the rights of man' (cited in Louis 1994: 41).

In addition to the gender-neutral approach of the original UN convention on 'trafficking human beings',[4] the French approach derives from the republican universalism embedded in the constitution and law, where all individuals are defined in terms of formal equality before the law.[5] In this frame, texts and policy actors do not mention the specific sex, race, religion, etc. of individuals. Politically appointed ministers and career civil servants generally consider republican universalism a major operating principle in policy formation. On the one hand, the official gender-neutral universalism in all legal areas makes it difficult to insert gender-specific language and ideas into policy discussions and in official texts. On the other hand, the gender-neutrality of universalism often hides the gender-biased approach of many actors to women's policy issues where gender stereotypes about men and women are the norm. In the area of prostitution policy, the gender-biased aspect of republican universalism is expressed, for example, by portraying women prostitutes as sexual objects, minors or victims, or by failing to focus on male clients as criminals.

The Socialist Deputy Minister of Justice, Michel Sapin, responsible for Penal Code reform, displayed the two sides of gender-biased universalism in an interview on the 1991 reform conducted by feminists in the AVFT. With regards to gender-neutrality, Sapin stated:

In so far as the Penal Code does not make any discrimination based on the sex of either the perpetrator or the victim of a crime, it is normal that women, no more than men, are not considered in a specific manner. In this context, legal provisions [from the Penal Code on violence against women] must be applied in a symmetric fashion for individuals of one or the other sex. (Cromer et al. 1992: 87)

With regard to gender-biased assumptions about women's vulnerability and women's child-bearing roles, he asserted that 'Women's particular situation is taken into consideration in the cases where, for objective reasons, it is necessary to do so. As it is the case in the definition of the vulnerable person. Vulnerability which comes from the state of pregnancy is obviously unique to women' (Cromer et al. 1992: 91).

In addition, Ministry of the Interior policy actors dealt with prostitution issues from a law enforcement perspective defined by the parameters of the abolitionist system: to criminalise pimping, trafficking and solicitation without impinging on the rights of prostitutes to work in private. In law enforcement practices prior to the 1994 reforms and despite the recommendations of the Pinot report, criminalisation was a more important focus than the respect of the rights of individual prostitutes.

Gendering the debate

The parliamentarians did not waver from a criminal justice and a gender-biased universal approach (Louis 1994: 64–7). The short parliamentary debate on prostitution focused primarily on penalising large-scale pimping and on the rights of male clients and individual pimps, with no mention of the rights of prostitutes. There was no discussion about the gendered nature of the system of prostitution or the potential for gendered power relations between male clients and female prostitutes.[6] Instead, one deputy referred to the complex relationship between a pimp and his 'prostitute girlfriend': 'In effect, it is not a relationship of a protector to protected, nor one based only on terror: there is some of that, but also there is affection, not even speaking of love' (cited in Louis 1994: 65).

In the discussions on changing the law on incarcerating boyfriends of *'prostituées'*,[7] deputies were concerned mostly with not punishing 'innocents' – used in masculine form – in the interest of protecting individual rights that emphasise the rights of men as clients and low-level pimps, rather than with women prostitutes. While the deputies supported increased penalties for organised crime behind pimping, the Socialist Minister of Justice and the deputies agreed that individuals pimps – *le proxénétisme simple* – should not be overly penalised: *surpénaliser* (Louis 1994: 66).

Policy outcome

The Penal Code reform adopted in July 1992 and put into effect formally on 1 March 1994 included a separate chapter on pimping – *proxénétisme et des infractions assimilées* (law no. 92-684). In the process of issuing implementation orders, the Conseil d'Etat (Council of State) changed the legal definition of soliciting under article R.265.8 of the Penal Code (*Prostitution et Société* October/November/December 1994: 26).

Women's movement impact

The final law incorporated several different women's movement demands (Chapter III, Section 2 du loi no. 92-684 du 22 juillet). It included all three proposals made by the Ministry of the Rights of Woman in the 1980s as well as a precise definition of pimping that would prevent the police from arresting the companions of prostitutes. All three of these positions had been supported by prostitute rights groups or women's groups. Implementation orders on the Penal Code reform issued by the Conseil d'Etat responded to another long-held demand of prostitutes, that the legal definition of solicitation preclude the routine and expensive fining of prostitutes. Henceforth, judges and police would have to show clear proof of public solicitation and undertake a more complex process of questioning (*Prostitution et Société* October/November/December 1994: 26).

These feminist policy outcomes occurred with little direct involvement of women or feminists. As Louis observes, 'the parliamentary commission that prepared the code did not call any feminists to its hearings' (1994: 44). The reporters for the commission were men and three of the thirty-eight members of the two commissions for both houses of parliament were women (Louis 1994: 44). Only male members of parliament participated in the debates on prostitution reform. Also, there was no evidence that any feminist groups were directly consulted in the pre-parliamentary process of elaborating the draft legislation. Thus, the impact of the women's movement was pre-empted in the final law.

Women's policy agency activities

Michèle Andrée was replaced by Véronique Neiertz when Prime Minister Michel Rocard resigned in July 1991 and was replaced by Edith Cresson (PS). The new Deputy Minister of Women's Rights and Daily Life did not participate in formulating the government's draft legislation or in the parliamentary discussions on the prostitution Penal Code reform and thus did not change the gender-neutral/biased frame of the policy debate. Like Andrée, Neiertz presented a feminist analysis of prostitution in an interview with the Mouvement du Nid (*Prostitution et Société* July/August/September 1999, no. 98: 12–13). The women's policy agency activities in the early 1990s, therefore, were marginal.

The deputy ministry in 1991 continued to have a cross-sectoral remit, combining a new portfolio on 'daily life issues' with women's rights. The ministry was relatively close to the Prime Minister's Office but distant from the president's. Like previous ministers, Neiertz's appointment was political, due to her connections in the PS, and the administrative capacity of the ministry was moderate. The new deputy minister had stronger feminist credentials than her predecessor, Andrée. She had been active in the women's rights section of the Socialist Party in the 1980s. At the same time, in a 1993 interview, she downplayed the need for a separate ministry. Femocrats in the ministry in 1993 observed also that she was even less interested in women's rights issues than Andrée. None the less, Neiertz was well-respected within the Socialist Party, particularly the Mitterrandist *courant*, and hence had some political clout with other cabinet ministers. She continued Andrée's focus on sexual violence, focusing most of the attention of her ministry on elaborating anti-sexual harassment legislation.

Women's movement characteristics

Although there was not a significant mass-based women's movement like the movements of the 1970s, feminist organisations and movements in the early 1990s continued to gain momentum, re-emerging as important players. By 1992, the relatively cohesive parity movement had increased public interest and elite support for calls to deal concretely with France's poor record in women's representation (Mazur 2001a). In addition, the AVFT had by 1992 become an important leader in the campaign for anti-sexual harassment legislation. The AVFT also formally turned its attention to prostitution politics, publishing articles on prostitution in its journal, *Projets Féministes*, on a regular basis. While prostitution was a relatively moderate priority for the AVFT at least, the women's movement organisations no longer had their close links to the left. The only significant counter-movement to women's rights issues was the anti-abortion movement (Robinson 2001), which showed little interest in prostitution policy.

Policy environment

The prostitution policy sub-system was dominated by criminal justice actors from the Ministries of Justice and the Interior with a gender-biased universalist approach to prostitution issues, which was incompatible with feminist positions on the issue. This policy sub-system was closed compared with the first two debates. Socialist François Mitterrand remained in the presidency for a second term until 1993. The Socialist Party had a majority in parliament from 1981 to 1986 and from 1988 to 1993 – moderate left-wing control.

Conclusion

The three debates show significant variation in the women's policy agency activities and women's movement impact. In the first debate (symbolic/dual response), the Deputy Secretary of Women's Status eschewed a feminist stance and made no effort to gender the debate on prostitution law enforcement and prostitute rights. Instead, the prostitute rights movements, in the context of a vital, mass-based women's movement, participated in the formulation of the Pinot report. Giscard's emphasis on individual rights also reinforced the demands of the prostitute rights movements. The gender-neutral yet gender-biased powerful law enforcement policy sub-system did not block the articulation of feminist policy, plausibly because the Pinot report was strictly advisory.

In the second debate (insider/dual response), although the Deputy Ministry of Women's Rights was not the only actor to gender the public discussion, Michèle Andrée did present feminist arguments in several different public arenas. Here women's groups and women's policy agency positions worked together. The policy outcome was not just to reject the regulation of prostitution but to formulate the all-party consensus in the context of feminist arguments. The ensuing 'action-research' sponsored by the Ministry of Health suggested that gendering health and prostitution issues and involving women in the process was not entirely anathema to the health policy actors.

The third debate (marginal/pre-emption) shows the importance of the gender-biased universalist culture and discourse of the law enforcement sub-system when concrete policy is being formulated. In this debate, relatively active and institutionalised women's policy agencies, particularly under Yvette Roudy, contributed to the formulation of legislation but were unable to introduce a gendered approach. Compared with the other two debates, women did not have significant roles in the policy discussions in the early 1990s. Still, the feminist recommendations of the Roudy ministry as well as the demands of the prostitute rights movement were incorporated into the final law in a gender-neutral context.

The analysis suggests that while active, institutionalised and feminist women's policy offices have the potential to gender policy debates and help women's movements' ideas and women to be accepted into policy processes, they do not by themselves guarantee feminist success. Also, feminist outcomes are not entirely products of a politically active women's movement, of left-wing governments or of powerful feminist women's policy offices. Women's movement successes occurred under both right-wing and left-wing governments at times when the women's movement was growing and in decline, and when women's policy agencies were relatively weak and strong. An active women's prostitute rights movement appeared to play an important role in all debates. The degree to which the dominant approach in the policy environment was compatible or not with feminist ideas made a difference in the first and third debates.

The analysis also indicates that when policy formation occurs on significant reforms like the Penal Code reform, rather than policy proposals or symbolic policy statements, dominant gender-biased universalism will block out weaker feminist approaches. Another factor which certainly played a role was the extent to which prostitution issues were a low priority for most policy actors. Government and society-wide inattention to the issues may have allowed feminist approaches to enter into less important policy discussions. In conclusion, prostitute rights movements, elite apathy, the dominant belief system of policy sub-system actors and the relative importance of the policy decision may be decisive factors in the extent to which women's policy agencies have the potential to bring women's interests into the political process and, in doing so, eventually make stable democracies more democratic.

NOTES

The research for this chapter was funded by a grant from the Women's Rights Services of the French Ministry of Social Affairs. Danielle Barichasse, Genevieve Comte, Béatrice Florentin, Catherine Lesterpt, Marie-Victoire Louis and Lilian Mathieu provided their crucial insights into French prostitution politics. Thanks go to Joyce Outshoorn and other RNGS members for their useful advice on earlier versions.

1. These are:
    1 strengthening prostitute rights to social security and fair treatment, 1970s;
    2 Penal Code reform of pimping and prostitution, 1970s and 1990s;
    3 defence of abolitionist position in international agreements on trafficking in women, 1990s to 2000;
    4 regulation of sexual tourism, early 1990s;
    5 regulation of child prostitution, 1990s;
    6 public health/AIDS and prostitution, 1988–91;
    7 re-instating the regulatory regime of prostitution, 1988–90;
    8 jurisdiction over prostitution policy, 1970s to present.
2. All translations are by the author.
3. There is some speculation about whether the movement was supported by organised crime. Ulla admitted in her memoirs several years later that she had been paid off (Falco 1991). Still, an active prostitutes' rights movement has re-emerged in the late 1980s and 1990s as well, suggesting the proclivity for French prostitutes to mobilise.
4. International documents formally cited in the Penal Code reforms, according to Louis (1994: 41), did not include gendered texts such as the 1979 UN Convention on the Elimination of Violence Against Women.
5. The 1999 parity amendment to the constitution challenges the gender-biased approach to French democracy; however, at the time of the Penal Code reform it obviously was not a part of the political landscape.

6. Louis found that there was 'no sexed analysis made', 'never any question of violence against women' (1994: 42) and that the term 'women's rights' was mentioned once, by a woman communist deputy who was talking about the right of women to choose to be a mother (p. 43).
7. The female form of prostitute was used in the parliamentary papers, suggesting that deputies assumed that individual prostitutes were all women.

8 The politics of prostitution and trafficking of women in Israel

Delila Amir and Menachem Amir

Introduction

Historically, up until the 1990s, prostitution was not a politicised issue in Israel. However, since the 1990s, trafficking in women for prostitution purposes emerged, as in many other countries, as the most important issue on women's agenda – violence against women. The old and new women's movements, NGOs and women in the Knesset (parliament) and in government succeeded in mobilising the public and pressuring parliament to enact laws against trafficking and traffickers and to render special services to trafficked women.

This relative success can be attributed to several factors, among them the vocal position of the Parliament Commission for the Status of Women, the mobilisation of citizen's advocacy groups for foreign labourers' rights (including those of trafficked women) and broadening of the definitional umbrella of 'violence against women' to include trafficking.

Israel is a society of immigrants from all 'corners of the world'. Each wave of immigration (e.g. one million Russians since 1988) included practising prostitutes, while the marginal status of the newcomers and their economic hardships increased the number of women who viewed prostitution as their only way to survive. Moreover, global movements of labour have not bypassed Israel (200,000 to date), among them a sizeable number of women trafficked for prostitution purposes (2,500–3,000 prostitutes annually). Many, 'lured' by promises of legitimate earning opportunities, found themselves forced into prostitution. Most of the women come from the former Eastern bloc, mainly Russia, Ukraine and Moldova (for statistics: Levenkron 2001).

Unlike in many other countries, the public and political debates on prostitution in Israel did not challenge the legal premises of the law or the law itself as a regulatory state mechanism. Criticism and debate focused on Section 2 of the law, location of practice, and more so on arbitrary police practices. Initially, trafficking was framed as a gender issue rather than as a women's issue. Only recently has it been framed within the

144

context of 'exploitation of women' and 'illegal activities', emerging as one of the hottest public and political issues. It has mobilised a wide range of citizens' groups, including feminist and other women's groups who organised a vocal political coalition calling for tougher legislation against traffickers and stiffer law enforcement as well as legal aid and shelters for trafficked women.

Israel inherited the British mandate criminal law. In 1949, the 'Prostitution and Abomination Law' was enacted, re-legalising heterosexual prostitution in all its forms (street and house prostitution, but not homosexual varieties, which remained illegal until 1954). In 1962, following a Supreme Court decision, prostitutes were prohibited from 'working under a roof' (in a house, even the prostitute's residence, a vehicle or a boat). The decision was subsequently enacted into law. Prostitution thus remained a street phenomenon, practised in backyards, beaches and highways.

While the practice of prostitution is legal in Israel, the state's regulative role is solely limited to the spatial and organisational dimensions of the 'trade' (Israeli Criminal Law 1966, sections 199–202), premised on a free-market transaction between two equal adult negotiators (prostitutes are not required to register or to undergo health checks). In practice, however, houses of prostitution are in full operation as are sexual escort services, a growing business throughout the country since the 1990s. Street and house prostitution are the target of arbitrary raids and arrests by local police who respond to citizen complaints about noise, blatant visible sexual encounters, disturbing behaviour in public places and the 'corruption of the morals of minors'.

The illegality of house prostitution is continually justified by the police and the public claiming that nothing can be done against prostitution, including the 'natural growth' of brothels attributed to increased demand and supply (Amir 2001). The resulting policy is one of benign neglect, periodically disrupted by a critical report and a small group of moral crusaders. Minors spotted in the 'trade' are under the jurisdiction of the Youth and Welfare Services as 'minors in need of care and protection'. As for the 'clients', they can be detained for investigation if found in a brothel, and charged with 'cohabiting with a minor' if the prostitute is a minor. The law forbids 'solicitation' of clients for sexual services, yet its vagueness makes it difficult to establish this charge. In turn, a prostitute can be charged with 'loitering' or 'disturbing the peace' and detained for up to forty-eight hours, and then released on bail. This leads to a 'revolving door policy' of work – arrest – work. Pimping, pandering and other types of 'living on the earnings of a prostitute' are also illegal: these charges are, however, only accepted following the testimony of the woman (which is very rare). Conviction can lead to imprisonment of up to three years. In reality this mandatory rule is bypassed, mostly, by plea-bargaining (Horowitz 1969). The power of enforcement is relegated to the local police authorities who deploy their 'moral squad' to regulate and control the practice of pimping and of prostitution, in effect regulating the 'sex business' under their jurisdiction.

Attempts to change the prostitution and abomination laws emanate mainly from the left liberal Knesset members. The reformers' principal goal is to legalise the practice of prostitution under a roof in order to ameliorate the working conditions of prostitutes: 'to save them from the harsh weather, from harassment, attack and robbery by clients, pimps and hate vigilante citizens' (Ben-Ito 1977). Additionally, the liberals strive to prevent police arbitrariness, harassment, extortion and corruption. These attempts are often brought as legal test cases before the courts. While court decisions have not changed the existing laws, they have provided more severe penalties for procurers and pimps. The courts and the police concern themselves mainly with law and order and with the public peace aspects of the various types of prostitution. The regulative approach re-mains the prevailing policy towards prostitution in Israel, accompanied by the demand for more punitive measures against pimps. Regulation remains local, based on the local prostitution scene and the occasional public and media outcries to enforce law and order and protect the public.

Selection of debates

The 1962 decision which exclusively legalised street prostitution set the framework for all future attempts to amend and change the consequences of this decision. From the ten major debates that have taken place in the Israeli parliament since then, we have chosen those debates which led to changes in the legislative policies and procedures pertaining to pros-titution and trafficking. The first of these is the debate in 1972, in the aftermath of the Six Day War of 1967, when the issue of prostitution first 'appeared' on the political agenda as an administrative decision, pertain-ing only to minors involved in prostitution.

The second is the 1976 debate following the public outcry against street prostitution in Tel Aviv. Framed as a disturbance to public 'peace and order', the government was compelled to appoint a state commis-sion to investigate the issue of prostitution and the state, which pro-duced a report. Although its outcome did not produce a change in public policy towards prostitution, the debate can nevertheless be identified as highly salient in re-framing future attempts to change relevant laws and to legalise the *de facto* existence of street and house prostitution.

Thirdly, after a period of dormancy between 1977 and the 1990s, with occasional media interest for sad and 'moral' stories, debate took off in the mid-1990s, leading to the Law Against Trafficking in Women for the Purpose of Prostitution (2001). In that period, mass immigration from the Soviet republics brought an influx of 'Russian' prostitutes who arrived as legal immigrants, conjoined with a growing number of trafficked women to change the structure and organisation of prostitution. The massive mobilisation of the already viable parliamentary committee on the 'Status of Women', as well as media women, women's movements and a plethora of civil anti-trafficking associations, not only politicised the issue but was also instrumental in enacting a new law against trafficking.

The three selected debates represent, on the one hand, the temporal–dynamic dimensions of the 'changing times' and at the same time the broadest arenas of action and change. They also seem to be the most salient, as all attracted much attention and were instrumental in setting the framework for future legislation and for the structure of prostitution in Israel.

Debate 1: 'The Agency for Teenage Girls in Distress', 1970–1972

How issue came to the public agenda

It should be remembered that from 1948 until 1968/9, prostitution was not defined as a 'social problem'. A minor problem in 1948, it increased with the arrival of approximately one million immigrants between 1948 and 1955, mainly from Middle Eastern and North African countries.

The 'young prostitution debate' emerged at the national level in the aftermath of the 1967 War, when the Ministry of Welfare, which finances most of Israel's welfare departments, defined the waywardness and delinquent behaviour of adolescent females as a 'national problem' highly concentrated in mixed Jewish–Arab towns. The national debate also assumed a local character: the 'Jerusalem debate' was formulated in terms of 'physical, mental and moral' harm to the girls as well as the damage to the 'image of the State as a Jewish State' (Protocol of the Jerusalem Municipal Committee on 'Girls in Distress'). This framework combined an educational and welfare vocabulary with a concern for the collective image of the new state as a Jewish state. Another discourse focused on 'national boundary crossing', not only the 'corruption of minors' but specific concern centring on Palestinian clients and pimps. These age and national boundary crossings called for state intervention and regulation 'to save the young prostitutes through special prevention and rehabilitation programmes'. Women social workers from the welfare services at the local and national levels along with the media raised the issue in the Knesset. Female Knesset-members (MKs) from left-wing parties in the Welfare Committee allied with other groups, mostly professionals, to pressure mayors and the Ministry of Welfare to establish the necessary services. Two of the active female MKs, representatives of the left, critically challenged the Minister of Welfare and the Minister of Internal Affairs, accusing them of blindness and indifference to adolescent prostitution, followed by an appeal from youth workers in Jerusalem who voluntarily initiated a special municipal service for 'girls in distress'. The Minister of Welfare responded that 'the problem of deviant girls is the anti-image of Israel, a negative reality for any society, but even more so for the State of Israel as a model State' (Knesset session 1969: 2708), adding that 'this phenomenon is a plague that afflicts our streets and stigmatises our city, especially the holy city of Jerusalem' (Knesset session 1921: 1148; Tene 1977).

By that time the ministry had established professional outreach services for street corner youth as well as a Jerusalem-based unit for 'Girls in Distress'. Female MKs and social workers continued to pressure the ministry to adopt the 'Jerusalem experiment' as a model for centres throughout the country, recognised and financed by the state. The state agency for 'Girls in Distress' was ultimately established in 1972. The initial intent was to integrate the service with existing youth services; however, the Director of Youth Services succeeded in convincing the Ministry of Welfare of the need for a special department and service for 'Girls in Distress', 'because of their special needs'.

The idea of a special service for adolescent prostitutes was also raised in parliament; however, instead of an ideological and partisan political debate focusing on the need for a special agency, the discourse was characterised by 'moral panic', emphasising the identity of the clients and pimps (Arabs) and the fact that the girls were transported to work in Arab territories. 'Panic' was also voiced about their 'tender age'. These debates were instrumental in the establishment of the National Service for 'Girls in Distress', a preferred euphemism for 'prostitutes'.

Dominant frame of debate

The debate surrounding the 'Girls in Distress' can be viewed as the first debate which defined prostitution as a social issue pertaining to age and gender that was national concern rather than as a legal issue. As mentioned above, prostitution was accepted as a 'natural' and 'given' practical response to, and an off-shoot of, a gendered sexuality that in some instances cannot be met through either legal or normatively sanctioned relationships – marriage and its equivalents. Formulated in these terms, the 'immorality' of the trade did not emerge as an issue. The debate surrounding the 'Girls in Distress' and its institutional manifestation introduced the moral aspects of the debate in relation to the ethnic identity of the clients and pimps, the 'moral panic' surrounding the age of the 'service providers', and the state's failure as 'protector'.

The third argument couched the debate in terms of the image of the Israeli state as a new model state which protects its youth and ensures their development as mature and civilised citizens of a modern state. One can also speculate that the social work background of these moral entrepreneurs contributed to a large extent to the particular framing of the issue as a moral, welfare educational and psychopathological issue, while the politicians framed the phenomenon in terms of collective identity and as an issue of 'state image'.

In summary, the framing of the first debate was age-specific – adolescent prostitutes, and re-framed as 'Girls in Distress' – client-specific – Arabs – and anxiety-specific – moral lacuna of the adolescents and collective image pollution. These frameworks were initially formulated and politicised by female social welfare professionals and politicians who also designed the state's response – special social services for 'girls in distress'. It was viewed as an internal administrative issue which did not require special legislation, but rather more proactive programmes designed to locate the girls and to place them in ambulatory or in-patient, institutional treatment programmes.

Gendering the debate

This first debate was entirely gendered: women were the first to raise the issue and open the debate, and their concern was not only with delinquency as such but with 'girls' and their sexual behaviour. The explanation of their deviant behaviour was based on a gendered pathology model and the response was gendered as well – special services for troubled girls. On the other hand, the clients and pimps were men, as were the politicians who insisted on couching the issue in terms of collective 'image'.

Policy outcome

The first two directors of the special service for young prostitutes – initially in Jerusalem – were active social workers with feminist views concerning the special needs of girls. By virtue of their organisational and political skills they succeeded in establishing special units in local welfare departments and in enlisting the help of the women's welfare-type organisations. Such services were then introduced to other locales, ultimately resulting in the development of a national headquarters for services for young prostitutes, which later developed into a national service for women in need and distress. Most important, one can argue, was the fact that for the first time in Israel the debate about prostitution was formulated as a social, physical, mental, emotional and moral problem – both for the girls involved and for society at large – permeating all governmental levels: government, parliament, local councils, as well as women's organisations, professionals, the media and the public at large.

Under the charismatic and active leadership of the municipal youth and welfare units, intensive outreach activities were initiated, resulting in the demand for treatment programmes. While programmes were developed, they did not evolve into a re-framing of the phenomenon of prostitution or of adult prostitutes nor into a shift from a politically dormant to a politicised issue.

Women's movement impact

Characteristic of traditional women's organisations, the existing women's movement organisations (the Organisation of Working Women and WIZO – Women's International Zionist Organisation) at the time of the first debate were mostly auxiliary to the major 'male' political parties. Their ideology and activities focused mainly on charity for women and children, and mobilised to provide afternoon recreational activities and vocational training to adolescent girls from poor or immigrant families. As they lacked even the embryonic characteristics of a feminist women's movement, it is difficult to classify the impact of these organisations on the first debate. Women within the state bureaucracy constituted the driving force in raising the issue and in its framing as an administrative service issue. They also gendered the debate by insisting on its gender-specificity, based on a mixture of professional-traditional approaches – pathologising the young women – at the same time creating for themselves an organisational and professional power base for addressing the unique needs of women. The collaborative coalition formed between female politicians, policy-makers, professionals and front-line service providers should also be noted. None the less, the absence of a feminist movement and a feminist agenda may partially explain the one-time nature of the effort in the absence of an organisational foundation for ongoing political activity. About a better classificatory category, co-optation will be used as the defining category for their activities.

Women's policy agency activities

At the time of this debate no single agency was responsible for policy with respect to women and a mandate to improve the status of women. Instead, various government units were responsible for welfare policies and services for women. It was the youth welfare unit within the Jerusalem municipality and on the national level in the Ministry of Welfare that assumed this role and succeeded in establishing both a new framework and new services. The programmes focused on family and individual treatment (e.g. school supervision, transferring the girls from their homes, working with youth centres). While both units were mainly staffed by women and headed by women, they did not promote feminist ideas or demands as such formulations were not voiced at the time. In terms of the model their role can therefore be classified as non-feminist.

Women's movement characteristics

As mentioned above, Israel's women's movements were associated with the major political parties. They were instrumental in developing particular services for women, mainly by empowerment without ideology and with hardly, if any, political training. Prostitution was not a priority. Feminist ideas at this stage centred mainly on equality and women's rights as well as childcare. A traditional second-wave feminist movement was still non-existent in Israel and feminist ideas, mostly from the USA, were just beginning to permeate, imported by female veterans of the 1968 students' movement and the women's movement who had immigrated to Israel. There was no counter-movement on the issue.

Policy environment

The debate, during a coalition government of the Labor Party and the religious parties headed by Golda Meir, took place in a closed policy environment. The debate developed within the psychiatric, social work, moral and national contexts and within an administrative framework. The dominant policy approach focused on the consequences for the girls and on how to minimise or prevent these in unprotected social areas and under disorganised social circumstances. The ideological and functional orientations of the women's movement were primarily towards services for 'normal conforming' women; deviant behaviour was relegated to 'the authorities'. The dominant policy approach was incompatible with that of the women's movement, emphasising a combination of pathology, circumstances and gender as an explanatory framework – accepting the vulnerability model and acting upon it.

Debate 2: The commission to reform the prostitution law, 1975–1977

How issue came to the public agenda

In 1974, the idea of a Commission on Prostitution emerged as a grass-roots idea, mostly from citizens who felt victimised by prostitutes who plied their trade in their backyards, 'engaged in visible sexual behaviour, made noise, violated private space, disrupted the public order and corrupted the morals of minors'.

In the summer of 1974 prostitutes in Tel Aviv were forced to move from their regular work locations, concentrated around certain streets (hotel areas), following tourists' complaints of harassment. To avoid police raids, they moved primarily into middle-class residential areas. The residents complained to the municipality and involved the media. The mayor in turn appealed to the Knesset and to the government 'to control the situation', suggesting they 'regulate' the practice by legalising the two existing red light districts. To expedite the proposed change, the mayor expressed his willingness to allocate special areas and to permit prostitutes to work in 'houses'.

In response, the Knesset's Judicial Committee proposed, with general consent, to appoint a commission to investigate the problem of prostitution. In February 1975 the Minister of Justice appointed a state commission 'to examine the subject of prostitution in Israel in all its aspects and to come up with suggestions that would ameliorate the situation and placate the citizens' (Ben Ito 1977: ii).

The commission consisted of a chairwoman (a district judge), the Tel Aviv district prosecutor (a woman), a female psychologist from the Department of Psychology at Hebrew University, the chief psychiatrist of the Ministry of Health, the chief of investigation of the Israel Police, the commissioner of corrections in the Ministry of Welfare and two criminologists. It was closed to the public yet it invited testimony from the mayor of Tel Aviv, physicians, psychologists, anthropologists, criminologists, rabbis, social workers and prostitutes.

Dominant frame of debate

The commission's mandate was to investigate all aspects of prostitution in general and the 'condition of prostitution in Israel' in particular. It reviewed numerous laws and regulations concerning the practice of prostitution, especially the spatial issue – or the legal solutions to the issue of the 'location' of the sexual transaction – the phenomenon of pimping, enforcement practices and the economic aspects of the sex services market, as well as recruitment channels and 'entry' motivations and circumstances. The dominant framework as defined by the commission centred on the prostitute's work location as well as her well-being as affected by her working conditions.

From its inception the commission refrained from a moral debate about the issue, adhering to a pragmatic stance relying on the British Wolfenden report on prostitution (1957) as a model of the pragmatic, mainly legal, approach. Consequently, the legal-judicial approach dominated the major underlying assumptions of the commission's deliberations (Sion 1977).

The commission held the position that prostitution was inevitable and therefore could only be regulated and not eradicated. The 'naturalistic' approach to male sexuality and the laws of 'demand and supply' were taken for granted as working assumptions. The commission also maintained a concern and a commitment to the welfare of young prostitutes, influencing considerations related to prevention and rehabilitation policies. The explanatory assumptions and theories about adolescent prostitution, as voiced by professionals in the first debate, were fully adopted by the commission.

Most of the commission deliberations focused on regulative laws of the sex trade, and its most important formative notion was de-regulation, that is, repealing the 1962 laws forbidding the practice of prostitution in private residences. The commission advocated that prostitutes be allowed to practise in their homes or in hotel rooms. Excluded were brothels and special zones as alternative and legitimate locations, based on testimonies of prostitutes objecting to brothels as proper locales for their practice and other testimonies. However, the commission excluded the option of street prostitution, to prevent blatant solicitation, and recognised the right of prostitutes to advertise their services, while voicing a harsh and punitive policy towards active recruiting and pimping.

Gendering the debate

The debate in the city council, in the Knesset which had authorised the commission and in the commission was permeated by a specific gendered perspective. The commission investigated only female and heterosexual prostitution; male prostitution was mentioned only in passing as a minor and non-relevant public issue. However, this gendered perspective lacked a feminist analysis as it did not address such issues as equality and power relations between women and men and the stereotyping of women. It uncritically accepted the motivational notion that women were forced into prostitution as a result of stressful personal and social conditions. However, unlike in the first debate, prostitutes were asked to voice their opinions and suggestions with regard to the regulatory role of the state (for them, the police) in policing their work, and their opposition to the commission's proposition to legalise brothels, and other structural features of the 'trade'.

Policy outcome

Pressures, initially local and then parliamentary, succeeded in producing the first in-depth and all-inclusive investigation of all aspects of prostitution in Israel. The appointment of the commission, its report and recommendations can be viewed as the first serious attempt to address the problem of prostitution as a policy issue, not only as a moral or a cross-boundary discourse, with some concerns for the working conditions of prostitutes. The commission's report, it is suggested, laid the broad foundation for reconsidering the prohibitionist elements embedded in the law, especially those regulating the 'locale' aspect of prostitution. Legalising 'indoor' practice, except for brothels, surfaced as the new discourse, and even more so as a 'mantra' for reformers of the 'prostitution scene', framing the aspired change as the 'institutionalisation of prostitution' (e.g. Poraz et al. 1998). The appointment of the commission stemmed from internal pressure within the government system. However, only one of the commission's recommendations was implemented – allowing prostitutes to advertise their work address, benefiting under the continuing legal circumstances only women providing escort services and illegal brothel owners rather than 'street' prostitutes.

Paradoxically, the expansion of house-brothel prostitution, as the main organising feature of Israel's prostitution scene, can be attributed in part to the commission's deliberations and recommendations that set in motion continuous debate about the right 'locale' for the practice as well as its organisational characteristics. The commission's serious deliberations and recommendations aimed at improving the prostitutes' conditions remained untouched.

Women's movement impact

The Israeli women's movements, including at the time the upcoming feminist movement, did not express a particular interest in the problem of prostitution as a women's issue. In their testimony, representatives of the 'old' women's movement, not represented in the Knesset Judicial Committee, proposed educational and rehabilitation programmes, as preventive measures, especially for young girls. While women as a category and as a separate constituency were perceived by the authorities as the most fit to tackle the issue of prostitution, resulting in the appointment of mostly women experts as commission members, none of the women's movements expressed an interest in the issue. This debate is therefore classified as co-optation.

Women's policy agency activities

In 1974 the first formal council 'for the status of women' was created, as an autonomous government authority, with a mandate to promote and advance women's issues as an integral part of government policies. The new agency was an outcome of a government Commission on the Status of Women (1972). In 1975 the position of Advisor for Women's Affairs was created in and budgeted by the Prime Minister's Office, becoming the Authority for the Status of Women in 1998. The Authority has a cross-sectional mandate to establish and to oversee a Women's Affairs Advisor in every government ministry; to lobby for women's affairs in government, especially to fund woman's activities and programmes (e.g. rape crisis centres, shelters for battered women, etc.); and to act as a supportive body to Knesset members in promoting women and women's issues as reflected in legislative activities.

The advisor position has always been filled by female lawyers known for their stance *vis-à-vis* women's issues, female public figures or activists. Despite these new appointments and institutions, their voice was not heard on the prostitution issue. It may be argued that, at the time, the issue seemed 'out of context' to the advisor, who perceived her role to represent women's issues at large, while prostitution and prostitutes were not on her agenda. Consequently, neither the advisor nor the women's movements were instrumental in ideologically gendering the debate. The non-ideological gendering – the focus on women – as we have shown, took place in the official framing, discourse, policy and selection of commission members and witnesses. Its role is therefore classified as symbolic.

Women's movement characteristics

The commission's deliberations took place against the backdrop of active and well-organised traditional women's movements, with their political party affiliations (Labour, Liberal, religious) and traditional activities (childcare, vocational training, legal advice, etc.) and the initial stages of the crystallisation of a basic feminist agenda which vehemently rejected any identification with a feminist ideology. The feminist movement in Israel at the time was in its early stages of development, pioneered by a small group of active feminists (mostly newcomers from the USA). These groups served as the basis for Israel's radical feminist movement which matured during the period of the third debate. Thus, during the second debate the issue of prostitution was defined as a regulatory-legal issue rather than as a political and a social movement issue. The benign attitude towards the issue characterised all women's movements, institutions and even activists to the extent that the newly formed civil rights association dismissed the issue, claiming that it was not a civil rights issue. There was no counter-movement on the issue.

Policy environment

The policy environment characterising this debate was similar to that of the first debate, concentrated in parliament, under a Labour/religious parties coalition under Rabin, especially the Judicial Committee. The latter unanimously and unequivocally supported the establishment of the commission, premised on a sexuality-gendered discourse and the state's benign regulatory role. The environment can be classified as relatively closed. The approach defined prostitution as a women's issue, from the perspective of 'women' as a differentiated social category or prostitution as the business of women. The issue was therefore relegated to women and provided women's groups the opportunity to voice their view. Unfortunately, however, the latter had not yet formulated their own agenda and political stance on the issue. Therefore, the movement approach did not clash with the dominant policy sub-system approach and can be regarded as compatible.

Debate 3: Trafficking in women and prostitution, 1994–2002

How issue came to the public agenda

As mentioned above, trafficking in women into Israel as sex workers increased consistently from the beginning of the 1990s as an organised enterprise by local and international criminal groups that use fraud and violence to entice and employ the women (Kempadoo and Doezema 1998; Skrobanek et al. 1997; Richard 2000). Women's groups and academics first drew public attention to this phenomenon and to its cruel and exploitative nature, pointing out the ongoing practice of buying and selling women as property and their sexual and violent abuse in addition to their horrific living conditions. The media were instrumental in exposing the exploitative and criminal characteristics of the 'business' and its roots in 'international organised crime'. Investigations of the scene were also carried out by NGO groups and by academics (Amir 2001; Klein 2001).

Following these expositions, feminist groups, NGOs and MKs accused the government, and especially the police, of indifference towards the new and growing sex industry, as well as to the plight of the trafficked women. The police manifested both apathy and tolerance, to the extent that the 'phenomenon' was justified as 'necessary and expedient'.

The report on the sex trade in Israel (Vandenberg 1997) revealed that almost all trafficked women were placed in brothels, housing between three and eight women, and in most cases caged, in effect totally controlled. It is important to remember that brothels and in-house prostitution are illegal in Israel. When arrested by the police, in arbitrary raids, the women are detained in prison without trial, at times for up to four months, before deportation.

Unlike the issue of prostitution, trafficking received media attention, including factual and statistical coverage and exposure which helped to sensitise the public to the issue and to mobilise new and old NGO groups. The veteran women's organisations were joined by a multitude of new associations specialising in treating violent men, rape crisis centres, shelters for battered women and the Association for Foreign Labourers' Rights. This newly established coalition pressured the government for more dignified detention procedures and facilities. They also joined efforts with the Committee for the Status of Women in promoting laws to criminalise trafficking in humans and to enact a special law against the trafficking of women for the purpose of prostitution. Instrumental in expediting the new laws against trafficking were external pressures by international bodies (the UN) in their reports which accused Israel of allowing and even facilitating the trafficking of women and pointing to the women's abhorrent living conditions and exploitation (Amnesty International 2000; US State Department 2001).

Dominant frame of debate

The framing of the debate can be identified as a cumulative, dynamic process formulated by and through a multiplicity of inputs: growing public awareness of organised crime activities, especially those involving trafficking of women and the sex trade in general; the exploitative and abusive nature of the trafficking business (recruitment, transfer, selling and buying); the exploitative and abusive working conditions of the trafficked women; the laxity and inefficiency of the government and its enforcement bodies. The dominant debate framework is multidimensional: legal, moral, human rights, exploitation, injustice, choice and social deprivation, the vulnerability of Israeli society, sex workers and foreign labourers. Unlike the focused uniform framing of the first two debates, the third one seemed so pervasive and all-encompassing that, on a different level, the dominant framework can be formulated as a deep sense of threat to the moral and symbolic order of Israeli society.

Gendering the debate

The debate was, and still is, mostly muted with respect to gendered relationships, power relations between women and men, the role of the state as regulator, violence against women and the disadvantaged status of women in both the private and public spheres. However, in contrast to the first two debates in which the gendering discourse was women-focused, in the current debate on trafficking men as a category and as a group appeared as the principal players. Thus, as a case in point, the week designated by the women's movements for consciousness-raising and increasing awareness about 'violence against women' (November 2001) developed into a protest against trafficking and prostitution. For the first time, the Feminist Coalition publicly raised the issue of 'men who buy sex', demanding severe punishments for the 'clients'. Additionally, male sexuality and violence were discussed in public meetings relating the persistence of trafficking to men's readiness or even eagerness for bought sex. Prostitutes were encouraged to appear in public and to 'tell their story' of their treatment by men.

The radical branch of the women's movement raised the issue of prostitution and pornography in public meetings, conferences and demonstrations, referencing it to the problem of trafficking. Prostitution, as a phenomenon, was also discussed in these meetings for the first time, from an abolitionist perspective. In these debates a new vocabulary surfaced – 'sex workers' replaced 'prostitutes' and 'trafficking' displaced 'trading or commerce with women'.

Policy outcome

Under multiple pressures, the Knesset, which had initially enacted a law 'against trafficking in humans' (2001), also enacted new laws and changes in the procedures pertaining to the treatment of arrested prostitutes, mostly trafficked women. The outcomes consisted of specific legislation 'against trafficking in women for the purpose of prostitution' and harsher punishment for trafficking in women – from six to twelve years of imprisonment. New procedures and arrangements were instituted, designed to ease the plight of trafficked women arrested or detained before deportation. Access to health services, the right to legal advocacy and other services were also added.

Another important outcome of the debate on trafficking was the renewed debate on the broader issue of prostitution, reformulated as a debate on men's sexuality and its resultant gender-exploitative institutions. It merits noting that from the 1990s, street work prostitution became marginal to the 'trade', while illegal in-house prostitution flourished undisturbed, as part of the trafficked sex business.

Women's movement impact

As mentioned above, the women's movement at large was instrumental in raising the issue of trafficking, in its politicisation and in mobilising an organised response to media exposure pertaining to its magnitude, criminal roots, organisational characteristics, the plight and exploitation of women involved and the indifference of the authorities.

The women's movement joined with the anti-trafficking coalition, holding street demonstrations in front of police stations, the Israel police headquarters and brothels. Its members continuously appear in the media and organise public debates and academic conferences. In this way the women's movement, as part of a broader coalition, not only politicised the issue but helped frame the debate, advocated new legislation and services and acted to ensure, with the support of female MKs, the desired legal and institutional changes. Women were highly involved in the legislative process. The women's movement, particularly its radical feminist branch, was also instrumental in redefining prostitution as a gender–power–sexuality issue. Some even expounded an abolitionist stance while others accepted the expansion of brothels, but demanded state regulation. The impact can be classified as a dual response.

Women's policy agency characteristics

The influence of the Advisor for Women's Affairs and of the Knesset Committee on the Status of Women (1992) on the debate and its legal and policy outcomes was considerable. The Committee for Women's Affairs, consisting of twelve MKs (including four men), was established in 1987 and to date is headed by a female MK with a strong commitment to women's issues. Its mandate is to initiate investigations and to propose laws and policies on all issues affecting women.

When the issue of trafficking was raised, a sub-committee was established to investigate the situation, headed by a left-wing female MK. This sub-committee toured brothels, heard testimonies from trafficked prostitutes and participated in public meetings addressing the issue. The sub-committee concluded its mission, proposing an addition to the 'Law against Trafficking in Humans', a special 'Law against the Trafficking of Women for the Purpose of Prostitution', and successfully receiving government assurance to provide needed services for incarcerated women before their deportation, and a secure hiding place for those willing to testify against their pimps, who would be liable to twelve years' of imprisonment. Both the government advisor and the Women's Status Authority played a major institutional role (parliament, government) in politicising the issue, formulating the needed policy changes (legal and services) and successfully pressuring for action.

Women's policy agencies incorporated pressures applied by the women's movement, proposed policies and succeeded in passing important legislation in the Knesset: laws against trafficking in humans and in women, services for arrested trafficked women, health and advocacy. This debate is therefore a case of insider status, within government and in the public arena – women's groups were able to operate without any counter-resistance from the cabinet and political parties in the Knesset. Even the ultra-right wing and the religious parties supported the law against trafficking.

Women's movement characteristics

Since the second debate, in the late 1970s, a new type of women's movement had appeared in the public arena – a radical feminist movement that gradually succeeded in ideologically radicalising the traditional women's movements. From the mid-1980s and throughout the 1990s numerous new women's groups appeared in the Israeli public arena, diverse in their political agendas, specific objectives and organisational features. They succeeded in networking and building *ad hoc* and long-term coalitions, creating a sense of solidarity and visibility. The coalition against trafficking in women (since 1997), together with the established Israeli women's network organisation, spurred a wider mobilisation on the issue of trafficking (it is important to note that all these groups, movements and organisations did not exist during the first and second debates). The movements are even more cohesive regarding issues of trafficking and prostitution. No counter women's groups have organised against this coalition, although abolitionist ideas against prostitution are voiced in radical feminist circles. Concomitantly, a new men's abolitionist organisation has appeared, joining the fight against trafficking. Both new groups, jointly with the women's 'Coalition', have for the first time raised the issue of pornography as an inherent part of the sex industry and its relationship to violence against women, rape and child sexual abuse.

Policy environment

Unlike in the first two debates, the policy environment of the third debate was intrinsically different and can be defined as moderately open. Women's agencies had matured politically, and were organisationally well established, efficiently networked in the media and in the community. The public sphere is permeated with new movements and organisations that have selected trafficking as their targeted issue. Even the traditional women's movements have become ideologically radicalised and have taken a politically activist stance. Both the Knesset and the government were encouraged, even compelled, by the women's movements to initiate new legislation and procedures involving trafficking, trafficked women and prostitution in general. This was not dependent on the composition of the government during the debate: in the mid-1990s Netanyahu was prime minister in a centre-right coalition with the religious parties; it was succeeded by the Labour/religious right coalition of Ehud Barak. The developments we observed on the policy level in the Authority for the Status of Women and in the women's movement were instrumental in bringing about policy outcomes. Moreover, the fact that the trafficking issue lent itself to a multiplicity of frameworks and discourses on the one hand, and touched core social values and basic existential fears such as exploitation, international criminal activity, smuggling, border crossing, boundary crossing, illicit markets, big money, corruption (moral and organisational), tarnished national image, exposure of the disruptive potential of male uncontrolled sexuality, on the other, created the opportune conditions for massive mobilisation and co-operation. These unique conditions helped create an open policy environment. The dominant policy approach was compatible with that of the women's movement.

Conclusion

A review of the three debates reveals the following: the multiple facets of the institution of prostitution did not constitute an issue in the first debate, it being focused instead on teenage prostitutes and the failure of Israeli social institutions to attend to the well-being of the 'weaker segment' of society. The reform was an administrative one accomplished by the Ministry of Welfare – a special social service, a local experiment expanded to become a national model.

The second debate focused on the government commission created to study prostitution and its regulation. The dominant legal framing of the debate focusing on a 'peace and order' discourse had an inhibiting effect on the commission deliberations and outcomes. It accepted prostitution as an inevitable phenomenon requiring some minor legal changes using a neutral yet gendered frame in its deliberations. The recommendations, permitting prostitutes to act as free agents, continue to permeate every discussion or mention of prostitution since. The representatives of the 'traditional women's movements' took the same accommodating approach evidenced in the first debate. The new women's movement at the time was in its infancy and concerned itself mostly with women's equality issues. The Authority for the Status of Women had just been established and added no input to the commission's deliberations and recommendations.

The third debate was a full-fledged gendered debate with a dual response, whereby women's policy activists in the Knesset and in the government, and the analysis and critique of 'old' and 'new' women's movements and of NGOs, initiated public politicised debates and mobilised grass-roots activists. The debate addressed the multiple characteristics and ramifications of the phenomenon of trafficking: its structural, cultural, economic and gendered dimensions, which enable a 'free market' of 'sexual slavery' licensed through a policy of benign neglect by the government and society at large, and often interpreted as protection of the 'sex business' entrepreneurs. The policy outcomes included policies and laws against traffickers and amelioration of the conditions of trafficked women. But alas, the entire 'sex industry' market is still in operation, with only relatively minor and sporadic 'difficulties' encountered by operators of, still illegal, house prostitution.

Contrary to the first two debates, the third debate was a huge public debate involving parliament, the cabinet, the bureaucracy, women's movements, grass-roots organisations and the media. This can be attributed to the radicalisation of the traditional women's movements and the emergence of new grass-roots movements on sexuality and human rights. The establishment of official agencies addressing women's issues also proved a decisive factor. The framing of the third debate had an inherently different perspective compared with the two other debates in that it related the phenomenon of prostitution to a gendered social structure which works against women's equality, economic security and empowerment, enhancing their multiple vulnerability.

While in all three debates 'entry' into prostitution is framed in terms of 'adverse social conditions', in the third debate men and a gendered structure are framed as the primary explanation, i.e. as a patriarchal structure. The policy outcomes of the debates can be seen as successful. The demand of the first debate for special services for young prostitutes was met. The mandate to investigate all aspects of prostitution and to formulate policy recommendations was fulfilled in the second debate. The recommendation to allow prostitutes to advertise their services was also accepted. However, while the commission's recommendation to allow house prostitution was rejected officially, paradoxically it is the main form of Israel's sex trade – albeit illegally.

During the third debate the women's policy agency, women in the Knesset and the women's movement succeeded in bringing about legislation against trafficking, facilities for detained trafficked women and increased penalties for those involved in the trafficking and sex trade business. For the first time, the 'blame' discourse shifted from women to men.

All three debates were gendered from their very inception, focusing primarily on women, shifting from teenage girls to the prostitute population and later to trafficked women and prostitution as a social institution. Male prostitution was mentioned only in passing despite surveys which uncovered the existence of teenage male prostitution, while the framing and discourse of the involvement of procurers, pimps and customers emphasised their role rather than their gender identity. A full-fledged gendered discourse was only evident in the third debate.

Women's policy agencies were involved in all debates, in different ways according to the changing policy environment. In the first debate, there was strictly speaking no women's policy agency, but women's concerns were taken care of by professionals in the administration and in the field. In the second debate the women's policy agencies coalesced with female MKs with a left and Liberal orientation, professionals in the Ministry of Justice and senior members of the commission. These actors exhibited their most active influence in the third debate, supported by their political resources in the parliament and in government which developed in the period between the second and the third debate.

Although Israel's women's movements were openly invited to participate and take a stand on all debates, their impact was negligible during the first and second debates as they were not interested in prostitution, focusing on working women and their children. It was only with the appearance of a second generation of radical feminists, politically skilled in networking and in 'coalition' building, that the women's movement as a mobilising force and as a pressure group became a major actor.

The first and second debates operated within a relatively small policy arena with a passive public, exposed only periodically through the media to the issue of prostitution. During the third debate, prostitution as a complex issue was widely publicised by women's movements, academia and other public entities. Sexuality as a feminist discourse and as an issue related to prostitution did not surface until the third debate when radical feminists, homo-lesbian organisations and academics raised the issue.

In summary, all the debates were initiated by women and for women who pressured for changes in the existing laws, procedures and services as well as for new legislation. Thus, the three debates can be defined as gendered, although gendering took on different meanings. In the thirty years covered by this analysis, one can delineate three gradual trends. There was a trend of viewing prostitution narrowly, focusing on a specific population towards a broader social and political issue. There was the development of a supportive policy environment through the establishment of new positions occupied by women in decision-making bodies. Finally, a feminist movement developed which radicalised the traditional women's movements and spawned new radical groups, networks and coalitions which made sexuality, trafficking and prostitution one of their main arenas of social and political activity.

9   Italy: the never-ending debate

Daniela Danna

Introduction

In 1958, a new law regulating prostitution, the Merlin law (L. 75/58), fought for by the socialist MP Lina Merlin, abolished the previous system of regulation that had been established in 1861, the year of Italy's unification (Gibson 1995). Since then the law has been only slightly modified. It is a classic abolitionist law, prohibiting not only trafficking and the exploitation of prostitution, but all forms of aiding and abetting with or without the intent of financial gain. Therefore it allows only street prostitution or prostitution by a woman in her own house or apartment. The decision to close the brothels and liberate the 2,500 women deprived of many of their civil rights by being obliged to reside in brothels was greeted as a liberation in the spirit of equality.

The Merlin law, which took ten years to be passed, never ceased to be an object of public debate, periodically emerging in the national media with articles, books, campaigns for the gathering of signatures to repeal and proposals for new laws. Defence of the law against repeated attacks by a very mixed public (though commonly composed of the right wing) who demanded the re-opening of the '*case chiuse*' (closed houses, i.e. brothels), has always been acknowledged as a feminist issue. Yet support for the 'Merlin' is much broader: it is also backed by the Catholic church and the majority of the Marxist (now post-communist) parties. Many Catholic volunteer associations, although they are hostile to feminism, work on prostitution. The women's movement of the early years also denounced prostitution, and caused a major scandal in 1981 when a documentary, *A.A.A. Offresi*, made with a hidden camera by a feminist movie co-operative, showed the endless stream of men with their requests in Veronique's room (Belmonti 1981). It was to be shown on the public channel Rai (Radio Televisione Italiana), but the Rai Vigilance Commission cancelled it. An indictment for breaching the privacy of Veronique's clients followed (at an early stage the accusation was even of aiding and abetting prostitution). The final sentence was passed in 1985, absolving the women on the film crew and the directors of the Rai who had scheduled the programme.

In the 1990s, the issue of prostitution became redefined by illegal immigration. The growing number of foreign prostitutes, especially from Nigeria and Albania, and recently from Moldova, added a note of urgency to the old and rather predictable debate on how to handle the question. A particular cause for concern is the phenomenon of debt-bondage (Kennedy and Nicotri 1999) and of women forced to prostitute themselves (Moroli and Sibona 1999). These have partially replaced the issue of the prostitution of minors, which has always received a lot of space as a recurring theme in the crime news of the press. But the issues of forced and underage prostitution (which in many cases overlap) are tightly interwoven with those of public order and decency.

During the 1990s, mobilisation of the inhabitants of neighbourhoods where street prostitution was expanding led to complaints to the police, but also to street demonstrations to intimidate the women or to chase them out of the area, sometimes with violent punitive expeditions. These were typically legitimated as the defence of public decency, nocturnal quiet and the innocence of the neighbourhood's children, as well as the protection of local women from harassment by clients, with an eye to the lowering of real estate values in the area where prostitution took place.

Selection of debates

The true initiators of the big debates, however, were the attackers of the Merlin law, always defeated but never surrendering. The periodical outcry for the re-opening of brothels had its first high point in 1973, when the Christian Democrat Party (Democrazia Christiana, DC) started gathering signatures to revise the Merlin law and re-open the brothels. Other campaigns followed, but without success. More recently, in 1998, the launching of another campaign for anti-Merlin signatures made news because it was sponsored by a local cell in Prato of the DS (Democratici di Sinistra, Democrats of the Left, formerly ex-communist party, now centre-leftist) (Farini 2000). This initiative was later 'excommunicated' by the party's secretary. In the same year, Federcasalinghe (Federation of Housewives), a large and very conservative group, launched a campaign to gather signatures for compulsory medical examinations of prostitutes, for the purpose of 'defending the family'. The women's movement has repeatedly expressed its opposition to compulsory health check-ups, which violate the dignity of prostitutes, and instead proposed compulsory check-ups of their clients. Opinion surveys on the issue also repeatedly show a

majority of the sampled population in favour of the re-opening of brothels. According to an IARD survey, 64.7 per cent of young people agreed
with a possible re-opening of brothels (Buzzi 1998: 64).

Meanwhile, prostitutes began to organise themselves. At the beginning
of the 1980s a small but very vocal transsexual movement called for a law
permitting sex and identity changes on documents, at a time when prostitution was the only feasible way for transsexuals and man-to-woman
trans-genders to earn a living. They obtained recognition of the sex-
change operation in 1982 (L. 164/82). In 1983 the Comitato per i diritti
civili delle prostitute (Committee for Prostitutes' Civil Rights, hereafter
Comitato) was founded in Pordenone, following a protest against violence
towards the street workers, and in particular, against the rapes that had
been occurring near the US military base area of Aviano, near Pordenone
(Teodori 1986). The Comitato was born in the wake of the feminist
movement of the 1970s, but did not have direct contacts with groups
of the feminist movement. Indeed, members of the Comitato viewed it
very suspiciously, although now one of the two leaders of the prostitutes,
Carla Corso, declared herself a feminist. This feeling was reciprocated:
as one feminist leader wrote: 'It is not possible to find contact points
other than a generic solidarity, with women who do not realise that their
struggle is aimed only at the concreteness of everyday life and that it
doesn't question the more dangerous field of male fantasizing'(Bocchetti
1995: 43).[1]

The initiative for the Comitato came from women who were not subjected to pimps, and they defended their choice of prostitution as a way
of earning a living, without, however, defining it as work. The Comitato's
goal has never been the official recognition of prostitution as work, but
rather the decriminalisation of aiding and abetting without purpose of
gain, which would render the work easier, less subject to police surveillance and oppression, and, in the long run, less stigmatised. In fact,
prostitution is still so stigmatised that many Italians think that it is
illegal.

The foundation of the Comitato and the conferences and debates they
organised in the following three or four years mark the highest point in the
political arena for Italian prostitutes. The Comitato asked for decriminalisation of the crime of aiding and abetting,[2] and the right to exercise prostitution indoors. Three leftist parties were sympathetic towards
these requests, and introduced bills with these demands in parliament.
The press took it for granted that a reform would be approved, but it
never was.

The number of bills introduced in parliament has been growing ever
since (up to twenty-two in the most recent legislature, 1996–2001), along

with a rise of the number of women on the streets in the late 1990s. Whenever a new proposal came from some prominent politicians, it was debated in the media.

In the summer of 1994, many city mayors took the initiative and ordered traffic police to target clients for the first time. Men loitering in cars were fined for disturbing traffic and a copy of the fine, including its reason, was sent to their homes so that their wives would be informed. Clients also risked being charged with aiding and abetting prostitution if they brought the women back to their spot in the streets and their cars were even confiscated as 'instruments for committing a crime'. The criminalisation of clients was stopped by a sentence of the Tribunal of Perugia (20 September 2000), declaring that aiding and abetting must apply only to third parties, and not to clients. Nevertheless, the practice continued, until a young man from Susegane whose car was taken away by the police, instead of going back to his parents' home, committed suicide by hanging himself. This was unanimously taken as a sign that the targeting of clients had gone too far (Mafai 2000).

Despite all these debates, no major change in the structure of the abolitionist law occurred. While the abolitionist principles have been upheld at the national level, more restrictive measures were taken at the local level, where some towns started to withdraw residence permits from foreign women working in the streets and to deport those without a valid residence permit as a part of a clamp-down on 'clandestini' (migrants without valid documents). At the same time the new phenomenon of foreign women loitering in the streets received a different, more articulated response. In Mestre a committee composed of all the interested parties (inhabitants, prostitutes, police, city government) was established in 1995 to negotiate a tolerance area for street prostitution (Signorelli and Treppete 2001). In the Emilia-Romagna region, the local government has co-ordinated city and health authority initiatives to help prostitutes and organised public seminars to exchange experiences and discuss the different views and possible solutions. Many other local governments have provided resources for information and aid projects of NGOs, in the spirit both of harm reduction and of Christian redemption (On the Road 1998).

For the purpose of this analysis, I shall focus on the three debates at the national level that led to policy output.

1 The offer of a 'protection permit' to stay in the country for the victims of traffickers, within the framework of a law regulating immigration (L. 40/98) with its art. 18, in 1996–9. It was approved in 1998 and implemented by a set of rules promulgated by the Ministry of Internal Affairs (DPR 394/99).

2 The criminalisation of the clients of prostitutes under sixteen years of age, within the framework of a law protecting underage persons from exploitation occurring during prostitution, pornography and sexual tourism (L. 269/98) in 1998.

3 The financing of projects to assist prostitutes, including, as its best accomplishment according to press reports, a helpline for victims of trafficking. This was the result of a parliamentary inquiry into the social and health aspects of prostitution, organised by the XII Commission (Social Affairs), composed of fifty MPs from the Chamber of the Deputies, in 1998–9.

All three debates are the most salient, the first two resulting in new articles of law, while the third one is a major step in combating trafficking while helping its victims, an issue very much alive among the public. The criterion for representativeness over the past three decades cannot be fully met, as there was no women's policy agency before 1984, and the debates bringing state decisions only took place at the end of the 1990s. As far as the representation of the different political arenas is concerned, there have been many local controversies and the outcomes have been too various to be unified, but the reason not to select these local debates is their low salience, in comparison with the decisions taken by the parliament. All three selected debates were widely addressed in the media.

The first two decisions were made under the rule of the centre-leftist coalition in the Prodi government (1996–8); the third was concluded under the first D'Alema centre-left government (1998–9). The May 2001 parliamentary elections resulted in a second Berlusconi government, a coalition between Forza Italia (FI, Forward Italy), the Alleanza Nazionale (AN, National Alliance) and the Lega Nord (LN, Northern League). All three parties advanced mainly restrictive and/or neo-regulationist (re-opening of brothels with compulsory medical checks) proposals in parliament to abolish the Merlin law. All cases are marked by the concern about foreign street prostitutes, as part of the overall scare about illegal migration.

Debate 1: Protection permits for victims of trafficking, 1996–1999

How issue came to the public agenda

The idea of granting protection permits for victims of trafficking was initially put forward at the beginning of the 1990s in international institutions such as the Council of Europe, the UN and the European Union.

The European Commission approved and recommended its adoption by member states in 1996 (European Commission 1996; European Union 1997). An Italian MEP, Maria Paola Colombo Svevo of the Partito Popolare Italiano (PPI, Italian People's Party), a centre Catholic party, was very active in putting forward the issue of new measures against trafficking. President of the NGO 'Irene', based in Milan, she acted at both the European and Italian levels. Irene is an organisation whose goal is the promotion of equal opportunities, including information and assistance to foreign women escaping forced prostitution. It has quietly adopted a strict abolitionist stand, disseminating information that equates prostitution with violence against women, but is apparently reluctant to launch press campaigns with these contents. However, it is not alone: the proposal to fight trafficking more efficiently has been promoted by other and more powerful Catholic NGOs such as Caritas and by 'lay' NGOs dealing with prostitution, including some feminist ones.

Dominant frame of debate

The awareness of the terrible conditions of what seemed to be the majority[3] of the foreign prostitutes working in the streets had already reached the public in 1990. The dominant frame in the public debate was the fight against foreign criminality, both petty crime and mafia-like big organisations. The violence used to force women to prostitute themselves has always been one of the crudest examples of the ferociousness of the so-called 'imported criminality'. The frame also included the typical 1990s issue of trafficked young women. The women selling sex for money now appeared clearly as victims of male deceit and violence, while in the 1980s the role and the discourse of the Comitato tried to promote an image of an independent and assertive prostitute, to which the women's movement reacted sympathetically.

Gendering the debate

It is not surprising that the initiative came from a female politician and a feminist, Anna Finocchiaro, Minister for Equal Opportunities. Prostitution was considered a women's issue, and female politicians are usually ready to respond in the public debate. Nevertheless, the first politician announcing the possibility in the new law to obtain a protection permit without denouncing anyone was the Minister of Internal Affairs, Giorgio Napolitano (DS). In the context of a meeting on 'urban safety' in 1997 he presented it as a measure to curtail the spreading phenomenon of prostitution. The debate in parliament was minimal: the awareness of a need to initiate new and more effective paths for dealing with traffickers was widespread. The gendering of the debates about prostitution was implicit, since the word employed in Italian to describe sex workers by nearly all the people who took part is the feminine 'prostitute', and not, as would otherwise be normal in the Italian language, a masculine 'prostituti', universal term for men and women. The very idea of prostitution implies that it is performed by women paid by men.

Policy outcome

The Turco–Napolitano law, next to raising the penalties for recruiting and trafficking foreigners with the intent of exploiting them as prostitutes or inducing them into the exploitation of prostitution (art. 10), grants victims of traffickers in general, not only for prostitution, a permission to stay and work or study in the country (art. 16). The article became art. 18 in the 'Testo unico sull'immigrazione' (Unified text on immigration). These protection permits are granted by the Questore, the local chief of police, on humanitarian grounds. This was also criticised by NGOs, because it takes too much time to follow the procedure and because the decision lies with the Questore. The only condition is that the victim must follow special courses for job training organised by NGOs belonging to a special list of about two hundred associations. The law gives funds to 'non-institutional subjects' to activate procedures to help the person to abandon prostitution. In fact, renouncing prostitution is the only condition for access to this measure, next to being in danger as a victim of violence and deceit.

The Comitato was very critical of the framing of prostitution as something from which women must be protected, a view typical of abolitionist (and Catholic) thought. The outcome was judged negatively because of the increased financing for the Catholic organisations which are in the majority on the NGO list, and the continuing stigmatisation of prostitution. There was a general agreement on defending the freedom to be a prostitute 'if this is the outcome of a free and conscious choice of the individual' (Fiorensoli 1998: 33).

Although the policy outcome of this decision is gender-neutral, the focus has been on young women victims of trafficking forced to prostitute themselves, rather than on other cases of forced prostitution including male teenagers, or the exploitation of one's labour power to pay a debt contracted for entering Italy illegally. The reason lies in the media appeal for everything connected with sex, the increasing visibility of street prostitution and the resulting (very often hypocritical) public scandal. The figure of the woman forced to prostitute herself attracts a kind of morbid and voyeuristic attention in the press.

Neither did the outcome settle the issue. The debate continued along the same lines (but without further decisions). In October 1998 the new D'Alema government was presented, and three of the six female ministers (the highest number ever in an Italian government) – Laura Balbo (Equal Opportunities, replacing Anna Finocchiaro), Rosa Russo Jervolino (Internal Affairs) and Livia Turco again (Social Affairs) – stated that they were going to work together on new proposals to solve the problem of trafficking, claiming that the previous governments had overlooked it. The first minister was a feminist sociologist belonging to the Verdi (Green Party), the second, a powerful member of the PPI, and the third, a DS Secretariat member. She declared they had joined forces to defend the dignity of women.

They collaborated with, and gave visibility to, an *ad hoc* commission: the Interministerial Table for the Fight against Trafficking, where representatives from Equal Opportunities, Social Affairs, Internal Affairs, Justice and Foreign Affairs ministries sat together with feminist jurists, judges from the National Board against the Mafia, psychiatrists and communication experts. Auditors were representatives of NGOs, administrators and politicians (notably from Mestre and Emilia-Romagna, which had approved the most progressive policies) and representatives from the Comitato and from the feminist association Orlando (Bologna). This Interministerial Table was established in February 1998 by Anna Finocchiaro (DS), the first Minister for Equal Opportunities, who declared that 'trafficking in women is a new and very serious problem, that we have to combat primarily with the punishment for reduction into slavery, instead of using the Merlin law'. This would avoid the feared parliamentary debate that could overturn the abolitionist implant of the prostitution policy completely.

On 9 March 1999 the three ministers jointly announced that they intended to enact more severe penalties for the perpetrators of forced prostitution, and that soon the protection of prostitutes who renounce their trade would be implemented by the approval of the administrative rules for the protection permits. Finally, in November 1999, an interministerial commission to implement art. 18 of L. 40/98 was established, with the mandate to lead the programmes of assistance and re-integration of NGOs and local authorities. The figures for 1998 are: 342 victims of trafficking came into contact with the police, 37 per cent of whom were under age, predominantly from Albania, Nigeria and former Yugoslavia. The number of protection permits granted – which in 1999 was 242 – rose to around 600 in 2000.

Women's movement impact

The objective of the decriminalisation of prostitution, except for exploiters, in other words a defence of the Merlin law, is the dominant view in the women's movement. It is also in line with the demand by feminist scholars of law for a radical reform towards a 'diritto leggero' – a 'light law'. This follows the principle of minimal intervention by the law on questions that should be left to the free will and conscience of the individual. The aim of these feminist scholars is to counteract the pervasiveness and inefficiency of the Italian legal system (Pitch 1998).

The result of the debate met these wishes of the movement actors. Among these were the Centri antiviolenza (Anti-violence Centres), the women's shelters, especially those from Bologna and Modena. Some activists in these shelters, which were originally based on volunteer work by feminists (and still are partly so), joined the voices calling to allow victims of trafficking to stay in the country, even if they do not denounce their traffickers (Fiorensoli 1998). These demands follow the practice of the Centri antiviolenza to empower women who have experienced violence by having them make their own decisions about how to deal with their batterers. As women also took part in the decisional arena, the first debate can be characterised, in terms of the model, as a case of dual response.

Women's policy agency activities

The proposal of a protection permit was promoted by Anna Finocchiaro (DS), the Minister of Equal Opportunities and a feminist, together with Livia Turco, Minister for Social Affairs, and it was sustained by Napolitano, Minister of Internal Affairs of the Prodi government (centre-left). The Ministry of Equal Opportunities is a cross-sectional organ of the state which has only moderate resources. A high focus was maintained on the issue by Finocchiaro (and Livia Turco), defeating, with the decisive support of Napolitano, all the attempts to allow the granting of such a permit only to those who denounced their traffickers (Finocchiaro 2000).

In this debate the role of the women's policy agencies has been an insider one, though the balance of power in this debate clearly swung towards the Ministry for Equal Opportunities and not towards the scattered voices of the women's movement. The agreement between NGOs (including feminist ones), female politicians concerned with this issue and the policy agencies has proved very effective in accomplishing a change of policy in favour of the victims of horrible crimes in need of protection from a life-threatening return to their country of origin, if expelled as *sans papiers*. The measure can be characterised as an emergency measure, a reaction to an extreme and new situation: the resurgence of what has been called (especially by Catholics) a new 'slave trade'. Women's movement groups found a good channel in the women's policy agency for introducing a more compassionate policy.

Women's movement characteristics

While the 'ecumenical' women's policy agencies stayed on in the public panorama and very often made prostitution a major issue, the women's movement, with its grass roots part in decline since the 1980s, has not made prostitution a hot issue, giving it a mid-level priority. There was also ambivalence in its views of prostitution: the view of the exchange of sex for money as oppression of women is still widespread among feminists, although there are more and more voices speaking for a normalisation of the trade. Roberta Tatafiore, the chief editor of the feminist magazine *Noidonne* (Us Women), has been the most prominent of these (Tatafiore 1994), taking a liberal position. The women's movement was still close to the left during this debate.

A backlash against feminism has been raging since the 1980s, and on the issue of prostitution there are many Catholic volunteer associations, with the characteristics of a social movement, who are very hostile to feminism. There is a counter-movement: the Catholic right and the fascist right are strongly opposed to feminism. They also oppose the harm reduction policies practised by non-Catholic NGOs. Guazzaloca, the right-wing mayor of Bologna elected in 2000, has cut all funds to the local women's shelter.

Policy environment

It was Livia Turco (DS), Minister for Social Affairs, who in 1996 introduced a 'justice permit' especially aimed at victims of trafficking who denounced their traffickers. Its duration is tied to the duration of the trial and expires with the sentence or after one year; it forbids working. It was adopted as part of the 'Dini Decree' on foreigners (D. L. 376/96), named after Lamberto Dini, prime minister of the centre-leftist coalition which held power from 1995 to 1996. Catholic organisations such as Caritas (Charity) and Gruppo Abel (Abel Group) protested against the denunciation clause; according to their (prior) demand, the permit should have been granted for reasons of protection alone. It was already possible to get a permit to stay in the country on humanitarian grounds, but this information is not well known among prostitutes and is little publicised, though there have been some cases of obtaining such a permit. In 1998, the new Turco-Napolitano law on immigration, named after its two minister-proponents, contained the protection permit without denunciation. Livia Turco, still Minister of Social Affairs, introduced the clause, being spurred by the Commission for Equal Opportunities.[4]

The centre-leftist government provided a moderately open policy subsystem on this issue, although it did afford the new law a high profile. The dominant approach to the issue matched that of the women's movement actors.

Debate 2: Criminalisation of clients of prostitutes under sixteen years, 1998

How issue came to the public agenda

Clients of prostitutes are no longer considered sacred cows whose behaviour must never be questioned. Blaming clients for the existence of prostitution is now a common discourse among both feminists and Catholics. Catholics have hailed the city mayors who, since 1994, have ordered the municipal traffic police to fine clients in order to reduce street prostitution. There were also signs of approval from feminists: the fact that the target of police action shifted from women to men was greeted with some satisfaction. But part of the feminist movement operating in this field has been fiercely opposed to the mayors' initiative: in 1998, when fines were imposed on clients in Bologna, the women's anti-abuse shelter (Case delle donne per non subire violenze) protested and abandoned the City Co-ordinating Committee on Prostitution, together with the Comitato and the MIT, an organisation of transsexuals. They held that an increase in repressive measures only worsened the working conditions of women on the streets and that the client represents an important point of contact for giving information to victimised prostitutes on how to escape their oppressors. But the criminalisation arrived on the policy agenda with an entirely different framing.

Dominant frame of debate

The debate that led to the penalisation of the clients of prostitutes under sixteen years old (under fourteen is statutory rape) was only partially connected with the role of clients and their possible guilt. Although the subject of underage prostitution is a common theme which has always surfaced periodically in newspaper chronicles (until the1990s, the focus was on Italian minors, especially from the South), the real debate in the press was the issue of child molestation, with much more attention given to male children than to female children. Consequently it was often used as a demeaning argument against the gay movement.

Gendering the debate

Anna Serafini and Daria Bonfietti were the MPs from the DS who introduced the law in 1996. It unified several different law proposals; both the left and the right converged on the measures, emulating the 'ecumenical' spirit of international agreements like the Programme of Action against Sexual Exploitation of Children for Commercial Purposes adopted by the World Conference on Childhood in Stockholm in 1996. The Minister for Internal Affairs, Rosa Russo Jervolino, also played an important role in promoting this law. The decision to make laws against what is called 'sexual exploitation of minors' was largely due to the pressure exerted by international organisations concerned with sex tourism regarding minors, such as UNESCO and End Child Prostitution and Trafficking (ECPAT).

On the domestic front, the parliament reacted to press reports of cases of the abuse and even murders of minors, and to the continuous hype about the use of the Internet to distribute pornography depicting minors and to initiate contacts with 'children', meaning underage subjects. In the press and elsewhere, the terminology for speaking about minors has increasingly eliminated the use of the term 'teenager' and substituted it with the term 'children'. Moreover, the debate was conducted along the lines of equating 'women and minors', turning the clock back to times when both these categories were legally powerless. In public discourse it is still common practice to group women and minors together.

The major issue that influenced the decision in this 'fight against child molestation', or against paedophilia, was a particularly ugly murder case involving an eight-year old boy murdered by his friend's father, in the summer of 1998 in the town of Ostia. The Penal Code was rapidly changed to introduce and toughen prison sentences for people who have sexual contact with minors,[5] or who possess pornography depicting them. No opposition has been voiced, either by the women's policy agencies or by the women's movement: the fight against child molestation is an issue against which hardly anyone takes a critical stand.

In the discussion on whether ignorance of the true age of a minor should be taken into consideration or not, the Senate voted in favour and the Chamber of Deputies voted against it. The latter had the last word, but only for reasons of perceived urgency. The final version of the law states that ignorance is not considered a reason for avoiding the punishment for paying a minor for sex. Ersilia Salvato, a feminist MP for RC (Rifondazione Comunista, Communist Refoundation), abstained from the vote, asking for more time to reflect rather than approve a law under the pressure of public opinion. MPs on the right (FI and AN) have expressed the same perplexities.

As in the case of the first debate, the law was not gender-specific, since the Italian constitution forbids discrimination on the basis of gender (also due to Lina Merlin). The measures for prostitutes are practically only implicitly gender-oriented, as clients are practically only men. In fact, the debate has been definitively gendered on the side of the female prostitutes, given the fact that a good share of street prostitution is in fact practised by transvestites and transsexuals, both appearing to be women. They were not mentioned very much in the debates: they are not victimised to the same extent as women, and they usually work without 'protection'. They mainly come from Italy, especially its southern part, and South America.

Policy outcome

The articles in the law against child molestation (paedophilia) (L. 269/98) that deal with prostitution (art. 2 and 4, which include crimes committed abroad) prescribe a stiffer prison sentence (six to twelve years) and a fine of 15,000–150,000 euros for exploiting minors and prison from six months to three years or a fine of up to 5,000 euros for those who pay a minor between fourteen and sixteen for sex, unless the accused is under age (younger than eighteen years old), which reduces the penalty by one-third. Another measure introduced is the institution of special 'anti-child molestation' police units.

The introduction of this measure was, above all, a formal change rather than a substantial change of policy on the national level: concrete examples of cases are limited to one in Padua. The implementation of this measure is impossible because the only agents who can make credible charges are the prostitutes themselves, and the police do not use female police officers as baits for customers.

The client issue resurfaced in 1999 when on 13 January the Interior Affairs Minister, Rosa Russo Jervolino, declared that a modification of the Merlin law was necessary to punish exploiters more harshly. Giuliano Amato (ex-PSI, now independent), the most prominent politician in the centre-left coalition who has ever declared such a position, intervened with a suggestion to penalise clients, and within days, Di Pietro (Lista Di Pietro) presented a corresponding bill in the Senate. The Amato proposal was immediately rejected by the feminist female politicians. Livia Turco in particular reacted promptly, and once again proposed the usual line of a decriminalisation of soliciting and of punishing aiding and abetting only in cases of true exploitation.

At the end of this month of debate, the newspapers reported that the ministers Balbo and Turco had received representatives of the Comitato, who were against client criminalisation. This occurred during meetings of a parliamentary commission instituted to acquire information on the issue of prostitution. The references to underage foreign prostitution were conspicuous: this leads us to my third selected debate.

Women's movement impact

Within the anti-child molestation legislative initiative, the particular proposal to penalise clients of underage prostitutes has not been put forward by the women's movement, not even by the anti-abuse shelters. Punishing clients was not on the agenda of the movement: feminists in general might find it appealing, but those who have reflected more deeply on the issue are against it. Neither part of the movement took part in the debate, so it is most apt to classify this debate as a case of no response. In general the women's movement considers the question of prostitution a cultural one, and does not trust the state to intervene with penal legislation, judging it ineffective for ending the prostitution of women to men.

Women's policy agency activities

The role of the women's policy agency in this debate was symbolic: not even the highest body, the Ministry for Equal Opportunities, intervened in the debate. The mandate of this cross-sectional organ of the state, which counts on only moderate resources, did not exclude expressing an opinion in this matter, but it remained silent, also on the more general issue of the criminalisation of clients. At that time the ministry was still headed by Anna Finocchiaro.

Women's movement characteristics

The second debate took place in the same period and stage of the women's movement, so its characteristics did not change: it was in decline and still close to the left. It remained ambivalent about the possibility of accepting a normalisation of the exchange of sex for money. This also goes for the presence of the anti-feminist backlash and the Catholic volunteer associations working on prostitution.

Policy environment

The dominant approach of the policy environment (the parliament) was quite hostile to that of the women's movement groups: a rejection by nearly all participants of the possibility of a more moderate intervention of the law on this delicate matter. The law was adopted in a climate of media hype, which pushed the authorities to show that they were 'doing something' against paedophilia, so the parliament acted in a rush. In this issue the policy sub-system was really closed to the women's movement's proposals, even though there was a centre-leftist government.

Debate 3: Financing of projects, 1998–1999

How issue came to the public agenda

The third debate started in parliament in 1998 when the XII Commission (Justice) of the Chamber of Deputies ordered an 'Inquiry to increase knowledge about the social and sanitary aspects of prostitution', to counter the increased presence of foreign prostitutes in the streets. The Minister for Equal Opportunities, Finocchiaro, had actively promoted the initiative, and opened the first meeting. The president of this commission, Marida Bolognesi (DS), had already been very much in contact with the NGOs, both Catholic and non-Catholic, dealing with prostitution.

During these hearings the deputies, mostly on the centre-left, listened to and interrogated experts, local administrators, mayors, members of organisations dealing with prostitution (harm reduction or 'salvation' work), including priests, and representatives of the Committee for Prostitutes' Civil Rights, called to inform the MPs of the current facts. The Anti-Violence shelter of Bologna and the Bolognese feminist association Orlando were also invited, though in the parliamentary acts only an intervention of a member of the first association is registered (Italia 1999). No other women's policy agencies' representatives, except the minister, took part in the gatherings.

Dominant frame of debate

The six hearings of the commission (Italia 1999) touched on all the aspects of prostitution, but the dominant frame centred on the issue of foreigners 'invading' the streets: many local administrators were primarily concerned with the disturbance to public order and citizens' protests. The sanitary problem was also mentioned by many experts.

Gendering the debate

The discussion was gendered both by deputies of the left and the right, and by the experts. There were repeated references to the 'male issue of sexuality in prostitution' (by female MPs Nardini and Valpiana, both RC, and Finocchiaro, DS), and also in connection with the health hazard of men refusing to use condoms and offering a higher price for sex without condoms. Tiziana Valpiana spoke about the degradation inflicted by the male gender on prostitutes, and at a certain point complained about the insufficient gendering of the debate: the fact that exploiters were men and the victims women was, in her opinion, systematically overlooked. This was a polemical exaggeration, since the very proposal by the Minister of Equal Opportunities, Finocchiaro, and the Minister of Internal Affairs, Turco, was conceived in terms of giving opportunities of self-determination to female victims of male violence (Finocchiaro 2000).[6]

But in the course of the debate MPs of the right did try to generalise it, affirming that the 'problem of male prostitution' was equally important (Carlesi, AN, Massidda, FI), or blaming the prostitute for all the problems concerned with her activity, when she freely chooses to enter the trade (Baiamonte, FI). There was a general consensus on distinguishing the cases of free and forced prostitution, and the focus of the debate remained on forced prostitution.

Policy outcome

The commission took a rather low-profile end decision, adopting three principles: harm reduction for reducing health hazards, education of clients via information campaigns, and maintenance of the Merlin law. It deliberated on a law proposal to finance new local programmes to help prostitutes in using the new possibility of the protection permit. Other measures to finance projects were taken at about the same time at the ministerial level. The three ministries held by women started information campaigns in the 'sending countries' (Nigeria and Eastern Europe) to warn young women. Courses to help the police improve their methods of intervention, and to oblige them to inform the women of the possibility of obtaining a protection permit, were also financed and initiated. In February 2000, a free of charge phone number was launched: women who wanted help to escape prostitution could call and obtain the necessary information. One hundred operators assured a twenty-four-hour presence.

Moreover, the Department for Equal Opportunities earmarked 8 million euros for 'social protection programmes' connected with art. 18 (the protection permits), most going to Catholic organisations.

Women's movement impact

The representative of the Anti-Violence shelter, Elsa Antonioni, underlined the continuity between sex for which women get paid and sex without payment. She defended prostitutes whose civil rights are still incomplete; for example, they face the risk of having their children taken away from them (Italia 1999). No other feminist voices were heard in this debate, and the plea for enhancing the civil rights of prostitutes was not taken up by the women's policy agencies.

However, as women from the Anti-Violence shelters and the Comitato did participate at several points in the procedure, and the outcome was in line with women's movement demands, this debate can be seen as a dual response. A side-effect has been the strengthening of the Catholic position, not considered a problem by women's movement actors, who seem resigned to its weaknesses in the NGO arenas. It does not have the resources of the Catholic NGOs to establish more refuges and to find work for those who manage to escape, even if the state helps with funding.

Women's policy agency activities

In the third debate, too, we can attribute to the women's policy agencies (in particular the Ministry for Equal Opportunities), the role of insider. The issue was important to them and the ministry took care to intervene in the drafting of the measure. Its characteristics had not changed since the second debate.

Women's movement characteristics

The third debate took place in the same period as the other two, and the characteristics of the movement did not change. Neither was this the case for the backlash and the Catholic volunteer organisations.

Policy environment

On this issue, the policy environment (the parliament with a centre-leftist government, plus the experts that brought information on prostitution to the MPs of the commission) showed a much more favourable attitude towards the proposed measure, so we can consider the policy sub-system open. The dominant approach matched the women's movement's view of the matter. On this issue both Catholics and non-Catholics agreed, and both felt a sense of urgency for adopting new measures against a phenomenon that sincerely worried the public opinion.

Conclusion

Under the centre-leftist government, the response of the state to the new issue of foreign prostitution and of trafficking in women has been slow but in line with the views of the feminists. Women's policy agencies, primarily the newly established Ministry for Equal Opportunities, have often intervened in the debate, and managed to put through their proposals. Nevertheless, the major player the state and women's agencies considered was not the (declining) women's movement, but the Comitato. The most important feminist voices that were heard in these debates were those of the associations that created women's shelters, who already collaborated with the Comitato.

There has been a minimum position defended by the Comitato, the women's movement and the women's policy agencies alike: to leave free space to prostitution with minimum state control. This principle has been defended in all of the three decisions under examination, if not completely maintained, as in the case of granting protection permits only to women who renounce prostitution. But the attempts to abolish the clause of the Merlin law punishing people who are involved with prostitutes and help them in their trade without exploiting them have all failed. Livia Turco affirmed her intentions again by endorsing the proposals of the Comitato just before the elections of May 2001, which the centre-left coalition lost. We can conclude by affirming that in the second half of the 1990s the leadership in the issue of prostitution in Italy was taken up by a strict co-ordination of female politicians and the newly created Department for Equal Opportunities, as a gendered response to what tended (and still tends) to be considered a mere issue of public order and crime. The possibility of granting protection permits to victims of trafficking is extremely helpful: it is true that even before the approval of this measure they could have applied for ordinary asylum when in danger of being returned to their own countries, but they are almost totally unaware of this possibility. Moreover, asylum is quite difficult to obtain. The presence of an *ad hoc* article in the immigration law should now compel the police to show them this possibility (though it rarely happens). It also gives legitimacy to public funding information campaigns aimed at foreign prostitutes, illustrating this possibility to escape violence. In summary, twice there was a dual response to the (weak) women's movement's demands and insider status exhibited by the Ministry for Equal Opportunities, and once only the Ministry had a symbolic role and there was no response to the women's movement. This difference can be accounted for by the general tendency of both the centre-left and the centre-right coalitions to show firmness in the matter of public order, which led to the criminalisation of clients of prostitutes under sixteen, or rather 'paedophiles', as they were called in the debate. The non-criminalisation approach of both the women's movement and the Ministry for Equal Opportunities was too weak in this particular political climate. The results of the other two debates can be considered great victories, given the fact that they are humanitarian measures that need financial resources from the state, in a general trend of reducing public expenses and welfare measures. Both the protection permits to victims of trafficking and the financing of projects on their behalf are 'softer' and more far-sighted measures spurred on by a growing public feeling against violence against female immigrants, whose situation with regard to traffickers was much publicised by the press, but which often overlooked the fact that many foreign women are willing to come to Italy to practise the trade of prostitution.

The question of limiting the damage to the Merlin law was the main concern of both the women's movement and the women's policy agencies, in particular the Ministry for Equal Opportunities, and this goal has been achieved, although the head of the new government, Berlusconi, within months of its accession to power, has already expressed himself in favour of a re-opening of brothels.

NOTES

1. She judged, however, the struggle for civil rights for prostitutes a legitimate struggle, reflecting the common opinion of the movement.
2. The High Court, Cassazione, in 1998 overruled a conviction for aiding and abetting against a prostitute who had organised an encounter between a client and another woman, declaring that two women working together should not be considered as aiding and abetting each other. This affirmed one of the principles that the Comitato fought for, but it was not very significant: lacking a parliamentary or governmental decision, a High Court ruling can easily be overturned by a later judgment.
3. It is controversial how many women have been trafficked and lured or forced into prostitution. Estimates vary from a rather small minority of around 7–8 per cent (Carchedi et al. 2000) to all the foreign prostitutes (Olivero 1997).
4. Elena Marinucci, the first president of the commission, has dedicated her political activity also to prostitution; she has embraced the request of the prostitutes' Comitato for decriminalising aiding and abetting without purpose of

gain. An MP for the PSI, she presented a law proposal with this intent in 1987, and was violently contested by the feminist Elvira Banotti and her little group 'Femministe in rivolta', who claimed that the client is a rapist.

5. Sex tourism has been mentioned, in an interview with Serafini, as a major element in the approval of these measures before the summer, as a measure to prevent the crimes that might be committed in the summer approaching (Martirano 1998).

6. The ministers' abortive proposals about a further decriminalisation of deeds concerned with the free exercise of prostitution were made in the same framework of responding to trafficking of women.

10 Voluntary and forced prostitution: the 'realistic approach' of the Netherlands

Joyce Outshoorn

Introduction

Prostitution has existed for a long time and will continue to do so. This requires a realistic approach on the part of government... prohibition is not the way to proceed... but one should allow for voluntary prostitution. The authorities can then regulate prostitution and the prostitution sector. It can then become healthy, safe, transparent and cleansed from criminal side-effects.

This quote is taken from a speech by the Minister of Justice, the Liberal Korthals, in October 1999, when he defended the repeal of the brothel ban in parliament (Handelingen Eerste Kamer (HEK) 1999–2000, 25437, 5-10-1999, 11). He added that all forms of forced prostitution would be combated vigorously. The quote presents in a nutshell the basic philosophy of current prostitution policy in the Netherlands, with its distinction between voluntary prostitution, to be regulated as sex work, and forced prostitution, to be prosecuted as illegal. The repeal was supported by the secular parties in parliament and opposed by the religious parties. Feminists in the Netherlands and the national women's policy agency supported the repeal of the ban, arguing that it is an important step forward in improving prostitutes' position.

The new legislation marks a profound shift from the abolitionist legislation in the Morality Acts of 1911, which outlawed brothels and made pimping a criminal offence. Prostitutes or clients were never liable to prosecution. The ban had been the result of the concerted campaign waged against regulated prostitution by Protestant and feminist groups around the turn of the twentieth century (de Vries 1997). However, abolitionism never proved effective. In the course of the twentieth century policy unofficially reverted to regulation, local authorities limiting the various types of prostitution to well-defined areas and condoning 'private houses', true to the time-honoured pragmatic approach of Dutch authorities to morally controversial issues in the absence of a consensus. The brothel ban survived the 'sexual revolution' of the 1960s, which had led to the repeal of other articles of the Morality Acts about contraception,

185

homosexuality and abortion. It was retained as a weapon for local authorities to threaten those 'houses' that did not maintain some degree of discretion. The Netherlands never signed the abolitionist UN Convention Against the Trafficking of Persons (1949), as state-regulated brothels for the military existed in the Dutch West Indies at the time (Haveman 1995: 98).

Not foreseen was the huge growth of the sex industry in the Netherlands from the late 1970s on. Confining prostitution to certain neighbourhoods was no longer effective, and its spread to other areas led to numerous citizens' protests. In an attempt to regain control, Rotterdam tried setting up an 'Eros Centre' and designating certain zones for prostitution, but the courts struck down the proposals, as they contradicted the brothel article of the Penal Code (van Mens 1992). Many other Dutch municipalities were faced with similar dilemmas. Their umbrella organisation, the powerful Vereniging van Nederlandse Gemeenten (VNG, Association of Dutch Municipalities), then started the lobby for repeal of the ban so the industry could be regulated.

From the early 1980s feminists rediscovered the issues of prostitution and trafficking of women, and came out in favour of lifting the ban. In 1981 some of them set up the Working Group Against Sex Tourism and raised the issue of the trafficking of young Thai and Philippine women. Prostitutes were increasingly recruited from the 'Third World' and it emerged that a number of them were being lured by false promises to work in the sex industry. At the Hague government conference on sexual violence in 1982, which included the issue of prostitution, three feminist demands on the issue were advanced: the repeal of the brothel ban in order to improve the position of prostitutes, higher penalties for traffickers so that offenders could be held in remand custody, and temporary residency permits for trafficked women in order to enable them to testify during the prosecution against their exploiters (Outshoorn 1998b: 195).

Selection of debates

The demand for repeal meant amending the Penal Code, which in the Netherlands has to be effected by parliamentary act, making parliament and cabinet the primary decision-making arena. The Netherlands has a multiparty system, in which no party has a majority by itself; a coalition cabinet is therefore inevitable to obtain a parliamentary majority. After elections the leadership of the potential coalition parties negotiate a pact for a new cabinet, which to a large extent determines the political agenda till the next elections. These negotiations are never easy as the party system is based on two cleavages – a social–economic divide and a religious–secular divide – and they often take many weeks. In order not to endanger the coalition, party discipline is usually strictly maintained. The cabinet is the major initiator of bills to the Second Chamber of parliament. If a bill passes, it then proceeds to the First Chamber, a house of review. The latter does not have the right of amendment, but can fail a bill. Up to 1994 cabinets always included the Christian Democrats (united in one party since 1977), who ruled with either the Liberals or the Social Democrats. It gave them a veto on any issue touching on the religious–secular cleavage, such as prostitution or abortion. Between 1994 and 2002 the Netherlands had two cabinets of Liberals, Social Liberals and Social Democrats, popularly known as 'purple' cabinets, bridging the social–economic cleavage.

Since the 1970s, the period under study, there have been six policy debates which have led to some kind of official output:

1 The report of the Commission Melai (Commissie Melai 1977), the government commission advising on the repeal of the 1911 Morality Acts. One of its unanimous recommendations – endorsed by the cabinet – was to maintain the ban on brothels.

2 The government policy plan on sexual violence (Nota Bestrijding Seksueel Geweld 1984), which called for a lift of the ban on brothels and a firmer policy against trafficking of women. It was drafted by the Directie Coordinatie Emancipatiebeleid (DCE, Department for the Co-ordination of Equality Policy), the women's policy agency.

3 The bill to modernise the Penal Code, including the article on pimping, of the Liberal/Christian Democrat cabinet Lubbers I (Handelingen Tweed Kamer (HTK), 1983–1984, 18202, nrs 1–3).

4 The debate on the amended Bill 18202,[1] introduced by the same cabinet, to repeal the ban on brothels. It was passed by the Second Chamber in 1987, but the First Chamber delayed debate until a new bill on the trafficking of 'persons' was drafted. The First Chamber rejected it in 1993.

5 The debate on Bill 21027 about the trafficking of persons (HTK, 1988–1989, 21027, nrs 1–3) introduced by the Liberal/Christian Democrat cabinet Lubbers II in 1989, passed in 1993.

6 The debate on Bill 25437, a renewed attempt to lift the ban on brothels, of the Socialist/Liberal/D66 cabinet Kok I, in 1997, passed in 1999 (HTK, 1996–1997, 25437, nrs 1–3). It took effect on 1 October 2000.

For the purposes of analysis, I have selected the last three debates, despite the fact that this choice does not cover the complete range of time under study. The 1977 report was not salient for prostitution; neither was the 1983 initiative. The 1984 debate on sexual violence attracted a huge debate because it addressed rape and domestic violence, but the paragraphs on prostitution were hardly noticed. The selected debates attracted widespread attention and debate; they determined all consecutive debates and are also more representative of the decisional arena, parliament and cabinet.

Debate 1: Bill 18202 on the repeal of the ban on brothels, 1983–1989

How issue came to the public agenda

In 1983 the Liberal Minister of Justice, Korthals Altes (not to be confused with his later successor Korthals), submitted to parliament a bill (18202) to modernise the Penal Code; it included the removal of the outdated penalty of work camps for pimps. During the parliamentary debate, the Christian Democrats proposed lifting the ban on brothels so that municipalities would be able to regulate prostitution more effectively. A majority supported the proposal, so the minister revised his bill. He resubmitted it in 1985, renaming it the 'Repeal of the brothel ban'.

The crux of the bill was an innovative distinction between 'forced' and 'voluntary' prostitution; the state should combat only the former and stop moralising about the latter by accepting it as work. The bill no longer spoke of 'vices', but about 'sexual acts for payment': these are criminal only if a 'person' is coerced into providing them, infringing the right of the prostitute to self-determination (HTK, 18202, nr 3, 11). The bill also provided a broader definition of the offence to include, along with force and coercion, abuse of authority or deceit to appropriate the earnings of the 'sexual acts' of prostitutes.

During the parliamentary debate the minister stressed the advantages of repeal: local authorities could tailor regulation to local needs and set standards for health and safety of the prostitutes. This would help to maintain public order and provide 'a realistic approach'[2] that accepts the existence of prostitution and offers security to prostitutes. Contracting parties can agree on conditions of work and pay, normalising the sex business. The minister was well aware that a prostitute cannot be a 'normal' worker, as one cannot hold her to deliver her services. The moment she says 'no', her constitutional right to bodily integrity is invoked, and neither client nor employer can force her to comply. The minister also introduced the (untranslatable) concept of the '*mondige prostituée*': the emancipated and assertive prostitute who identifies as a sex worker, in contrast to the exploited victim of forced prostitution (HTK, 18202, nr 32a).[3] This concept was later developed to mark the difference between

Dutch prostitutes and prostitutes from non-EU countries, who by implication are framed as docile and oppressed.

Dominant frame of debate

The Second Chamber debated Bill 18202 in 1987,[4] a debate in which three frames on prostitution competed. Firstly there was the traditional moral frame of the religious parties defining prostitution as a moral vice; the state should aim at abolishing prostitution and protect women as the weaker party or victims. Brothels should not be allowed. The parties were divided, however, on how 'realistic' one should be. The Christian Democrats opted for realism, maintaining that prohibiting prostitution had never worked in the past, so it is better to regulate to 'protect' the prostitutes. Secondly, parties from the left employed the feminist sexual violence and domination frame. But they also held that prostitution could be work; to bridge the contradiction in the framing they deployed the distinction between voluntary and forced prostitution. This enabled them to take a pro-legalisation position instead of the abolitionist position which logically follows from the sexual domination framing. Finally there was the new frame of sex work prevalent in all the secular parties. It stressed prostitution as the private affair of citizens; the state should only intervene to set standards on working conditions and fight forced prostitution. All agreed the sex trade should be normalised. The dividing line between the secular parties was the feminist perspective: is prostitution mainly discussed in neutral market terms (the Liberals) or does it focus on women's work, talking about improving working conditions, unionisation and collective bargaining (the left)?

Gendering the debate

All frames were gendered, the major difference being that the traditional morality frame and the sexual domination frame view women as victims, while the sex work frame allows for a modern sex worker who knows what she is doing. They also differed in their view of clients and sex-club owners. In traditional moral and abolitionist discourse clients had been males lusting after sex, while brothel keepers and traffickers were seen as unscrupulous men. The religious parties still gendered them as male, but made no reference to sexuality. In the sexual domination discourse clients are sexist men seeking to subjugate women through (oppressive) sex, and brothel keepers and traffickers are the male guardians of the patriarchal order. In both discourses women are denied sexual agency. In the sex work frame no reference was made to what is exchanged in the sex work encounter: it de-genders and de-sexualises the issue. Prostitutes are competent sex-providers, the client a normal customer no different to one looking for a doctor or hairdresser. Female MPs from the secular parties did bring the male client into the debate, but the minister and the male MPs did not rise to the bait (Outshoorn 2001a: 165). The bill, speaking of 'persons' engaging in sexual acts, retained its gender-neutral framing.

Outside parliament the lobby of the VNG did not employ a gendered discourse, but used a law and order frame enabling it to demand regulation. The women's movement, which had developed a co-operation with the civil servants of the DCE since the Hague conference on the issue, employed a gendered sex work frame. This frame, and the distinction between voluntary and forced prostitution, was the product of a dialogue between the femocrats, feminist activists, researchers and lawyers in the field. It then found its way into the policy papers of the agency and was subsequently inserted in Bill 18202. The consensus about sex work among Dutch feminists can be ascribed in part to doubts about the sexual domination frame, which turns prostitutes into powerless victims on whose behalf feminists are supposed to act. But it was also the consequence of individual prostitutes speaking out and making the case for sex work. Few feminists were willing to ascribe 'false consciousness' to them. The sex work framing was also compatible with the dominant feminist discourse about rights and self-determination. For policy-makers the sex work discourse makes it easier to develop policy solutions than does the sexual domination frame, which only allows for abolition, but that was dismissed as ineffective.

Policy outcome

The Second Chamber passed the bill in 1987, with only the orthodox Protestant parties opposed. However, in 1989 the bill ran into trouble in the First Chamber where the Christian Democrats opposed the sex work frame and wanted state intervention to guard public morals. Furthermore, the bill would make it impossible for municipalities to refuse to license brothels. Other parties observed that the wording of the article defining 'coercion' differed from the definition in the article in the Penal Code about trafficking. The minister, concurring with this legal problem and aware that his majority was at stake, agreed to postpone debate till the new bill on trafficking, due in the Second Chamber, was introduced in the First Chamber (HEK, 1988–1999, 18202, nr 39a). The articles defining prostitution and trafficking were to be harmonised and both bills debated in conjunction.

Women's movement impact

During the parliamentary debate female MPs were spokespersons for three of the four major secular parties and they were successful in promoting the goal of improving the position of prostitutes and stressing the need to rid the profession of its traditional stigma. They also came out in favour of the sex work framing. In the First Chamber there were no female spokespersons, as men still made up the majority of members. The women's movement groups involved in the issue supported the bill, as it had adopted their framing and met the demand for the repeal of the brothel ban. The first debate is therefore a case of dual response: women were active in the policy process and movement demands were met.

Women's policy agency activities

During the first debate, the women's policy agency was part of the Ministry of Social Affairs and Employment. The Hague conference had been an initiative of its political head at the time, the Social Democrat Hedy d'Ancona, who was a founder member of the first feminist group of the second wave of feminism in the Netherlands, Man-Vrouw-Maatschappij (Man-Woman-Society). Her successor, the Liberal Annelien Kappeyne van de Coppello (cabinet Lubbers I), adopted her platform on sexual violence. The director of the agency was a female professional civil servant who had served as the permanent secretary of the erstwhile Emancipation Commission, the predecessor of the permanent advisory council to government on women's affairs, the Emancipation Council. Many of the civil servants had a background in the women's movement and can be regarded as 'femocrats' (Outshoorn 1994). The agency had a considerable budget to fund women's movement initiatives, including those in the area of prostitution and trafficking. Women's public policy in the Netherlands has always been conceived of as intersectoral policy; working with other departments was therefore regular strategy (Outshoorn 1995).

The DCE adopted the three feminist demands of the Hague conference and inserted the crucial distinction of forced and voluntary prostitution into its 1984 paper on sexual violence and into the major policy paper on the status of women (Beleidsplan Emancipatie 1985). Both papers called for the repeal of the brothel ban. In interviews several femocrats recall that at first they felt ambivalence about the sex work position, as they found it hard to believe it was work women would do voluntarily (Outshoorn 2001a). Talking to feminist activists and prostitutes convinced them that lifting the ban and regulating prostitution as work were the best ways of improving prostitutes' position.

The women's policy agency initiated and funded innovative research on the issues of prostitution and trafficking, resulting in three major studies (Buijs and Verbraken 1985; Pheterson 1985; Vanwesenbeeck 1986). The DCE subsidised the First World Whores Congress in Amsterdam in 1985, a trade union for prostitutes, the Rode Draad (Red Thread) (1986) and the Stichting tegen Vrouwenhandel (Foundation against Trafficking of Women) (1987), all feminist initiatives. Given its advancement of the feminist demands and the successful framing of the cabinet bill, the first debate is an insider case.

Women's movement characteristics

The women's movement had been at its zenith in the 1970s; in the early 1980s it had consolidated its position when many movement groups set up formal organisations and started to specialise in various issue areas. New national coalitions of traditional women's associations and second-wave groups were formed around issues of economic independence and women's work in 1984. However, neither prostitution nor trafficking was high on the agenda of the movement. The Anti-Sex Tourism Group and the Foundation against Trafficking of Women consisted of a small number of dedicated researchers, social workers and lawyers, who were soon acknowledged as experts in the field (Outshoorn 1998b: 195). A support group for the Red Thread, the Roze Draad (Pink Thread), was established by Amsterdam feminists working on the issue since the early 1980s (Verbeek 1996). Although the members of these groups were able to generate considerable media coverage during the debates of the 1980s, the issues were not much debated within the women's movement. During this period the movement was close to the left, but had increasingly good ties to the other secular parties. There was no counter-movement on the issue save for the religious parties.

Policy environment

The policy sub-system around prostitution had always been closed: at the local level it is controlled by the mayor, the attorney-general and the police. Reform of the Penal Code is under the control of the traditionally conservative Ministry of Justice. In this debate, however, the compatibility between the Liberal minister's party ideology and the feminist sex work discourse made for access. Moreover, parliament was open to lobbying, and the cross-sectoral mandate of the DCE enabled it to promote the demands, helped by women-friendly counterparts in the Ministry of Justice and the Ministry of Health and Welfare. The government was headed by a Liberal/Christian Democrat coalition. The dominant approach within the policy sub-system matched with that of the women's groups involved.

Debate 2: Bill on the Trafficking of Persons, 1989–1993

How issue came to the public agenda

After the debate on trafficking in 1982 at the Hague conference, the issue made its way into the DCE policy papers, where it was defined as the prime example of forced prostitution as well as a contravention of the basic human rights of sexual self-determination and bodily integrity of women (Beleidsplan Emancipatie 1985: 49). Awareness emerged that effective action against trafficking encountered barriers at the local level. Police were not giving it priority, and victims of trafficking, mainly women from the Far East and Latin America, were reluctant to report the offence as they were often without papers. Complaints from feminist activists and sympathetic police officers led to a working party of the five attorney-generals of the Netherlands (Outshoorn 1998b: 196). It came up with new directives to facilitate prosecution of traffickers and produced a feasible definition of trafficking. Moreover, temporary residency permits became obtainable for victims willing to act as witnesses against their traffickers in 1988, after pressure from the DCE and the Foundation against Trafficking of Women.

Legal change remained necessary to broaden the definition of trafficking in the Penal Code and to raise the sentences for traffickers. At first the Minister of Justice, Korthals Altes (Liberal Party) was reluctant to act, but after pressure in the Second Chamber from the Standing Committee for Women's Equality Policy (who in turn had been lobbied by femocrats from the DCE) in 1988, he introduced Bill 21027 on the Trafficking of Persons[5] in 1989. The bill included a revised definition of the offence and a higher penalty, raising it from five to six years of imprisonment.

The Trafficking of Persons Bill also followed the distinction between forced and voluntary prostitution and its definition of coercion. A person who

brings another by way of violence, threat of violence or takes advantage by abuse of authority or deceit, into the prostitution business, or any action undertaken of which he or she knows or in reason can be aware of that the other will land up in the prostitution business, is guilty of trafficking, and can be sentenced to six years of imprisonment. (HTK, 1988–1999, 21027, nr 2, art. 1)

In the memorandum to the bill the minister pointed out that in the past culpability had been independent of whether or not trafficking occurred against the will of the woman. The new article now exempted those cases in which the woman voluntarily enters prostitution. The minister defended the gender-neutral phrasing on the grounds that boys and men were also being trafficked.

Dominant frame of debate

A change in the cabinet in 1989, with a new coalition taking over (Christian Democrats and Social Democrats – Lubbers III), led to the postponement of the parliamentary debate. The new Minister of Justice, Hirsch Ballin (CDA), had major reservations about defining prostitution as sex work. He amended the bill by mixing elements from the repeal of brothels bill with the new trafficking draft, radically changing its intent (HEK, 1990–1991, 21027, 11-12-1990). Firstly, he departed from the distinction between voluntary and forced prostitution where non-EU women were involved. In those cases he assumed trafficking, as women from 'Third World' countries (later he also included women from Eastern and Central Europe) are vulnerable because of poverty and therefore easy prey to deceit. Trafficking, according to the minister, can be determined by comparing a possible victim of trafficking with the situation of the '*mondige*' Dutch prostitute, such as not having personal financial means or passport or a valid visa, and working in bad conditions. The figure of a migrant woman coming to work as a prostitute in the Netherlands for economic reasons was thus defined away (HEK, 1991–1992, 21027, nr 10, 21-2-1992). Secondly, he made it possible for municipalities to reinstate the ban on brothels in their territories, in response to those religious municipalities who did not want brothels there.

These innovations led to fierce opposition when the bill was debated in the Second Chamber in 1992. The dominant framing was in terms of the victimisation of 'Third World' women and the problems of migration. The secular parties tried to reinstate the distinction between forced and voluntary prostitution so that it would include the work of non-EU women. They objected in no uncertain terms to the attempt to re-introduce a ban on brothels at the local level, pointing out that this clashed with the repeal of the brothel ban already passed by the Second Chamber. They also maintained that the Penal Code was not intended for drafting and implementing immigration policy.

Gendering the debate

Despite the gender-neutral formulation of the offence of trafficking, all parliamentarians referred to 'women' during the debate. The Christian Democrats discussed trafficked women in terms of deceived victims, and by designating all women from non-EU countries as victims, they could oppose the coming of non-EU sex workers to the Netherlands by asserting it was the best way to stop trafficking. In this way they linked trafficking to illegal migration. The spokeswoman of the CDA feared an 'uncontrollable stream of foreign prostitutes' and their minister spoke of the 'open flank' of Dutch immigration policy (HTK, 1991–1992, TK 81, 4994; 5001). The other parties maintained that not all 'Third World' women were victims of trafficking and pointed out that this ignored the distinction between forced and voluntary prostitution. Nobody at this stage raised the race and ethnic aspects of migration: that it is about black and brown and Asian women catering for the sexual demands of predominantly white men. Why there was male demand for women from abroad and 'lack of supply' of women living in the Netherlands was also not debated.

Policy outcome

Despite these objections, the bill passed in the Second Chamber as the Social Democrat Party decided to support it.[6] As party to the cabinet, it did not want to offend the minister of their coalition partner. In the First Chamber, however, all parties except the minister's ripped the bill apart on all contentious points. Constitutionally the First Chamber cannot amend bills, but by intimating it would fail both the trafficking and the repeal bills (now debated in conjunction), it forced the minister to produce a series of amendments himself. Even that was insufficient to save both bills. The minister had to withdraw Bill 18202 repealing the ban on brothels and to remove the offending articles from the trafficking bill.[7] The result was a bill against trafficking of persons with higher penalties for traffickers and a more precise yet more inclusive definition of coercion and deceit in 1993. The ban on brothels remained on the books.

Women's movement impact

The demands of the women's movement groups were partly met by the higher penalties and the improved definition. However, the removal of the distinction between forced and voluntary prostitution for non-EU prostitutes detracted from its framing. The gender image of the non-EU sex worker reverted to that of victim, not allowing for a voluntary migrant sex worker.

During this debate, several women and women's groups were involved in the policy process. The parliamentary Standing Committee for Women's Equality Policy pressured the reluctant minister into action. Action by feminist lawyers, partly organised within the Clara Wichmann Institute, a feminist legal institute (originally funded by the DCE), the scholars of the feminist legal journal *Nemesis* and the Foundation against Trafficking led to the guidelines of the attorney-generals and the temporary residency permits. They supplied the First Chamber with some very effective legal ammunition and continued to provide the major research on the issues. Female MPs took the lead in parliament.

Because of the cabinet change during the legislative process, the second debate is hard to classify. The demands of the movement were met, with the exception that no allowance was made for voluntary prostitution in the case of 'Third World' women. Despite this, the second debate can be classified as one of dual response.

Women's policy agency activities

The women's policy agency had survived the cuts in government in the 1980s, although it lost its state secretary in 1986 when it came to reside directly under the Minister of Social Affairs and Employment. He gave the DCE free rein to continue its work on the issue, as did a new director, a female civil servant with an interest in the women's movement. With the advent of the cabinet Lubbers III in 1989, the Social Democrat Elske ter Veld became the new junior minister. A feminist from the trade union movement, she gave priority to social-economic issues and provided little support to her femocrats working on sexual issues (Outshoorn 2001a). This, and opposition from the new Minister of Justice, led to a decline in activity and effectiveness. Prostitution and trafficking disappeared from the policy papers of the women's policy agency. Only in the international arena (UN Commission on the Status of Women, Council of Europe) did it – in conjunction with the Ministry of Foreign Affairs and Development – continue to further the framing in terms of voluntary and forced prostitution. The Netherlands provided financial support for the Global Alliance against Traffic in Women (not to be confused with the abolitionist Coalition against Trafficking in Women which is based on the sexual domination framing of prostitution).

It is difficult to assess the role of the DCE in the second debate because of the cabinet change of 1989. It continued to support movement demands and it was able to influence the content of the original bill, but it lost influence and was not able to prevent Hirsch Ballin's revision of the trafficking bill. One must conclude it had a marginal status.

Women's movement characteristics

The second debate saw the women's movement going into decline in the early 1990s. Only a number of specialised groups and professional organisations, many of them state-funded, remained active, although a broader and well-informed feminist public continued to exist. Feminist discourse had also become part of mainstream discourse, as evidenced in debates on sexual violence and on work and care.

Neither prostitution nor trafficking was a prominent issue in the movement during the second debate. There is little evidence that the larger feminist community was aware of or objected to the exclusionary move in the new bill. As a whole the movement was close to the left, although it maintained its autonomous status. There was no counter-movement on the issue either: combating trafficking is a typical valence-issue (on which people agree on the goals, but not on the methods to achieve them).

Policy environment

Compared with the situation during the first debate, opportunities for influence of the DCE deteriorated. The Ministry of Justice had the lead in drafting the bill and consulted with the DCE until the cabinet change of 1989; after the take-over by Hirsch Ballin there was no further consultation with state secretary Ter Veld on the issue. Parliament remained accessible and open to the lobbying of the movement's groups, but was far less open because of the imposition of party discipline during the uneasy coalition cabinet of the Christian Democrats and the Social Democrats. The policy environment can therefore be characterised as closed. The dominant approach in the policy sub-system was compatible with that of the movement groups, but not on all points.

Debate 3: Bill 25437 on the repeal of the brothel ban, 1997–2000

How issue came to the public agenda

After the elections of 1994 the repeal of the brothel ban became part of the coalition pact of the new 'purple' cabinet (Kok I) as it was high on the agenda of all three parties. The lobby for repeal had remained strong and local authorities started to anticipate the repeal by setting standards for sex clubs and occasionally raiding their premises in search of underage prostitutes or women without valid papers.

The bill was introduced in the Second Chamber in 1997 (HTK, 1996–1997, 25437, nrs 1–3). It adopted most of the ill-fated Bill 18202 and reinstated the distinction between forced and voluntary prostitution. The memorandum to the bill advocated a 'realistic approach without moralism', limiting the role of the state to eliminating forced prostitution. Its aims were to control and regulate the exploitation of prostitution, to fight forced prostitution more effectively, to protect minors from sexual abuse and to 'protect' (not 'improve') the position of prostitutes. The repeal would allow for setting standards and licensing at the local level. Turning voluntary prostitution into work would lead to the normalisation, control, cleansing and regulation of the sex business.

The memorandum showed a shift of concern from women to the sexual abuse of minors. In the Netherlands the age of consent for sexual activity is sixteen, but from the age of twelve, it is only an offence if the minor registers a complaint. For paid sex, the minister proposed doing away with the complaint requirement, making paid sex with anybody under the age of sixteen illegal. As for the category of non-EU prostitutes, there was no prohibition on them working in a brothel, but brothel keepers – like all employers in the Netherlands – are not permitted to employ illegal workers. Therefore only women with valid papers would be able to work in the sex business. The cabinet did not intend to grant work permits to non-EU sex workers or legalise already present migrant prostitutes without papers.

Dominant frame of debate

The Second Chamber debated the bill in 1999; the dominant frame was now sex work. Its proponents stressed that prostitution is hard and exacting labour, demanding certain skills and requiring a certain degree of toughness. They accepted that it was 'special work' in an 'exceptional branch', 'as sexual service directly touches on physical and mental integrity involved in sexuality'.[8] Given constitutional restraints, a prostitute does not have to deliver services if she chooses not to do so. Therefore it can never be 'fitting work' a woman could be required to do in order to retain her social security benefits, a source of worry to MPs from the religious parties.

The work frame led to problems when it came to the matter of age. Normally children in the Netherlands are allowed to work from the age of fifteen and the age for consensual sex is sixteen. For sex work an amendment raised the age to eighteen, making paid sex with a minor illegal. Employing a minor as a sex worker, or purchasing sex from a minor, was defined as forcing the minor into prostitution. Making sex work illegal for minors could only be done by focusing on the sexual aspect of the work, an aspect given little attention in the sex work frame which tends to ignore that prostitution is about sex. The female Labour MP introducing the successful amendment justified it by arguing that prostitution differs from consensual sex between minors: 'making a discovery tour with your boyfriend [at age fifteen] is something totally different to having sex with somebody for money twenty times a day'.[9]

The sex work discourse also set the frame about the non-EU women prostitutes. They were regarded no longer as victims, but as illegal workers. The Green Left Party attempted to legalise the estimated 10,000–15,000 non-EU prostitutes in the Netherlands, but all other parties were opposed to this. This was also the only party to deconstruct the implicit racial character of the distinction between illegal and legal prostitutes and to point out that predominantly 'black' women were catering to predominantly white men. Ironically, by wanting to legalise the migrant prostitutes, the Greens reinforced the definition of the issue as illegal migration. By refusing these women work permits, the government can be seen to say that working was not what these illegal migrants were doing, which contradicts the sex work frame.

The only other discourse that challenged the sex work discourse was the local autonomy versus central authority debate. Leaving regulation and enforcement to the municipalities created the space for the religious parties to attempt to revive the ban on brothels at the local level, but this was successfully resisted by the secular parties, who invoked constitutional law that stipulates that the Penal Code is binding for the whole territory of the Netherlands.

The First Chamber saw the Christian Democrats attempting to dislodge the sex work frame by arguing that allowing brothels was a naïve and risky attempt to control so-called sex businesses,[10] while those in favour saw it as a pragmatic and realistic approach that would eliminate bad practices. Green Left spokesperson Bob van Schijndel (also a member of the board of the Red Thread) pointed out that the debate had shifted from 'improving the position' of prostitutes to the 'protection' of prostitutes and that all the talk about licensing and enforcement turned the issue into one of public order once again (HEK, 1999–2000, 25437, EK 1, 4). The minister maintained that repeal was the best way of gaining control over the situation and made his statement about the expected effects of the bill cited at the beginning of this chapter.

Gendering the debate

In this third debate the predominant gendering was about the emancipated sex worker and the female victim of trafficking. A new image also emerged: that of the illegal immigrant who comes to the Netherlands only to earn money in a disreputable way. According to the majority in parliament, giving them work permits is not in the national interest. The Green Left and the spokeswoman from the Social Democrat Party were the only MPs to gender the demand for sex and question male desire (Outshoorn 2001b: 486).

In contrast to the two earlier debates, the third debate gave the work of the prostitute new meaning. It emerges as a very personal service involving skill and hard work. New also is the construction of the sexuality of minors, with the separation of paid sex and the kind of experimental sex girls have with boys as teenagers. With the increased emphasis on child sexual abuse, however, teenagers are once more turned into children, in need of protection against the lusts of adults. These appear as unsexed, thus hiding the fact that it is predominantly men who sexually abuse children. This is a remarkable shift in the discourse if one remembers that the whole issue started off with feminists worrying about male sexual abuse of women.

Policy outcome

As was to be expected, the legislation passed in both chambers, with the predictable voting pattern along the secular–religious cleavage. Provided they meet certain standards, brothels are now legal. Municipalities are authorised to set up local regulation of the sex business within their jurisdiction. The only concession to the opposition was to postpone the date of the law taking effect to 1 July 2000 (later postponed to 1 October) to give the municipalities more time for drafting their local regulations (*Staatsblad* 1999).

Women's movement impact

During the third debate women participated regularly, reflecting their increased presence in parliament and the cabinet. The drafter of the new bill was a female minister; female MPs successfully claimed the right to be spokesperson on the issue. Feminists continued their lobbying efforts and the Foundation maintained its expert status. The major demand of the women's movement groups – repeal to improve the position of prostitutes – was met by the passing of the bill. The demand of the

Foundation to legalise illegal prostitutes and grant sex workers from non-EU countries work permits was not fulfilled. The lack of debate on these points among the broader women's movement public makes it hard to assess whether these demands were supported by a wider feminist public. It is unlikely that this is the case, as there is no reason to expect that opinion would diverge from the overwhelming consensus in parliament on this issue. I would therefore classify the third debate as dual response: women's groups were accepted in the policy process and the outcome of the debate met the major demand of the movement: repeal of the ban.

Women's policy agency activities

During the third debate the DCE was still within the Ministry of Social Affairs and Employment and it had retained its staff and money. Since 1994 its political head was the Social Democrat minister Melkert. His priority was women's employment, but he became interested in the issue of trafficking during the UN Women's Conference in Beijing in 1995. In that year he appointed a new director for the DCE who had no prior experience in the women's movement. She restructured the existing networks between movement and agency, making for strained relations between the two.

Because of Melkert's interests, the DCE regained access in the policy arena and was consulted by the Ministry of Justice on the new bill, as demonstrated by references in the memorandum to the bill and parliamentary proceedings. The new Minister of Justice, Winnie Sorgdrager, a Social Liberal, was also more sympathetic to women's issues than her predecessor. The DCE continued to support the repeal of the ban on brothels, but was silent on the issue of the legalisation of the illegal immigrants and the work permits. This is not surprising as it would have meant opposing its minister (who was also responsible for working permits for non-EU residents) and cabinet policy. In terms of the model, the DCE can be said to have regained insider status. It continued to support the movement's most important demand and its original framing of the issue.

Women's movement characteristics

By the mid-1990s a mobilised women's movement had disappeared and the institutionalised organisations were directly affected by the reorganisation of the women's policy network, leading to loss of access and expertise when jobs were cut. Two of the most important organisations working on prostitution were able to continue their work: the Clara Wichmann

Institute and the Foundation against Trafficking of Women, both funded by other departments (the Ministry of Justice and the Ministry of Health, Welfare and Sport). The Red Thread led a marginal existence, but after parliamentary questions obtained a small grant from the DCE in 1997. There was still a small attentive feminist public intent on maintaining its gender framing of the debate, but prostitution remained a minor issue for the wider feminist public. Most remaining organisations were close to the left, but were necessarily more oriented to other actors in their environment. In predominantly religious local municipalities a counter-movement emerged opposing the repeal; it found its allies in the Christian Democrat and orthodox Protestant parties.

Policy environment

With the re-establishment of the contacts between the DCE and the Ministry of Justice the policy arena was more open than during the second debate. The proponents of legalising brothels, including the feminist groups, joined forces in the Landelijk Platform Prostitutie (National Platform for Prostitution), consisting of the De Graaf Stichting, the Rode Draad, the Foundation against Trafficking of Women and the Nederlandse Stichting tot Bestrijding van Seksueel Overdraagbare Aandoeningen (Netherlands Foundation for the Campaign against STDs). The future employers of the sex branch also joined: the Vereniging van Exploitanten van Relaxbedrijven (Association of Entrepreneurs of Relax Businesses) and the Stichting Man, Vrouw en Prostitutie (Foundation Man, Woman and Prostitution), a clients' association. The Platform functioned in the best corporatist tradition as a negotiating partner for government, delivering expertise and information in exchange for influence. During the third debate the coalition of the Social Democrats, Social Liberals and the Liberals was in power; it won a second term in 1998. The dominant approach of the policy sub-system matched with that of the women's movement.

Conclusion

After nearly twenty years of debate, the Netherlands have legalised prostitution, making only forced prostitution a criminal offence. Voluntary prostitution is seen as sex work, and municipalities have been delegated the responsibility of licensing brothels and setting up safety and health standards. The definition of trafficking, the most blatant form of forced prostitution, has been adjusted to facilitate prosecution and now carries heavier penalties so that suspects can be held in remand custody. The outcomes all meet the original demands of the women's movement: the repeal of the brothel ban, higher penalties for traffickers, temporary residency permits for trafficked women prepared to act as witnesses against the traffickers, and more inclusive definitions of force and coercion in the Penal Code. The movement was always in favour of legalising prostitution as sex work, as this was seen as the first step to improve the position of prostitutes.

However, none of the demands was ever prominent on its agenda. Throughout all three debates several small but well-organised and dedicated groups pursued these demands, lobbying and bringing their expertise into the policy process. Their demands were supported by the DCE, except for the recent demand for the legalisation of illegal sex workers in the Netherlands and work permits for sex workers from non-EU countries. The movement's framing was highly successful, having become the cornerstone of prostitution policy in the Netherlands.

Three aspects need to be highlighted in accounting for the very successful Dutch case of state feminism. Firstly, in all three debates the role and priorities of the political leadership of the agency proved crucial to the impact of the DCE. In the second debate, when its political leader lost interest in the issue and a powerful antagonist emerged, it was not able to maintain the movement frame and lost its influence on the draft of the trafficking bill. In the other two debates the political leadership actively pursued the feminist prostitution agenda and facilitated the groups active on the issue. Secondly, the outcome was also very much determined by the congruency of the movement frame with that of other major actors, such as the VNG and the secular parties in parliament. All wanted to achieve the same demands, although not always for the same reasons. Thirdly, women's movement groups remained cohesive on the issue. For the reasons given in the paragraph on the first debate, the sexual domination frame disappeared from the debates and the sex work frame emerged as the dominant feminist framing. The DCE was therefore not confronted by the difficulty of dealing with a divided movement.

What the consequences of the recent reforms will be is not yet clear. Trafficking of women, run by organised crime, continues (Mensenhandel 2002), and although the instruments for a more effective anti-trafficking policy are now available, the issue has no high priority for the police. Implementation of the repeal of the brothel ban is under way, leading to new debates. Conservative municipalities are testing the possibilities of non-compliance. All cities are experiencing shifts in the prostitution market, from brothels to escort services and street walking as sex bosses and illegal sex workers try to avoid control. Feminist groups have seized the new situation as an opportunity to re-open debate about improving working conditions and various (state) agencies are incorporating prostitution as work in tax rules, social security, health and safety rulings and credit supply for new entrepreneurs. The largest confederation of trade unions is prepared to promote unionisation of sex workers in co-operation with the Red Thread.

Will recognising prostitution as work clean up the business, improve the position of prostitutes, and make the work healthy and safe? Or will it lead to new forms of state control and continued intervention by the underworld? Parliament has already passed the requirement of obligatory identification for prostitutes, which does not apply to other citizens. Shifting patterns of prostitution practices appear to be making many prostitutes more vulnerable to abuse. It will require continual pressure from movement groups and their allies to maintain the intent of the law and keep authorities and police interested in its enforcement and alert to the indignity of forced prostitution.

NOTES

1. For the amendments: HTK, 1985–1986, nr 5, 24-9-85; nr 6, 24-9-85.
2. HTK, 1985–1986, 18202, nr 10, 24-2-87, 2.
3. The minister had used it before in the Standing Committee on Women's Equality Policy, in HTK, 1987–1988, 32e vergadering, Vaste Commissie voor het Emancipatiebeleid, 1-2-88, 20.
4. HTK, 1986–1987,18202, TK 66, 3478–3502 (2-4-87); final vote, 3511 (7-4-87).
5. HTK, 1987–1988, 32e vergadering, Vaste Commissie voor het Emancipatiebeleid, 1-2-88, 20.
6. HTK, 1991–1992, 21027, TK 80, 20/21-5-92. For the vote: TK 80, 26-5-92.
7. For the letter of withdrawal: HEK, 1993–1994, 18202, nr 127, 16-11-93. For the debate in the First Chamber: HEK, 1993–1994, EK 3, 12-10-93; EK 5, 26-10-93; EK 12, 7-11-93; final vote, EK 12, 524.
8. HTK, 1998–1999, 25437, TK 45, 28-1-99, 3104. For the parliamentary debate: HTK, 1998–1999, 25437, TK 44, 27-1-99, TK 45, 28-1-99; final vote, TK 49, 2-2-99.
9. Marleen Barth (PvdA) made this point, followed by others: HTK, 1998–1999, 25437, TK 45, 28-1-99, 3141. Her amendment to raise the age of consent passed during the final voting.
10. Hirsch Ballin (CDA), now member of the First Chamber, HEK, 1999–2000, 25437, EK 1, 5-10-99, 4.

11   State feminism and central state debates on prostitution in post-authoritarian Spain

Celia Valiente

Introduction

In Spain, state intervention in the policy area of prostitution has been varied. In 1935, during the first democratic regime of Spanish history, the
so-called Second Republic (1931–6), prostitution was prohibited (Decree
28 June). From the mid-1930s to 1975 Spain was governed by a right-
wing authoritarian regime headed by Franco which actively opposed
women's rights. In 1941, the prohibitionist law of the Second Republic
was suppressed by Decree 27 March. Prostitution was tolerated and put
under the surveillance and control of the police. On 18 June 1962, Spain
ratified the 1949 United Nations (UN) Convention for the Suppression
of the Traffic in Persons and of the Exploitation of the Prostitution of
Others. Decree 168 (24 January 1963) modified the Penal Code according to the 1949 UN Convention. Broadly speaking, Spanish legislation on
prostitution was abolitionist from 1963. In this view, prostitutes were not
legally defined as criminals, in contrast to people who promote the prostitution of others or benefit from it; they are punished accordingly – up to
six years in prison (Cebrián Franco 1977: 116; Carracedo Bullido 2001:
151–4). State and society also make serious efforts to help women stop
working as prostitutes. Such abolitionist legislation considers prostitution
as an affront to people's dignity; it is then irrelevant whether prostitutes
voluntarily consent to prostitution or not (Carracedo Bullido 2001: 152–
4). However, abolitionism was imperfect, because even if prostitutes were
not legally defined as criminals, Act 16/1970 of 4 August on social menace
and rehabilitation (Ley de Peligrosidad y Rehabilitación Social) considered prostitutes (and other categories of people) as individuals dangerous
to society. Prostitutes could be confined to special centres, or, alternatively, be sent into internal exile, as judges could forbid them to live in a
given place.

The (imperfect) abolitionist legislation did not change with the transition to democracy and the consolidation of the democratic regime. In
1995, Spain moved away from its former abolitionist position, since most

behaviours around prostitution, such as pimping, were decriminalised (except in the case of the prostitution of minors and those defined as legally incapacitated, like the mentally handicapped or disturbed; hereafter 'legally incapacitated people'). Subsequent legal changes focused on the fight against the traffic of women for the purposes of sexually exploiting them.

The reforms in central state legislation on prostitution since the mid-1990s were undertaken by governments formed by parties of different ideological colours: the social democratic Spanish Socialist Workers' Party (Partido Socialista Obrero Español, PSOE) up to 1996 and the conservative People's Party (Partido Popular, PP) since then. The impact of the women's movement on these legal changes was very small (but not negligible). The same was true with regard to the influence on prostitution policies by the main women's policy agency of the central state, the Women's Institute (Instituto de la Mujer, WI).

Selection of debates

The period of study for this chapter is post-authoritarian Spain from 1975 to the present. The main central state piece of legislation on prostitution is the Penal Code, which defines some behaviours related to prostitution (but not prostitution itself) as crimes. Recently, the phenomenon of high numbers of women being trafficked into Spain and forced into prostitution makes the Immigration Act the second most important legislative instrument regarding prostitution (but considerably less central than the Penal Code).

Both the Penal Code and the Immigration Act are made or reformed in parliament. Thus one institution dominates the policy area regarding prostitution at the central state level. Parliament is composed of two chambers: the lower chamber, the Congress of Deputies, and the upper chamber, the Senate. The former is much more important than the latter. Members of the Congress of Deputies are elected by proportional representation under the D'Hondt system with closed and blocked lists. The vast majority of senators are elected by a majority system. Although different units have the power to initiate legislation, in post-authoritarian Spain most laws have been initiated by government. Political parties dominate parliamentary life (Heywood 1995: 99–101; Newton and Donaghy 1997: 45–72).

Three main reforms in the policy area of prostitution have taken place in post-authoritarian Spain: the 1995 enactment of a new Penal Code; the 1999 reform of this new Penal Code; and the 2000 approval of a new

Immigration Act. Because of its wider scope, the 1995 reform is the most important of the three legislative changes. The first change, the new Penal Code of 1995, reformed Spanish legislation on prostitution, distancing it from the imperfect abolitionist past as it decriminalised behaviours around prostitution that had been considered crimes in the past (such as pimping). The only behaviour around prostitution that is still defined as a crime is the promotion of the prostitution of minors or of those legally incapacitated. The 1995 Penal Code abolished the 1970 Social Menace and Rehabilitation Act that considered prostitutes to be individuals dangerous to society.

The 1995 Penal Code regarding prostitution was revised in 1999, the second major change. This reform increased the punishment for crimes relating to the prostitution of minors and legally incapacitated people. This 1999 legal change defined a new crime: that of trafficking people with the aim of sexually exploiting them. The 1999 revision increased penalties when prostitution crimes were committed by criminal organisations. Other proposed amendments, such as the recriminalisation of the promotion of adult prostitution, were discussed prior to the 1999 reform but not approved. The third legislative change was the new Immigration Act of 2000, which offers permanent residence and work permits to illegal immigrants trafficked into Spain and forced into prostitution if they denounce their traffickers or co-operate with public authorities in the prosecution of these traffickers.

Since 1975 in Spain policy-makers have enacted two other measures in the area of prostitution, but these measures are significantly less important than the three aforementioned legal reforms. Article 2 of the Organic Act 5/1999 of 13 January on the reform of the Criminal Trial Act (Ley de Enjuiciamiento Criminal) states that police officers can work under an assumed identity (*identidad supuesta*) while investigating prostitution crimes committed by criminal organisations.[1] This measure is considerably less relevant than the other three because it deals with a procedure to combat a type of prostitution crime but is not a broad attempt by the state to intervene in the social reality of prostitution (as are the other three). Organic Act 8/2000 of 22 December on the reform of the 2000 Immigration Act did not modify the article of the Immigration Act that refers to people who have been trafficked into Spain with the purpose of being sexually exploited and who denounce their traffickers. Organic Act 8/2000 only changed the number of this article.

Spanish policy-makers have not regulated free prostitution as a profession (or as sex work), nor is it likely that the current conservative government will do so in the near future. On 19 February 2002, the Minister of Labour and Social Affairs, Juan Carlos Aparicio Pérez, declared that 'prostitution lacks the characteristics of a profession which can be performed freely and voluntarily'. He also stated that prostitution is a 'set of circumstances that propitiates violence and the trafficking of people' (*El País* 20 February 2002: 24).[2]

In this chapter I shall examine the public debates leading to the three aforementioned legislative changes: the enactment of the 1995 Penal Code the 1999 reform of the Penal Code and the approval of the 2000 Immigration Act. The three debates were selected for analysis following the RNGS criteria of decisional system importance, life cycle and issue area salience. With regard to decisional system importance, all debates took place partly in parliament, the main institution making central state policy on prostitution. Regarding life cycle, although the second wave of the women's movement has been active and women's policy machineries have been functioning since the 1980s (the Women's Institute was created in 1983), the three selected debates took place in the 1990s. These are the most important policy deliberations regarding prostitution, thus overriding the criterion of the life cycle, also given the fact that no debates with policy outcomes took place in earlier years. In terms of issue area salience, I have already mentioned that the 1995, 1999 and 2000 legal reforms are the most important legal changes related to prostitution in post-authoritarian Spain (although the 1995 reform is definitely the most central of the three).

It is worth remembering that the legal structure in Spain is a codified system. In common law systems (for instance, those of the United Kingdom and the United States), judges build case law and great importance is placed on precedent. In contrast, in code law systems, judges are supposed to apply the principles of the code and laws in each particular case. The source of the law is therefore not precedent but what is written in the codes and other pieces of legislation. This is why it is important to study the public deliberation and debates on prostitution reform in Spain prior to the main changes in the codes and other laws regarding prostitution.

The sources for this chapter include the three parliamentary debates prior to the three aforementioned legal reforms, legislation, published documents from the WI and from groups of the women's movement, as well as interviews with a member of the WI directive team and members of the women's movement and other associations of civil society active in the area of prostitution. I have also consulted all daily issues of *El País* (the main national newspaper) between 1994 and 2000 and collected all references to prostitution.

Debate 1: The elaboration of the 1995 Penal Code, 1994–1995

How issue came to the public agenda

In 1994 the socialist government presented a new Penal Code as a legislative project. The existing code was a substantially modified version of the one instituted in 1848. This PSOE project contained several reforms regarding prostitution. Firstly, it no longer defined promoting the prostitution of others or benefiting from it as criminal behaviour, except in the case of prostitution of minors and legally incapacitated people. Secondly, it intended to punish people who force others to be prostitutes. Therefore, this project implicitly distinguished between voluntary and forced prostitution (Carracedo Bullido 2001: 155–7). It also tacitly stated that the role of the penal law was to fight the latter (but not the former) and to combat any type of prostitution performed by minors or legally incapacitated people. Finally, this project abolished the 1970 Social Menace and Rehabilitation Act which considered prostitutes and other categories of people as individuals dangerous to society.

Dominant frame of debate

The parliamentary debate that led to the new Penal Code contained hardly any reference to prostitution. Articles on prostitution are included in the Penal Code under Title VIII of Book II on 'Crimes against Sexual Freedom'. When parliamentarians discussed this part of the Penal Code in the mid-1990s, they debated other issues than prostitution, such as rape. Very few amendments were presented to the articles on prostitution. These amendments were of minor importance and did not attempt to change the regulation of prostitution made by the new Penal Code. The PP, at that time the major party in the opposition, emphasised that it was especially concerned about the protection of minors (Intervention of PP Senator Ms Vindel López on 10 October 1995) (Delgado-Iribarren 1996: 2135). References to prostitutes were made in the debates on other articles of the Penal Code on other issues. The PSOE praised the Spanish legislation that defined rape as a crime regardless of the profession of the victim. As such, the rape of a prostitute is defined as rape in the penal law and could be prosecuted. The PSOE accused the PP of not supporting the legal possibility that a prostitute could be raped. The PP denied that accusation (Interventions of PSOE Senator Mr García Marqués and PP Senator Ms Vindel López of the conservative group on 25 October 1995) (Delgado-Iribarren 1996: 2401, 2403).

Gendering the debate

The (scant) debate was not gendered at all. Participants did not mention women or men explicitly. In this debate, references to prostitution were made in very general and abstract terms, and coined in gender-neutral legal language. The same was true concerning the people who worked as prostitutes or who participated in the business of prostitution.

Policy outcome

The new Penal Code was approved by Organic Act 10/1995 of 23 November by the votes of members of parliament from all parties except the PP, who abstained from voting for reasons that were unrelated to prostitution. Articles on prostitution from the 1994 project were included in the 1995 Penal Code with hardly any change.

Women's movement impact

Generally speaking and with some exceptions, prostitution was an issue of low priority during the authoritarian period for the Spanish women's movement as a whole. Unlike in other countries, in Spain the majority of (but not all) feminists discussed prostitution only rarely up to the late 1980s, and scarcely since then.

Up to the late 1980s, most members of the Spanish feminist movement conceptualised prostitution as an extreme form of women's exploitation which undermines the status of all women in society (whether prostitutes or not). The long-term goal to be achieved was therefore the eradication of prostitution (Garaizábal 1991). This position usually coincided with the abolitionist legal approach (Montero 1986; Oliván 1986; Partit Feminista de Catalunya 1986; Miura 1991).

The abolitionist position is supported by some feminist groups today, the most visible and active of which is the Commission for the Investigation of Violence against Women (Comisión para la Investigación de Malos Tratos a Mujeres). Some women's associations, whose main aim is to deliver services to prostitutes, are also abolitionist. The best known of these organisations is the Association for the Reintegration of Female Prostitutes (Asociación para la Prevención, Reinserción y Atención a la Mujer Prostituta, APRAMP). Members of APRAMP do not define their group as a feminist association (interview Rocío Mora Nieto and María Morales Moreno, APRAMP, Madrid, 4 April 2002). APRAMP can be seen as a part of the (non-explicitly feminist) branch of the women's movement. Other associations characterised by their members as feminist and providing services to prostitutes also support abolitionism, such as the Institute for the Promotion of Specialised Social Services (Instituto para la Promoción de Servicios Sociales Especializados, IPSSE) (interview Helena Barea, IPSSE, Madrid, 8 April 2002).

Prostitutes have traditionally received support and services from female religious associations and charities that are not usually considered part of the organised women's movement, including the Little Teresa Association (Asociación Villa Teresita), which is also abolitionist (interview Mercedes Gascue, Little Teresa Association, Madrid, 15 April 2002).

Since approximately the late 1980s, some feminists have stated that there are two types of prostitutes: those who perform this task voluntarily and those who are forced into prostitution by others. The state should actively fight forced prostitution but not free prostitution. These feminists conceptualise free prostitutes as sex workers and have demanded that the state treats them in the same way as other workers, for example allowing them to contribute to the social security system (Garaizábal 1991; Pineda 1995: 108–9; Forum de Política Feminista 2001). This position coincides with a legal approach aimed at regulation. The most vocal representative of this perspective today is the Collective in Defence of Prostitutes' Rights Hetaira (Colectivo en Defensa de los Derechos de las Prostitutas Hetaira). The regulation position has also been defended by some prostitutes (interview Concepción García Altares, Collective in Defence of Prostitutes' Rights Hetaira, Madrid, 30 April 2002; Olga-Prostituta de Madrid 1986).

It is important to note that not all groups in civil society active on the issue of prostitution are either abolitionist or supporters of regulation. Some associations have not publicly taken any position on the matter and their members hold different (or even contrasting) views. This is the case with some female religious organisations that provide services to prostitutes, such as the Hope Project (Proyecto Esperanza) administered by the Order of Worshipping Nuns (Congregación de Religiosas Adoratrices) (interview Aurelia Agredano Pérez, Hope Project, Madrid, 11 May 2002). The same is true for Cáritas, which is the main charity of the Catholic church formed by religious and lay women and men (interview Francisco Cristóbal Rincón, Cáritas, Madrid, 26 April 2002).

The policy content of the 1995 Penal Code coincided with the goals of those in the women's movement in favour of regulation but only to a certain extent. The position of these members and leaders in the women's movement (but not that of the members of abolitionist groups) supported the 1995 decriminalisation of behaviours regarding this matter, such as promoting the prostitution of others or benefiting from it. People in favour of regulation would also approve the differentiation implicitly made by the 1995 Penal Code between free and forced prostitution.[3] In contrast, abolitionist activists believe that prostitution is hardly ever (or never) voluntary, so the state has to fight any type of prostitution instead of investing in the battle against the forced variety. Both activists advocating regulation and abolition agreed with the suppression of the 1970 Social Menace and Rehabilitation Act which considered prostitutes as individuals dangerous to society.

Representatives of the women's movement did not participate directly in the (little) parliamentary debate preceding the treatment of prostitution by the 1995 Penal Code. Some women's groups unsuccessfully attempted to introduce their ideas and discourses in the debate. For instance, in 1995 the abolitionist feminist group Commission for the Investigation of Violence against Women presented in the Congress of Deputies a report against the anti-abolitionist measures included in the proposal of the Penal Code (*Mujeres* Number 18, second quarter, 1995: 17). Members of this commission and other abolitionist feminists held several meetings with socialist parliamentarians and (unsuccessfully) attempted to persuade them to change the articles of the project that decriminalised behaviours around prostitution, such as promoting it or pimping. The same parties also tried to lobby female socialist parliamentarians selectively in this direction (interview Rosario Carracedo Bullido, Commission for the Investigation of Violence against Women, Madrid, 26 March 2002). In 1994 and 1995 the commission organised public conferences on prostitution around the country to raise awareness among the public about the problems surrounding prostitution. To run these conferences, the commission received financial aid from the WI (Instituto de la Mujer 1996b: 226–27).

Thus, with the articles on prostitution in the 1995 Penal Code partly coinciding with some of the goals of the regulation sector of the women's movement, but not directly including women's movement groups in the policy process, the state's response to the women's movement was one of pre-emption during this debate.

Women's policy agency activities

The WI was officially created in 1983 (Act 16 of 24 October). The WI has been the main central state women's policy agency since its establishment. The scope of the WI is very broad, because it has five comprehensive goals: to promote policy initiatives for women through formal enactment of policy statements; to study all aspects of women's situation in Spain; to oversee the implementation of women's policy; to receive and handle women's discrimination complaints; and to increase women's knowledge of their rights. The WI is a permanent bureaucratic agency (Valiente 1995, 1997, 2001a, 2001b; Threlfall 1996a, 1998). Up to 1988 it was a part of the Ministry of Culture and between 1988 and 1996 a part of the Ministry of Social Affairs. These ministries are two of the least important in the Spanish state. Since the WI was not a ministry but a unit within a ministry, it has generally been distant from major power centres. In the mid-1990s, the WI had already acquired an extensive staff and budget. Between 1993 and 1996, the WI director was Marina Subirats, a sociology professor specialising in gender and education who had links with the feminist movement and the PSOE.

Up to 1995, prostitution was a topic of low priority for WI state feminists. This is reflected in the very modest (but not negligible) coverage of the topic by the WI periodical *Mujeres* (Women) and the annual report of WI activities, *Memorias*. The WI position and goals on prostitution tended to coincide with those of the abolitionist sector of the women's movement. This coincidence is reflected in the first gender equality plan (1988–90).[4] This plan mentioned prostitution frequently and contained numerous references to abolitionist ideas and goals. For example, it defined prostitution as 'a crime against the dignity of the people' (Instituto de la Mujer 1988b: 34) and stated that 'in general terms, it [prostitution] is not an option in life chosen freely and it leads the person who practises it to an extreme situation of exploitation at social, economic and psychological levels' (p. 33). The plan identified a general objective for prostitution policy: 'to resolutely help people who practise prostitution to enjoy a normal way of life, above all, by making possible their voluntary abandonment of their predicament' (p. 33). For concrete policy, this plan formulated two goals: 'the reform of the Penal Code to emphasise the criminal nature of exploitative behaviour in prostitution of persons under eighteen years of age', and 'the express annulment of the section of the 1970 Social Menace and Rehabilitation Act regarding prostitution'. The second gender equality plan (1993–5) contained very few references to prostitution and did not propose any legislative reform in this policy domain (Instituto de la Mujer 1993b).

As said, the new Penal Code contained anti-abolitionist reforms: the decriminalisation of behaviour around prostitution, such as promoting the prostitution of others or benefiting from it; and the implicit distinction between forced and free prostitution. As shown in WI documents, the WI position was abolitionist. Therefore the anti-abolitionist aspects of the 1995 reform could not have come from the WI.

The two legislative goals proposed in the first equality plan (the emphasis on the fight against the prostitution of minors and the suppression of the 1970 Social Menace and Rehabilitation Act) were achieved with the

1995 Penal Code. However, this was approved only in 1995, five years after the theoretical completion of the first equality plan. This delay, and the fact that the second gender equality plan was already in its third and final year of application as well as not containing the two aforementioned legislative goals, suggests that the WI did not have a significant impact in the 1995 Penal Code regarding these two goals. The conclusion therefore is that the WI was unable to insert its preferences and definitions of the issue of prostitution into the new Penal Code. Since some WI goals and positions coincided with some of the aims and views of abolitionist groups of the women's movement, the WI activities should be characterised as marginal.

Women's movement characteristics

After emerging in the 1960s and early 1970s, and growing from 1975 to the early 1980s, the Spanish women's movement moved into a stage of consolidation. Nevertheless, the Spanish feminist movement, while not negligible, has been historically weak, its activities involving only a minority of women. The movement has occasionally shown some signs of strength, however. For example, since the 1970s it has organised national feminist conferences regularly attended by between 3,000 and 5,000 women. Nevertheless, in comparison with other Western countries, the movement in Spain has not achieved high visibility in the mass media or initiated many public debates. In the 1990s, most of the feminist groups were very close to the left, but this was not the case for the non-feminist branch of the women's movement. This branch is composed of groups that are close to the left, the right and to no party at all. Therefore, the women's movement as a whole was close to the left (Threlfall 1985, 1996a; Scanlon 1990; Kaplan 1992).

Prostitution was an issue of low priority for the women's movement in its entirety. The women's movement was divided on the issue, since movement organisations active on the issue substantially disagreed on the frame (abolition/regulation/neither of these) and policy proposals. To my knowledge, no counter-movement to the feminist movement was active around the issue of prostitution.

Policy environment

The debate under study took place in parliament, which has some characteristics of closed policy sub-systems: parliamentary proceedings are codified through regular meetings and rules, and participation is limited to leaders of political parties with parliamentary representation. As mentioned, there was very scant debate in parliament prior to the enactment of the 1995 Penal Code. This dominant deliberation was very general, abstract and gender-neutral. The discourses on prostitution by the women's movement and the WI were more varied, elaborated, concrete and gender-sensitive. Given the general and vague nature of the parliamentary debate, the approach was compatible with the deliberation that took place in the women's movement and the WI. As mentioned, at the time of the discussion prior to the 1995 Penal Code the party in office was the PSOE. The 1993–6 PSOE government was a minority government supported in parliament by the regionalist Catalan coalition of parties, Convergence and Union (Convergència i Unió, CiU).

Debate 2: The 1999 reform of the Penal Code, 1997–1999

How issue came to the public agenda

On 17 October 1997, the conservative government (in power since 1996) presented a bill in parliament on the reform of the section of the 1995 Penal Code on crimes against sexual freedom. This reform referred to many issues (such as sexual harassment) and not only to prostitution. Regarding prostitution, the proposal increased the penalties in four cases: the crime of promotion of prostitution of minors and legally incapacitated people; the crime of forced prostitution when perpetrated by public authorities or civil servants taking advantage of their positions within the state; prostitution crimes committed with the purpose of profit; and the circumstance when the person who has parental authority, guardianship or fosterage over a prostitute younger than eighteen years or a legally incapacitated individual, does not actively attempt to stop him/her acting as a prostitute. The bill defined a new crime: that of trafficking people for the purpose of sexually exploiting them. The proposal explicitly referred to the frequency with which crimes related to prostitution were linked with the execution of sexual attacks and abuses against victims. The reform extended the negative prescription for prostitution crimes when victims were minors. The bill included a definition of prostitution: acts of sexual meaning performed with one or more individuals in exchange for an economic reward of any type. Finally, the proposal classified as a crime an act that had been illegal up to 1995, but legal since then: the promotion of adults' prostitution.

Dominant frame of debate

The debate on the reform of the Penal Code only marginally dealt with the issue of prostitution, dwelling on other topics, especially around the new crime of corruption of minors that the PP wanted to define. The (very scant) deliberation on prostitution included arguments against the definition of prostitution contained in the bill. The PSOE denounced the fact that the definition of the proposal was so broad that it would also include clients' behaviour. Penalising (male) clients seemed to be abhorred by socialist representatives. The PSOE argued that any definition of prostitution has to specify not only that sex is exchanged for money, but also a temporal element of 'persistency, permanence or frequency' (Intervention of PSOE deputy Ms Fernández de la Vega – *Diario de Sesiones del Congreso de los Diputados*, plenary session, sixth parliamentary term, 12 February 1999: 7044). The regionalist coalition of parties Canary Islands Coalition (Coalición Canaria, CC), the mixed group[5] and the PSOE held that the definition of the bill was imprecise and did not contain the requirement of full sexual intercourse. Apparently (and surprisingly), the three groups implied that full sexual intercourse was necessary in the case of prostitution.[6] The regionalist Basque Nationalist Party (Partido Nacionalista Vasco, PNV) argued that prostitution was a clear concept for any person and therefore perfectly coined: the exchange of sex for money.[7] For this and other reasons, the four aforementioned political organisations demanded the withdrawal of the definition of prostitution from the bill.

These four political organisations also opposed the proposal to define the promotion of adults' prostitution as a crime. Several arguments were used. If the exercise of prostitution by adults was not a crime, the promotion of adults' prostitution should not be a crime either. The law had to distinguish between forced prostitution (which had to be prosecuted) and free prostitution and behaviours around it (such as the promotion of this type of prostitution) that should not be criminalised because these belong to the realm of the private behaviour of consenting adults. The criminalisation of the promotion of adults' prostitution would imply the criminalisation of behaviours such as running a newspaper that published advertisements on prostitution services. These types of behaviours should not be criminalised because they are widely accepted in Spanish society.[8]

Gendering the debate

There were no special references to gender or women's issues in the parliamentary deliberations that led to the 1999 reform of the Penal Code. Instead, a highly gender neutral frame was taken throughout the discussions which produced the legal reform. For example, no reference was made to the fact that the overwhelming majority of prostitutes are women and most clients (of female and male prostitutes) are men. There were no references to women or gender in the 1999 Act.

Policy outcome

In parliament, a new version of the original bill was prepared and became Organic Act 11/1999 of 30 April. Organic Act 11/1999 was very similar to the original bill except on four points. Firstly, the Act does not define the promotion of adults' prostitution as a crime. Secondly, it does not include a definition of prostitution. Thirdly, it increases the penalty when crimes related to prostitution are committed by criminal organisations or associations. Lastly, the Act does not increase penalties when crimes related to prostitution are executed with the purpose of profit.

Women's movement impact

As was the case in the elaboration of the 1995 Penal Code, representatives of the women's movement did not take part directly in the debate that preceded the 1999 reform of the Penal Code. However, female deputies with connections with the feminist movement and/or who had defined themselves in public as feminists participated in the parliamentary debate. This was the case of the PSOE deputy María Teresa Fernández de la Vega and of deputy Cristina Almeida Castro – representative of the United Left (Izquierda Unida, IU), which is a coalition of parties to the left of the PSOE.

The content of the 1999 reform partly coincided with some (but not most) of the aims of the feminist movement. Most feminists were not against the definition of a new crime made by the 1999 reform: that of trafficking people with the aim of sexually exploiting them. The majority of feminists also did not oppose the intensification of the fight against the prostitution of minors or the special zeal with which the state would prosecute and punish prostitution crimes committed by criminal organisations. Most feminists thought that these measures either were in the right direction or were useless (but not harmful). The same could be said of the increase in penalties for prostitution crimes perpetrated by criminal associations.

However, the coincidence between the content of the 1999 reform and some of the goals of the feminist movement should not be overstated. The majority of the aims of the feminist movement were not satisfied by the 1999 legislative change. The abolitionist branch of the women's movement wanted parliamentarians to restore an abolitionist legislation. The 1999 reform did not re-introduce this type of legislation in Spain. The regulation branch of the women's movement wanted the state to define free prostitutes as sex workers and to recognise their workers' obligations (such as contributing to the social security system) and workers' rights (for example entitlement to retirement pensions). The 1999 Act did not make any significant step in the direction of regulating prostitution as sex work either.

In sum, two reasons suggest (with some qualifications) that the state reaction to the women's movement in the 1999 reform of the Penal Code was a case of dual response. Firstly, female deputies with links with the feminist movement participated in the parliamentary deliberation on prostitution prior to the enactment of Organic Act 11/1999 of 30 April, although representatives of the feminist movement did not directly take part in this debate. Secondly, the 1999 reform included in the Penal Code some (but not most) of the goals of the women's movement.

Women's policy agency activities

The characteristics of the WI were the same as during the first debate except for the leadership. In 1996 the PP appointed Concepción Dancausa as the WI director. She was a former civil servant with no ties with the feminist movement and with no previous significant experience in the policy area of women's rights. The third gender equality plan (1997–2000) paid very limited attention to the issue of legal reform in the area of prostitution (less than the first plan but more than the second plan). Under the heading of violence, the third plan explicitly talked about the grave problem of women and girls who are trafficked and forced into prostitution. In this and other situations, women are unable to enjoy the same rights as men. The plan stated that trafficked women are in an extremely vulnerable position that makes them potential victims of physical violence. As a goal in this policy area, the plan recommended in very general terms the adoption of measures to eliminate the traffic of women with the aim of sexually exploiting them (Instituto de la Mujer 1997: 73–4, 78). The definition of the crime of trafficking women with the purpose of forcing them into prostitution of the 1999 reform of the Penal Code coincided with the general proposals on prostitution of the third gender equality plan. This was not the case for the remaining measures on prostitution included in the 1999 reform. Therefore, according to the information provided by public WI documents, the WI was not the only or the main actor which set the agenda of this legal reform or set the content and tone of the 1999 legislative change.

As mentioned, the goal in the third equality plan of fighting the traffic of women and girls with the objective of sexually exploiting them was not opposed by members of the women's movement. This was the only instance in which the WI was an advocate for women's movement goals in the policy-making process on the reform. I therefore conclude that the WI incorporated (although in a very limited way) women's movement goals into its own positions. All in all, in this debate, the WI was marginal.

Women's movement characteristics

The characteristics of the women's movement were unchanged since the first debate. The movement was in the stage of consolidation and as a whole was close to the left. Prostitution was a low-priority issue within the movement, and moreover, the movement was divided on the issue. There was no significant counter-movement against the reform of the Penal Code on prostitution.

Policy environment

The debate prior to the 1999 reform of the Penal Code took place in parliament, which generally speaking is a closed policy sub-system. The dominant approach was compatible with the discourse elaborated by the women's movement and the WI, although the dominant discourse was not gendered in contrast to the latter ones. In 1996, the PP came into power, forming a minority government with three regional parties or coalition of parties CC, CiU and PNV (although the latter withdrew its support of the government in the middle of the legislative term) that parliament approved. The PP has been in power since then.

Debate 3: The 2000 Immigration Act, 1998–2000

How issue came to the public agenda

In February and March 1998, the IU, the CiU and the mixed parliamentary group presented in parliament three bills for a new Immigration Act. At that time, the older Immigration Act of 1985 was, according to many policy and social actors, outdated and no longer in line with the social reality of increasing numbers of immigrants coming to Spain. The three bills did not contain any reference to prostitution. On 18 November 1998, the PP in government presented an amendment to the three bills. According to this amendment, illegal immigrants who have been trafficked into Spain and forced into prostitution would not be expelled from Spain under two circumstances: if they denounce their traffickers or if they co-operate with public authorities in the prosecution of these traffickers, providing relevant information or testifying against them. These illegal immigrants would be allowed to choose between returning to their country of origin or remaining in Spain with residence and work permits. The PP amendment did not ask these illegal immigrants to give up prostitution in order to be granted residence and work permits.

Dominant frame of debate

The parliamentary debate that preceded the new Immigration Act (enacted in 2000) referred not to prostitution but to many other immigration issues. The public debate outside parliament only rarely referred to the prostitution article of the bill. To my knowledge, no political and social actor opposed the amendment on prostitution proposed by the PP. This consensus can be interpreted as a sign of an agreement among the main political and social actors on the following points: that many immigrants were illegally being trafficked into Spain with the purpose of being sexually exploited; and that these immigrants would not denounce their traffickers or co-operate with the traffickers' prosecution unless given very strong incentives to do so, because these trafficked women were strictly controlled and terrified by their traffickers.

Gendering the debate

In general, the references to prostitution within the public debate prior to the 2000 Immigration Act were coined in gender-neutral terms. Participants in this public deliberation spoke about trafficked 'foreigners' or 'immigrants' instead of trafficked women. The same was the case for the proposals that became the 2000 Immigration Act, and the references in the 2000 Immigration Act to trafficked prostitutes.

Policy outcome

On 4 November 1999, the three bills were unified into a new one which contained the amendment on trafficked people forced into prostitution presented by the PP. The new bill became Organic Act 4/2000 of 11 January on immigration. Article 55 of the Act contains the prostitution amendment presented by the PP.

Women's movement impact

Members of the women's movement did not directly participate in the parliamentary debate on the Immigration Act. Most women's groups active around the prostitution issue were not against the citizenship rights given by article 55 of the Act to trafficked people forced into prostitution who denounce their traffickers or co-operate with authorities on their traffickers' prosecution. In not including representatives of the women's movement in the deliberation of the aforementioned article but in coinciding with (only) a goal of the women's movement, the state response to women's mobilisation was that of pre-emption.

Women's policy agency activities

The women's policy agency characteristics were the same as in the second debate. The third gender equality plan (1997–2000) contained proposal number 7.3.2 regarding women who have been trafficked into Spain and forced into prostitution: 'to study the viability of the establishment of a temporary residence permit for victims of traffic forced into prostitution who have shown willingness to testify in legal processes [against their traffickers]' (Instituto de la Mujer 1997: 79). With article 55 of the Act, legislators not only fulfilled this 7.3.2 WI proposal but went further. Legislators not only studied the WI proposal, but proposed offering some of these trafficked victims work and residence permits. The WI successfully pressurised law-makers to insert its demands into state legislation (interview Dolores Pérez-Herrera Ortíz de Solórzano, WI, Madrid, 19 April 2002). Women's groups active in the policy area of prostitution agreed with the WI proposal number 7.3.2 and article 55. Thus the WI's role can be regarded as insider.

WI documents that speak about illegal immigrants trafficked into Spain and subjected to sexual exploitation often employ a gendered language. These documents frequently talk about 'women' when referring to these immigrants, and link the issue of trafficking women to the wider phenomena of violence against women and the commercialisation of women's bodies and sexuality (see for instance Dávila 2001: 22–3).

Women's movement characteristics

Given the similar time frame of the second and third debates, the characteristics of the women's movement in the third debate were similar to the second debate.

Policy environment

Since the second and third debates took place at approximately the same time, their policy sub-systems were similar (closed). The PP was still the majority party and formed the cabinet. The parliamentary discussion and the deliberation in the women's movement and in the WI were compatible but not exactly matching or the same, because the former was gender-neutral and the latter was gendered.

Conclusion

This chapter has shown that in post-authoritarian Spain the women's movement has had a modest impact on the debates on prostitution that preceded the major legal changes in this policy area at the central state level. It is true that the content of the 1995, 1999 and 2000 reforms studied in this chapter coincided with some of the goals of the women's movement. However, this coincidence has to be interpreted with extreme caution. Prostitution is an issue of low priority for most of the groups of the women's movement. The part of the movement concerned with prostitution is profoundly divided on the issue. Different groups have supported radically different goals in this policy area (abolitionism, regulation or neither of the two). Therefore, with the possible exception of prohibition, any measure undertaken by the state will coincide with a goal of at least one group of the women's movement. The women's movement or people close to it have participated directly in the debates on prostitution to a very limited extent (only in the second debate). Two reasons can account for this limited participation: the closed nature of the policy sub-system (parliament) in which decisions were made, and to a lesser extent the little debate and mobilisation of the women's movement as a whole around prostitution.

The impact of the Women's Institute on the debate previous to the 1995, 1999 and 2000 reforms on prostitution has also been very modest. In the three cases, the WI's goals coincided with some of the objectives of the women's movement. Since the women's movement came up with almost all conceivable demands regarding prostitution, any WI objective will match with at least one goal advanced by a group. The WI has been able to insert its positions into only one parliamentary debate on prostitution: the deliberation that preceded the 2000 Immigration Act. None the less, the 2000 legal reform is the least important of the three legal changes studied in this chapter and the measure was preceded by hardly any public discussion on prostitution. The closed nature of the parliamentary setting to outsiders' influence and the low priority conferred by the WI to the issue of prostitution explain the relatively minor role of the WI in the debates on prostitution reform.

The small impact of both the women's movement and the WI in the deliberations around prostitution policies has to be understood in the context of the marked lack of public discussion on the topic at the central state level. The main prostitution reforms were not undertaken separately, but were part of much wider legislative moves: the elaboration of a new Penal Code (1995), the modification of this Penal Code (1999) and the enactment of a new Immigration Act (2000). As shown in this chapter, little reference was made to prostitution in the public deliberations prior to the 1995 and 1999 reforms, and hardly any before the 2000 measure.

Since the late 1990s the focus of state policies on prostitution has shifted markedly towards the fight against the trafficking of people for the purpose of sexual exploitation. Whether this new attention to one aspect of the matter (trafficking) instead of another (prostitution itself) would foster public debate or contribute to devitalise it is an open question. The answer will depend to some extent on whether, in contrast with the past, the women's movement and the Women's Institute adopt the fight against the traffic of women as one of their own high priorities.

NOTES

I would like to thank the staff of the library of the Women's Institute (Centro de Documentación del Instituto de la Mujer) for their valuable help in the search for sources for this chapter.

1. According to article 81 of the 1978 Constitution, an Organic Act (ley orgánica) regulates, among other matters, fundamental rights and public liberties. An absolute majority of the lower chamber, in a final vote of the whole project, is necessary for the approval, modification or derogation of an Organic Act. For an ordinary – not organic – Act, only a simple majority is required.
2. Unless otherwise stated, in this chapter all translations from Spanish to English are made by Celia Valiente.
3. The coincidence of some of the reforms enacted by the 1995 Penal Code and the aims of the regulation groups of the women's movement is shown in Garaizábal (1991: 10).
4. A gender equality plan is a policy instrument. It contains gender equality measures to be applied during a given period by some ministries. In Spain three central state gender equality plans have been applied, between 1988 and 1990, 1993 and 1995, and 1997 and 2000 (Instituto de la Mujer 1988b, 1993b, 1997). When the period of implementation of the plans ends, the application of them is evaluated (Instituto de la Mujer 1990b; 1996b).
5. Parliamentary groups conduct most parliamentary work. In general, they are formed by deputies or senators from a party or coalition. If a party or coalition does not have the necessary number of members of parliament to form a parliamentary group, its representatives are included in the mixed group (Grupo Mixto) (Newton and Donaghy 1997: 52).
6. Amendment number 30 by the CC, and amendment number 31 by Ms Almeida Castro from the mixed group (*Boletín Oficial de las Cortes Generales – Congreso de los Diputados*, sixth parliamentary term, 16 February 1998, Series A (Bills), Number 89–8: 45).

7. Amendment number 23 presented by the PNV (*Boletín Oficial de las Cortes Generales – Congreso de los Diputados*, sixth parliamentary term, 16 February 1998, Series A (Bills), number 89–9: 25).

8. Intervention of PSOE deputy Ms Fernández de la Vega and CC deputy Mr Mardones Sevilla (*Diario de Sesiones del Congreso de los Diputados*, plenary session, sixth parliamentary term, 12 February 1998: 1044, 1049); Amendment number 17 presented by the PNV (*Boletín Oficial de las Cortes Generales – Congreso de los Diputados*, sixth parliamentary term, 16 February 1998, Series A (Bills), number 89–8: 23); Amendment number 31 presented by deputy Ms Almeida Castro from the Mixed Group (*Boletín Oficial de las Cortes Generales – Congreso de los Diputados*, sixth parliamentary term, 16 February 1998, Series A (Bills), number 89–8: 27).

12 Criminalising the john – a Swedish gender model?

Yvonne Svanström

Introduction

A state with 'feminism without feminists' is how Sweden at times has been pictured (Gelb 1989, in Florin and Nilsson 1999: 64–5). In a country as organised as Sweden, extra-parliamentary groups and other protest groups seem to be absorbed by the state and there is no place for militant feminism. Since the 1960s the Swedish state has partly integrated what has been called a 'Swedish gender equality discourse'. This led to a number of changes in laws, a Ministry of Equal Status in 1976, a Parliamentary Commission on Equal Status in the same year, and the creation of the Equal Opportunities Ombudsman in 1980. It has been argued that a number of 'policy entrepreneurs' and feminist agents were necessary to spread ideas on gender equality and to politicise the issue (Florin and Nilsson 1999: 65, 73). However, this gender equality policy mainly focused on women's right to work and equal pay; issues of sexuality were less debated.

This chapter will show that there was more or less unanimous support among the feminists in the established political parties for seeing prostitution as patriarchal oppression of women. Opinions have diverged on *how* to deal with this question, whether non-criminalisation, criminalisation of both parties or just criminalising the john was the right way to proceed. To legalise prostitution has never been an issue among feminists in parliament during the past thirty years. It was not until the 1990s that prostitution as sex work became a loud argument in the debate, mainly used by feminists and debaters outside parliament. This chapter will discuss the debates leading up to the unique Swedish law that criminalises the purchase of sexual services.

Selection of debates

Since 1918 prostitution policies in Sweden have been decided at the national level. As in almost every other Western European country, Sweden

had locally governed regulation systems in the nineteenth century, retained until 1918 (Svanström 2000). All decisions affecting prostitution
after that date were made by the national government (Månsson and
Linders 1984: 153; SOU 1995: 15: 55–70).

Generally speaking, the Swedish policy process relies heavily on inquiry
commissions in the preparation and drafting of legislation. Commissions
can be established at the request of parliament or by the government;
however, it is the relevant minister who appoints the commission and
draws up its instructions. In the case of prostitution the Minister of Social Affairs appointed a commission, consisting of one person, assisted
by experts. In this respect the policy process was more closed than when
members of the commissions are representing the political parties, or
representatives of major interest groups. At the same time, openness of
the process is achieved by the 'remiss' system of consultation: interested
parties are invited to submit their views on the proposals of the commissions. Organisations may submit their opinions even though they have
not been asked.

For this study, three debates were selected at the national government
and parliament level, which cover the period 1981 to 1999. From the
1970s some debate occurred, for instance when the city of Malmö conducted a major investigation into illegal clubs and enterprises in 1975, or
when the same city tried to establish local regulations concerning prostitution in 1996. There was also the debate on the so-called sauna clubs in
1987 when a law was passed to stop the spread of AIDS (which meant the
prohibition of clubs where sexual intercourse was 'made available'). In
1997 the so-called KAST project began, where the clients in prostitution
are, among other things, offered counselling.

However, some debates have been more important than others.
The first debate concerns the official investigation into prostitution,
starting in 1981 and ending in 1983 with a law against public pornographic shows (SOU 1981: 71; SFS 1983: 1617). The second debate starts in 1995 with a second official investigation into prostitution and ends in 1998 with a proposal for a Violence against Women
Act (SOU 1995: 15; SOU 1997/98: 55). The third debate begins
with the said proposal and ends with the ensuing law that was passed
on 1 January 1999 (SFS 1998: 408). These debates are representative of the policy sub-system since they have all taken place in
parliament, the primary decisional system in Sweden. They are also
representative of the range and salience of the issue, and are spread
evenly over the period since prostitution became a parliamentary
issue.

Debate 1: The first commission on prostitution, 1981–1982

How issue came to the public agenda

One of the reasons for the appointment of a commission to investigate prostitution was the criticism of another commission investigating sexual offences in 1976 (SOU 1976: 9). The latter wanted to soften the rape charge and suggested lower penalties. The investigation was severely criticised, above all by the women's movement. Twelve different women's organisations came together and demanded a new official commission and a second commission investigating prostitution. There was a big media debate. The topic of economic crime, such as the black economy surrounding the sex industry, and young girls being used in prostitution, was given much space (Månsson and Larsson 1976; Nilsson and Öijer 1977; Thomsson 2000: 53–7).

The commission that was appointed was to map out the problems of prostitution, especially child and youth prostitution, and the possibly increasing problem of procuring. The reasons for prostitution were also to be discussed. Further, the law concerning public pornographic exposures was to be investigated, and sex clubs charted (SOU 1981: 71: 9, 31–3). The one-woman commission had a committee of ten experts and a secretarial staff, but only two women among them. The commission finished its work in 1981, and its official report was published that same year (SOU 1981: 71). However, after a disagreement within the commission, all experts except one had left the commission and published their work separately. The results were made available to a larger public only after pressure from women's organisations (DsS 1980: 9; Borg et al. 1981: 15).

In her report, the commissioner stated that prostitution was not a 'woman question', but a question of human dignity. Nor was it a question of gender equality: if it were, the solution would be to encourage male prostitution and 'everybody can see that this is an absurd thought' (SOU 1981: 71: 136). The reasons for prostitution were seen to lie in a combination of a commercial society with a special gender pattern. The clients were said to be 'all men'. Contrary to what was assumed, there had been no increase of young women in prostitution; in fact prostitution had declined during the previous decade (SOU 1981: 71: 136–7). The commission advised against criminalisation. It might have a deterrent effect on the clients, but it would risk further stigmatisation of the women, and prostitution would go underground. The problem of defining prostitution, of drawing a line between 'private sexuality and prostitution', would make criminalisation difficult. However, men who bought sexual services from drug-addicted women should be punished. Prostitution was nevertheless incompatible with 'the ideas of individual freedom and equality among all that have prevailed in our country for a long time' (SOU 1981: 71: 144–5). Another suggestion was to increase public information on prostitution to change attitudes in society. Tax revenue laws (to demand income tax from prostitution) could also be used to make women quit prostitution. The law on pimping should be relied on more. Further, it was suggested that the rent law be changed to force landlords to end the contract when hearing that the apartment was used for pimping or as a brothel. An additional purpose of the commission had been to map the organisation of the sex clubs; the commission suggested the outlawing of public pornographic shows (SOU 1981: 71: 16–17).

When the commission's report was presented in parliament, it had been preceded by the separate publication by the experts who had left the commission. According to the remaining expert in the commission, the schism within the group stemmed from political differences. The official commissioner held 'classical liberal views on humans' – the women were in prostitution as a result of exercising their free will (Brunnberg et al. 1981: 26: Persson 1981: 216). After pressure from the women's movement, a popularised but fuller version of the experts' results was published in 1981. None of the experts and the secretaries participating in the debate was in favour of criminalisation (Månsson and Linders 1984: 154).

The experts' separate report was debated in parliament, and a female Social Democrat, stating that she was 'representing the organised women's world', said that a number of women's organisations planned to send in a 'remiss' on the experts' report, without being officially invited to do so. The female Minister of Social Affairs, who also saw herself as 'representing the united women's world', answered that the 'one-man [*sic*] commission' had to be given time to finish *her* work. Whether the government would take the women's organisations' 'remiss' into consideration was to be decided later (RP 1980: 33: 53–9).

In the 'remiss' process a number of women's organisations were represented, from both the old and new movement, including the political parties' women's organisations. Many were in agreement that preventive measures were necessary. The recommendation not to criminalise prostitution was supported by a number of police and judicial authorities and also by the Equal Opportunities Ombudsman (Jämställdhetsombudsmannen, JämO), the Social Democratic Party

(Socialdemokraterna) and the Conservative Party Women's Federation (Moderatkvinnorna), the Swedish Federation for Gay and Lesbian Rights (RFSL, Riksförbundet för Sexuellt Likaberättigande) and the Swedish Association for Sex Education (RFSU, Riksförbundet för Sexuell Upplysning). In favour of criminalising the john were, among others, the women's federations of the Centre Party (Centerkvinnor), the Left Party (Vänsterkvinnorna) and the Liberal Party (Liberala kvinnor), the Fredrika Bremer Association and the Alla Kvinnors Hus (Shelter for Battered Women) (Proposition 1981/82: 187: 42–5).

The government's bill was presented in parliament in May 1982 and more or less agreed with the suggestions of the commission. The bill prohibited public pornographic shows. It also provided state financial support for the organisation of a co-ordination group for questions on prostitution, and for research projects concerning the clients and young women at risk of becoming prostitutes (Proposition 1981/82: 187: 1–4, 27; 1981/82: 50 SOU; 1981/82: 56 JuU). During this period a number of party bills about the proposal were put forward in parliament. The majority requested state support for social projects against prostitution and prohibition of public pornographic shows and sex clubs. However, different demands were also heard: the Conservatives wanted to criminalise prostitution altogether (M 80/81: 1252; 80/81: 1367; 80/81: 403; 80/81: 1246; 80/81: 1254; 81/82: 2430).

The reception of the bill was mixed. The Minister of Social Affairs for the non-socialist government (who was also the chairperson of the Centre Party's women's federation) introduced the bill. Among other things, she stated that 'prostitution is a human problem – not a man or a woman problem, and it must be fought'. Further, she declared that 'prostitution is an expression of contempt for women . . . sexuality becomes a merchandise and the woman a thing among others that can be bought'. Prostitution stood in contradiction to the ongoing societal work for gender equality (RP 1982: 159: 152–3). Although not a woman's issue, the minister still underlined that the woman was the most exploited and vulnerable part in prostitution. She was supported by the Liberals, who stated that sexual purity had disappeared, but been replaced by a commercialisation of sexuality: 'to let a message of human beings as sexual merchandise come across in the name of sexual liberty is a double standard in new clothing'. The left observed that the original official investigation into prostitution 'was the mountain that brought forth a mouse – at least concerning actual suggestions from the government'. However, the proposal was passed with minor changes and the law against public pornographic shows was enacted on 1 July 1982 (SFS Ordningslag 1993: 1617).

Dominant frame of debate

In the parliamentary debate, prostitution was presented as a human question, both by the one-woman commission and in the government's bill. Prostitution was placed within the gender-equality framework, and by calling prostitution a human question, politicians wanted to get away from the focus on women in prostitution and include the men, the clients. The bill and the investigation focused on heterosexual prostitution. However, regarding the reasons for prostitution the government proposal stated that it was a combination of a patriarchal society and an economic restructuring of society, along with the commercialisation of sexuality and of human beings. The one-woman commission also emphasised the free individual choice to enter prostitution – either as a seller or as a client. However, the current situation was also seen as a development from the so-called sexual revolution, where prostitution was seen as the commercialisation of sexual freedom, and had to be fought. Homosexual prostitution between men was touched on very briefly in the inquiry, and in the experts' report; it was seen, among other things, as a result of heterosexual society's contempt of homosexuality (Borg et al. 1981: 510).

Gendering the debate

The debate was gendered in the sense that the reasons for prostitution were generally seen to lie in a patriarchal society, where women were subject to men's oppression both economically, sexually and in the work structure. It was pressure from the women's movement that initiated the official investigation in the first place. In the parliamentary debate representatives from all parties used arguments such as 'commercialisation of women's bodies', 'counterproductive to equality', 'contempt of women' (RP 1982: 159: 152). However, both men and women were seen as victims of a commercialised society in which individuals were objectified. To eliminate prostitution, an overall change of gender roles in society had to come about. Karin Söder, the Minister of Social Affairs, stated that 'prostitution cannot be seen as a woman's question. However, at the same time I want to emphasise that the woman is the most exploited and vulnerable exposed party in prostitution' (RP 1982: 159: 153). Thus, there was an interesting contradiction in the discussion, where a patriarchal and commercial society was the ground for prostitution, but the question was to be regarded as a human question, which in a sense degendered it. Prostitution was seen as a social question, like drug abuse or any other societal problem.

Policy outcome

On 1 July 1982 the law prohibiting public pornographic shows came into effect. There was no criminalisation of prostitution, which also had been strongly opposed in the investigation, the experts' separate report and the government proposal.

Women's movement impact

A coalition of thirteen of the autonomous and party-organised women's movements had participated in gendering the debate by questioning an ongoing official investigation, and requesting a separate investigation into prostitution. The organisations were representatives from both the 'old' and 'new' women's movement and turned to the Ministry of Justice with their demands. Although the organisations held different political positions, they were able to agree on the issue of rape and prostitution (Thomsson 2000: 51, 55). A number of women participated in the parliamentary debate and women's organisations participated in the 'remiss' process, although most of them represented the 'old' women's movement. Some supported the suggestions of the government; others wanted the john to be criminalised. In the first step, the government met the demands of the women's movement when it initiated a separate investigation into prostitution. This result can be described as a dual response in the initiating stage, since not only were the demands from the women's movement met, but some of them were also included in the 'remiss' procedure. However, not all representatives of the women's movement were included; the autonomous women's movement was also not included and did not submit any opinions to government (Prop. 1981/82: 187: 36).

Women's policy agency activities

The period 1981–2 saw a reconstructing of the WPAs. When the non-socialist coalition won the election in 1976 it established a parliamentary Gender Equality Committee. The gender equality question was moved from the prime minister's cabinet, and a cross-sectional Minister of Gender Equality without a portfolio was established in 1981. An advisory unit to the minister was organised, which meets four times a year, where the posts are held by representatives from twenty-eight different organisations. Also a Gender Equality Unit (Jämställdhetsenheten) was established at the Department for Labour. Since then the organisation of the WPA has remained more or less the same. Karin Andersson from the Centre Party was given the post of Minister of Gender Equality, and at the same time held the post of Minister for Immigration (Pincus 1998: 17–19). The law on gender equality had been established in 1980 (SFS 1991: 433), as had the Equal Opportunities Ombudsman (JämO); its main goal was to fight gender discrimination in the workplace. The Equal Opportunities Ombudsman had been involved in the 'remiss' process when the 1981 proposal concerning prostitution was discussed and supported the preventive measures against prostitution. It was also in favour of the proposal not to criminalise prostitution. The women's policy agency's activity must be characterised as symbolic, since it did not participate in the discussion.

Women's movement characteristics

During the first debate the women's movement can be considered as consolidated in the sense that the 'old' movement had institutionalised organisations (such as the Fredrika Bremer Association and the political parties' women's organisations). The 'new' women's movement had also consolidated its structure and had the endurance and the strength to mobilise the different organisations around a mutual issue. It worked together with representatives from the political parties' women's organisations, and was mainly socialist or left (Thomsson 2000).

Traditionally the Swedish women's movement has been characterised as being more concerned with women's right to work than with questions concerning sexuality (Hirdman 2001; Isaksson 2001). However, the question of prostitution seemed to be high on the agenda at this particular point in time, and different women's organisations were able to unite on the issue in the initial stages. When the state response came, several parts of the movement participated in the debate, but their responses were now different. Thus, the movement was cohesive in the beginning and divided at the end of the debate. There was little outside opposition to the movement's demands and no counter-movement.

Policy environment

The SDP, with a few short breaks, had been in power since the 1930s. However, in 1976, the year before the commission to investigate prostitution was appointed, the Social Democrats lost the election. Sweden acquired a new government consisting of a coalition of the Liberals (Folkpartiet), the Centre (Centerpartiet) and the Moderate (Conservative) (Moderaterna) parties. Its prime minister was from the Centre Party. In 1981–2 the coalition comprised the Liberals and the Centre Party alone. The policy sub-system was closed, but the women's movement was involved in some of the 'remiss' processing. The discussion was gendered. The policy approach within the policy sub-system can be characterised as matching, since the demands of the movement were met, with little resistance, and the general attitude was one in favour of social policies.

Debate 2: The second commission on prostitution and the proposal for a Violence against Women Act (*Kvinnofrid*), 1995–1998

How issue came to the public agenda

After the proposal and the ensuing law of 1982 a number of bills were introduced in parliament in which the request to criminalise the client recurred frequently. During the period 1983–93 more than fifty party and member bills concerning prostitution were proposed, and of those about thirty proposed the criminalisation of the john. These came from representatives of all parties, sometimes both men and women from the same party, sometimes only women, but never groups of men alone.

The periods 1984–7 and 1990–2 were intense periods of parliamentary party and member bills. These were of three types: requests to criminalise only the client, requests to criminalise both parties, and requests calling for a new official investigation into prostitution. To criminalise only the prostitute, regardless of sex, was never an option. In 1993 the Parliamentary Committee of Justice's (Justitieutskottet) 'remiss' recommended that the matter be further investigated (1992/93: JuU15).

The Minister of Social Affairs and Gender Equality, Bengt Westerberg (Liberal Party), officially set the commission its task on 11 March 1993. It was to map the prevalence of both hetero- and homosexual prostitution in Sweden, and discuss the problem and reasons for prostitution. Furthermore, the commission had to investigate whether criminalisation could be an appropriate measure to fight prostitution or whether other solutions were to be recommended. It also had to investigate how to communicate informative work to the general public on prostitution nationally and internationally (SOU 1995: 15: 37). The commission was another so-called 'one-woman commission' headed by a senior civil servant (formerly the Equal Opportunities Ombudsman), and her expert group contained an equal number of women and men (SOU 1995: 15: 3; Gould 2001: 439).

Soon after it had become known that there was to be an official commission, another bill was put forward in parliament. This bill was different in character from the earlier party bills. Its support cut across party lines and the proposers of the bill were women from the SDP, the Left Party and the Liberals (1992/93: Ju622). They argued that there were already sufficient grounds for criminalisation of the john. This should not have to wait until after the commission had reached its conclusions. Nevertheless, the Parliamentary Committee on Justice later rejected the bill (and the additional 1992/93: Ju616) on exactly those grounds: there was no reason for parliament to make a statement on a question which was under investigation (1993/94: JuU03).

After two years of investigation the report from the one-woman commission proposed that both parties, the prostitute and the client, should be criminalised (SOU 1995: 15: 224). It would be 'peculiar' if only one party was seen as guilty of a crime, while the other was innocent. The effect of criminalisation would also be greater if both parties were included. The commission also suggested using another term to describe prostitution: gender or genital trade (*könshandel*).[1] This would focus on both parties in the transaction, the seller and the client. Since prostitution traditionally signified the woman in a heterosexual sex trade, this new term would also make it possible to include homosexual prostitution. It has been suggested that a 'fear of the foreign' was an important characteristic of the investigation and the ensuing debate in parliament (Gould 2001). There were elements of this, but the presence of gender equality arguments in the discussion was more frequent. Two of the experts on the commission disagreed with the final result (SOU 1995: 15: 241).

On the same day the report was made public two prominent experts attacked the results in an article in the liberal morning paper *Dagens Nyheter*. Both writers had been involved in the 1977 commission and were among those who had left that earlier commission. In their article they stated that to criminalise both parties obscured what prostitution was really about – men's power and men's sexuality. Rather, criminalisation of the buyer would mark a 'historical turning point in relation to that double standard which always had permeated the patriarchal society, which is the basis of the existence of prostitution' (Månsson and Olsson, *Dagens Nyheter* 14 March 1995). The editorial in the social democratic evening paper *Aftonbladet* the same evening stated that only the clients ought to be criminalised and that few women in the streets had chosen their situation freely (Karin Andersson, *Aftonbladet* 14 March 1995). The next day the *Dagens Nyheter*'s editorial stated that 'to punish them [the women] is to punish the victims. If criminalisation is seen as necessary to make a social "impact", it would be enough to penalise the purchase' (Arne Höök, *Dagens Nyheter* 15 March 1995).

The 'remiss' procedure was completed by November 1995, and only two of the sixty-four organisations involved supported the commission proposal. They were the Women's Forum and the Stockholm Police

Authority (S97/8122/IFO). The majority was opposed to any kind of criminalisation, but some also wanted to criminalise only the client. The Equal Opportunities Ombudsman, the Public Health Institute, the Central Committee of the Church of Sweden, and the Liberal, Centre and Social Democratic parties' women's organisations supported the criminalisation of the john.

After the 1995 commission report had been severely criticised in the media, party and member bills continued to be delivered in parliament. On 2 October 1996 another bill supported by all political parties' women's organisations (except the Conservatives') proposed a bill suggesting the criminalisation of the john. Other bills had made the same request in early 1995 and late 1996, with representatives for the Liberals, Centre and Social Democrats (1994/95: A802; 1994/95: A820; 1996/97: A806; 1996/97: Ju714; 1996/97: Ju718; 1996/97: Ju917). The Parliamentary Committee on Justice had dismissed these bills on the grounds that the question had been investigated, and it was still being prepared in government (1996/97: JuU11). In the following parliamentary debate in April 1997 it was obvious that female MPs were disturbed by the fact that the expected government's bill took so long. One woman from the Green Party stated that 'the mission for us women in parliament is now to see to it that government speeds up the drafting of a bill' (RP 1996/97: 86).

The proposal by the government that came in May 1998, *Kvinnofrid* (Violence against Women Act), had as part of its overall proposal about violence against women the suggestion that only the client in a prostitution relationship should be criminalised (Prop 1997/98: 55: 15). The government argued that 'although prostitution as such is not a wanted occurrence in society, it is not reasonable also to criminalise the one who, at least in most cases, is the weaker party and is used by others who want to satisfy their own sexual urges' (Prop. 1997/98: 50: 104).

Dominant frame of debate

When the recommendation to criminalise prostitution came from the official investigation into prostitution in 1995, the media criticised the proposal. The argument was that few women had freely chosen to be streetwalkers and that the victims should not be punished. In the 'remiss' procedure a minority supported the commission's proposal; the majority refuted the idea of criminalisation of both parties, but a substantial group recommended the criminalisation of the john. The suggestion of criminalising only the john could be heard again towards the end of the debate, as it had been forcefully during the mid-1980s and early 1990s.

It became especially evident in the ensuing government bill. The frame seemed to be a question of criminalisation: none at all or of the client.

Gendering the debate

The debate was highly gendered when it re-emerged. Female MPs were united across party lines in their proposal to criminalise the john. Although the commission had as one of its tasks also to investigate homosexual prostitution, the majority of the debate concerned heterosexual prostitution. When the report from the commission was presented, a major characteristic of the debate was rather an attempt at de-gendering, or neutralising the question, by the suggestion of criminalising both parties, which would repress the woman in prostitution even more. It was pointed out that the commission itself was in disagreement, and that when the chairperson talked about free choice and equality she missed the point. Prostitution was a question of oppression, and prostitutes and their clients would not become more equal if they were both criminalised.

Policy outcome

The processing of the commission's report took a long time. The government also chose to wait for the investigation into violence against women (*Kvinnofrid*, SOU 1995: 60) before drafting a bill. Along with other proposals concerning violence against women, it also suggested the criminalisation of the client, or rather the 'buying of sexual services'. The penalty would be fines or imprisonment for no more than six months (SOU 1997/98: 55: 15). The proposal thus contradicted the recommendation that had been made by the commission in 1995.

Women's movement impact

The intense lobbying in parliament mainly came from representatives from the women in party politics and the women's organisations of the political parties. Both female and male MPs proposed bills together, but there were also bills supported by only the women's party organisations. In 1997 a bill was proposed that united all women's party organisations except the Conservatives (1996/97: Ju718). ROKS (the National Organisation for Women's Shelters and Young Women's Shelters in Sweden) has a regular yearly meeting with women in parliament. In 1992, 1994 and 1995 the criminalisation of the john was on the agenda of these meetings (ROKS 2002). Both ROKS and the Fredrika Bremer Association were part of the 'remiss' procedure and wanted to criminalise the john.

The state response could be seen as co-optation since the main demand from the women's movement (to criminalise the client) was not met by the commission. Still, part of the women's movement was invited to participate in the 'remiss' procedure, and others participated without being invited.

Women's policy agency activities

The Minister for Gender Equality, Westerberg, gave the task of investigating prostitution to the commission. He was the leader of the Liberal Party and the first man to hold the post of Minister of Gender Equality. He was also the Minister of Social Affairs, and took an active public interest in gender equality affairs. He had a prominent position as a politician, and the gender question was given much attention. Nevertheless, it was in his position as the Minister of Social Affairs that he initiated the investigation into prostitution. The commission's task was 'in an unbiased way [to] investigate whether criminalisation of prostitution' was an adequate measure to fight prostitution. However, it also stated that to criminalise the buyer alone would most likely make way for blackmail, and was thus not to be recommended (SOU 1995: 15: 225, 257). The unbiased nature of criminalisation thus was limited in its scope from the outset. The commissioner was a former Gender Equality Ombudsman, and a femocrat. The WPA initiated the commission, but the commission was not feminist from the women's movement perspective, since their demands were to initiate legislation to criminalise the customer, rather than to initiate another commission. One debater stated that 'many had expected that the new prostitution commission would take the remaining step and criminalise the client' and the proposal was met with surprise. 'The Swedish gender equality politics weakest fixed star – gender neutrality – was applied to history's most unequal situation!' (Kristina Hultman, *Aftonbladet* 26 April 1996). The WPA must be characterised as non-feminist in the sense that it was involved in the issue of prostitution, at least enough to initiate a commission. However, the outspoken demand from the women's movement to criminalise the john was clearly already disregarded in the guidelines of the commission.

Women's movement characteristics

During the early 1990s the so-called *Stödstrumporna,* a 'secret feminist network', gained much media attention. However, on their agenda was restoring women's political representation in parliament, whereas questions of sexuality in terms of prostitution were less discussed (Ulmanen

1998). Within parliament, some of the women's organisations within the parties continued to present bills to criminalise the john. The strength to join forces on this question across party lines suggests that the movement was in a stage of consolidation. Although it was a coalition of women from different parties, the Moderate (Conservative) Party Women never joined in. So in terms of being left or right, the women's movement was closer to the left, since all parties but the Moderate Women could unite.

The issue was high on the agenda for the organised women's movement within parliament. In at least two cases the issue united women across party lines, and during the period investigated here it happened in 1996. Women from the Left Party, the Greens, the Liberals, the Christian Democrats, the Social Democrats and the Centre Party requested the criminalisation of the john (1996/97: Ju718). The movement can be seen as divided in the beginning, since their bills were not all suggesting the criminalisation of the john. However, towards the end of the debate they joined in a mutual bill and can be seen as cohesive. There was a weak opposition within parliament; most joined in a general feeling of wanting to better the situation for women.

Policy environment

When the commission to investigate prostitution was given its task there was a non-socialist coalition government in power. Nevertheless, the Minister of Gender Equality (in his position as Minister of Social Affairs) requested the investigation. In 1994 Sweden again had a socialist government and the fact that gender equality was high on the agenda is demonstrated by the fact the vice prime-minister, Mona Sahlin, was also made Minister of Gender Equality. The project of gender mainstreaming was initiated. However, at the end of 1995, the vice prime minister resigned after an affair involving the private use of government credit cards and some private debts which was given much attention in the media. The Minister of Gender Equality was moved to the Ministry of Labour. This emphasised that gender equality was again a question of equality in working life and given a less prominent position; the vice prime minister no longer held the position (Ulmanen 1998). The policy sub-system was closed, but the women's movement participated in the remiss process. The dominant political approach during this debate changed. The party in power changed from conservative to social democratic. From what must be seen as an incompatible fit, with an official investigation initiated against the wishes of the women's movements, a fit emerged when the government's bill proposed the criminalisation of the john. However, this fit only came about through extensive lobbying from women in parliament.

Debate 3: The proposal for *Kvinnofrid* (Violence against Women Act) to the Law against Purchasing Sexual Services, 1997/98–1999

How issue came to the public agenda

The proposal for a Violence against Women Act came in February 1998 and was presented by the Minister of Gender Equality, Ulrika Messing, and the prime minister, Göran Persson. It was debated in parliament at the end of May that same year. The bill contained suggestions to counteract violence against women, sexual harassment in work and prostitution (SOU 1997/98: 55). It received attention in the media, and one of the conservative editorials, written by a woman, stated that the government 'confessed to radical feminism' (Susanna Popova, *Svenska Dagbladet* 8 March 1998; cf. Gould 2001).

After the proposal had been presented it was followed by a number of party and member bills. The Greens, the Centre Party, the Social Democrats and the Left Party were all in support of the proposal, the Christian Democrats, the Conservatives and the Liberals were against. However, the Liberals were divided by sex, and the Liberal women delivered a bill supporting the proposal (1997/98: Ju708). On 24 March 1998, the Parliamentary Committee on Justice considered and recommended the government proposal, but also stated that criminalisation alone could not reduce prostitution (1997/98: JuU13 Kvinnofrid).

When the proposal was presented in parliament the media emphasised the consensus among the parties concerning violence against women (Unsigned, *Göteborgsposten*, 29 May 1998: 37). However, the issue of criminalising the client in prostitution caused debate in parliament (RP 1997/98: 114). The Moderate Party and the Liberals were against criminalisation. The Christian Democrats supported criminalisation of both parties in prostitution. The arguments were that prostitution would go underground and become more difficult to control and that the proposal seemed to be more symbolic rather than realistic. The Christian Democrats argued that every person is responsible for his or her actions, thus both parties should be criminalised.

Those in support of the proposal, the Left, the Social Democrats, the Greens and the Centre Party, argued that two-thirds of the current prostitution business was already carried out underground, and that the new law would decrease the demand for sexual services. Women have the right to be the mistresses of their own sexuality, although it was emphasised that prostitution was *not* about *women's* sexuality. Other characteristics of the debate were the references to the current and expected future situation in Europe, the 'permissive attitude' within the EU, and the risk of its spreading to Sweden (RP 1993/94: 86). The Swedish law was seen as the 'antidote' for what were perceived as 'liberal' tendencies (RP 1998/99: 59). The problem of trafficking and foreign women being transported to Sweden for prostitution was also discussed (RP 1998/99: 43).

After the bill was passed by parliament, the debate in the media took off. Compared with the debate in 1995 it was now more intense. Critical voices were heard in May and June 1998. There was a debate between a well-known female debater on issues on sexuality, together with a sex worker, and two women from the Left Party. According to the first pair, the law would stigmatise a group of workers – the sex workers. They criticised what they saw as the political arguments for the law, the selling of women's bodies. Women in prostitution did *not* sell their bodies, they sold sexual services. The supporters of the law were pictured as middle-class feminists, who endorsed the traditional division of women into whores and madonnas (Petra Östergren/Lilian Andersson, *Aftonbladet* 11 May and 15 June 1998). They were countered with the argument that research and verdicts from *other* prostitutes gave a distinctly different picture, and that their article lacked an analysis of male society and the acknowledgement that sexuality was formed on economic, social and psychological terms together.

However, there were reasons to take the 'prostitution lobby' seriously, since to see prostitution as oppression of women was unusual south of the Swedish border (Marianne Eriksson and Ina Lindroth, *Aftonbladet* 30 May 1998).

There was also support for the law. A 'former prostitute' stated that the law would be supportive: 'Perhaps we [women in prostitution] will not be doubted about being abused when prostitution in itself is seen as abuse.' When in the future it became less acceptable to buy women's bodies, fewer johns would demand sex services and the market would decline (Jenny Günay, *Dagens Nyheter* 6 August 1998).

On 1 January 1999 the law against purchasing sexual services came into force (Lag 1998: 408). Two women representatives of the SDP stated in parliament that 'everybody knows that the whole of Europe follows the "Swedish model" when it comes to drugs, [and the model is] now completed with the fight against prostitution'. Also, the women stated that 'Sweden takes the leading position when it comes to fighting prostitution' (RP 1998/99: 45).

Dominant frame of the debate

Comparisons with Europe and other ways of thinking about prostitution were made to a greater extent than before. However, it was also noted that the Dutch argument (just as the Swedish argument) was to improve the conditions for the women in prostitution. A new framework had entered the Swedish debate, and prostitution could now also be discussed in terms of a profession, as work. The debate was also more heated than before, but the proponents of the sex work view were mostly to be found in the media rather than in parliament. Most of the debaters in parliament and in the media were women. As one journalist described it, the American Sex Wars had entered the Swedish debate concerning pornography, but also that concerning prostitution (Ulrika Lorentzi, *Bang* 1998: 2).

Gendering the debate

The debate was gendered in that the discussion concerned women and men in prostitution. The collective strength of women in changing the oppression of women in prostitution was emphasised. The chairperson of the Social Democratic Women stated that the expected law was a good example of what could be attained when women held 50 per cent of the seats in politics, and when 'women issues' became political questions in their own right (RP 1997/98: 114). The Minister of Gender Equality, Ulrika Messing, stated that the decision about to be made was historic, and would make a difference: 'I believe that in twenty years today's decision will be described as the big leap forward to fight violence against women and to reach *Kvinnofrid*' (Women's peace) (RP 1997/98: 114). She also emphasised the importance of years of lobbying by women in politics and women in volunteer organisations. There were still very few references to homosexual prostitution. The split between different opinions was evident and was mostly stressed by feminists and other debaters in the media, whereas most women in parliament were in agreement.

Policy outcome

The government's bill included the criminalisation of the client, and parliament subsequently voted for the law to criminalise the buying of sexual services. This law came into effect on 1 January 1999. Parliament accepted the proposal with 181 votes in favour of the proposal and 92 against, while 63 members were absent. The majority of those voting against the proposal belonged to the Moderate or Liberal parties

(89 votes). The Christian Democrats abstained from voting (RP 1997/98: 115).

Women's movement impact

The women's movement's goal was the criminalisation of the john; this was supported by both the party women and organisations such as the National Organisation for Women's Shelters and the Young Women's Shelters in Sweden (Angela Beausang, *Aftonbladet* 27 September 1997). The women in the organised party movement were also involved in the process and could participate in the voting on the law. The women's movement impact must be characterised as dual response. However, some feminist debaters outside parliament but present in the media supported a view of prostitution as sex work.

Women's policy agency activities

By the end of the 1990s the Minister of Gender Equality was connected to the Ministry of Labour, a less prominent position than before. The Minister of Gender Equality, Ulrika Messing, presented the proposal for a Violence against Women Act in parliament. Although the Minister of Gender Equality seemingly had less impact than before, Messing herself participated in the debate, both inside and outside parliament, and emphasised Sweden's unique way of handling prostitution: 'There is no other country which has tried the road we are now entering. We shall set an example in gender equality questions by criminalising prostitution in the way we do' (RP 1997/98: 114). She participated in gendering the parliamentary debate, but also the media debate. The role of the women's policy agency can be classified as insider and feminist.

Women's movement characteristics

The women's movement in parliament was still consolidated and close to the left. All women in parliament except the conservatives supported the issue, and argued for the criminalisation of the john. The Social Democratic Women was the group that seemed to take the lead in promoting the question. However, many of the men in parliament (especially within the Green Party and the Left) supported the proposal to criminalise the john. The view within parts of the movement itself was that it was now sufficiently strong to have the power to influence men in parliament, and have them vote in the direction of the movement.

The issue was high on the agenda, and debated constantly both in parliament and in the media after the proposal was presented. Women from different parties forged alliances, and some even went against their party's line to vote according to their feminist views on the matter. However, the movement must be seen as cohesive at the beginning of the debate and divided at the end. The split became evident in the discussion on the proposal in parliament, where the liberal women were accused of withdrawing from the collective decision to support the proposal. The counter-movement to the proposal must be seen as moderate. Both women and men within the Moderate Party argued forcefully against the proposal, calling it 'symbolic'. At the same time, the opposition stated that it assumed that the proposal would be voted through in parliament (RP 1997/98: 114).

Policy environment

After the election in 1998 the SDP formed a minority government, with the support of the Left. However, the Social Democratic Women assumed the lead in promoting the issue of prostitution, and at the SDP congress in 1997, the chairwoman of the Social Democratic Women pushed through the proposal to criminalise the john – against the party leaders. In an interview she stated that she thought the results of the congress would influence other men in parliament: 'I would like to see the male member of parliament who wants to go against this proposal – unless he is a conservative' ('Kriminalisera torskarna', *Aftonbladet* 16 September 1997). The policy sub-system was closed. The political parties' women's organisations could and did participate in the voting on the law, but the autonomous movement could not. The dominant approach and that of the women's movement fitted because of the extensive pressure exercised by feminist women *inside* parliament on the dominant approach.

Conclusion

The three debates on prostitution in Sweden show that the women's movement has been a strong force in putting the issue on the political agenda. In all debates, the movement received policy satisfaction from the state, but not necessarily in the way they wanted. The women's movement was involved in the process in all three debates. The women's policy agencies had a marginal position in the first debate and an insider's role in the last two debates. Their impact, however, must be seen in relation to the women's movement, which was much larger.

Nevertheless, in the last debate the Gender Equality Minister presented the proposal, and took part in the debate with a strong feminist perspective, supporting the goals of the women's movement – both in parliament and in the media. Although not perhaps always in the forefront, the women's policy agencies have not been working *against* the women's movement and its goals. In the case of the second commission on prostitution, it had a different definition of gender equality and feminism than did parts of the women's movement.

The women's movement has emphasised the issue, although with varying intensity, during all selected debates. The lobbying for criminalising the john, however, came after the first investigation into prostitution in the early 1980s. The first commission on prostitution in 1981 looked upon prostitution as a social question, but from a distinct gender perspective. Nevertheless, both commissions were beset with conflicts and arguments within the expert group, and between the experts and the appointed commissioner. When the long-standing goal of the criminalisation of the john was finally achieved in 1999, the closeness to the left and a Social Democratic government was evident, but the Social Democratic Women also had to fight their own party comrades to obtain support on the issue. The criminalisation of the john must be seen as the result of steady lobbying by the women's movement, and not as a part of a 'feminist state policy'.

The impact of the law is now on the agenda, where critical voices argue that, although street prostitution has decreased, hidden prostitution has increased (BRÅ-rapport 2000: 4; SoS-rapport 2000: 5). In parliament there are now bills proposing criminalisation of the selling of sex (1999/2000: Ju717; 2001/02: Ju291), but also bills that want to increase state action against trafficking of women and to work against a legalisation of prostitution, both in the EU and in the UN (2001/02: Ju267; 2001/02: Fi219; 2001/02; Ju299; 2001/02: U308). On this evidence, criminalising the john is not the end of the prostitution debate in Sweden.

NOTES

I want to thank Professor Diane Sainsbury at the Department of Political Science, Stockholm University, for her help. This chapter presents the first results from a larger, recently begun project: 'To trade in sex: regulation, liberalisation or criminalisation? Prostitution politics in Sweden 1930–2000' financed by the Riksbankens Jubileumsfond; by the chapter Vetenskapsrådet (VR), through the research programme Gender, Citizenship and Public Policies 1848–1998, and VINNOVA, through the group FOS for (Feminist Organisation Studies), headed by Professor Anna Wahl at the Stockholm School of Economics.

1. The word 'kön' in Swedish being equivalent both to the English word sex (gender) and genitals, but not to the word sex (as in sexual intercourse).

13 The invisible issue: prostitution and trafficking of women and girls in the United States

Dorothy McBride Stetson

Introduction

US politics is striking in the absence of discussion of prostitution in public debate. In comparison with other aspects of sexuality, such as pornography, rape, child abuse or lesbian rights, prostitution has been low on just about everybody's agenda: moralists; law reformers; police; feminists. A majority of the public considers prostitution immoral, and the politicians seem content to leave the long-standing criminalisation regime in place (Weitzer 2000). Activists campaigned briefly for decriminalisation in the 1970s, but soon feminists were divided over policy options (Hobson 1987; Baldwin 1992). Most agreed that prostitution is the product of male domination. Liberal feminists, however, accepted the fact that some women choose prostitution, and supported removal of legal and social burdens on that choice. Radical feminists, on the other hand, rejected the idea that free choice is possible and considered prostitution, along with rape, sexual harassment, pornography and child sexual abuse, to be part of systematic sexual exploitation of women by men.

In the 1980s, prostitutes' rights groups formed; the most famous was Margo St James' COYOTE (Call Off Your Old Tired Ethics). They demanded complete decriminalisation and the guarantee of their right to engage in what they considered sex work. Little changed in the laws (Weitzer 1991). The high point of the campaign occurred in 1994 when the San Francisco Board of Supervisors formed a Task Force on Prostitution to examine alternatives to criminalisation (Weitzer 1999). The prostitutes' advocates dominated the task force which quickly recommended decriminalisation. In conventional form, the politicians ignored the report. COYOTE found few allies in the women's movement; only a minority of the feminists saw prostitution as a normal occupation (Larum 1998). Most sided with anti-prostitution groups, some organised by former prostitutes, who considered prostitution as a form of violence against women (Holsopple 1999).

Selection of debates

The US federal structure places primary responsibility for what are called 'police powers' with the state governments. While there are, potentially, fifty-one (including the District of Columbia) different policies relating to prostitution, in this area of policy, like so many others, the federal government sets standards and guidelines. In 1919 Congress passed the Standard Vice Repression Act which took a strong stand against prostitution (DeCou 1998). After this, every state enacted laws to control and prohibit prostitution. These laws, which, for the most part, remain intact, criminalised selling and buying sex, solicitation, pimping and related activities. In the 1970s, there was some discussion of reform of these laws, but only minor changes resulted (Rosenbleet and Pariente 1973; Wandling 1976; Murray 1979; Weitzer 2000). An exception was the establishment of a system of regulated prostitution in rural areas of Nevada (Symanski 1985). Since then, the states have paid little attention to their prostitution laws. Even in the late 1980s, when many states empanelled gender bias commissions to review criminal and civil law and legal practices for their effects on women's status, only Florida's commission included prostitution as a subject for study. As a result, Florida statutes were amended to give a person the right to sue for damages against another who coerced her into prostitution (Florida Supreme Court 1990; Baldwin 1992).

While prostitution has not been on policy agendas, trafficking for prostitution has attracted some attention in Congress exercising its constitutional power to regulate interstate commerce and immigration. An ancient law – the Mann Act – remains on the books (Langum 1994; Beckman 1995; Conant 1996). When enacted in 1910, this Act was called the 'White Slave Traffic Act' (United States 1910). It was the culmination of a series of statutes dating back to 1875; at the time, the discourse on the issue likened the fate of women brought into the country or a state to Africans brought to the USA earlier in the century as slaves. The Mann Act (which today still takes its name from its 1910 sponsor in the Congress) made it a federal felony knowingly to

transport or cause to be transported or aid or assist in obtaining transportation for, or in transporting, in interstate or foreign commerce, or in any Territory or in the District of Columbia, any *woman or girl for the purpose of prostitution or debauchery, or for any other immoral purpose to induce, entice, or compel such woman or girl to become a prostitute or to give herself up to debauchery, or to engage in any other immoral practice* . . . (italics added).

In contrast to lack of policy debates on prostitution, there have been several debates on trafficking in the past thirty years. I have selected three for this study: the Protection of Children against Sexual Exploitation Act 1976–8; the Sexual Abuse and Pornography Act of 1984; and the Trafficking Victims Protection Act of 1998–2000.[1] These represent the policy sub-system since they all have taken place in Congress, the primary decision system in the USA on trafficking. They are representative of the range and salience of this 'invisible issue'. There is one from each decade – the 1970s, 1980s and 1990s – and they are the only debates to produce changes in federal policy relating to trafficking for prostitution.

Debate 1: Sexual exploitation of children, 1976–1978

How issue came to the public agenda

By the 1960s, the FBI had cut back on enforcing the federal ban on trafficking of women (Grittner 1990). People could be arrested for transporting only women, not men, across state lines. Because, technically, one could violate the law by crossing a state line with a girlfriend for a romantic weekend, the Mann Act criminalised what many men were doing. When they did make an arrest, the FBI was criticised for arbitrary enforcement. In addition, the moral outrage that had given rise to the Mann Act, and the Act itself, seemed out of touch with the sexual revolution and changes in the status of women (Young 1998).

By the 1970s the problem of trafficking for prostitution was back in the national headlines. In 1973, Gail Sheehy published what might be called an exposé about prostitution called *Hustling: Prostitution in Our Wide Open Society*, which was also made into a TV movie. She followed this with a series of articles about girls lured to New York and put into prostitution. Somewhere along the line, the idea of a 'pipeline' of traffic in girls (usually portrayed as blondes) from states like Ohio, Michigan and Minnesota to become hookers for Times Square pimps (usually portrayed as black) in New York caught the public imagination. A crusade by Al Palmquist, a Minneapolis police detective and self-styled preacher, seemed to resurrect the idea of white slavery and debauchery and put a 'seventies' face on it (Palmquist 1978).

As intriguing as this story was, it did not propel the Mann Act to the congressional agenda for action. Rather, that story begins with the publication of another book, *For Money or Love* by Robin Lloyd (1976). This was a study of boy prostitution and suggested a connection with child pornography. Congress had already taken up the issue of child sexual abuse and runaways. The Child Abuse Prevention and Treatment Act of 1974 established a centre for gathering information and assisting states in education and reporting with grants for specific programmes. Soon connections were made between teenage runaways, child pornography and juvenile prostitution. A series of news stories in the *Chicago Tribune* revealed that the most serious problem with prostitution was for boys, not girls. The networks took up the topic of teenage prostitutes, and a bill was drafted to include sexual abuse of children – defined as use in pornography or sending child pornography across state lines – as a federal criminal offence. Another player in the arena was Judianne Densen-Gerber, director of the Odyssey Institute and a psychiatrist who had been active in promoting an anti-child pornography protection bill (Geiser 1979).

Congress convened hearings; it was only during those hearings that the idea of amending the Mann Act arose. Policy-makers found evidence of the use of children in making pornographic films and magazines. Next, it was alleged that children were being brought into the country and across state lines to produce this pornography. Most of the child victims were boys, and no federal law adequately punished producers or distributors of child pornography. The Mann Act prohibited the transport of women but did not apply to minors, at the time, defined as persons under sixteen years of age. Policy-makers agreed that the 1978 Act would introduce the anti-pornography provision into child abuse law and amend the Mann Act to extend to trafficking in minors.

Dominant frame of debate

The dominant frame of the debate in the congressional hearings in 1977 focused on a redefinition of the pornography question from the usual contest of free speech versus morality enforced by the Supreme Court to a problem of sexual abuse of children. In 1973 the Court had established guidelines for regulation of obscenity under the First Amendment guarantees of freedom of speech and the press (*Miller vs. California*). These were a compromise in the dilemma but have made it difficult for government to limit the sale of pornography by and for adults. With evidence of child pornography, the campaigners portrayed a definite harm going beyond questions of personal morality and outweighing First Amendment freedoms of the purveyors.

Congressional advocates pictured themselves arrayed against a massive industry, a dark underworld where innocent children were bought and sold as commodities. Such children were especially vulnerable to child molesters and chicken hawks – men who prey on boys. Policy actors readily accepted the assumption of a connection between posing for pornographic pictures and being exploited as prostitutes. The only way to fight this enemy would be through a federal law which would punish the pornographers and extend the Mann Act to cover children.

Gendering the debate

For the most part the debate was not gendered. What gender references there were referred to boys. Examples of exploited children showed boys being preyed on by adult males – child molesters and chicken hawks. Witnesses claimed that child sex and pornography were basically boy–man phenomena. Police reported that most instances of coerced prostitution involved boys, despite the news outside Congress about the Minnesota pipeline. Inside the hearing rooms, the series of investigative reports by the *Chicago Tribune* on victimisation of boys was read into the record. Girls as victims were largely ignored with a couple of exceptions. The director of a National Coalition for Children's Justice said that girls were the subject of the hardest core pornography and subject to rape. Judianne Densen-Gerber opened one hearing with graphic testimony and examples of girls portrayed in sexually explicit photographs in magazines such as *Lollitots* and in cartoons from *Hustler*. The chair of the hearings cut her demonstration short claiming lack of time. Thus, the tenor of the debate seemed to counter the assumption that girls were the only victims of pornography and trafficking. A strong case was made that boys deserved equal protection of the Mann Act with girls. While radical feminists agreed that child prostitution and pornography were sexual abuse, they linked such abuse to the overall exploitation of women (Rush 1980; Brownmiller 1999). Contrary to congressional views, however, they pointed out that the victims were overwhelmingly female and the offenders male. They did not participate in the policy debate to express these views and took little interest in it.

Prostitutes had begun to organise in the early 1970s, claiming that prostitution was a privacy issue, and in 1973 the National Organisation for Women (NOW) passed a resolution calling for decriminalisation. The issue remained low on the NOW agenda, and there was no serious effort for reform. Later in the 1970s, divisions arose among feminists over prostitution (Baldwin 1992). In 1977 Women against Violence against Women (WAVAW) began an anti-pornography campaign that led to the formation of Women against Pornography (WAP). They agreed that pornography and prostitution were all aspects of male sexual domination. A small but devoted group led by Kathleen Barry became abolitionists, likening prostitution to sexual slavery (Barry 1979). It is interesting that much of the same language used by radical feminists to describe trafficking in women was used by Congress to describe child (boy) victims of sexual exploitation.

Policy outcome

In January 1978, the Congress enacted the Protection of Children against Sexual Exploitation Act (United States 1978) which made it a crime to 'employ, use, persuade, induce, entice, or coerce any minor to engage in, or assist any other person to engage in, any sexually explicit conduct for the purpose of producing any visual or print medium depicting such conduct'. It also prohibited shipping child pornography across state lines. The key provision relating to trafficking was Section 2433, the amendment to the Mann Act adding a new offence: 'Any person who transports, finances in whole or part the transportation of, or otherwise causes or facilitates the movement of, any minor in interstate or foreign commerce . . . with the intent that such minor engage in prostitution; or that such minor engage in prohibited sexual conduct . . .' (United States 1978).

This formally redefined child pornography as sexual abuse, rather than morality/free speech and extended the prohibitions on trafficking of minors to include boys as well as girls.

Women's movement impact

Only two women participated in the policy debate over child sexual exploitation: Representative Elizabeth Holtzman (Democrat, New York) was the sole female member of the congressional committees that considered the issue; Judianne Denson-Gerber was the only woman presenting testimony. Men dominated the process; women were token participants, not enough to consider this a procedural state response for descriptive representation.

Those movement activists who were aware of the new policy were ambivalent about its relation to their goals. They did not oppose the extension of the Mann Act to boys as well as girls, but disagreed with Congress's claim that the principal victims of sexual exploitation were boys. Kathleen Barry's response is representative. She concluded that congressional attention in the 1970s to child sexual abuse through pornography and prostitution underscored the policy-makers' refusal to treat prostitution of adult women as sexual exploitation (Barry 1995: 225). At the same time she noted that the new law provided some resources to be used to help girls treated as adult prostitutes by pimps and customers. Rather than coinciding with (or being in opposition to) movement goals, the policy outcome was irrelevant. Therefore in the first debate, the state made no response to the women's movement.

Women's policy agency activities

The women's policy agency most likely to be involved in the debate over sexual exploitation of children was the National Commission on the Observance of International Women's Year 1975–7. Other women's policy agencies, such as the Women's Bureau and the Citizens Advisory Commission on the Status of Women (both inside the Department of Labor and devoted to improving the status of women workers), were attached to specific departments. The National Commission was a cross-sectional body, advisory to the president and Congress, created by congressional statute to convene conferences and develop a plan of action with respect to International Women's Year. The budget was sufficient to cover conference and publication expenses with little else. While the leadership was predominantly feminist, the commission had a mandate to take up a variety of issues relating to women's rights and status. Perhaps because of the growing controversy among feminists themselves, neither prostitution nor pornography was among these. The commission developed a plank relating to child abuse, endorsing treatment and prevention programmes. This women's policy agency did not contribute to the policy debate nor did it take a stand on the central question of trafficking of women in the USA. Thus the agency took a symbolic role in the debate over child sexual exploitation.

Women's movement characteristics

In the mid-1970s, the women's movement was at the zenith of its growth. This was reflected in the large number of organisations, events and activities and a series of victories in federal legislation (Costain 1992; Rosenfeld and Ward 1996). Movement participation in leftist organisations and the Democratic Party was also growing, as evidenced by their active presence at the 1976 Democratic presidential nominating convention. Nevertheless, the head of the party, President Jimmy Carter, was not warm to this feminist presence, and conflicts developed over his agenda, particularly on abortion funding questions (Stetson 2001c). This moderately close relationship persisted until the end of the Carter administration. Prostitution, pornography and child abuse were not high on the movement agenda. When discussed they produced divisions among movement activists which may account for their reluctance to place this as a high priority for action. With a weak feminist presence on the topic at hand, there was the absence of a counter-movement as well.

Policy environment

The left was in power during this debate, holding the presidency and both houses of Congress; the policy-making sub-system was moderately closed. In the absence of leadership from the White House or any administrative agencies, individual policy entrepreneurs drove the process of deliberation and debate. These activities centred in the congressional committees where the chairs (members of the majority party) controlled the agenda and determined who could participate. These prominent committee and sub-committee chairs worked with constituents, interest group representatives and other members of Congress to push their bill through the steps in the legislative process. The dominant norms favoured non-partisan treatment of children's sexuality and agreed that adults using children for sex was abuse and not protected by privacy rights. This dominant approach was compatible with the approach of feminists who commented on the issue (Rush 1980); the two approaches differed over the relation of issues of child sexual exploitation to women's rights.

Debate 2: Child Sexual Abuse and Pornography Act, 1984–1986

How issue came to the public agenda

Following the 1978 Act, the child pornography issue did not stray far from Congress's agenda. Leaders received reports that the new legislation had stimulated US Customs to be more vigilant in keeping child pornography out of the country. Yet it seemed to have little effect on the home-grown products. In 1982, the Supreme Court upheld a New York law that provided criminal penalties for distributing child pornography, affirming that there were different First Amendment standards for child pornography (*New York vs. Ferber*), and Congress strengthened the 1978 law with the Child Protection Act of 1984 (Campagna and Poffenberger 1988). By definition, selling representations of children in sexual modes was prohibited; no longer was it necessary for prosecutors to prove that pictures, either photographs or films, of children were obscene according to the *Miller* standards. It also raised the age of majority with respect to federal law to eighteen from sixteen. When signing this bill President Reagan (Republican) announced the establishment of a federal commission to examine the harm of pornography, headed by the Attorney-General, Edward Meese.

In 1985, backers of even stronger legislation were active. Their goal was to remove the requirement of a commercial purpose to the sexual exploitation in order to have a conviction. One of the sponsors was Republican John McCain, of Arizona. His bill would have given victims of child exploitation the right to sue abusers for damages in civil court. Upon recommendation of the Meese Commission, this debate again provided the opportunity to amend the Mann Act (US Department of Justice 1986: 481–3). While the commission devoted little of its huge two-volume report to the question of trafficking or the Mann Act, they pointed out that men and boys were used in prostitution and in making pornography. They explained that controlling prostitution and pornography was the purpose of the statute. Thus, it made sense in terms of equal protection law that, although women and girls may be the majority of the victims of sexual exploitation, there was no reason not to extend the protections of the Mann Act to males. This was consistent with President Reagan's plan, two years after the defeat of the Equal Rights Amendment to the Constitution in 1983, to remove sex-specific references from the Federal Code. The report concluded that by removing the references to 'immoral purposes' the Act would be better enforced because the concern about arbitrary punishment by over-zealous prosecutors would be diminished.

Dominant frame of debate

This pedigree for Mann Act revision rendered it non-controversial. The dominant frame of the debate focused on the problem of child pornography and paedophiles who exploit children. The policy actors worked to redefine the issue of child pornography as a moral issue, departing from its 1978 definition as child abuse. At a time when the Meese Commission advocated removing the language of morality from the Mann Act, the policy actors emphasised the immorality of child sexual exploitation. Evidence was presented about organisations that promoted sex with children (motto: 'sex before eight or it's too late') and a network of child pornography recipients and paedophiles with international connections (especially from Scandinavian countries and the Netherlands). Policy solutions offered in the hearings ranged from additional social services and education programmes to better law enforcement. It was on this latter theme that references finally were made to the Mann Act, referred to in these 1985 hearings as 'White Slave Act cases'. By improved law enforcement, the FBI would help make the Act more credible and get the local police to take child pornography and prostitution cases more seriously.

Gendering the debate

Gender ideas were rare in this policy debate. A paedophile was defined as 'a person, either man or woman' who 'has a sexual interest in children and takes pride in that interest'. Usually, however, examples and images were of men: 'His association is very similar to that of a man–woman dating relationship. He spends money, gives gifts, and generally buys the companionship of the victim' (US Congress, Senate 1984: 53). The objects of their attention were discussed mostly in gender-neutral terms: child, children, victim. Otherwise there were scattered references to women, including a comment by Victoria Wagner, executive director of Seattle's youth and community services programmes and the only woman to testify, that there was little interest in victimisation of prostitutes 'because they were women'. This observation seemed to make little impression on the other policy actors at the hearings. The only other woman in the hearing room during the policy debate was Lindy Boggs (Democrat), a Representative from Louisiana.

The National Broadcasting Corporation (NBC) reported on mass production of pornography ('Silent Shame: the Sexual Abuse of Children') in 1984. Otherwise, the attention of the media and the women's movement was not on the child pornography/prostitution issue. Rather, radical feminists captured the media's interest with their efforts to ban pornography that exploited and degraded women. Aided by their libertarian and moralist allies respectively, the battle between so-called free speech feminists and the anti-porn feminists was waged in Minneapolis in 1984 and again in Indianapolis in 1985. Kathleen Barry's campaign to bring international traffic in women to the public agenda earned her a spotlight in the *New York Times* (Klemesrud 1985). But, just as the media had little interest in Congress's attention to child pornography, child prostitution and the Mann Act, so Congress was unaffected by the media's interest in prostitution and pornography that exploits women. So, while the media were beginning to note concerns about the sexual exploitation of women, for federal policy actors the issue of trafficking in women remained largely invisible.

Policy outcome

After the 1986 Act, the Mann Act now provides:

Whoever knowingly transports any individual in interstate or foreign commerce, or in any Territory or Possession of the United States, with the intent that such individual engage in prostitution, or in any sexual activity for which any person can be charged with a criminal offence, shall be fined under this title or imprisoned not more than five years or both. (US 1986, Sec 2421).

The Act also prohibits coercion or enticement and transportation of minors (under eighteen) for prostitution or criminal sexual activity. In addition, the 1986 Act strengthened federal criminal law pertaining to buying or selling sexual representations of children and their use in advertising or through the mail.

Women's movement impact

Anti-pornography feminists linked pornography to sexual abuse and prostitution. While they could have contributed to the debate on the 1986 law, they were largely disinterested in the congressional discussions. No woman effectively participated; there were only token appearances at committee hearings. In the end, neither side in the feminist 'pornography wars' was particularly happy or disappointed in the 1986 Act: while not offensive, the outcome was considered irrelevant. Therefore, the movement's impact on the state was no response.

Women's policy agency activities

The only federal women's policy agency during the consideration of the Child Sexual Abuse and Pornography Act was the Women's Bureau. There is no reason to expect that the bureau would have taken part in this debate. From their remote location in the Department of Labor and their mandate to promote the status and rights of women workers, bureau staff would be unlikely even to be aware that the question of pornography, prostitution and the Mann Act was on the agenda. As a single issue agency it has used its moderate resources to work directly with women's advocacy groups on conventional themes of equal pay and working conditions, with special attention to giving women more opportunities to train for non-traditional occupations. Even with this agenda, the bureau was in a passive mode; President Reagan placed a non-feminist in the leadership. Thus with no attention to the debate, this agency was symbolic.

Women's movement characteristics

After 1983, radical feminists had dispersed and no longer had a national presence. Many feminist organisations remained, but membership began to decrease along with the attention of the media. At the same time, the Washington DC-based interest groups were consolidating their organisations and agendas into a strong Women's Lobby (Costain 1992). Feminists were very close to the Democratic Party in the wake of the

Geraldine Ferraro nomination for vice president. The threats posed to women's rights by the administration of President Reagan and the right wing brought many feminist groups together at regional and local levels. Nothing had changed the feminist position that child pornography and prostitution were abuse and exploitation. However, the issue of child pornography and prostitution and the Mann Act was so low on the movement's agenda that it was invisible. Finally, with no movement demands, it is impossible to locate counter-movement demands.

Policy environment

The policy sub-system is the same as in the first debate, that is, a moderately closed process that centres on Congress and its specialist committees and individual policy entrepreneurs in charge of these committees. The dominant approach in that sub-system emphasised the immorality of child pornography and prostitution, a position distant from the feminist perspective of women's freedom from oppression and exploitation. To insert this frame in the debate would have required a change in the underlying paradigm. In addition, unlike during the first debate, the left was not in power: Republicans had the majority in the Senate and, with President Reagan, a stronghold in the executive.

Debate 3: Trafficking in women and children, 1998–2000

How issue came to the public agenda

The issue of trafficking in women came to the public agenda of Congress in the late 1990s from two directions: international organisations – especially the United Nations and the Organisation for Security and Co-operation in Europe (OSCE) – and media reports of cases showing that the USA had become a destination country. For instance, in 1996 Russian women who had answered an ad for jobs in the USA were found in a massage parlour in Bethesda MD; in 1998, the Cadena family was arrested for operating a brothel with girls from Mexico forced to service men in North Carolina, South Carolina and Florida. International conferences, usually including personal testimony of victims, brought attention to the increase in sexual trafficking from countries in the former Soviet bloc, as well as Asia and Latin America. In 1998, concurrent resolutions in the House of Representatives and the Senate called upon the Justice Department to prepare a report on the cases of trafficking in the USA.

The same year, the Democrat President Bill Clinton issued a directive entitled: 'Steps to Combat Violence against Women and Trafficking in Women and Girls'. With this, he gave responsibility for the issue of trafficking to the President's Interagency Council on Women (Interagency Council or IAC). The Interagency Council was a women's policy office created to implement the 1995 Beijing Plan of Action in the United States. Housed in the Department of State, its chair was Madeleine Albright, Secretary of State, and the honorary chair was First Lady Hillary Rodham Clinton. A deputy director of the council was assigned to the trafficking issue, and there was a working group representing the departments of Justice, State, Labor, Health and Human Services and the US Agency for International Development. Another working group in the Department of Justice studied exploitation of workers including sexual exploitation.

The Interagency Council proposed a three-part framework for policy – (1) prevention through funding research to gather information on the issue, (2) protection through specific projects for social services, and (3) prosecution – to enhance the enforcement of existing laws. It prepared a bill to authorise this plan; Democrat sponsors Senator Paul Wellstone and Representative Louise Slaughter set the policy process in motion.

Chris Smith, a Republican congressional representative from New Jersey and delegate to the OSCE, was also impressed with what he learned at international conferences about sexual trafficking. He drafted a bill to strengthen criminal law in the USA and to authorise the president to sanction countries which contribute to the trafficking problem. As chair of the Human Rights Committee in the House of Representatives, he was in a position to push his bill through a series of congressional hearings.

Dominant frame of debate

Despite the existence of the Mann Act, the federal government had traditionally approached trafficking prosecutions as immigration matters. Immigration officials had little sympathy for the victims, seeing them as willing participants trying to get into the USA by any means rather than victims of international criminal gangs (Young 1998). Officials would round up the individuals brought illegally into the country and send them back. Having removed the victims, there was little opportunity to prosecute traffickers in federal courts. Advocates of new legislation in the State Department and Congress agreed to redefine the issue as a matter of human rights, not immigration. Smith called forcible and/or fraudulent trafficking in women and children for the international sex trade 'one of the world's most serious and widespread human rights problems' (US Congress, House of Representatives 1999: 1). Others labelled the practice a form of slavery or involuntary servitude. With this, it was a short conceptual leap to call coerced prostitution a form of coerced labour. Once that was established, it followed that the new law should extend to other forms of coerced labour as well as sex labour.

All agreed that this was primarily an international problem, promoted by international organised crime and tolerated, even aided, by foreign police, immigration officials and even national governments. Nevertheless, the USA was involved as a recipient country for over 50,000 women and children (Richard 1999). Senator Wellstone and others noted that this growing problem was the dark side of globalisation and free trade, exacerbated by the low status of women and poverty, especially in the former Soviet bloc countries and the developing world. Proponents of the new legislation argued that the USA needed to strengthen and direct its criminal laws towards the traffickers and stop punishing the victims. Proponents also signed on to the prevention, prosecution and protection scheme, and all bills provided for changes to immigration practice to assist victims. Only Smith's bill established new criminal penalties for traffickers and authorised the president to sanction and deny aid to countries that lent them assistance. He used the Religious Freedom Act of 1998, which had been promoted by Christian groups to fight persecution in foreign countries, as a model for these sanctions. The administration was dead set against such sanctions.

Gendering the debate

From the beginning, the debate was gendered – it was about the trafficking of women and children. Most policy actors portrayed the women as naïve and destitute, usually from poor communities in poor countries being sold as commodities. Traffickers would entice these women from their homes with promises of jobs in other countries; then they would be kidnapped, transported across the borders by gangs, and made to service many men to repay a huge debt or held as prisoners. If they turned to the police, the victims were treated with contempt as criminals themselves.

Thirteen women's rights groups formed an informal coalition to lobby Congress on the trafficking bill.[2] At first they focused on Senator Wellstone who had introduced the Clinton administration's bill and was an ally of feminists on other issues including violence against women. They were critical of the Wellstone/administration bill on a number of fronts, but their primary concern was the definition of trafficking (interview Twiss Butler 7 June 2001; Shenon 2000). To these feminists, prostitution itself was sex exploitation that affects the status of all women. The Wellstone/administration bill defined trafficking as *only* those instances of transporting women for prostitution through force, coercion, fraud or deception. Frank Loy, Undersecretary of State for global affairs, countered the feminist demand, asserting that 'the key in trafficking is not the act itself of sexual exploitation. It is the act of the use of force, or fraud, and artifice to get people across borders' (US Congress, Senate 2000: 22).

Policy outcome

Neither the administration nor Wellstone was receptive to the feminists' efforts to change the definition. Led by Equality Now (Jessica Neuwirth), the Feminist Majority (Eleanor Smeal) and the Protection Project (Laura Lederer),[3] the feminists turned to Representative Chris Smith. Smith, prominent in the anti-abortion movement, was not a natural ally of the feminists. But on the issue of trafficking, he and his allies, many from faith-based organisations, were more in tune with feminist thinking than the administration or the leading Democrats. At the same time, Smith's staff negotiated with the administration to extend the bill's coverage to all forms of coerced labour. The negotiations between the women's rights coalition and the Smith camp produced a two-tier definition of sex trafficking that set it apart from the other forms of trafficking. *Sex trafficking* would mean 'the recruitment, harboring, transportation, provision, or obtaining of a person for the purpose of a commercial sex act'. *Severe sex trafficking* would mean 'a commercial sex act induced by force, fraud, or coercion or in which the person induced to perform such act has not attained eighteen years of age'.

The Trafficking Victims Protection Act of 2000 (United States 2000) went into effect in October 2000 with little opposition. In fact, there was so little opposition that policy actors promoting the controversial renewal of the Violence against Women Act coupled their bill to the trafficking bill in one package. In its final form the provisions were gender-neutral, and included the administration's demand that it cover all forms of coerced labour, not just sex. The preamble recognised that women and girls were disproportionately victims of trafficking. The two-tier definition of sex trafficking was included, but the protections, sanctions and penalties of the new law applied only to *severe sex trafficking*. The Act gives authority to the president to impose sanctions on governments in countries of origin, transit or destination who fail to meet minimum standards in combating the trade.

Women's movement impact

Policy-making on trafficking thus involved settling two main conflicts important to feminists: (1) whether coercion should be part of the definition of sex trafficking or not; and (2) whether sex trafficking should be combined with coerced labour under a common definition or not. The final policy resolved these in line with feminist demands. The Act contained a definition of sex trafficking that did not require coercion and it retained the idea that trafficking for sex was a separate form of trafficking with special impact on women's rights and status. At the same time, with the two-tier definition of trafficking, the bill's provisions applied only to severe or coerced prostitution. Thus, although the feminists supported the Trafficking Victims Protection Act as better than nothing, they were disappointed in it as a tool for fighting against sex exploitation.

Movement activists were accepted as representatives of women's interests during the policy process. They negotiated with the senior congressional staff in charge of the bill and were successful in gaining some of their goals (interview Laura Lederer, Director, Protection Project, 6 June 2001; interview Twiss Butler, national staff of NOW, 7 June 2001). In addition, women as individuals and representatives of various organisations such as NOW and the Protection Project testified at committee hearings. Thus the movement impact in this third debate was dual response.

Women's policy agency activities

Unlike in the first two debates on the Mann Act, there was a high-level women's policy agency active on the trafficking issue. The President's Interagency Council (IAC) had been established in 1996 to monitor US compliance with the Plan of Action of the UN conference on women in Beijing. The IAC was composed of people from the Departments of Justice, State, Labor, Health and Human Services and US Agency for International Development (AID). When the trafficking bill was in Congress, Madeleine Albright was chair and the IAC was housed in the Department of State. President Clinton established a special task force in the IAC on trafficking in women and girls to represent the administration on the issue. Thus the trafficking bill was part of the mandate of the agency. The IAC was an administrative body, with high-level female leadership including First Lady, Hillary Rodham Clinton, as honorary chair. The council did not have a separate budget, and worked with staff reassigned from other agencies within the Department of State. The two leaders – Teresa Loar, Senior Co-ordinator for International Women's Issues, and Anita Botti, Deputy Director of International Women's Initiatives and chair of the Interagency Task Force on Trafficking in Women and Girls – had no connections with the feminist organisations or interest in the women's movement activism.

On the trafficking issue, the IAC represented President Clinton and Secretary of State Albright, not the women's movement. Thus the IAC worked to de-gender the debate, calling for language that treated sex trafficking as another form of coerced labour. As Anita Botti said: 'It's not just women who are trafficked.' While sex is what gets the attention, she noted, the IAC worked to frame the issue as a work/economics issue (interview Anita Botti, 29 August 2000). Botti for one believed this was necessary to gain support for the bill. Women's movement representatives presented themselves to the IAC in an effort to counter this approach, but did not receive a warm reception. Botti preferred the approach of Human Rights Watch and Amnesty International to that of the feminist coalition who considered all prostitution as exploitation and wanted to abolish it. Those on the feminist side saw the IAC as a closed group, uninterested in their input. Thus the women's policy agency in the third debate worked to de-gender the policy debate, not to bring women's status to the fore, and it was successful in inserting gender-neutral ideas into the final bill. The IAC's position not only did not coincide with women's movement goals, it opposed them. Thus it can be classified as a non-feminist women's policy agency.

Feminists active in this policy debate were unable to explain the lack of support they received from the IAC and the Clinton administration (interview Twiss Butler, 7 June 2001; interview Laura Lederer, 6 June 2001; interview Pamela Shifman (Equality Now), 21 June 2001). The IAC and State Department defended their opposition to the feminist definition of trafficking in terms of foreign policy. The debate on the Smith bill was coming to a close just before the final negotiations on the protocol on trafficking, a supplement to the UN Convention against Transnational Organised Crime. The USA did not take a leadership role in this debate but wanted to support allies such as the Netherlands and Germany who had decriminalised prostitution and, US officials apparently believed, would oppose any definition of trafficking that did not separate coerced from 'voluntary' prostitution. In December 2000, many US allies, and the USA itself, approved language, inspired by the radical feminist view, which became part of the final document. In the UN protocol, consent of the victim is irrelevant to the definition of sex trafficking.[4]

Women's movement characteristics

In the late 1990s, the US women's movement remained in the position of consolidation which had characterised it since the 1980s. The resources and energy were in the women's lobbying organisations based in Washington, DC (Disney and Gelb 2000). At the same time, trafficking had an international dimension which attracted non-governmental organisations (NGOs) like the Coalition against Trafficking in Women with affiliated organisations in other countries. Feminists remained divided on the question of prostitution, but fourteen prominent women's lobbying organisations agreed to work together and supported the compromise in the Smith bill.

For the movement as a whole and for the women's rights lobby in particular trafficking was an issue of middle-level priority. The campaign to renew the Violence against Women Act, which was taking place at the same time, had a much higher priority and profile with movement rank and file members and the public at large. There was little opposition and no counter-movement to speak of.

Policy environment

The policy sub-system in this debate was different from those in the other debates in that it included both executive and legislative structures: the State Department and the congressional committees. The chief players were the heads of the congressional committees and sub-committees. Their staffs worked with other legislators and representatives from the executive agencies, in this case the Interagency Council and the Human Rights desk of the State Department which monitors other governments' compliance with human rights standards. The dominant approach these players shared was that trafficking was a human rights issue. Frequently gendered, this approach was similar to that of the movement organisations who maintained that prostitution was sexual exploitation of women. With respect to matters of human rights, there was a culture of compromise and bipartisan co-operation. Being moderately open, the sub-system was accessible to established lobbying groups such as the coalition of women's rights groups interested in the trafficking bill. Both houses of Congress were in the hands of the Republicans during the debate, with a Democrat in the presidency.

Conclusion

The three debates on trafficking in the USA offer little support for the state feminism hypotheses. In the first two debates – which are remarkably similar to each other – the state did not act to further women's movement goals. Women's policy offices provided no links between movement activists and substantive and procedural responses. In the third debate, movement organisations were active and successful in gaining access to the process and changing the policy content. They did this, however, in the face of an active and non-feminist women's policy agency. Thus, in comparison with abortion and job training debates (Stetson 2001a, 2001c), women's policy agencies have failed as allies for the women's movement on the issue of prostitution and trafficking of women.

What factors account for these results? After early forays promoting decriminalisation, feminists dropped prostitution as a policy issue and found themselves engaged in internal conflicts over pornography. The dominant frame of the debates on child sexual exploitation, pornography and trafficking was gendered to focus only on boys. While women's movement actors had access to a feminist discourse on the topic it was remote from the dominant frame; hence the growing and consolidating movement remained otherwise engaged. In this situation, a women's policy agency could have stepped in to offer a feminist gender perspective, but the machinery in the USA has tended to be either specialist if permanent, such as the Women's Bureau, or temporary if cross-sectional, such as the various commissions appointed by the president. Such a cross-sectional agency under the Democratic Clinton administration was in a position to assist women's movement activists as the White House Office of Outreach had done in the 'partial birth' abortion debate (Stetson 2001c). However, the partisan divisions on sexuality do not easily align with feminist perspectives. In many ways, this has long been the situation with sexuality issues in the USA. The left party – the Democrats – and American liberal politicians see sexuality as a private matter and oppose government involvement. As it turned out they were much more concerned about trafficking in coerced sweat shop labour than they were in sex trafficking. The IAC working closely with the top Democrats in the administration reflected this viewpoint.

This left the feminists to find allies on the right. It is not the first time that women's rights advocates have found themselves working with religious leaders and moralists in trying to limit sexual exploitation of women. During the 1980s, feminists promoting anti-pornography ordinances in Minneapolis and Indianapolis lined up with Phyllis Schlafley and the anti-Equal Rights Amendment and anti-abortion Eagle Forum. Thus, while at first they demurred, eventually the feminists worked with Republican Chris Smith and organisations such as the International Justice Mission that seek to bring a moral aspect to US foreign policy. Prior to the first hearings on the Smith bill, bill supporters organised a pre-hearing event on Capitol Hill. Sharing the stage were right-wing moralist William Bennett and feminist Gloria Steinem, both denouncing trafficking as modern-day sex slavery. Rather than hinder women's movement success, the fact that the left was out of power (at a time when the movement was closer to the left than it had ever been) helped achieve the dual response from the state despite opposition from the women's policy agency.

NOTES

1. The others were: the Child Abuse Prevention and Treatment Act of 1974; a 1994 amendment to the Mann Act making it a crime for US citizens to go to foreign countries to have sex with children; and the Telecommunications Act of 1996 which makes it a crime for any communications facility to induce a minor to engage in prostitution.
2. Equality Now; Planned Parenthood Federation of America; International Women's Health Coalition; NOW; Women's Environment and Development Organisation; Catholics for a Free Choice; Protection Project; Coalition against Trafficking in Women; Sisterhood is Global Institute; National Black Women's Health Project; Feminist Majority; Gloria Steinem; Center for Women Policy Studies.
3. The Protection Project, housed at The Johns Hopkins School of Advanced International Studies, has produced a data bank of laws on prostitution and trafficking from countries around the world. Its feminist director, Laura Lederer, was one of the major policy actors throughout the debate on the Trafficking Act.
4. It reads as follows:

(a) 'Trafficking in persons' shall mean the recruitment, transportation, transfer, harbouring or receipt of persons, by means of the threat or use of force or other forms of coercion, of abduction, of fraud, of deception, of the abuse of power or of a position of vulnerability or of the giving or receiving of payments or benefits to achieve the consent of a person having control over another person, for the purpose of exploitation. Exploitation shall include, at a minimum, the *exploitation of the prostitution of others or of other forms of sexual exploitation,* forced labour or services, slavery or practices similar to slavery, servitude or the removal of organs.

(b) The consent of the victim of trafficking in persons to the intended exploitation set forth in sub paragraph (a) of this article shall be irrelevant where any of the means set for in sub paragraph (a) have been used. (United Nations 2000)

14   Comparative prostitution politics
and the case for state feminism

Joyce Outshoorn

Introduction

After presenting the results of thirty-six debates on prostitution from
twelve countries, this chapter returns to the original question that motivated the RNGS research project: do women's policy agencies matter? If
they do, the results make the case for state feminism: governments can be
effective in promoting an agenda in favour of improving women's status.
The analyses also enable us to answer the question as to the conditions
in which effectiveness occurs.

In the preceding chapters all authors have provided an in-depth analysis of the politics of prostitution in their countries. Here their findings
have been adapted for the purpose of the analysis of this chapter. Such an
adaptation invariably entails a loss of detail and runs the risk of eliminating important cultural aspects of the politics in a country. To minimise
this risk, all authors, being the most familiar with the national context
of 'their' debates, have provided the classification of their findings within
the conceptual framework of the RNGS project. The resulting measure-
ments will be compared to examine the hypotheses presented in chapter 1 aimed at assessing the effectiveness of the women's policy agencies.
The impact of the women's movement actors will then be determined
across debates and countries, after which the role of the women's policy agencies in the debates making for movement success is assessed.
Movement success will be related to the characteristics of the women's
movement; then the characteristics of the agencies are analysed to determine which ones are associated with impact. Finally the approach
of this study, which uses policy debates as units of analysis, is assessed
by comparing it with the approach which takes states as the point of
departure.

The first section of this chapter will analyse the politics of prostitution, providing an overall view of the policy arenas involved in the various
countries and examining the routes of the issue to the political agenda
of the decision-makers. The prevailing prostitution regime prior to the

re-emergence of the issue and the dominant framings are also discussed. The second section is devoted to the gendering of the policy debates. A major hypothesis underlying the RNGS conceptual framework is that gendering has an effect both on the content of the policy and on access of women in the policy process. The typology of the effectiveness of the women's policy agency (see figure 1.3 in chapter 1) is based on this assumption. It is important to assess how the debates are gendered; only when debates are gendered in such a way that lets women's movement actors and activists in and results in outputs congruent to their demands, does the hypothesis hold. The gendered frames will therefore be compared with the demands of women's movement actors, and the linkages to both substantive and descriptive representation will be examined. In this study no standard is given to classify whether certain demands, frames, goals, strategies or policies are feminist or not. Following the discussion of women's movements in chapter 1, the standard applied here for classifying impact is in the terms of the demands of women's movement actors and activists in each country.

The third section will explore the composition of the women's movement and its connection to the issue of prostitution over the three decades studied.[1] The fourth section will examine the hypotheses of the framework to establish the case for state feminism, using the five hypotheses outlined in chapter 1. To enable the analysis, the major overall findings are presented in a series of tables relevant to each hypothesis, and discussed. In the final section the advantages of taking debates, instead of nation-states, as the unit of analysis are discussed and the major findings of this study summarised in terms of their contribution to the theory of state feminism.

The politics of prostitution

Prior to the re-emergence of prostitution as an issue on the public agenda, all states under study had policies on prostitution. Most states had abolitionist regimes that criminalised prostitution-related activities, such as brothels and pimping, but not the prostitute herself (Australia, Austria, France, Israel, Italy, the Netherlands, Spain and Sweden), although often severe limits were set to soliciting. Canada, Finland, Great Britain and the United States also made the prostitute liable to prosecution. In Canada and Finland she could be prosecuted under a vagrancy act. All of these policies were enacted in law, either through the national criminal code or special acts on vagrancy or 'street offences'; this meant that any attempt at legal change has to go through parliament, making it, with the incumbent cabinet, the major decisional arena.

At the same time, it is important to realise that the actual practice of prostitution was much more widespread than can be read off the books; local authorities often condoned prostitution-related activities, opening up space for corruption of local officials and police. In several countries local ordinances could – and did – set up additional barriers; in these cases the decisional arena would be the local council. In this study two debates took place in a local setting (the cities of Vienna and Helsinki) and two at the state level of a federal state (New South Wales and Victoria in Australia). (See table 14.1.)

Prostitution as a political issue did not make it to the political agenda of the incumbent governments in the same period in the different countries. Australia, France, Israel and Italy were the first countries where renewed public debate took place in the early 1970s and where the issue became part of the political agenda; Austria adjusted its Penal Code in 1975. In Britain, Canada, Finland, the Netherlands and Sweden the issue arrived on the political agenda in the early 1980s, while in Spain this only happened in the mid-1990s. In the USA there was little public debate about prostitution and only minor changes occurred at the state level during the 1970s. All attention was then focused at the federal level around trafficking of minors for the purpose of prostitution.

The major route of the issue to the political agenda was by reform of criminal codes and acts relating to vagrancy, as part of the broader and international mood to modernise criminal law in a more humanitarian and liberal spirit, a trend that lasted from the 1960s into the next decade. Incumbent governments, after pressure from civil liberty groups and usually also from left and liberal political parties, entered reform bills in the legislatures. Reform of the Penal Code (Austria, the Netherlands) or vagrancy laws in which prostitution was ranked as a social disease along with alcoholism (Finland) led to the removal of what were perceived as anachronistic offences with outdated penalties such as work camps. In Australia too, a reform act on illicit public behaviour such as vagrancy and prostitution was drafted by the state government of New South Wales after a lobby of civil liberty groups and feminists. In the same vein, the British government removed from the books the imprisonment penalty for loitering and soliciting in the early 1980s after numerous abortive attempts by private members' bills in the 1970s. Canada had to repeal its act in which the status offences were covered, which was held by the courts to be in conflict with the 1960 Bill of Rights. The government responded by retracting the act, but immediately inserted new penalties for prostitution in the Criminal Code. In Sweden a reform commission attempted to soften penalties for rapists, which outraged feminists. They pressed government to set up an official commission of inquiry on prostitution

268   *Joyce Outshoorn*

Table 14.1 *Prostitution debates by country*

Australia		
	AUS 1	Legalisation of street soliciting in New South Wales, 1968–79
	AUS 2	Legal brothels in Victoria, 1984
	AUS 3	Slavery and sexual servitude, 1995–9
Austria		
	AUT 1	Amendment of the Penal Code, 1984
	AUT 2	Vienna's prostitution law, 1991
	AUT 3	Social insurance law, 1998
Britain		
	BR 1	Abolition of imprisonment of prostitutes, 1979–82
	BR 2	Kerb crawling as an offence, 1985, 2001
	BR 3	Sexual servitude, 2001
Canada		
	CA 1	Fraser report, 1983–5
	CA 2	Bill C-49, 1985
	CA 3	Youth in prostitution, 1992–6
Finland		
	FI 1	Repeal of Vagrant Act, 1984–6
	FI 2	Sex Crime Act, 1993–8
	FI 3	Helsinki Municipal Ordinance, 1995–9
France		
	FR 1	Prostitute rights/law enforcement, 1972–5
	FR 2	Public health/AIDS: debate on regulation, 1989–90
	FR 3	Penal Code reform on pimping and solicitation, 1991–2
Israel		
	IS 1	Teenage girls in trouble, 1970–2
	IS 2	Commission on prostitution law reform, 1975–7
	IS 3	Trafficking of women and prostitution, 1994–2002
Italy		
	IT 1	Protection permits for victims of trafficking, 1996–9
	IT 2	Criminalisation of clients of prostitutes under sixteen, 1998
	IT 3	Financing of projects, 1998–9
Netherlands		
	NL 1	Repeal of the brothel ban, Bill 18202, 1983–9
	NL 2	Trafficking of persons, Bill 21027, 1989–93
	NL 3	Repeal of the brothel ban, Bill 25437, 1997–2000
Spain		
	SP 1	Elaboration of the Penal Code, 1994–5
	SP 2	Reform of the Penal Code, 1997–9
	SP 3	The 2000 Immigration Act, 1998–2000
Sweden		
	SW 1	First commission on prostitution, 1981–2
	SW 2	Second commission on prostitution, 1995–8
	SW 3	Violence against Women Act/law on the purchase of sexual services, 1997–9
USA		
	US 1	Sexual exploitation of children, 1976–8
	US 2	Child Sexual Abuse and Pornogaphy Act, 1984–6
	US 3	Trafficking in women and children, 1998–2000

reform. In Spain the authoritarian Franco Penal Code had survived the transition to democracy in the 1970s; its modernisation finally took place in the 1990s when the Socialist government introduced the long-due overhaul in parliament.

In four countries the issue followed a different route to the political agenda. In abolitionist France prostitution landed on the national political agenda after a police crackdown on prostitutes in Lyons. It led to the first organised protest movement of prostitutes of the era. The government then set up a commission of inquiry into prostitution. In similarly abolitionist Italy, prostitution was hardly ever off the agenda; since the enactment in 1958 of the Merlin law, which abolished brothels, there have been numerous attempts by right-wing MPs to legalise these again. These never met with success, as support for the Merlin law from women's groups, the left and the Catholic church was always stronger. In Israel citizens' protest and left-wing MPs induced the government to set up services for 'girls at risk', following a moral panic about prostitution of young girls in mixed Jewish/Arab areas after the Six Day War. In the USA prostitution as such did not reach the political agenda (with the exception of Nevada, which legalised prostitution outside the major cities in 1971). The first debate about trafficking for prostitution, framed as the sexual abuse of children, led to congressional hearings in 1977 and a subsequent change in anti-trafficking law to include minors.

Gendering the prostitution issue

A major strategy of women's movement actors was to gender the policy debates on prostitution, in the expectation that once they established that the issue was about women, women would be included in the policy process, as well as obtaining policy results in line with their demands. This relationship is also assumed in the conceptual framework employed in this study. Are these underlying hypotheses valid? This will first be examined for the matter of access: did women's movement actors succeed in gendering the dominant frame of the first debate, and did they gain access at the end of the debate? Did they maintain or accomplish this in the second debate and did they also manage to do so in the third debate? In order to establish this, the dominant frame at the beginning of the first debate is compared with the outcome of the first debate on whether this was gendered or not, and then compared with the access of women into the policy arena in the three debates.

Prior to the rise of the new women's movement and the re-emergence of the prostitution issue, its dominant frame was not necessarily gendered. At the outset of the first debates the dominant frame about prostitution was that it was either a social problem (the debates in Israel, Finland, France, Sweden), a potential threat to public health and order (Austria, Italy) and to minors at risk because of trafficking for prostitution (the US debates), or it carried the progressive frame of the modernisers: the state should not interfere in the private life of its citizens. The reformers' aim was to redraw the boundaries between the public and the private sphere (the debates in Australia, Britain, the Netherlands, Spain). In the Canadian debate this boundary was also at stake, but here the old boundary prevailed.

At the end of the first debate no fewer than nine of the twelve debates had become gendered. One of these (the US debate) was gendered towards boys, making the majority of prostitutes (women) invisible. The three exceptions are the debates in Austria, where the old law and order/public health frame remained intact; Britain, where despite non-gendering, the prison penalty for loitering and soliciting was removed from the books; and Spain, which decriminalised prostitution except for the prostitution of minors and the mentally ill under legal custody, without referring to women. At the end of all three non-gendered debates, no women or women's movement actors had gained access in the decisional arena. In the gendered debates access was established in all cases, save for the US case, where the gendering towards boys hardly legitimated entry of women. This all is consistent with our underlying hypothesis. (See table 14.2.)

In the second debate women gained access in six cases, and in all of these cases the debate was gendered successfully. In four of the six cases in which women did not gain access, the debates were indeed not gendered. The two odd cases here are the Italian and Austrian debates. In Italy the debate was gendered, but towards boys, again hardly conducive to women's access in the arena. In Austria, the debate, about Vienna's new prostitution ordinance, was gendered but as women's movement actors were hardly interested in the issue at the time, there was no push towards representation. So the outcomes of the second debate also support the hypothesis that gendering towards women is conducive to access.

In the third debates women gained access in nine cases, and in all of these cases the debate was gendered towards women. The three exceptions are the debates in France, Spain and Canada. All three of these debates were not gendered. Overall, it can be concluded there is strong support for the hypothesis that successful gendering by women's movement actors is conducive for their representation.

The results also show that access in a previous debate does not automatically guarantee access in the next debate. In six of the nine cases where the issue was gendered in the first debate, access was also secured in the second debate. The three exceptions are the debates in Australia,

Table 14.2 *Gendering and access to policy arena*

Dominant frame 1st debate	Outcome of framing at end of 1st debate	Access in outcome of 1st debate	Access in 2nd debate/ gendered or not	Access in 3rd debate
Australia: public/private behaviour balance: civil liberties	Gendered: no penalties for prostitute	+ (dual)	– (different arena state) (pre-empt) Not gendered	+ (dual)
Austria: law and order/public health	No new gendered frame	– (no response)	– (pre-emption) Gendered	+ (dual)
Britain: penal reform	Not gendered: no penalties for prostitutes	– (pre-emption)	– (no response) Not gendered	+ (dual)
Canada: public order/private freedom	Gendered: no penalties for prostitute	+ (dual)	+ (co-optation) Gendered	– (no response)
Finland: social problem	Gendered: no penalties for prostitutes	+ (dual)	+ (dual response) Gendered	+ (co-optation)
France: gender neutral frame with social aid for prostitutes	Gendered: consideration of prostitute rights	+ (dual)	+ (dual response) Gendered	– (pre-emption)
Israel: social problem	Gendered: services for girls in trouble	+ (co-optation)	+ (co-optation) Gendered	+ (dual)
Italy: illegal migration, women/law and order	Gendered: women as victim of trafficking	+ (dual)	– (no response) Gendered, but towards boys	+ (dual)
Netherlands: no state intervention in private behaviour	Gendered: voluntary and forced prostitution	+ (dual)	+ (dual) gendered	+ (dual)
Spain: no state intervention in private behaviour	Not gendered: no penalties for prostitutes	– (pre-emption)	– (pre-emption) Not gendered	– (pre-emption)
Sweden: human and social problem	Gendered with no penalties for prostitutes	+ (dual)	+ (co-optation) Gendered	+ (dual)
USA: minors at risk for trafficking	Gendered, but focused on boy victims	– (no response)	– (no response) Not gendered	+ (dual)

N = 36

Notes Steps for analysis:

1. dominant frame at beginning of debate juxtaposed to outcome of framing at end of first debate
2. did gendering affect access of women/include women? When issue is about women, are they included? (determined by looking at gendering of first debate and inclusion in second; and in gendering of second debate with inclusion in the third debate)

Italy and the USA. The Australian case is inconclusive, as the second debate took place in a different state. In the USA the debate focused on child sexual abuse and in Italy it was gendered towards boys, so hardly conducive towards women's access. In the remaining three debates, in Austria, Britain and Spain, women had no access either in the first or the second debate.

However, when linking the second to the third debate, the picture is more erratic. Only in the Finnish, Israeli, Dutch and Swedish debates, all gendered, did access carry over into the third debate. Women in the Canadian and French debates lost access in the third debate. Both third debates were de-gendered, the Canadian one focused on youth and child sexual abuse, the French on Penal Code reform in a resolutely gender-neutral frame. All of the second cases in which women had no access changed into success stories in terms of access in the third debate. As mentioned, the positive relationship between gendering and access applies in all of these cases.

In addition to the question about the relationship between gendering and access, the other important relationship to explore is that of gendering and policy content, the second underlying hypothesis of the framework. Do the gendering and the policy outcome coincide with women's movement actors' goals? After all, not all gendering is to the liking of women's movement actors or activists, as in the case of masculine gendering or when the gendering contains negative images of women and femininity. To look into this, the goals of the women's movement actors were compared with the gendered outcomes of the three debates. (See table 14.3.)

Prostitution became redefined quite rapidly: the majority of the first debates, generally occurring during the 1970s and early 1980s, became gendered, with the exceptions of the debates in Austria, Britain and Spain. During the second debates, gendering took place in Austria, but not in Britain and Spain. In the USA and in Italy the second debate was gendered in the 'reverse' direction: it focused on boys. With the single exception of Canada, all of the third debates were gendered.

In all debates where gendering did not occur, or masculine gendering obscured female prostitution, the goals of the women's movement actors did not coincide with the policy outcomes of the debates, save for the first British debate. Four of these cases (the two US debates, the third Canadian and the second Italian debate) were about the sexual abuse of minors; the women's movement was not opposed to the outcomes, but these did not address its demands. In the first Austrian debate there were no demands yet by women's movement actors on the issue of prostitution. In Canada the second debate was gender-neutral: with both clients and prostitutes liable to prosecution when they 'communicate' publicly about

Table 14.3 *Gendered debates and policy outcomes*

Country/movement goals	Debate 1	Debate 2	Debate 3
1 Gendered all three debates, sustained over three debates; outcomes coincide with women's movement actors' goals			
Australia			
Repeal of laws against prostitutes	Penalties for soliciting abolished	Brothels to be regulated as other business, but penalties for street prostitution	Higher penalties for traffickers and sexual servitude
France			
Maintenance of abolition with recognition of prostitutes' rights	Recommendations on social services for prostitutes	Proposal to repeal abolition and call for regulation	Penal Code reform with higher penalties against abusive clients, better definition of pimping and soliciting in favour of prostitutes
Netherlands			
Legalise voluntary prostitution as sex work; fight forced prostitution	Insertion of distinction into policy documents	Higher penalties for traffickers but non-EU prostitutes regarded as illegal migrants/victims	Brothels legalised and prostitution regulated as work
Spain			
At first no demands; retain abolition	Decriminalisation of pimping; prostitutes no longer in Penal Code as social menace in need of rehabilitation	Higher penalties for prostitution of legal minors and traffickers	Permanent residency and working permit for victims of trafficking if they help prosecution
Sweden			
Against legalisation of prostitution and for criminalising clients	No further criminalisation of prostitution	Recommendation to criminalise clients	Law against purchasing sexual services

(cont.)

Table 14.3 (*cont.*)

Country/movement goals	Debate 1	Debate 2	Debate 3
2 Gendered two of the three debates, demands partly met in these debates			
Austria			
Recognition of prostitution as legal trade/sex workers' rights	Stricter law against pimping (no women's movement demands)[a]	Limitation of street prostitution in Vienna; registration and health checks of prostitutes	Rights for prostitutes in social security and equitable taxation
Finland			
Regulation allowing client criminalisation	Removal of penalties for prostitutes	Criminalisation of pimping and limited criminalisation of clients	Ban on prostitution in city limits: clients and prostitutes liable for prosecution
Italy			
Retain abolition but decriminalise aiding and abetting prostitution	Higher penalties for traffickers and residency permits for victims of trafficking	Higher penalties for child molestation and exploitation of minors[b]	Service provision for trafficked women
3 Gendered third debate only; demands met in first and third debate			
Britain			
Unequal treatment of prostitute under law	Repeal of imprisonment penalty for street soliciting[a]	Kerb crawling made offence, prostitutes also liable to prosecution[a]	Higher penalties for traffickers and new offence of sexual servitude

4 Gendered third debate only; demands met in third debate

Israel	Help prostitutes and fight trafficking	Services set up for help of young girls in 'trouble'[c]	Recommendations to legalise indoor prostitution.	Higher penalties for trafficking in women
United States	Divided: NOW for decriminalisation; radical feminists are abolitionist	Criminalised the use and exploitation of minors for sexual purposes[a]	Expansion of Mann Act to include all persons trafficked across state borders[a]	Trafficking act with definition separating sex trafficking from other forms of trafficking and retaining coercion[b]

5 Gendered only first debate; demands only met in this debate

Canada	Remove discriminatory laws against prostitutes	Recommendations to remove prostitution from criminal code and social services	Criminalisation of communication about prostitution for clients and prostitutes[a]	Youth in prostitution/child sexual abuse; Act overshadows women in prostitution[a]

N = 36

[a] Not gendered
[b] Gendered towards boys
[c] No demands of women's movement present

a deal, the outcome was in opposition to women's movement actors' goals. The second British debate made all participants in kerb crawling liable to prosecution.

In the cases where gendering did occur, policy satisfaction was also achieved. The only exception to this finding is the second Austrian debate: it was gendered, but led to an unsatisfactory policy outcome when street prostitution in Vienna was curbed and prostitutes had to be registered. The pattern of the outcomes therefore speaks very much in favour of the positive relation between gendering and a positive policy outcome, thus supporting the second underlying hypothesis of the conceptual framework.

Table 14.3 enables us partially to capture the trend of prostitution policy across states since the early 1970s. Overall, selling sex is no longer a crime, with the exception of the USA, although states certainly regulate when and where it is legal to do so. Seven of the states have toughened the penalties for traffickers (Italy, the Netherlands, Spain, Australia, Britain, Israel and the USA); in the latter four, developments within the UN were highly instrumental in putting trafficking on the political agenda in recent years. Another notable development is the stronger concern of the 1990s about the protection of legal minors and the concern about child sexual abuse, which figured broadly in the USA, Canada, Britain, Italy and Spain, and played a role in the third Dutch debate.

In prostitution regimes, the selected states fall mainly into two groups. Australia (i.e. New South Wales, Victoria, Australian Capital Territory), Austria, the Netherlands and Spain have made openings to allow for sex work in various ways, tending towards legalising prostitution. The first three underwent major changes, allowing for prostitution between consenting adults, sex work and brothels (in Austria limited to Vienna). Spain's new Penal Code allows for distinguishing between forced and voluntary prostitution, moving away from its (imperfect) abolitionism since 1994. The other countries have maintained their older policies. In Israel prostitution is still not legal, but authorities follow a policy of 'benign neglect', resorting to zoning and allowing prostitution 'under a roof' in recent years, resulting in a shift from street prostitution towards houses. France and Italy have not legalised brothels, retaining their traditional abolitionism. Sweden and Finland remain opposed to the legalisation of prostitution, and the former has even extended the Criminal Code to include clients, while Finland seems to be moving in a similar direction. In Canada prostitutes are no longer liable to prosecution, but at the same time it was made almost impossible for them to do their work. After minor changes in the early 1970s, the USA and Britain have not moved further in the direction of decriminalisation.

The only convergence between states is the trend towards more severe penalties for traffickers and persons holding individuals in sexual servitude; France increased the penalties for abusive clients. And a few states are recently providing aid to victims of trafficking: Italy, Spain and the Netherlands.

Women's movements

The re-emergence of the prostitution issue seems to coincide with the emergence of the second wave of feminism; careful examination of the formation of the first feminist organisations of the second wave and the rise of public debate on prostitution shows, however, that the picture is more complicated. Looking at the timing of the first debate on prostitution and the stage of the new women's movement, the emergence of the issue and the movement ran parallel in Australia, France and the USA, all occurring in the 1970s. The parallel is also in evidence in Austria and Finland, where issue and movement emerged a decade later. The first significant debates in Canada, the Netherlands and Sweden happened when the new women's movement had already consolidated itself; this occurred in the mid-1980s. In Spain this was also the case, but in the 1990s. In Britain the new women's movement was already in decline when the first debate was in full swing and settled in the early 1980s. Decline had also set in for the Italian feminist movement when trafficking made the political agenda in the mid-1990s. In Israel the issue came to the agenda during a period of consolidation of the traditional women's movement, which was entrenched within left-wing parties in the early 1970s; new-style feminism only came into being in the 1980s.

Within the broader women's movement, prostitution was never an issue where consensus has been reached, with often sharp controversy between warring factions. Moreover, among movement actors there are often so-called traditional women's movements which have their roots in earlier eras of mobilisation, such as the auxiliary women's organisations of political parties and trade unions, housewives' organisations and social-religious women's groups. Also involved were independent feminist political groups whose ancestry dates back to the suffrage movement of the first part of the twentieth century. Some of these organisations were interested in prostitution and subscribed to older framings, defining prostitution as a moral, social or public health issue.

Within the new feminism of the second wave, the various tendencies emerged at different periods in the countries studied here, and its radical feminist or socialist feminist manifestations also followed different paths and timetables. As emerges from the chapters, all of these positions have led to different framings of the issue of prostitution and trafficking, and to different demands. This makes complicated the assessment of whether the goals of the various women's movement actors were met. In each country study authors had to take an unambiguous decision on how to score the variables in each debate. Australia's debates may serve as a case in point: well-settled mainstream organisations such as the Women's Electoral Lobby (WEL) and feminists within the Australian Labor Party participated in the debates alongside radical feminists. The mainstream was for allowing brothels and regulating the sex trade, while the radical feminists were in favour of removing penalties for prostitutes but opposed to regulation – from whose viewpoint is the outcome then judged?

The cohesiveness of the movement around the issue was a variable in the conceptual framework. From the overall comparative analyses it emerges that in Australia, Finland, Israel and the Netherlands, women's movement actors were unified throughout all three debates, agreeing on the issue within a given debate, despite the fact that all of them had liberal-, socialist- and radical feminist organisations. In Spain and Italy the actors were never unified; many feminists adhered to traditional abolitionism, while others were in favour of regulating prostitution as work. It should be noted that in Spain all three debates took place in a very short time span in the mid-1990s. This also applies to Italy, but here debate among feminists dates back to the abolitionist Merlin law. In Canada, movement actors were divided in the first and third debates along the familiar divide of sex work/sexual domination, and only moderately cohesive during the second debate on soliciting and street prostitution. In Austria, Britain and the United States, the actors were divided during the first two debates, while in the 1990s one voice became dominant, presenting a more cohesive view.

This is not surprising for Britain and the United States, as sexual servitude and trafficking of women have all the trappings of valence issues, most people agreeing on the goal if not on the methods. Austria's third debate, ending tax discrimination and allowing prostitutes coverage under social security, united women's movement actors as the measure put an end to discrimination against prostitutes, even if it also made the idea of sex work more mainstream. In France, movement actors could agree on prostitutes' rights and higher penalties for pimping. They were cohesive in the first and third debates; in the second, about doing away with abolitionism in favour of some kind of regulation, they were predictably not cohesive. In Sweden there is more or less unified and strong opposition to prostitution, although considerably less so when it came to concrete proposals. Many hesitated about expanding criminalisation during the second debate, but in the end agreed on the final proposal criminalising the client. The third debate started off with this cohesion, but it evaporated when several actors opposed the outcome of the Act which prohibited the purchasing of sex.

Viewing the history of the debates across the three decades, it is also obvious that the issue of prostitution never had much priority among women's movement actors. Among the thirty-six debates, it had a high or medium priority in only eight cases; in all others priority was low. In three of the high-priority cases the issue was about combating trafficking and sexual servitude: they are the third debates of Australia, Britain and Israel. The other cases with high priority all took place in Sweden and in Finland (the second and third debates), and in all of these, criminalisation of clients figures prominently. Sweden is the only country where the issue had high priority in all three debates. All of the high-priority cases took place in the 1990s and early 2000s.

Prostitutes' movements

After the re-emergence of prostitution as a political issue, prostitutes' movements mobilised in eight of the states studied: Australia, Austria, Britain, Canada, France, Italy, the Netherlands and the USA. Although these movements were not separately mapped as actors, a closer look does suggest that their demands, usually aimed at facilitating prostitutes' work, were met in a number of the debates. This has been the case in Australia in the second debate, when brothels were legalised in Victoria in the mid-1980s (in the first debate no prostitutes' group was yet present). It also occurred in Austria, where the Vienna city ordinance of 1991 allowed for brothels and zones for prostitution and when prostitutes gained social insurance rights in 1998; France, where the 1998 reform of the Penal Code came up with a more precise definition of pimping and allowed for prostitutes' rights; and the Netherlands, where the ban on brothels was repealed, a long-favoured measure of the prostitutes' trade union.

In all four countries an alliance was established between prostitutes' groups and (part) of the women's movement, and in all four, the policy agency was favourably disposed towards the prostitutes' rights movement, the Dutch agency even subsidising the trade union over a considerable period. In Italy the assistance for prostitutes adopted after the parliamentary inquiry of 1999 also was in line with demands from the movement. It had support from the women's policy agency on the issue, but not from the women's movement.

In the other three countries the movement made little headway. In Britain the 1982 Criminal Justice Act abolished the use of imprisonment for soliciting, a move favoured by the prostitutes' movement; it soon turned against them, however. No women's policy agency participated in the process. In Canada the women's policy agency and the prostitutes' movement opposed the anti-soliciting legislation of 1985; in the USA the movement has not achieved its aims (see also Weitzer 1991). It appears that the support of a women's policy agency, especially if also backed by women's movement actors, can make a difference for prostitutes' rights.

Women's movement actors and the state: the case for state feminism

This section sets out to address the major goals of the study. One is to determine and explain variations in the impact of women's movement actors in gaining both substantive and descriptive representation, i.e. in terms of policy satisfaction and access to the decisional arena. The other is to trace whether women's policy agencies intervened in the various debates and helped women's movement actors to achieve their goals, answering the question of whether states can actually help to improve women's status, in other words, whether state feminism exists. In analytical terms, the women's policy agency is treated as the intervening variable. In order to discuss the outcomes systematically, the five hypotheses formulated in chapter 1 will each be examined. To enable this analysis, the findings of the chapters have been scored on the various characteristics and typologies explained in chapter 1 and appendix 1, using the policy debate as unit of analysis. The discussion of the hypotheses will be aided by tables summarising the findings at each stage.

First of all, it was hypothesised (H.1) that women's movements in democratic states have tended to be successful in increasing both substantive representation, as demonstrated by policy content, and descriptive representation, as demonstrated by women's participation in policy-making process, that is, dual response.

In nineteen of the debates (52.7%, a majority of the cases) the debate ended in a full response, providing access into decisional arenas for women's movement actors and more or less meeting their demands about prostitution. In addition, five more debates led to women's participation at some stage of decision-making, and six other debates delivered substantive success. Only in six debates (16.6%) were women's movement actors ignored, gaining neither access nor policy satisfaction. There is therefore substantial support for the first hypothesis. (See table 14.4.)

The second hypothesis takes on the role of the women's policy agencies, the intervening variable in the conceptual design. It (H.2) states that women's movements in democratic states have tended to be more successful where women's policy agencies have acted as insiders in the

Table 14.4 *Women's movement and state responses in thirty-six policy debates*

Country	Dual response	Co-optation	Pre-emption	No response
Australia	AUS 1; AUS 3		AUS 2	
Austria	AUT 3		AUT 2	AUT 1
Britain	BR 3		BR 1	BR 2
Canada	CA 1	CA 2		CA 3
Finland	FI 1; FI 2	FI 3		
France	FR 1; FR 2		FR 3	
Israel	IS 3	IS 1; IS 2		
Italy	IT 1; IT 3			IT 2
Netherlands	NL 1; NL 2; NL 3			
Spain	SP 2		SP 1; SP 3	
Sweden	SW 1; SW 3	SW 2		
USA	US 3			US 1; US 2

policy-making process, that is, have gendered policy debates in ways that coincide with women's movement goals. To analyse their role, their activities and characteristics were classified in a four-fold typology (see figure 1.3, p. 17) based on two dimensions: whether or not the agency shared the goals and demands of women's movement actors and whether or not they were able to insert these into the debates. The results were then combined in table 14.5 with the impact of the women's movements for the next step in the analysis.

In no fewer than thirteen of all the nineteen successful debates (the dual responses) the women's policy agency had an insider role (68%). In two more successful cases the agency played a marginal role; in four others the agency had a symbolic role. The final dual response case was the third US debate, where the agency had a non-feminist role, but despite it women's movement actors won out. The only case in which the women's agency had an insider role but did not lead to a dual response, was the third Spanish debate, where cabinet and parliament enacted a new immigration act that pre-empted movement demands. Overall, these findings support the hypothesis that insider agencies produce successes for the women's movement actors in terms of both access and policy substance.

When the movement encountered no response, it was in the six debates where the women's policy agency only had a symbolic role, strengthening the support for the hypothesis. Co-optation and pre-emption occurred in nine debates, spread quite equally over the roles the agency played.

What makes for successful women's policy agencies? On the basis of the conceptual framework, it was hypothesised (H.3) that women's policy agencies with greater administrative capability and institutional capacity

Table 14.5 *Women's policy agencies and movement impact*

	Insider	Marginal	Symbolic	Non-feminist
Dual response	13 debates: AUS 1; AUT 3; BR 3; CA 1; FI 1; FI 2; FR 2; IS 3; IT 1; IT 3; NL 1; NL 3; SW 3	2 debates: NL 2; SP 2	3 debates: AUS 3; FR 1; SW 1	1 debate: US 3
Co-optation		1 debate: CA 2	2 debates: FI 3; IS 2	1 debate: SW 2
Pre-emption	1 debate: SP 3	3 debates: AUT 2; FR 3; SP 1	2 debates: AUS 2; BR 1	
No response			6 debates: AUT 1; BR 2; CA 3; IT 2; US 1; US 2	

N = 35 (IS 1 not scored, no women's policy agency in existence)

as defined by type, proximity and mandate, would be more effective in providing linkages between women's movements and policy-makers than agencies with lesser administrative capacity. (See table 14.6.)

The women's policy agencies had a cross-sectional mandate in thirty-two of the thirty-five cases (89%), were of the bureaucratic type in twenty-one cases (66%) and were located close to power in twenty-two cases (62%). In twenty-four cases (68%) they have medium to good administrative capacity and twenty-six cases (74%) feminist leadership; in twenty-two cases (62%) prostitution was within their policy orientation. But successful agencies have other characteristics than the less successful ones. Insider agencies differ quite noticeably from symbolic agencies; all had a cross-sectional scope compared with only three-quarters of the symbolic type, and much more frequently a policy orientation that includes prostitution (78% to 46%). Symbolic agencies are more often of the bureaucratic type (69% to 50%) and are closer to power than the insider agencies (76% to 57%). This appears contradictory, as closeness to power was thought to increase the potential of the women's policy agency, but it can be accounted for by the fact that some women's policies might be positioned close to power within the bureaucracy (France and Australia spring to mind) but have no other means to develop political clout. The major difference between insider and symbolic agencies is in policy

Table 14.6 *Characteristics of women's policy agencies*

Debate	Scope		Type		Power		Administrative capacity		Leadership		Policy orientation	
	Cross-sectional	Single issue	Bureaucratic	Political	Near	Distant	Medium/high	Low	Feminist	Non-feminist	Within	Outside
Insider	14	–	7	7	8	6	10	4	11	3	11	3
Marginal	6	–	4	2	2	4	4	2	4	2	3	3
Symbolic	10	3	9	4	10	3	9	4	10	3[a]	6	7
Non-feminist	2	–	1	1	2	–	1	1	1	1	2	–
Total	32	3	21	14	22	13	24	11	26	9	22	13

N = 35 (IS 1 not counted: no existing WPA)

[a] FI 3 Leadership changed half way: counted as non-feminist leadership here

orientation: prostitution was within the policy orientation of the insider agencies in eleven of the fourteen (78%), compared with only six of the fourteen (46%) symbolic agencies. Inclusion of prostitution in an agency's policy orientation most likely provides motivation to tackle the issue and develop expertise on it; it probably also contributes towards establishing legitimacy for the agency to intervene in other departments on the issue.

Compared with marginal agencies, insider agencies more frequently have feminist leadership (nine of fourteen cases – 78%, to four of six – 66%), are closer to power (eight of fourteen – 57%, to two of six – 33%), have more resources (ten out of fourteen – 71%, to four of six – 66%) and prostitution within their policy orientation (eleven of fourteen – 78%, to three of six – 50%), and are more often of the political type (half to a third). So on the whole there is considerable support for the third hypothesis.

The fourth hypothesis (H. 4) states that variations in women's movements' characteristics and/or policy environments explain variations in both women's policy agency effectiveness and movement success in increasing women's representation. It is examined in two steps. First of all, the characteristics of the women's movement are mapped and related to the women's policy agency's activities in table 14.7, as it is expected that the latter would be more effective when women's movements are in the stage of emergence and growth, close to the left, cohesive on the issue, and give the issue priority, while faced with a weak counter-movement.

Contrary to expectation, stage does not seem to make much difference in explaining the variation. Closeness to the left differs from 71% (ten of fourteen) for insiders to 91% (twelve of the thirteen) of the symbolic cases, which runs contrary to expectation; five of the six marginal cases also show closeness to the left.[2] Neither was priority very important: in the insider cases only four of the ten (40%) saw prostitution as a high priority, but this also goes for six of the thirteen (46%) symbolic cases. In none of the six marginal cases did the issue have high priority. The absence of a counter-movement makes no difference for the insider cases; for marginal and symbolic cases the relation was contrary to what was expected (in two-thirds of the marginal cases and 61 per cent of the symbolic ones there was no counter-movement). So variations in the characteristics of the women's movement hardly account for the effectiveness of the women's policy agency.

Secondly, the women's policy agency activities are related to the policy environment to check out explanations for variation, as it was also hypothesised that a more open policy environment, the left in power or sharing power, and the compatibility of the dominant approach in the policy sub-system with that of the women's movement, would make for a more effective role. (See table 14.8.)

In line with the hypothesis, an open or moderately open policy sub-system was present in eleven of the fourteen (78%) insider cases, as opposed to only one of six (16%) of the marginal cases and seven of the thirteen (53%) symbolic cases. The left in power or sharing power seems to enhance the effectiveness of the agency: this was the case in 85% of the insider cases, as opposed to only 61.5% for the symbolic cases. However, the left was also in power, or sharing it in the marginal cases, in no fewer than four of the six cases, (but there are only six cases here, as opposed to twelve insider cases). Compatibility of the approaches also makes for greater effectiveness of the agencies: matching or compatible approaches occur in all but one of the insider cases (92%) and in only six of the thirteen (46%) symbolic cases. There are four cases in the marginal category where the approaches were compatible (none matched), with only one case of incompatibility. Overall therefore, policy environment is an important variable when accounting for variation in the effectiveness of the women's policy agency.

To check for further explanation for variation, women's movement characteristics were also compared with movement impact (table 14.9) and policy environment (table 14.10). Movement impact does not turn out to be directly related to stage. In nearly all cases the movement was close to the left (thirty-two of thirty-six cases – 88%), and priority low (high priority occurred in only seven cases – 19.4%), so that these characteristics can hardly explain movement success. The only characteristic conducive to movement impact was cohesion on the issue. When the movement was unified on the issue, a dual response occurred in 79% of the cases; in all of the six no response cases, the movement was divided on the issue.

When movement impact was related to policy environment, the following emerged (table 14.10). An open and moderately closed policy sub-system occurred in 73% of the cases of dual response (fourteen of the nineteen cases), compared with only one of the five cases of co-optation, one of the six pre-emption cases and half of the six of the no response cases. The left was also more often in power in the cases of dual response (78%), but the left was also in power or sharing it in four of the six no response cases and in six of the eleven co-optation and pre-emption cases (55.5%). The matching or compatible women's movement actors' approach to the issue proves to be highly important: in all but one of the dual response cases the approach was incompatible. Of the six no response cases, five (83.3%) had an incompatible approach (as compared with half of the co-optation cases and half of the four pre-emption cases).

Table 14.7 *Women's movement characteristics and women's policy agency activities*

	Stage			Closeness to left		Priority		Cohesive	Divided	Counter-movement	
	Emerging/ re-emerging	Growth	Consolidation decline	Very close/ close	Not close	High/ moderate	Low			Yes	No
Insider	5	4	5	10	4	4	10	10	4	7	7
Marginal	2	2	2	5	1	–	6	2	4	4	2
Symbolic	6	4	3	12	1	3	10	6	7	8	5
Non-feminist	–	1	1	2	–	1	1	1	1	3	–
Total	13	11	11	29	6	8	27	19	16	21	14

N = 35 (IS 1 not scored, no existing WPA)

Table 14.8 *Policy environments and role of women's policy agency*

	Party sub-system			Party in power			Dominant approach		
	Open	Moderately closed	Closed	Left in power	Left shares power	Left out of power	Matches	Compatible	Incompatible
Insider	3	8	3	7	5[a]	2	7	6	1
Marginal	–	1	5	2	2	2	–	4	1
Symbolic	1	6	6	4	4	5	1	5	7
Non-feminist	–	1	1	1	1	0	2	–	1
Total	4	16	15	14	12	9	10	15	10

N = 35 (IS 1 not scored, no WPA existing)
[a] IS 3 scored on latter and decisive part of debate

Table 14.9 *Women's movement characteristics and movement impact*

	Stage			Closeness to left		Priority		Cohesive	Divided	Counter-movement	
	Emerging/ re-emerging	Growth	Consolidation decline	Very close/ close	Not close	High/ moderate	Low			Yes	No
Dual response	6	8	5	17	2	5	14	15	4	12	7
Co-optation	2	3	–	4	1	2	3	3	2	3	2
Pre-emption	3	2	1	5	1	–	6	2	4	6	–
No response	3	1	2	6	–	–	6	–	6	3	3
Total	14	14	8	32	4	7	29	20	16	24	12

N = 36

Table 14.10 *Policy environment and movement impact*

	Party sub-system			Party in power			Dominant approach		
	Open	Moderately closed	Closed	Left in power	Left shares power	Left out of power	Matches	Compatible	Incompatible
Dual response	3	11	5	8	7	4	10	9	1
Co-optation	–	1	4	1[a]	2	2	–	2	2
Pre-emption	–	1	5	2	1	3	–	4	2
No response	–	3	3	4	2	–	–	2	4
Total	3	16	17	15	12	9	10	17	9

N = 36
[a] SW2 scored as in power (was out of power at beginning of debate)

Table 14.11 *Women's movement characteristics and policy environments linked to women's movement success/dual response*

		Dual response (%)		
		Yes	No	Total (n)
Priority of issue	Yes	75	25	100 (8)
	No	46	54	100 (28)
Cohesive on issue	Yes	75	25	100 (20)
	No	25	75	100 (16)
Policy sub-system	Open/moderately open	74	26	100 (19)
	Closed	29	71	100 (17)
Dominant approach	Matches/compatible	66.6	33.3	100 (27)
	Incompatible	11	89	100 (9)

N = 36

Therefore, the policy environment variables are more closely associated with movement impact than the characteristics of the movement. It can be concluded that the fourth hypothesis is only partially substantiated: of the women's movement characteristics, cohesion is the only important factor, while all three aspects of the policy environment contribute to the impact of the women's movement. In other words, the usefulness of the independent variables in explaining variation for both movement impact and the activities of the women's policy agency lies mainly in the policy environment indicators; the only women's movement indicator making a difference is the cohesion of the movement.

To test the fifth and final hypothesis, whether women's policy agencies are necessary and effective linkages between movements and state responses, it is necessary to show that variations in movement characteristics and policy environments do not have an independent relationship to state responses. To examine this, two tables were designed. First of all, table 14.11 presents an overview of those independent variables that are related to women's movement impact, as measured by dual response. The characteristics which do not account for variation, have been excluded. Secondly, table 14.12 presents the same variables, but now controlling for the role of the women's policy agency, and is now contrasted with the findings of table 14.11.

From table 14.11 it can be seen that movement actors are likely to achieve a dual response when it is cohesive on the issue, the issue has a high priority, their goals are compatible or match the dominant approach of the policy sub-system and when this sub-system is open to their lobbying. When controlling for women's policy agency activity in table 14.12,

Table 14.12 *Effects of women's movement characteristics and policy environment on women's movement success, controlling for women's policy agency activities*

| | | Women's policy agency activities | | | | | |
| | | Insider/marginal Dual response (%) | | | Symbolic/non-feminist Dual response (%) | | |
		Yes	No	Total (n)	Yes	No	Total (n)
Priority of	Yes	100		100 (4)	50	50	100 (4)
issue	No	69	31	100 (16)	22	78	100 (11)
Cohesive on	Yes	69	31	100 (12)	57	43	100 (7)
issue	No	50	50	100 (8)	0	100	100 (8)
Policy	Open/	92	8	100 (12)	43	57	100 (7)
sub-system	moderately						
	closed	50	50	100 (8)	13	87	100 (8)
Dominant	Matches/	90	10	100 (18)	30	70	100 (10)
approach	compatible						
	Incompatible	0	100	100 (2)	20	80	100 (5)

N = 35 (IS1 not scored – no women's policy agency present)

we find that movements that give prostitution high priority and whose approach matches or is compatible with the policy sub-system frame still need an insider/marginal agency to help them to a dual response and avoid co-optation, pre-emption or no response. The agencies are also of help when the policy sub-system is open, but in that case movement actors can be quite successful without agency support. There is therefore considerable support for the final hypothesis: women's policy agencies are necessary and effective linkages between movement and state response. If the movement was unified on the issue, the agency was less necessary, and movement actors still achieved a dual response even when faced by a hostile or indifferent agency.

Nation-state patterns

This study took policy debates as a point of departure for the analysis of the effectiveness of women's policy agencies, not assuming beforehand that differences between state patterns determine movement outcomes, but making these an object for comparative empirical analysis. Are nation-state patterns in evidence?

When one looks at the impact of the women's movement (see table 14.4), it is clear that, with the exception of the Netherlands, no other movement obtained a dual response in all three debates, i.e. both satisfaction of its policy demands and representation in the policy arena. In Australia, Finland, France, Italy and Sweden, movements scored two dual responses. Furthermore, in no country did a movement see its demands for policy or representation completely ignored, although it did happen to the Canadian and the US women's movement actors in two debates. The Finnish and French actors were successful in the first two debates, while the British and the US actors were kept out during the first two debates (although it should be noted that US women's movement activists were not particularly interested in the child prostitution issue). But in none of the cases where two of the three debates ended in a dual response is a pattern over time in evidence. There is also no evidence of cumulative success: a dual response in the first debate did not guarantee one in the next debates (see table 14.4).

When one looks at the role of the women's policy agencies, it can be observed that no one women's policy agency had the same role in all three debates. Three of them had an insider's role in at least two debates: Finland (but here it was a different agency in each debate), Italy and the Netherlands. It does emerge that agencies were relatively more successful in the third debates: in addition to the three countries already mentioned, this occurred in Austria, Britain (a new WPA, established under the new Labour government), Israel and Sweden. The more depressing stories come from the other side of the Atlantic. Canada's federal agency had an insider's role in the first debate, but lost influence in the consecutive ones. The US agency is the only agency that never had an insider's role in the selected debates.

As strong patterns are lacking, the nation-state does not appear to be the primary variable affecting the impact of the women's movement in prostitution policy. The findings do not allow for generalisations about national policy styles, thus lending support to the usefulness of analysing debates, policy sub-systems and their environment in detail to account for impact. Further research on the basis of the empirical material of this study in the future will be able to answer more fully the question of which variables are most important in explaining the variance in the outcomes of each debate.

Towards a theory of state feminism

This book set out to answer the question of whether women's policy agencies have been effective in advancing the goals of women's movement actors and activists in the area of prostitution policy and enhancing women's access to representation in policy-making arenas. In the background to this query is the debate about governments' role in improving women's status: is there such a thing as state feminism? The results of the study have confirmed the underlying hypotheses of the model employed: gendering policy debates is conducive both for the access of women's movement groups and activists into the policy process and for the attainment of their demands. From the research it emerged that women's movement actors have been successful in increasing both substantive representation (favourable policy outcomes) and descriptive representation (participation in the process); only in one-fifth of the cases studied were movement actors and activists ignored on both counts. They were more successful when women's policy agencies acted as insiders in the policy process, aiding favourable policy outcome and access. In all of the cases where the movement met with no response, the agency had only a symbolic role. It was also found that movement success could not be accounted for in terms of the stage of movement development, closeness to the left, priority given to the issue, or to the presence of a counter-movement; the important factor is movement cohesion on the issue.

Effective agencies are more likely to be of the cross-sectional type, allowing for intervention in other departments and policy arenas, to have prostitution included in their policy orientation and to have feminist leadership. These proved of more importance than their proximity to the locus of power within government or their administrative capacity. Effectiveness was shown to be dependent on the policy environment, especially if the dominant approach or issue frame of the latter was compatible with that of the women's movement actors. The presence of the left in the incumbent government was not a very convincing factor: although it was present in the majority of the insider cases, it also occurred in the majority of the other cases. This outcome lends support to the supposition that issues around sexuality appear to lie on a different dimension in politics than the left–right divide, and that the left is not always one's best friend on these issues.

Finally there is considerable support for the effectiveness and necessity of agency support for women's movement activists in achieving their aims. Therefore, overall, the case for state feminism is supported by the study: women's policy agencies with a cross-sectional mandate, feminist leadership and a policy orientation that includes prostitution do help. They are not a necessary condition for impact if women's movement actors are unified and operate in an open policy environment with a similar issue frame or approach. If these factors are lacking, women's policy agencies can make the difference between achieving actors' goals and non-fulfilment. Further ongoing research in other areas of women's public policy, currently being undertaken by members of the RNGS, will be able to tell us how these findings concur with the outcomes on other issues, or are at odds with the outcomes, making prostitution a special issue for politics, policy, and women's movements actors and activists.

NOTES

With special thanks to Dorothy McBride Stetson and Amy Mazur for reading an earlier draft of this chapter.

1. The chapter closely follows the analysis in the final chapter of Stetson (2001a). This will ensure comparability in the future, when the state feminism thesis will be examined across the issues the RNGS has selected in its project (see chapter 1 of this book).
2. A caveat to this finding is that researchers may not have used the same interpretation of what closeness to the left entailed, despite the independent variable indicators (see appendix 1). In the later stage of the RNGS project this will be analysed in more detail. It may well be that closeness to the left is only important when the left is in power or shares power, but then again measurement of the variable will have to be validated.

Appendix 1   Independent variable indicators

CLUSTER ONE: WOMEN'S MOVEMENT

STAGE

1 Emerging/re-emerging: Formation of new organisations; rehabilitation of older organisations towards new goals.
2 Growth: Expansion in numbers of organisations, activities.
3 Consolidation: Organisations have structure, endurance and regular support; institutionalised in community and government arenas.
4 Decline/abeyance: Decrease in organisations' members and activities over the period. Latent organisational activity primarily by individuals.

CLOSENESS TO LEFT

1 Very close: Feminist groups formally ally with or work with political parties and/or trade unions of the left. Ideas from the feminist movement are taken up by left-wing parties in party platforms. Feminists have internal power positions in the left-wing parties.
2 Close: Feminist groups formally ally with or work with political parties and/or trade unions of the left. They do not have internal power positions in the parties or unions and if the left takes up the ideas of feminist movements they do so without stating so and bring these ideas to fit the party line.
3 Not close: Feminist movement and the left are remote or hostile to each other.

PRIORITY OF ISSUE

1 High: Issue is one of the top priorities of the women's movement and serves to forge alliances among the various wings and tendencies.
2 Moderate: Not a uniting issue, but is a priority for some activists and organisations.

3 Low: Not a priority for any organisation, but mentioned by some. Not on the agenda. Not present at all on agendas of individuals and organisations in the movement.

COHESION

1 Cohesive: Movement organisations active on the issue agree on the frame and/or policy proposals.
2 Divided: Movement organisations active on the issue disagree on the frame and/or policy proposals.

COUNTER-MOVEMENT

1 Strong: Prevalent and proactive movement aimed at issue or issues taken up by different parts of the women's movement.
2 Moderate: Counter-movement less active against women's movement issues.
3 Weak: Nearly moribund or non-existent.

CLUSTER TWO: POLICY ENVIRONMENT

POLICY SUB-SYSTEM

1 Open: Organisation is amorphous, no common rules or conventions; participation is wide and changing with a variety of interest group representatives and free agents. Power balance shows no clear chain of command.
2 Moderately closed: Organisation is more clearly defined but changing over time. Participation shows some regular actors but some free agents around. Power balance shows several actors trying to dominate the group but no single line of command.
3 Closed: Codification of system through regular meetings and rules. Participation is limited with few free agents. Power balance shows one major actor controls policy space and parameters of the arena.

DOMINANT APPROACH FIT

1 Matching: Dominant approach of policy debate is gendered in terms that are similar to frames of movement demands.
2 Compatible: Dominant approach of policy debate is not gendered in terms that are similar to movement frames but in terms that are not in conflict with movement frames.
3 Incompatible: Dominant approach of policy debate is gendered in terms that conflict with (oppose) movement frames in the debate.

PARTY IN POWER

1 Left in power: Left-wing parties have majority in popularly elected legislative chambers and the presidency/executive.
2 Left shares power: Left-wing parties participate in coalition government, or may have the popularly elected chambers only and not the president. In the USA the left may have majority in only one elected chamber of the legislature.
3 Left out of power.

Appendix 2 Worksheets

WORKSHEET 1: SELECTION OF POLICY DEBATES
FOR STUDY

(one for each issue area: abortion, prostitution, job training, political representation)

Step 1: Issue area universe of major policy debates
A. Who and/or which institutions/policy sub-systems make the most important decisions about this issue.

Step 2: Universe of debates
List of debates that come up before these institutions/actors/sub-systems?
Base criteria: (1) debates take place in public arenas such as the legislature, courts, news media, policy party conferences or electoral campaigns; (2) debates occur when a women's policy agency was in existence; (3) debates end with an official state decision, including, for instance, legislation, an executive order, a court ruling or a government policy proposal.

Step 3: Selection of representative debates
Criteria for representativeness: (1) decisional system importance; (2) life cycle; (3) issue area salience.
Criteria used:
List of debates (at least three if possible; determined by resources of group).

WORKSHEET 2: POLICY DEBATE INFORMATION

(Complete one for each debate)
1. Policy debate
2. Appeared on public agenda
3. Endpoint government decision
4. WPA(s) in existence over time period
5. Debate sites: organisations/level of government

6. Documents and other sources used
7. Describe policy debate in three stages:
   - Dominant frame at the beginning of debate
   - How frame changes
   - Frame at end of debate
   a. What is the problem, what is it that needs fixing? Wrong, injustice, threat, situation that needs corrective action?
   b. Who is to blame for the problem?
   c. What should be done? Corrective action.
   d. Content of gendered debate:
      1. Images of women and what they are like.
      2. How men and women are different from each other; how men and women are NOT different.
      3. The ways gender systems shape situations/identities.
      4. How to correct? Challenges to male domination?
      5. Challenges to traditional gender roles?
   e. Is gendered debate feminist?
8. Gendering and policy debate
   a. Who presented gendered issues? (groups, individuals, networks, publics, WPAs, women's movement, trade unions, etc.)
   b. Centrality of gendering to the debate?
   c. Effect on law and legislation?
   d. What was the position of the women's movement on this policy debate?
9. Women's participation (How did women participate in this policy debate, not necessarily feminist women, and did they advocate some aspects of women's interests in the debate?)
   Individuals
   Groups
   Networks
   Publics

WORKSHEET 3: VALUES FOR MODEL VARIABLES

Policy debate name and dates:
Endpoint government decision:
1. IVI-WM Women's Movement
Mapping the women's movement: what are the major organisations, movements, individuals of the women's/feminist movement and what are the major ideas espoused by this constellation of actors?
The following information should be gathered as well:
Stage (emerging, growth, consolidation/decline)

Close of WMO to the left and/or political parties/groups that espouse social equality

Strength of counter-movement

Priority of issue to movement agenda

Cohesion of movement

2. IVII-PE Policy Environment

Policy sub-system:

A. Structure: who are the major actors, dominant structures and patterns of interaction? (open, moderately closed, closed)

B. Dominant approach fit: what was the dominant approach used by the policy actors in the sub-system? To what degree does it fit with the positions of the women's movement and WPAs? (matching, compatible, incompatible)

3. Intervening variable: Women's policy agency characteristics:

If more than one WPA, information should be gathered on each.

Scope (single issue, cross-sectional, other?)

Type (political, administrative, other?)

Proximity (closeness to power – position in government hierarchy?)

Administrative capacity (budget, staff, administrative divisions, field offices, women's groups, subsidies, etc.?)

Individual leadership (feminist, political, bureaucratic, etc.?)

Policy mandate (major policy orientation)

Women's policy agency activities (insider, marginal, non-feminist, symbolic)

WPA gendered policy debate?

WPA promoted women's movement goals?

4. Dependent variable: Women's movement impact (dual response, co-optation, pre-emption, no response)

Were women (individuals, group, networks, constituencies) advancing some aspect of women's interests in policy-making process?

Policy action achieved women's goals or not?

References

A GOVERNMENT DOCUMENTS

AUSTRALIA

C. of A. Commonwealth of Australia. Parliament. *Hansard*
NSWPD. New South Wales Parliament *Debates*
VPD. Victoria Parliament *Debates*

BRITAIN

Hansard, http://www.parliament.the-stationery-office.co.uk/pa/cm/cmhansrd. htm

FINLAND

Gov. prop. 246/1984, Hallituksen esitys Eduskunnalle päihdehuoltolaiksi
Gov. prop. 6/1997, Hallituksen esitys oikeudenkäyttöä, viranomaisia ja yleistä järjestystä kohdistuvia rikoksia sekä seksuaalirikoksia koskevien säännösten uudistamiseksi
Law (41/1986) *Päihdehuoltolaki*. Helsinki: Säädöskokoelma
Parliamentary law initiative (31/1996 Diet) Lakialoite 31/1996 vp.: Paula Kokkonen ym.: Lakialoite rikoslain 20 luvun 8 §:n muuttamisesta
Parliamentary documents 1984–1998, Helsinki: Eduskunta. (From the 1994 Diet onward, all parliamentary documents except committee minutiae are available at http://www.eduskunta.fi)

ISRAEL

Law against Trafficking in Human Beings 2001, Jerusalem, The Knesset

NETHERLANDS

Beleidsplan Emancipatie 1985, HTK, 1984–1985, 19502, nr 2
Handelingen Eerste Kamer (HEK), jaargangen 1982–1999
Handelingen Tweede Kamer (HTK), jaargangen 1982–1999
Nota Bestrijding Seksueel Geweld (1984), HTK, 1983–1984, 18452, nrs 1–2
Staatsblad 1999, 464 (9-11-99)

300   References

SPAIN

Diario de Sesiones del Congreso de Los Diputados
Instituto de la Mujer 1986; 1988a; 1989; 1990a; 1991; 1992; 1993a; 1994; 1995;
    1996a, Annual Reports of the Women's Institute Activities
Instituto de la Mujer 1988b; 1993b; 1997, Gender Equality Plans
Instituto de la Mujer 1990b; 1996b, Gender Equality Plans: Evaluations

SWEDEN

Parliamentary bills
M 80/81: 1246 *om behandling av rapporten Prostitutionen i Sverige*
M 80/81: 403 *om förbud mot offentlig pornografisk framställning*
M 80/81: 1252 *om åtgärder mot prostitution*
M 80/81: 1254 *om åtgärder mot prostitutionen*
M 80/81: 1367 *om förbud mot offentlig pornografisk framställning*
M 81/82: 2430 *vis åtgärder mot prostitutionen (prop. 1981/82:187)*
1992/93: Ju616 *Kriminalisering av prostituerades kunder*
1992/93: Ju622 *Prostitution*
1994/95: A802 *Jämställdhet*
1994/95: A820 *Jämställdhetsfrågor*
1996/97: A806 *Ökad jämställdhet*
1996/97: Ju714 *Prostitution*
1996/97: Ju718 *Kriminalisering av könsköp*
1996/97: Ju917 *Åtgärder mot kvinnovåld och våld mot barn*
1997/98: Ju708 *Kriminalisering av de prostituerades kunder*
1999/2000: Ju717 *Prostitution*
2001/02: Fi219 *Människohandel för sexuella ändamål som ett nytt politikområde*
2001/02: Ju267 *Handeln med kvinnor*
2001/02: Ju291 *Försäljning av sexuella tjänster*
2001/02: Ju299 *Bekämpning av trafficking*
2001/02: U308 *Legaliseringen av prostitution*

Proposals (Betänkanden)
1981/82: 50 SoU om vissa åtgärder mot prostitutionen (prop. 1981/82:187 delvis)
1981/82: 56 JuU om offentlig pornografisk föreställning m.m. (prop. 1981/82:187
    delvis jämte motioner)
1992/93: JuU15 Kriminalisering av prostitution
1993/94: JuU03 Övergrepp på kvinnor och barn
1996/97: JuU11 Våldsbrott och brottsoffer
1997/98: JuU13 Kvinnofrid

Government bills (Propositioner), commission reports
    and remiss
DsS 1980: 9 (*Prostitutionen i Sverige: en rapport utarbetad. inom Prostitutionsutred-
    ningen*), 1980, Stockholm, LiberFörlag/Allmänna förl
Proposition 1981/82: 50 *om vissa åtgärder mot prostitutionen*

Proposition 1983/84:105 om ändring i brottsbalken m.m. (sexualbrotten)
S97/8122/IFO (*Sammanställning av remissyttranden över prostitutionsutredningens betänkande Könshandeln SOU 1995:15*)
SOU 1976: 9 (*Sexuella övergrepp: förslag till ny lydelse av brottsbalkens bestämmelser om sedlighetsbrott: betänkande avgivet av Sexualbrottsutredningen*) 1976, Stockholm: LiberFörlag/Allmänna förl
SOU 1981: 71 (*Prostitutionen i Sverige: bakgrund och åtgärder: betänkande av Prostitutionsutredningen*) 1981, Stockholm: LiberFörlag/Allmänna förl
SOU 1995: 15 (*Könshandeln: betänkande av 1993 års prostitutionsutredning*), 1995 Stockholm: Fritzes
SOU 1995: 17 (*Homosexuell prostitution: en kunskapsinventering: rapport för 1993 års prostitutionsutredning*), 1995 Stockholm: Fritzes
SOU 1995: 60 (*Kvinnofrid: slutbetänkande av Kvinnovåldskommissionen*) 1995, Stockholm: Fritzes
SOU 1997/98: 55 *Kvinnofrid: Regeringens proposition* 1998

Parliamentary protocols (RP, Riksdagsprotokoll)
Riksdagsprotokoll 1980: 33
Riksdagsprotokoll 1982: 159
Riksdagsprotokoll 1993/94: 86
Riksdagsprotokoll 1996/97: 86
Riksdagsprotokoll 1997/98: 5
Riksdagsprotokoll 1997/98: 114
Riksdagsprotokoll 1997/98: 115
Riksdagsprotokoll 1998/99: 43
Riksdagsprotokoll 1998/99: 45
Riksdagsprotokoll 1998/99: 59

Laws (Lagar och förordningar)
SFS (Svensk författningssamling) Jämställdhetslag 1991: 433
SFS Lag 1998: 408 om förbud mot köp av sexuella tjänster
SFS Ordningslag 1993: 1617 (replacing the earlier law 1982: 1172)

USA

Florida Statutes 2001. Prostitution: Coercion. Title XLVI, Chapter 796.09
Miller vs. California 413 US 15 1973
New York vs. Ferber 458 US 747 1982
US Congress, House of Representatives 1977, *Sexual Exploitation of Children.* Hearings before the Subcommittee on Crime of the Committee on the Judiciary. May 23, 25, June 10, September 20
  1985, *Child Victims of Exploitation.* Hearing before the Select Committee on Children, Youth, and Families. October 31
  1999, *Trafficking of Women and Children in the International Sex Trade.* Hearings before the subcommittee on International Operations and Human Rights of the Committee on International Relations. September 14

US Congress, Senate 1977, *Protection of Children Against Sexual Exploitation*. Hearings before the Subcommittee to Investigate Juvenile Delinquency of the Committee on the Judiciary. May 27, June 16

1984, *Child Pornography and Pedophilia*. Hearings before the Permanent Subcommittee on Investigations of the Committee on Governmental Affairs. November 29–30

Child Pornography and Pedophilia. Hearing before the Permanent Subcommittee on Investigations of the Committee on Governmental Affairs. February 21

2000, *International Trafficking in Women and Children*. Hearings before the Subcommittee on Near Eastern and South Asian Affairs of the Committee on Foreign Relations. February 22; April 4

United States 1910, *Statutes at Large*. White Slave Traffic (Mann) Act. 36 Stat. 825–27

1978, *Statutes at Large*. Protection of Children against Sexual Exploitation Act (PL 95–225). 92 Stat. 7–9

1986, *Statutes at Large*. Child Sexual Abuse and Pornography Act (PL 99–628). 100 Stat. 3510–12

2000, *Statutes at Large*. Traffic Victims Protection Act of 2000 (PL 106–386). 114 Stat. 1466–91

B   GENERAL

Aitken, Jan 1978, 'The Prostitute as Worker', in Women and Labour Conference, *Women and Labour Conference Papers, May 1978*, North Ryde (NSW): The Women and Labour Conference Convenors, pp. 240–8

Allen, Judith 1990, *Sex and Secrets: Crimes Involving Australian Women Since 1880*, Melbourne: Oxford University Press

Alliance of Five Research Centres on Violence 1999, 'Violence Prevention and the Girl Child: Final Report' (December)

Amir, M. 1999, 'The Economy of Prostitution in Israel: Market and Organizational Aspects', report to the Conference on Trafficking in Women and on Prostitution organized by the Women's Study Network, Haifa, June (in Hebrew)

2001, 'Organized Crime in Israel', *Hachali Mishpat Law Journal* 2: 1–14

Amnesty International 2000, *Human Rights Abuses Affecting Women in Israel's Sex Industry*, 18 May

Appelt, Erna 1995, 'Frauen und Fraueninteressen im korporatistischen System', in *Bericht über die Situation der Frauen in Österreich. Frauenbericht 1995*, edited by Bundesministerin für Frauenangelegenheiten/Bundeskanzleramt, Vienna: Bundesministerium für Frauenangelegenheiten, pp. 610–18

Asia Watch and the Women's Rights Project 1993, *A Modern Form of Slavery: Trafficking of Burmese Women and Girls into Brothels in Thailand*, New York: Human Rights Watch

Bachrach, Peter and Morton S. Baratz 1970, *Power and Poverty: Theory and Practice*, New York: Oxford University Press

Baldwin, Margaret A. 1992, 'Split at the Root: Prostitution and Feminist Discourses of Law Reform', *Yale Journal of Law and Feminism* 5: 47–120

Barry, Kathleen 1979, *Female Sexual Slavery*, Englewood Cliffs, NJ: Prentice-Hall
1995, *The Prostitution of Sexuality*, New York: New York University Press

Bashevkin, Sylvia 1998, *Women on the Defensive: Living through Conservative Times*, Toronto: University of Toronto Press

Bastow, Karen 1995, 'Prostitution and HIV/AIDS', *HIV/AIDS Policy & Law Newsletter*, 2, 2, available at http://www.walnet.org/csis/papers/bastow-aidslaw.htm (accessed 8 March 2001)

Beckman, Marlene D. 1995, 'The White Slave Traffic Act: Historical Impact of a Federal Crime Policy on Women', *Women & Politics* 4: 85–101

Beckwith, Karen 2000, 'Beyond Compare? Women's Movements in Comparative Perspective', *European Journal of Political Research* 37: 431–68

Bell, Shannon 1994, *Reading Writing and Rewriting the Prostitute Body*, Bloomington: Indiana University Press

Belmonti, M.G. 1981, *Veronique*, Milan: Sperling & Kupfer

Ben-Ito, H. 1977, *Report of the Government Commission to Investigate the Problems of Prostitution*, Jerusalem: The Ministry of Justice (in Hebrew)

Bergqvist, Christina, Anette Borchorst, Ann-Dorte Christiansen, Viveca Ramstedt-Silén, Nina C. Raaum and Auōor Styrkársdóttir (eds.) 1999, *Equal Democracies: Gender and Politics in the Nordic Countries*, Oslo: Scandinavian University Press

Bindman, Jo 1998, 'An International Perspective on Slavery in the Sex Industry', in Kempadoo and Doezema (eds.), pp. 65–9

Bocchetti, A. [1983] 1995, 'Che cos'è il separatismo', in Bocchetti (ed.) *Cosa vuole una donna. Storia, politica, teoria. Scritti 1981–1995*, Milan: La Tartaruga, pp. 41–54

Borg, Arne, Folke Elrein, Michael Frühling, et al. 1981, *Prostitution: beskrivning, analys, förslag till åtgärde*, Stockholm: Liber Förlag

BRÅ-rapport 2000, *Förbud mot köp av sexuella tjänster: tillämpningen av lagen under första året*, Stockholm: Fritzes

Brezany, Elfriede 1987, 'Horizontal', *Sozialarbeit in Österreich* 77: 21–3

Brock, Deborah R. 1998, *Making Work, Making Trouble: Prostitution as a Social Problem*, Toronto: University of Toronto Press

Brownmiller, Susan 1999, *In Our Time*, New York: Dial Press

Brunnberg, Elisabeth, Hanna Olsson and Karin Widerberg 1981, 'Samtal kring prostitutionsutredningen', *Kvinnovetenskaplig tidskrift* 2: 26–31

Brussa, Licia 1991, *Survey on Prostitution, Migration and Traffic in Women: History and Current Situation*, Strasbourg: Council of Europe, EG/PROST (1)2

Buijs, Heleen and Annemarie Verbraken 1985, *Vrouwenhandel. Onderzoek naar aard, globale omvang en de kanalen waarlangs vrouwenhandel in Nederland plaatsvindt*, The Hague: Ministerie van Sociale Zaken en Werkgelegenheid

Bundesministerium für Justiz (ed.) 1983, *Prostitution – Zuhälterei. Fachtagung im Bundesministerium für Justiz am 18.10.1982*, Vienna: Bundesministerium für Justiz

Burt, Sandra 1998, 'The Canadian Advisory Council on the Status of Women: Possibilities and Limitations', in Manon Tremblay and Caroline Andrew (eds.) *Women and Political Representation in Canada*, Ottawa: University of Ottawa Press, pp. 115–44

Buzzi, C. 1998, *Giovani, affettività, sessualità. L'amore tra i giovani in un'indagine IARD*, Bologna: Il Mulino

Cabiria 1999, *Rapport d'Activité 1999*, Lyons

Campagna, Daniel S. and Donald L. Poffenberger 1988, *The Sexual Trafficking in Children: an Investigation of the Child Sex Trade*, Dover, MA: Auburn House Publishing

Canadian Advisory Council on the Status of Women 1984, *Prostitution in Canada*, Ottawa: CACSW

Carchedi, F., A. Picciolini, G. Mottura and G. Campani (eds.) 2000, *I colori della notte. Migrazioni, sfruttamento sessuale, esperienze di intervento sociale*, Milan: Franco Angeli

Carracedo Bullido, Rosario 2001, 'Legislación penal española', in Dirección General de la Mujer de la Comunidad de Madrid (ed.), *Simposio internacional sobre prostitución y tráfico de mujeres con fines de explotación sexual*, Madrid: Dirección General de la Mujer de la Comunidad de Madrid, pp. 149–59

Carver, Terrell and Veronique Mottier (eds.) 1998, *Politics of Sexuality: Identity, Gender, Citizenship*, London and New York: Routledge

Caul, Miki 1999, 'Women's Representation in Parliament: the Role of Political Parties', *Party Politics* 5, 1: 79–98

Cauly, Martine 1974, *Commission–Action Sociale (Lutte contre le proxnétisme)*, Paris: Publication of the Conseil National des Femmes Françaises, 2 February

Cebrián Franco, J.J. 1997, *Prostitución y Sociedad*, Barcelona: ATE

Chapkis, Wendy 1997, *Live Sex Acts: Performing Erotic Labor*, New York: Routledge

Cobb, R.W. and C.D. Elder 1972, *Participation in American Politics: the Dynamics of Agenda-Building*, Baltimore: The Johns Hopkins University Press

Cohen, Y. 1967, 'Open Treatment of a Deviant Girl', *Social Problems* 9: 13–22 (in Hebrew)

Collier, David 1991, 'New Perspectives on the Comparative Method', in D.A. Rustow and K.P. Erickson (eds.), *Comparative Political Dynamics: Global Research Perspectives*, New York: Harper Collins, pp. 7–31

Collier, David, and James E. Mahon 1993, 'Conceptual "Stretching" Revisited: Adapting Categories in Comparative Analysis', *American Political Science Review* 87: 845–55

Commissie Melai 1977, Derde Interimrapport: Prostitutie, The Hague: Staatsdrukkerij

Commission of the European Communities 2000, 'Combating Trafficking in Human Beings and Combating the Sexual Exploitation of Children and Child Pornography', *Proposal for a Council Framework Decision*, http://europa. eu.int/comm/avpolicy/regul/new_srv/sexcom.pdf (accessed 3 October 2001)

Committee Report 1986, *Irtolaislain kumoamisen vaikutuksia selvittävän toimikunnan mietintö*, Komiteanmietintö 1986:46, Helsinki: Valtion painatuskeskus

Conant, Michael 1996, 'Federalism, the Mann Act, and the Imperative to Decriminalize Prostitution', *Cornell Journal of Law and Policy* 5: 99–118

Considine, Mark and Brian Costar (eds.) 1992, *Trials in Power: Cain, Kirner and Victoria 1982–1992*, Carlton: Melbourne University Press

Coppel, Anne, Lydia Braggiotti, Isabell de Vincenzi, Sylvie Besson, Rosemary Ancelle and Jean-Baptiste Brunet 1990, *Recherche-action, prostitution et santé publique, rapport réalisé à la suite d'une recherche-action effectué à la demande et avec la participation de femmes prostituées parisiennes avec l'appui de La Direction Générale de la Santé et l'Agence Française de Lutte Contre le SIDA*, Paris: Ministère des Affaires Sociales

Corbin, Alain 1978, *Les filles de noce, misère sexuelle et prostitution*, Paris: Montaigne

Costain, Anne 1992, *Inviting Women's Rebellion: a Political Process Interpretation of the Women's Movement*, Baltimore: The Johns Hopkins University Press

Coulter, Emilie 1997, 'The Status of the Status of Women Canada: Co-opting Our Agenda', *Kinesis*, May: 3–7

Council of State 1984, Valtioneuvoston pöytäkirja 129/1984. 29.11.1984. Helsinki: Valtioneuvoston arkisto

Cromer, Sylvie, Odile Krakovich and Marie-Victoire Louis 1992, 'Entretien avec M. Sapin, Ministre délégué à la justice, concernant la réforme du code pénal', *Projets féministes* 3 (October): 87–103

CSCE 1999, *Briefing on Trafficking in Women*, Washington, DC: Federal Document Clearing House, Inc., 28 June

Cutrufelli, M.R. 1997, *Il denaro in corpo*, Milan: Marco Tropea Editore (reprint of M.R. Cutrufelli, *Il cliente. Inchiesta sulla domanda di prostituzione*, Rome: Editori Riuniti, 1981)

Daly, Mary 2000, *The Gender Division of Welfare: the Impact of the British and the German Welfare States*, Cambridge: Cambridge University Press

Dávila, Pilar 2001, 'Apertura del simposio', in Dirección General de la Mujer de la Comunidad de Madrid (ed.), *Simposio internacional sobre prostitución y tráfico de mujeres con fines de explotación sexual*, Madrid: Dirección General de la Mujer de la Comunidad de Madrid, pp. 21–6

Davis, Sylvia and Martha Schaffer 1994, 'Prostitution in Canada: the Invisible Menace or the Menace of Invisibility?', unpublished paper, available at http://www.walnet.org/csis/papers/sdavis.html (accessed 8 March 2001)

De Vincenzi, Isabelle 1989, 'Sida et prostituées: revue des données françaises', *Bulletin epidémologie hebdomadaire* 40: 165–6

DeCou, Kate 1998, 'US Social Policy on Prostitution: Whose Welfare is Served?', *Civil and Criminal Confinement* 24: 427–53

Delacoste, F. and P. Alexander (eds.) 1987, *Sex Work: Writings by Women in the Sex Industry*, San Francisco: Cleiss Press

Delegation for the Prevention of Intoxicant Abuse 1984, Irtolaislaista ja prostituutiosta. 7.5.1984/H.T. Päihdeasiain neuvottelukunta, asiakirjat 1978–87. Helsinki: Valtioneuvoston arkisto

Delgado-Iribarren, Manuel (ed.) 1996, *Ley Orgánica del Código Penal: Trabajos parlamentarios*, Madrid: Cortes Generales

Della Porta, Donatella and Mario Diani 1999, *Social Movements: an Introduction*, Oxford: Blackwell

Dick, Hildegund 1991, 'Die autonome Frauenbewegung in Wien. Entstehung, Entfaltung und Differenzierung von 1972 bis Anfang der 80er Jahre', Ph.D. thesis, University of Vienna

Disney, Jennifer Leigh and Joyce Gelb 2000, 'Feminist Organizational "Success": the State of US Women's Movement Organizations in the 1990s', *Women and Politics*, 21: 39–76

Doezema, Jo 1998, 'Forced to Choose: Beyond the Voluntary v. Forced Prostitution Dichotomy', in Kempadoo and Doezema (eds.), pp. 34–51

Dohnal, Johanna 1992, 'Männer entscheiden, welche Heilige, welche Hure ist', in *Wiener* 7 (6 March): 21

Duchen, Claire 1986, *Feminism in France from May 1968 to Mitterrand*, London: Routledge & Kegan Paul

Dulude, Louise 1988, 'The Status of Women under the Mulroney Government', in Andrew Gollner and Daniel Salle (eds.), *Canada under Mulroney: an End of Term Report*, Montreal: Véhicule Press, pp. 253–64

ECP (English Collective of Prostitutes) 1997, 'Campaigning for Legal Change', in Scambler and Scambler (eds.), pp. 83–103

Edelman, Murray 1964, *The Symbolic Uses of Politics*, Urbana and Chicago: University of Illinois Press

Edwards, Susan 1987, 'Prostitutes: Victims of Law, Social Policy and Organised Crime', in Pat Carlen and Anne Worrall (eds.), *Gender, Crime and Justice*, Buckingham: Open University Press, pp. 43–56

1996, *Sex and Gender in the Legal Process*, London: Blackstone Press

1997, 'The Legal Regulation of Prostitution: a Human Rights Issue', in Scambler and Scambler (eds.), pp. 57–82

Eisenstein, Hester 1990, 'Femocrats, Official Feminism and the Uses of Power', in Watson (ed.), pp. 87–103

1996, *Inside Agitators: Australian Femocrats and the State*, Philadelphia: Temple University Press

EU: Justice and Home Affairs 2001, 'Trafficking in Women: the Misery Behind the Fantasy: from Poverty to Sex Slavery', *A Comprehensive European Strategy*, http://europa.eu.int/comm/justice_home/new/8mars_en.htm (accessed 3 October 2001)

Europap-UK 1999a, 'UK Final Report 1998–1999', compiled by Hilary Kinnell. available at http://www.europap.net/

1999b, 'Trafficking and Sexual Exploitation: Response of Europap-UK to Points Raised at the Home Office Seminar', 15 October 1999, available at http://www.europap.net/

2002, 'Transportation of Sex Workers to be Criminalized', by Hilary Kinnell, available at http://www.europa.net/

European Commission 1996, *Report of the Conference on Trafficking in Women*, 10–11 June 1996, Vienna (CAB./183/96-en)

European Union 1997, *The Hague Ministerial Declaration on European Guidelines for Effective Measures to Prevent and Combat Trafficking in Women for the Purpose of Sexual Exploitation*, Ministerial Conference, The Hague, 24–26 April

Falco, Denise Pouillon 1991, 'La position de l'Union contre le trafic des êtres humains', *Cette violence dont nous voulons plus*, 11–12: 46–50

Farini. D. 2000, 'Nove proposte sulla prostituzione. Alcune posizioni di opinion maker italiani', http://www.regione.emilia-romagna.it/oltrelastrada (9 May)

Farley M. and V. Kelley 2000, 'Prostitution: a Critical Review of the Medical and Social Science Literature', *Women and Criminal Justice* 11, 4: 29–64

Federal/Provincial/Territorial Working Group on Prostitution 1998, *Report and Recommendations in Respect of Legislation, Policy and Practices Concerning Prostitution-Related Activities*, Ottawa: Ministry of Justice

Feigl, Susanne 2001, *Frauen sichtbar machen. 10 Jahre Frauenbüro der Stadt Wien/ MA 57*, Vienna: Frauenbüro

FEN 1988, *Le féminisme et ses enjeux*, Paris: Centre Fédéral de la FEN

Finocchiaro, A. 2000, 'Prefazione', in Carchedi et al. (eds.), pp. 11–15

Finstad, Liv 1981, 'Den svenska prostitutionsutredningen', *Kvinnovetenskaplig tidskrift* 2: 32–38

Fiorensoli, M.P. (ed.) 1998, *Donne ch'avete intelletto d'amore. Confronto e riflessioni sulla prostituzione a partire da un punto di vista di donne*, proceedings of the conference at, Modena, 7 November 1998, Rome: Il paese delle donne

Florida Supreme Court 1990, *Gender Bias Study Commission*, Gainesville: Florida Supreme Court

Florin, Christina and Bengt Nilsson 1999, 'Something in the Nature of a Bloodless Revolution . . . How New Gender Relations Became Gender Equality Policy in Sweden in the Nineteen-Sixties and Seventies', in Rolf Torstendahl (ed.), *State Policy and Gender System in the Two German States and Sweden 1945–1989*, Uppsala: University of Uppsala, Department of History, pp. 11–77

Fondation Scelle 1998, *Memento de 16 associations françaises face a la prostitution*, Paris: Fondation Scelle

Forum de Política Feminista (ed.) 1991, *Prostitución: Debate y propuestas del movimiento feminista*, Madrid: Forum de Política Feminista

Franzway, S., D. Court and R.W. Connell (eds.) 1989, *Staking a Claim: Feminism, Bureaucracy and the State*, Sydney: Allen & Unwin

Fraser, Paul 1985, *Report of the Special Committee on Pornography and Prostitution, Vol. II*, Ottawa: Minister of Supply and Services

Frauen in Wien 1996, *Zahlen, Fakten und Probleme*, edited by the Women's Office Vienna, Vienna: Women's Office Vienna

Frauenbericht 1985, *Bericht über die Situation der Frau in Österreich*, edited by Bundeskanzleramt, Vienna: Bundeskanzleramt

1995, *Bericht über die Situation der Frauen in Österreich*, edited by Bundesministerin für Frauenangelegenheiten/Bundeskanzleramt, Vienna: Bundesministerium für Frauenangelegenheiten/Bundeskanzleramt

Frauenhandel 1996, edited by Bundesministerin für Frauenangelegenheiten, Vienna: Bundesministerium für Frauenangelegenheiten

Gamson, William A. 1975, *The Strategy of Social Protest*, Homewood, IL: The Dorsey Press

Garaizábal, Cristina 1991, 'La prostitución: un debate abierto', in Forum de Política Feminista (ed.), *Prostitución: Debate y propuestas del movimiento feminista*, Madrid: Forum de Política Feminista, pp. 6–10

Gardiner, Frances (ed.) 1997, *Sex Equality Policy in Western Europe*, London and New York: Routledge

Geiser, Robert L. 1979, *Hidden Victims: the Sexual Abuse of Children*, Boston: Beacon Press

Gelb, Joyce 1989, *Feminism and Politics: a Comparative Perspective*, Berkeley: University of California Press

Geller-Schwarz, Linda 1995, 'An Array of Agencies: Feminism and State Institutions in Canada', in Stetson and Mazur (eds.), pp. 40–58

Gibson, M. 1995, *Stato e prostituzione in Italia 1860–1915*, Milan: Il Saggiatore (translation of *Prostitution and the State in Italy: 1860–1915*, New Brunswick: Rutgers University Press, 1986)

Giroud, Françoise 1976, *Cent mesures pour les femmes*, Paris: La Documentation Française

Gorjanicyn, Katrina 1992, 'Legislating Social Reform: Guns, Grog and Prostitution', in Considine and Costar (eds.), pp. 127–43

1998, 'Sexuality and Work: Contrasting Prostitution Policies in Victoria and Queensland', in Carver and Mottier (eds.), pp. 180–9

Gottweis, Herbert 1997, 'Neue Soziale Bewegungen in Österreich', in Herbert Dachs, Peter Gerlich, Herbert Gottweis, et al. (eds.), *Handbuch des politischen Systems Österreichs. Die Zweite Republik*, Vienna: Manz, pp. 342–58

Gould, Arthur 2001, 'The Criminalisation of Buying Sex: the Politics of Prostitution in Sweden', *Journal of Social Politics* 30, 3: 437–56

Grittner, Frederick K. 1990, *White Slavery: Myth, Ideology, and American Law*, New York: Garland Publishing

Guadagnini, M. 1995, 'The Latecomers: Italy's Equal Status and Equal Opportunity Agencies', in Stetson and Mazur (eds.), pp. 150–68

Guadilla, Nati Garci 1981, *Libération des femmes: Le MLF*, Paris: Presses Universitaires de France

Guigni, Marco 1995, 'Outcomes of New Social Movements', in Hanspeter Kriesi, Ruud Koopmans, Jan Willem Duyvendak and Mario Giugni (eds.), pp. 207–37

Gwinnet, Barbara 1998, 'Policing Prostitution', in Vicky Randall and Georgina Waylen (eds.) *Gender, Politics and the State*, London: Routledge, pp. 80–99

The Hague – Ministerial Declaration on European Guidelines for Effective Measures to Prevent and Combat Trafficking in Women for the Purpose of Sexual Exploitation, Ministerial Conference, The Hague 24–26 April 1997

Häkkinen, Antti 1995, *Rahasta – vaan ei rakkaudesta. Prostituutio Helsingissä 1867–1939*, Keuruu: Otava

Hapala, Michaela 1986, 'Rechtliche und praktische Möglichkeiten der Besteuerung von Prostituierten und Zuhältern', in *Öffentliche Sicherheit* 8 (August): 1–4

Harcourt, Christine 1999, 'Whose Morality? Brothel Planning Policy in South Sydney', *Social Alternatives* 18, 2: 32–7

Harding, Sandra 1986, *The Science Question in Feminism*, Ithaca and London: Cornell University Press

Hauer, Gudrun 1987, 'Frauenberuf Prostitution', *Die Linke*, 10: 12

Hausegger, Traude 1995, 'Zu wessen Schutz, in wessen Namen? Die "geregelten" Arbeitsbedingungen von Prostituierten und ihre Konsequenzen', in *Frauenbericht 1995. Bericht über die Situation der Frauen in Österreich*, edited by

Bundesministerin für Frauenangelegenheiten/Bundeskanzleramt, Vienna: Bundesministerium für Frauenangelegenheiten, 551–6

Haveman, Roelof 1995, 'Slavernij of reguliere arbeid?', *Nemesis* 11: 97–102

Hazani, M. 1989, 'Deviant Companionship and Interaction across an Intergroup "Seam": Arab Pimps and Jewish Prostitutes', *Plural Societies* 19, 1: 55–73

Helsinki City Council 1998, Sääntötoimikunnan järjestyssääntöehdotus 4.3. 1998. Helsinki

1999a, Järjestyssääntö. Erilliset liitteet. Liitteet, kaupunginvaltuusto 1.9.1999. Helsinki

1999b, Kaupunginhallituksen mietinnöt 6 – 1999. Helsingin kaupunginvaltuston asiakirjat. Helsinki

1999c, Kaupunginvaltuuston keskustelupöytäkirja 1.9.1999. Helsinki

Henniquau, Laurence 1986, 'Note à l'attention de Madame la Ministre', Interministerial Correspondence, 17 January, Mimeograph, 1–10

Hernes, Helga 1997, *Welfare State and Woman Power*, Oslo: Norwegian University Press

Heywood, Paul 1995, *The Government and Politics of Spain*, London: Macmillan

Hirdman, Yvonne 2001, *Genus: om det stabilas föränderliga former*, Malmö: Liber

Hobson, Barbara Meil 1987, *Uneasy Virtue: the Politics of Prostitution and the American Reform Tradition*, New York: Basic Books; reissued in 1990, Chicago: Chicago University Press

Holli, Anne Maria 1999, 'The Debate on Gender Equality within the Armed Forces – a Case Study of Finland', in Bergqvist et al. (eds.), pp. 233–49

2001, 'A Shifting Policy Environment Divides the Impact of State Feminism in Finland', in Mazur (ed.), pp. 183–212

Holsopple, Kelly 1999, 'Pimps, Tricks and Feminists', *Women's Studies Quarterly* 27: 7–52

Home Office 1956, *Sexual Offences Act 1956*, Norwich: HMSO

1959, *Street Offences Act 1959*, Norwich: HMSO

1984, *Politics and Criminal Evidence Act 1984*, Norwich: HMSO

1998, *Human Rights Act 1998*, available at http://www.hmso.gov.uk/acts/acts1998/19980042.htm

2000a, *Safeguarding Children Involved in Prostitution*, published jointly by the Home Office, the Department of Health, the Department for Education and Employment, and the National Assembly of Wales, available at http://www.homeoffice.gov.uk/circulars/2000/2000.htm

2000b, *Setting the Boundaries: Reforming the Law on Sex Offences* Vol. I, July

2001a, *Criminal Justice and Police Act 2001*, available at http://www.hmso.gov.uk/acts/acts2001/20010016.htm

2001b, *Select Committee on European Scrutiny*, Third Report, Select Committee Report, 17 July, available at http://www.parliament.the-stationery-office.co.uk/pa/cm/cmhansrd.htm

2002, *Secure Borders, Safe Haven: Integration with Diversity in Modern Britain*, Home Office White Paper CM 5387 2002, available at http://www.official-documents.co.uk/document/cm53/5387/cm5387.pdf

Horovitz, M. 1969, 'Female Crimes', *Journal of Israeli Criminological Society* 9, 1: 3–10

House of Commons 1985, *Minutes of Proceedings and Evidence of the Legislative Committee on Bill C-49*, First Session of the Thirty-third Parliament, 1984–1985, Ottawa: Speaker of the House of Commons, Queen's Printer for Canada

House of Commons 1996, *Hansard*, June 10, Ottawa: Speaker of the House of Commons, Queen's Printer for Canada

Hubbard, Phil 1998a, 'Community Action and the Displacement of Street Prostitution: Evidence from British Cities', *Geoforum* 29, 3: 269–86

1998b, 'Sexuality, Immorality and the City: Red-Light Districts and the Marginalisation of Female Street Prostitutes', *Gender, Place and Culture* 5, 1: 55–72

Hughes, D.M. and C.M. Roche (eds.) 1999, *Making the Harm Visible: the Global Exploitation of Women and Girls: Speaking Out and Providing Services*, Kingston, RI: Coalition against Trafficking of Women

Inglehart, Ronald 1990, *Culture Shift in Advanced Industrial Society*, Princeton: Princeton University Press

Isaksson, Emma 2001, 'Kvinnokultur – identitet och feministiska alternativ i den nya kvinnorörelsen', conference paper presented at the Gender, Citizenship and the State Conference, Skepparholmen, Stockholm, 5 February

Italia 1999, *Indagine conoscitiva sugli aspetti sociali e sanitari della prostituzione, (audizione del Comitato per i diritti civili delle prostitute e dei rappresentanti delle organizzazioni sindacali), 1–6 e documento conclusivo (28 luglio 1999)*, Camera dei deputati, Commissione affari sociali

Järvinen, Margaretha 1987, *Fallna kvinnor och hållna kvinnor. Polisen och prostitutionen i Helsingfors åren 1965, 1975 och 1980–95* (Publikationer från Institutet för kvinnoforskning nr. 2), Åbo: Åbo Akademi

1990, *Prostitution i Helsingfors: en studie i kvinnokontroll*, Åbo: Åbo Akademis förlag

Jeffreys, Sheila 1997, *The Idea of Prostitution*, Melbourne: Spinifex Press

Jenness, Valerie 1993, *Making It Work: the Prostitutes' Rights Movement in Perspective*, Hawthorne, NY: Aldine de Gruyter

Jenson, Jane 1989, 'Ce n'est pas un hasard: the varieties of French feminism', in J. Howorth and G. Ross (eds.), *Contemporary France*, London: Frances Pinter, pp. 115–43

1996, 'Representations of Difference: the Varieties of French Feminism', in Threlfall (ed.), pp. 73–114

Kaplan, Gisela 1992, *Contemporary Western European Feminism*, London: UCL Press and Allen & Unwin

Kelly, Liz 1988, *Surviving Sexual Violence*, Cambridge: Polity Press

Kelly, Liz and Linda Regan 2000, 'Stopping Traffic: Exploring the Extent of, and Response to, Trafficking in Women for Sexual Exploitation in the UK', Police Research Series Paper 125, London: Home Office

Kelly, Liz, R. Wingfield and Linda Regan 1995, *Splintered Lives: Sexual Exploitation of Children in the Context of Children's Rights and Child Protection*, Ilford: Barnardo's

Kempadoo, Kamala and Jo Doezema (eds.) 1998, *Global Sex Workers: Rights, Resistance, and Redefinition*, London: Routledge

Kennedy, I. and P. Nicotri 1999, *Lucciole nere. Le prostitute nigeriane si raccontano*, Milan: Kaos

King, Gary, Robert O. Keohane and Sidney Verba 1994, *Designing Social Inquiry: Scientific Inference in Qualitative Research*, Princeton: Princeton University Press

Klein, N. 2001, *Report to the Parliamentary Committee on Trafficking In Women*, Jerusalem: The Parliament, 25 August

Klemesrud, Judy 1985, 'A Personal Crusade Against Prostitution', *New York Times*, June 24: 16:2

Köpl, Regina 1999, 'Das Ende der Bescheidenheit? – 20 Jahre institutionelle Frauenpolitik in Österreich', *Österreichische Zeitschrift für Politikwissenschaft* 1, 28: 63–74

2001, 'State Feminism and Policy Debates on Abortion in Austria', in Stetson (ed.), pp. 17–38

Kriesi, Hanspeter, Ruud Koopmans, Jan Willem Duyvendak and Mario Giugni (eds.) 1995, *New Social Movements in Western Europe*, London: UCL Press

Kugler, Iris (n.d.), 'Prostitution – ein Überblick', unpublished manuscript

Langum, David J. 1994, *Crossing over the Line: Legislating Morality and the Mann Act*, Chicago: University of Chicago Press

Larsen, E. Nicolai 1991, 'The Politics of Prostitution: a Qualitative Analysis of the Development of Bill C-49 in Four Canadian Cities', Ph.D. thesis, University of Manitoba

Larum, Kari 1998, 'Twelve Step Feminism Makes Sex Workers Sick: How the State and the Recovery Movement Turn Radical Women into Useless Citizens', in B.M. Dank (ed.) *Sex Work and Sex Workers*, New Brunswick: Transaction Press, pp. 7–36

Legardinier, Claudine 1989, 'Quand les pouvoirs publics s'en mêlent', *Prostitution et société* April/May/June: 17–21

1991, 'La presse écrite au coeur du débat', *Prostitution et société* January/February: 4–5

1997, *La prostitution*, Toulouse: Editions Milan

Levenkron, N. 2001, *Trafficking in Women in Israel: an Update Report*, Tel Aviv: Hotline for Migrant Workers

Lijphart, Arend 1971, 'Comparative Politics and Comparative Method', *American Political Science Review* 65: 682–93

1975, 'The Comparable Cases Strategy in Comparative Research', *Comparative Political Studies* 8: 481–96

Lloyd, Robin 1976, *For Money or Love: Boy Prostitution in America*, New York: Vanguard Press

Lombroso, C. and G. Ferrero [1893] 1927, *La donna delinquente, la prostituta e la donna normale*, Turin: Bocca

Louis, Marie-Victoire 1991, 'Prostitution et droits de la personne', *Cette violence dont nous voulons plus* 11–12: 3–10

1994, 'A propos des violences masculines sur les femme: ébauche d'une analyse féministe du nouveau code pénal', *Projets féministes* 3 (October): 40–69

Lovenduski, Joni 1986, *Women and European Politics: Contemporary Feminism and Public Policy*, Brighton: Wheatsheaf

1995 'An Emerging Advocate: the Equal Opportunities Commission in Great Britain', in Stetson and Mazur (eds.), pp. 114–31

Lovenduski, Joni and Pippa Norris (eds.) 1993, *Gender and Party Politics*, London: Sage

Lowman, John 1998, 'Prostitution Law Reform in Canada', http://users.uniserve. com/~lowman/ProLaw/prolawcan.htm (accessed 25 February 2002)

McAdam, Douglas, John McCarthy and Mayer N. Zald (eds.) 1996, *Comparative Perspective on Social Movements: Political Opportunities, Mobilizing Structures, and Cultural Framing*, Cambridge and New York: Cambridge University Press

McFerran, Ludo 1990, 'Interpretation of a Frontline State: Australian Women's Refuges and the State', in Watson (ed.), pp. 191–205

McGinnis, Janice Dickin 1994, 'Whores and Worthies: Feminism and Prostitution', *Canadian Journal of Law and Society* 9, 1: 105–22

Mackay, Fiona and A. Schaap 2000, 'The Local Politics of Prostitution in Two Scottish Cities', paper presented at the Joint Sessions of the European Consortium of Political Research, Copenhagen, 14–19 April

MacLaren, John 1986, 'The Fraser Committee: the Politics and Process of a Special Committee', in J. Lawman et al. *Regulating Sex: an Anthology of Commentaries on the Findings and Recommendations of the Badgley and Fraser Reports*, Vancouver: School of Criminology, Simon Fraser University, pp. 39–54

McLeod, Eileen 1982, *Women Working: Prostitution Now*, London: Croom Helm

Mafai, M. 2000, 'Riaprite quelle case', *La Repubblica*, 15 September

Mansbridge, Jane 1996, 'What is the Feminist Movement?', in M. Marx Ferree and B.B. Hess (eds.) *Feminist Organizations: Harvest of the New Women's Movements*, Philadelphia: Temple University Press, pp. 27–33

Månsson, Sven-Axel and Annulla Linders 1984, *Sexualitet utan ansikte: könsköparna*, Stockholm: Carlsson & Jönsson

Månsson, Sven-Axel and Stig Larsson 1976, *Svarta affärer: utredning om vissa klubbars och näringsställens sociala betydelse och struktur*, Malmö: Socialförvaltningen

Martirano, D. 1998, 'E la legge antipedofili rischia di slittare', *Corriere della Sera*, 29 July

Mathieu, Lilian 1999, 'Une mobilisation improbable: l'occupation de l'église Saint-Nizer par les prostituées lyonnaises', *Revue française de sociologie* 40, 3: 225–50

Matthews, Roger 1986, 'Beyond Wolfenden? Prostitution, Politics and the Law', in Roger Matthews and Jock Young (eds.) *Confronting Crime*, London: Sage Publications, pp. 188–210

Mattila, Mikko 2000, *Policy Making in Finnish Social and Health Care: a Network Approach*, Helsinki: Helsinki University Press

Mazur, Amy G. 1995, 'Strong State and Symbolic Reform in France: le Ministère des Droits de la Femme', in Stetson and Mazur (eds.), pp. 76–94

2001a, 'Drawing Lessons from the French Parity Movement', in Jocelyne Praud (ed.) *Contemporary French Civilization*, special issue, Summer/Fall: 201–20 (ed.) 2001b, *State Feminism, Women's Movements and Job Training: Making Democracies Work in a Global Economy*, New York and London: Routledge

MCCOC 1998, The Model Criminal Code Officers Committee of the Standing Committee of Attorney Generals, *Model Criminal Code Chapter 9 (Offences Against Humanity)*, http://law.gov.au/publications/Model_Criminal_Code/index.htm (accessed April 2002)

Mens, Lucie van 1992, *Prostitutie in bedrijf: organisatie, management en arbeidsverhoudingen in seksclubs en privéhuizen*, Delft: Eburon

Mensenhandel 2002, *Eerste rapportage van de Nationaal Rapporteur*, The Hague: Bureau NRM

Mény, Yves 1992, *La corruption de la république*, Paris: Editions Fayard

Merlin, L. 1989, *La mia vita*, edited by Elena Marinucci, Florence: Giunti

Minister of Justice and Attorney General of Canada 1983, 'Justice Minister Tables Pornography and Prostitution Proposals and Names Special Committee', News Release, June 23, Ottawa: Minister of Justice and Attorney General of Canada

Ministry of Justice 1984, Lausunto luonnoksesta päihdehuoltolaiksi. Diaarionumero 2800/43/84 OM. Helsinki: Oikeusministeriö

1993, *Seksuaalirikokset. Rikoslakiprojektin ehdotus.* Oikeusministeriön lainvalmisteluosaston julkaisu 8/1993. Helsinki: Hakapaino Oy

1994, Lausuntopyynnöt rikoslakiprojektin ehdotuksesta seksuaalirikoksia koskevien säännösten uudistamiseksi. Diaarionumero 862/41/80. Helsinki: Oikeusministeriö

Ministry of Welfare 1976, *The Treatment of Girls in Trouble: Report to the Knesset (Parliament) Committee for General Services.* February (in Hebrew)

Miura, Asunción 1991, 'Abolicionismo, integración y propuestas sobre la prostitución', in Forum de Política Feminista (ed.), *Prostitución: Debate y propuestas del movimiento feminista*, Madrid: Forum de Política Feminista, pp. 11–15

Molyneux, Maxine 1998, 'Analyzing Women's Movements', in Cecile Jackson and Ruth Pearson (eds.) *Feminist Visions of Development: Gender, Analysis and Policy*, London: Routledge, pp. 65–88

Montero, Justa 1986, 'Defendamos a las prostitutas, condenemos la prostitución', paper presented at the Encuentros en Carabanchel: Violencia contra las mujeres, Madrid, 22–24 January

Moroli, E. and R. Sibona 1999, *Schiave d'Occidente. Sulle rotte dei mercanti di donne*, Milan: Mursia

Murray, Alison 1998, 'Debt-Bondage and Trafficking: Don't Believe the Hype', in Kempadoo and Doezema (eds.), pp. 51–64

Murray, Ellen F. 1979, 'Anti-Prostitution Laws: New Conflicts in the Fight Against the World's Oldest Profession', *Albany Law Review* 43: 360–87

Näre, Sari 1994, 'Pornografiakeskustelusta bordellikeskusteluun. Kaupallinen seksi vietti-ja rakkauseetoksen taistelukenttänä', in Sara Heinämaa and Sari Näre (eds.) *Pahan tyttäret. Sukupuolitettu pelko, viha ja valta*, Tampere: Gaudeamus, pp. 34–65

1998, 'Seksibaarien seksuaalipolitiikkaa', in Taava Koskinen (ed.) *Kurtisaaneista kunnian naisiin. Näkökulmia Huora-akatemiasta*, Helsinki: Yliopistopaino, pp. 219–32

Näre, Sari and Jaana Lähteenmaa 1995, 'Seksityötä baarien yössä – kiista seksibaareista', in Jaana Lähteenmaa and Laura Mäkelä (eds.) *Helsingin yö*, Helsinki: Helsingin kaupungin tietokeskus, pp. 173–200

Neave, Marcia 1994, 'Prostitution Laws in Australia: Past History and Current Trends', in Roberta Perkins, Garrett Prestage, Rachel Sharp and Frances Lovejoy (eds.) *Sex Work and Sex Workers in Australia* Sydney: University of NSW Press, pp. 67–99

Newton, Michael T. and Donaghy, Peter J. 1997, *Institutions of Modern Spain: a Political and Economic Guide*, Cambridge: Cambridge University Press

Neyer, Gerda 1996, 'Korporatismus und Verbände. Garanten für die Stabilität eines sexistischen Systems?', in Teresa Kulawik and Birgit Sauer (eds.) *Der halbierte Staat. Grundlagen feministischer Politikwissenschaft*, Frankfurt am Main and New York: Campus, pp. 82–104

Nilsson, Christer and Björn Öijer 1977, 'Allt kan köpas och säljas. En granskning av prostitutionsdebatten i Studio S och dagspress vintern 1976/77', unpublished term-paper, Journalisthögskolan, Stockholm

Norris, Pippa 1987, *Politics and Sexual Equality: the Comparative Position of Women in Western Democracies*, Boulder, CO: Rienner
  1997, 'Equality Strategies and Political Representation', in Gardiner (ed.), pp. 46–59

O'Connell Davidson, Julia 1998, *Prostitution, Power and Freedom*, Cambridge: Polity Press

O'Neil, Maureen and Sharon Sutherland 1997, 'The Machinery of Women's Policy: Implementing the RCSW', in Caroline Andrew and Sanda Rodgers (eds.) *Women and the Canadian State*, Montreal: McGill-Queen's University Press, pp. 197–219

O'Neill, Maggie 1997, 'Prostitute Women Now', in Scambler and Scambler (eds.), pp. 3–28

Olga-Prostituta de Madrid 1986, 'Sobre mis experiencas y vivencias en la prostitución', in Institut Valencià de la Dona (eds.) *Debates sobre la prostitución: Valencia, 16, 17 y 18 enero de 1986*, Valencia: Institut Valencià de la Dona, pp. 75–6

Oliván, Montserrat 1986, 'Sobre la prostitución: ¿Trabajadoras del sexo?', paper presented at the Encuentros en Carabanchel: Violencia contra las mujeres, Madrid, 22–24 January

Olivero, F. 1997, *La tratta delle donne straniere immigrate in Italia*, in F. De Stoop (ed.) *Trafficanti di donne*, Turin: Ed. Gruppo Abele, pp. 157–71

On the Road 1998, *Manuale di intervento sociale nella prostituzione di strada*, Capodarco di Fermo: Comunità edizioni

Orloff, Ann Shola 1993, 'Gender and the Social Rights of Citizenship: the Comparative Analysis of Gender Relations and Welfare States', *American Sociological Review* 58: 303–28

Ostner, Ilona and Jane Lewis 1995, 'Gender and the Evolution of European Social Policies', in Stefan Leibfried and Paul Pierson (eds.) *European Social Policy: Between Fragmentation and Integration*, Washington, DC: Brookings Institution, pp. 159–93

Outshoorn, Joyce 1994, 'Between Movement and Government: "Femocrats" in the Netherlands', in Hanspeter Kriesi (ed.) *Yearbook of Swiss Political Science*, Berne, Stuttgart and Vienna: Paul Haupt Verlag, pp. 141–65

1995, 'Administrative Accommodation in the Netherlands: the Case of the Department for the Coordination of Equality Policy', in Stetson and Mazur (eds.), pp. 168–86

1998a, 'Furthering the "Cause": Femocrat Strategies in National Government', in Jet Bussemaker and Rian Voet (eds.) *Gender, Participation and Citizenship in the Netherlands*, Aldershot: Ashgate, pp. 108–22

1998b, 'Sexuality and International Commerce: the Traffic in Women and Prostitution Policy in the Netherlands', in Carver and Mottier (eds.), pp. 190–200

2001a, 'Regulating Prostitution as Sex Work', *Acta Politica* 36, 2: 155–80

2001b, 'Debating Prostitution in Parliament', *European Journal of Women's Studies* 8, 3: 473–91

Palmquist, Al 1978, *The Minnesota Connection*, New York: Warner Books

Parliamentary Law Committee minutiae 1998, Eduskunnan lakivaliokunnan pöytäkirjat 1998 valtiopäivillä. Helsinki: Eduskunta

Partit Feminista de Catalunya 1986, 'Prostitución', paper presented at the Encuentros en Carabanchel: Violencia contra las mujeres, Madrid, 22–24 January

Pateman, Carol 1988, *The Sexual Contract*, Stanford, CA: Stanford University Press

Pernthaler, Peter 1975, 'Die Zuständigkeit zur Regelung der Angelegenheiten der Prostitution', *Österreichische Juristen-Zeitung* 11: 287–93

Persson, Leif G.W. 1981, *Horor, hallickar och torskar: en bok om prostitutionen i Sverige*, Stockholm: Norstedt

Petten, Angela and Liz Jefferson 1995, 'NAC: Issues and Strengths', *Canadian Dimension* 29 May: 19–21

Pheterson, Gail 1985, *Mannenadel en Vrouweneer. Over het stigma Hoer*, The Hague: Ministerie van Sociale Zaken en Werkgelegenheid

(ed.) 1989, *A Vindication of the Rights of Whores*, Seattle: Seal Press

1996, *The Prostitution Prism*, Amsterdam: Amsterdam University Press

Phillips, Anne 1991, *Engendering Democracy*, Oxford/Cambridge: Polity Press

1995, *The Politics of Presence*, Oxford: Clarendon Press

Phoenix, Joanna 1999, *Making Sense of Prostitution*, London: Macmillan

Picq, Françoise 1993, *Les Années-Mouvement: Libération des femmes*, Paris: Seuil

Pincus, Ingrid 1998, *Från kvinnofrågor till könsmaktstruktur: den svenska jämställdhetspolitikens utveckling 1972–1997*, Örebro: Kvinnovetenskapligt forum, Högsk

Pineda, Empar 1995, 'Algunas reflexiones sobre el estado actual del feminismo en España', *Género y Sociedad* 3: 95–116

Pinot, Guy M. 1976, '*Mission d'information sur la prostitution*', Report, Mimeograph

Pitch, T. 1986, 'La sessualità, le norme, lo stato. Il dibattito sulla legge Merlin', *Memoria* 17: 24–41

1998, *Un diritto per due*, Milan: Il Saggiatore

Pitkin, Hanna Fenichel 1967, *The Concept of Representation*, Berkeley: University of California Press

Poraz, A. et al. 1998, 'Suggestions to Change the Laws of Prostitution in Israel', presented to the Knesset, 14 June

Prostituiertengewerkschaft in Österreich 1987, 'Wir haben viele Pflichten und keine Rechte', Interview mit der Wiener Vertreterin des Verbandes Manuela', *Die Linke* 10 (6 June): 11–12

Przeworski, Adam 1991, *Democracy and the Market: Political and Economic Reforms in Eastern Europe and Latin America*, Cambridge: Cambridge University Press

Pugh, Martin 2000, *Women and the Women's Movement in Britain*, New York: Palgrave

Ragin, Charles 1987, *The Comparative Method: Moving Beyond Qualitative and Quantitative Strategies*, Berkeley: University of California Press

Rankin, Pauline and Jill Vickers 2001, *Women's Movements and State Feminism: Integrating Diversity into Public Policy*, Ottawa: Status of Women Canada, http://www.swc-cfc.gc.ca-publish-research (accessed 10 May 2002)

Raymond, Janice 2001, 'Guide to the New UN Trafficking Protocol', Coalition Against Trafficking in Women, http://www.catwinternational. org/un_protocol.pdf

Refuveilles, Danièle 1991, 'La position du RPR–Secrétariat National à l'Action Féminine', *Cette violence dont nous voulons plus* 11–12: 56

Richard, Amy O'Neill 1999, 'International Trafficking in Women to the United States: a Contemporary Manifestation of Slavery and Organized Crime', November (photocopied report)

Richard, A.Q. 2000, *International Organised Crime and its Involvement in Trafficking Women and Children Abroad*, Washington, DC: US State Department, Center for the Study of Intelligence, 23 September

RNGS 2002, *'Research Network on Gender Politics and the State: Project Description'*, January

Robertson, James R. 1999, *Prostitution*, Ottawa: Library of Parliament, Parliamentary Research Branch, 82-2E

Robinson, Jean 2001, 'Gendering the Abortion Debate: the French Case', in Stetson (ed.), pp. 87–110

ROKS (Riksorganisationen für Kvinnojourer i Sverige) 2002, http://www.roks. se/index.html, 2 April

Rosen, Ruth 1982, *The Lost Sisterhood: Prostitution in America 1900–1918*, Baltimore: The Johns Hopkins University Press

Rosenberger, Sieglinde 1986, 'Frauen fordern – Männer geben (vielleicht): Gedanken zur Quotenregelung', in Anni Bell (ed.), *Furien in Uni-Form? Dokumentation der 3. österreichischen Frauensommeruniversität*, Innsbruck: Studienverlag, pp. 263–8

Rosenbleet, Charles and Barbara J. Pariente 1973, 'The Prostitution of the Criminal Law', *The American Criminal Law Review* 11: 373–427

Rosenfeld, Rachel A. and Kathryn B. Ward 1996, 'Evolution of the Contemporary US Women's Movement', in M. Dobrowski and I. Walliman (eds.) *Research in Social Movements, Conflict and Change* Vol. XIX, Greenwich CT: JAI Press, pp. 51–73

Rush, Florence 1980, *The Best Kept Secret: Sexual Abuse of Children*, Englewood Cliffs, NJ: Prentice Hall

Sainsbury, Diane (ed.) 1994, *Gendering Welfare States*, London: Sage
    1996, *Gender Equality and Welfare States*, Cambridge: Cambridge University Press

Sartori, G. 1970, 'Concept Misformation in Comparative Politics', *American Political Science Review* 74: 1033–53

Saunders, Kay 1982, *Workers in Bondage: the Origins and Bases of Unfree Labour in Queensland 1824–1916*, St Lucia: University of Queensland Press

Saunders, Kay and Ray Evans (eds.) 1992, *Gender Relations in Australia: Domination and Negotiation*, Sydney: Harcourt Brace Jovanovich

Sawer, Marian 1990, *Sisters in Suits: Women and Public Policy in Australia*, Sydney: Allen & Unwin
    1995, 'Femocrats in Glass Towers? The Office of the Status of Women in Australia', in Stetson and Mazur (eds.), pp. 22–39

Sawer, Marian and Abigail Groves 1994, *Working from Inside: Twenty Years of the Office of the Status of Women*, Canberra: Australian Government Publishing Service

Scambler, Graham and Annette Scambler (eds.) 1997, *Rethinking Prostitution*, London: Routledge

Scanlon, Geraldine M. 1990, 'El movimiento feminista en España, 1900–1985: Logros y dificultades', in Judith Astelarra (ed.) *Participación política de las mujeres*, Madrid: Centro de Investigaciones Sociológicas and Siglo XXI, pp. 83–100

Schattschneider, E.E. 1960, *The Semisovereign People: a Realist's View of Democracy in America*, New York: Holt, Rinehart & Winston

Scott, Joan W. 1986, 'Gender: a Useful Category of Analysis', *American Historical Review* 91, 5: 1053–75

Shamsullah, Ardel 1992, 'Politics in Victoria: Parliament, Cabinet and the Political Parties', in Considine and Costar (eds.), pp. 11–24

Shaver, Frances M. 1993, 'Prostitution: a Female Crime?', in Ellen Adelberg and Claudia Currie (eds.) *In Conflict with the Law: Women and the Canadian Criminal Justice System*, Vancouver: Press Gang, pp. 153–73

Sheehy, Gail 1973, *Hustling: Prostitution in Our Wide-Open Society*, New York: Delacorte Press

Shenon, Philip 2000, 'Feminist Coalition Protests US Stance on Sex Trafficking Treaty', *New York Times* 13 January: A5

Shrage, Laurie 1994, *Moral Dilemmas of Feminism: Prostitution, Adultery and Abortion*, London: Routledge

Siegmund-Ulrich, Sylvia 1994, 'Geschlechterdifferenz und Chancengleichheit', in Bundesministerium für Frauenangelegenheiten (ed.), *Frau und Recht. Dokumentation der Enquete der Bundesministerin für Frauenangelegenheiten und des Bundesministers für Justiz*, Vienna: Schriftenreihe der Frauenministerin, Bd. 4, 63–78

Signorelli, A. and M. Treppete 2001, *Services in the Window: a Manual for Interventions in the World of Migrant Prostitution*, Trieste: Asterios

Sion, A. 1977, *Prostitution and the Law*, London: Faber & Faber

Skrobanek, S., Nataya Boonpakdee and Chutima Jantareero 1997, *The Traffic in Women: Human Realities of the International Sex Trade*, London: Zed Books

Snow, David A. and Robert D. Benford 1992, 'Master Frames and Cycles of Protest', in Aldon D. Morris and Carol McClurg Mueller (eds.) *Frontiers in Social Movement Theory*, New Haven: Yale University Press, pp. 133–55

SoS-rapport 2000, *Kännedom an prostitution 1998–1999*, Stockholm: Socialstyrelsen

Soziale Absicherung 1996, *Soziale Absicherung von Prostituierten*, edited by Bundesministerin für Frauenangelegenheiten, Vienna: Bundesministerium für Frauenangelegenheiten

Soziale Aspekte 1996, *Soziale Aspekte der Lebenssituation von Prostituierten*, edited by Bundesministerin für Frauenangelegenheiten, Vienna: Bundesministerium für Frauenangelegenheiten

Stahl, A. 1978, 'Prostitution of Young Immigrants in Israel', *Megamot* 24, 4: 202–25

Standing Committee on Justice and the Solicitor General 1990, *Minutes of Proceedings and Evidence* (Review of Section 213 of the Criminal Code), Issue No. 42, Ottawa: House of Commons

Status of Women Canada 2000, 'Women's Program Funding Guidelines: Areas of Focus of the Women's Program', Status of Women Canada homepage, available at http://www.scw-cfc.gc.ca/wmnprog/guidtx2e.htm (accessed 2 February 2000)

Stephenson, M. 1998, *The Glass Trapdoor: Women, Politics and the Media during the 1997 General Election*, London: Fawcett

Stetson, Dorothy McBride (ed.) 2001a, *Abortion Politics, Women's Movements and the Democratic State: a Comparative Study of State Feminism*, New York: Oxford University Press

2001b, 'Federal and State Women's Policy Agencies Help to Represent Women in the United States', in Mazur (ed.), pp. 271–92

2001c, 'US Abortion Debates 1959–1998: the Women's Movement Holds On', in Stetson (ed.), pp. 247–66

Stetson, Dorothy McBride and Amy Mazur (eds.) 1995, *Comparative State Feminism*, London, Thousand Oaks and New Delhi: Sage

2002, 'Defining Women's Movements Cross-Nationally and Over Time: Lessons from the Project of the Research Network on Gender, Politics and the State', paper presented at the Canadian Political Science Association Annual Meeting, Toronto, 29–31 May

Stockinger, Michael 2001, 'Menschenhandel und Prostitution', in *Zebratl Informationsblatt des Vereins Zebra*, H. 4, S. 6–10

Stokes, Wendy 2002, 'The Government of the United Kingdom: the Women's National Commission', in Shirin Rai (ed.) *Mainstreaming Gender, Democratizating the State? International Mechanisms for the Advancement of Women*, Manchester: Manchester University Press

Sullivan, Barbara 1994, 'Contemporary Australian Feminism: a Critical Review', in G. Stokes (ed.) *Australian Political Ideas*, Kensington: University of New South Wales Press, pp. 152–67

1995, 'Commercial Sex and the Law: a Case for Decriminalisation', *Social Alternatives* 14, 3: 23–6

1997, *The Politics of Sex: Prostitution and Pornography in Australia since 1945*, Melbourne: Cambridge University Press

1999, 'Prostitution Law Reform in Australia: a Preliminary Evaluation', *Social Alternatives* 18, 3: 9–14

2001, '"It's All in the Contract": Rethinking Feminist Approaches to Contract', *Law and Context* 18, 2: 112–28

2003, 'Trafficking in Women: Feminism and New International Law', *International Feminist Journal of Politics* 5, 1: 67–91

Svanström, Yvonne 2000, *Policing Public Women: the Regulation of Prostitution in Stockholm 1812–1880*, Stockholm: Atlas/Akademi

Symanski, Richard 1985, *The Immoral Landscape: Female Prostitution in Western Societies*, Toronto: Butterworths

Tálos, Emmerich 1997, 'Sozialpartnerschaft. Kooperation – Konzertierung – politische Regulierung', in Herbert Dachs, Peter Gerlich, Herbert Gottweis, et al. (eds.) *Handbuch des politischen Systems Österreichs. Die Zweite Republik*, Vienna: Manz, pp. 432–51

Tarrow, Sydney 1998, *Power in Movement: Social Movements, Collective Action and Politics*, New York and Cambridge: Cambridge University Press

Tatafiore, R. 1994, *Sesso al lavoro*, Milan: Il Saggiatore

Tene, P. 1986, *'Lins in Trouble' – Treatment Considerations*, Akademai: Hebrew University (in Hebrew)

Teodori, M.A. 1986, *Lucciole in lotta. La prostituzione come lavoro*, n. p.: Sapere

Thomsson, Ulrika 2000, 'Rätten till våra kroppar. Kvinnorörelsen och våldtäktsdebatten', *Kvinnovetenskaplig tidskrift* 4: 51–63

Threlfall, Monica 1985, 'The Women's Movement in Spain', *New Left Review*, 151: 44–73

1996a, 'Feminist Politics and Social Change in Spain', in Threlfall (ed.), pp. 115–51

(ed.) 1996b, *Feminist Politics and Social Transformation in the North*, London and New York: Verso

1998, 'State Feminism or Party Feminism? Feminist Politics and the Spanish Institute of Women', *The European Journal of Women's Studies* 5, 1: 69–93

Toth, Birgit 1997, 'Die Prostitutionsgesetze der Länder. Kompetenz – Systematik – Grundrechte', Ph.D. thesis, University of Vienna

Truong, Thanh-Dam 1990, *Sex, Money and Morality: the Political Economy of Prostitution and Tourism in South East Asia*, London: Zed Books

Ulmanen, Petra 1998, *(s)veket mot kvinnorna och hur högern stal feminismen*, Stockholm: Atlas

United Nations (UN) 1993, *Directory of National Machinery for the Advancement of Women*, Vienna: Division for the Advancement of Women

1999 *Global Programme against Trafficking in Human Beings*, Vienna: United Nations Office for Drug Control and Crime Prevention

United Nations 2000, *Protocol to Prevent, Suppress and Punish Trafficking in Persons, Especially Women and Children, Supplementing the United Nations Convention Against Transnational Organized Crime*

US Department of Justice 1986, *Attorney General's Commission on Pornography: Final Report*. Washington, D.C., July

US State Department 2000, *Victims of Trafficking and Violence Protection Act*

US State Department 2001, *Trafficking in Persons Report 2001-Israel*, (tier 3), Washington, D.C.: US State Department

Valiente, Celia 1995, 'The Power of Persuasion: the *Instituto de la Mujer* in Spain', in Stetson and Mazur (eds.), pp. 221–36

1997, 'State Feminism and Gender Equality Policies: the Case of Spain (1983–95)', in Gardiner (ed.), pp. 127–41

2001a, 'Gendering Abortion Debates: State Feminism in Spain', in Stetson (ed.), pp. 229–45

2001b, 'Job Training Debates in Spain: a Closed Gender-Neutral Policy System and Distant Feminist Demands Block Women-Friendly Outcomes', in Mazur (ed.), pp. 111–30

Vandenberg, M. 1997, *Trafficking in Women to Israel and Forced Prostitution*, Jerusalem: Israel Women's Network

Vanwesenbeeck, Wilhelmina M.A. 1986, *'Wiens lijf eigenlijk?'. Een onderzoek naar dwang en geweld in de prostitutie*, The Hague: Ministerie van Sociale Zaken en Werkgelegenheid

Varsa, Hannele 1986, *Prostituution näkymätön osa: miesasiakkaat: lehti-ilmoitteluprostituution asiakkaista*, Helsinki: Tasa-arvoasiain neuvottelukunta (Naistutkimusmonisteita 5/1986)

Verbeek, Hansje 1996, *Goede bedoelingen. Zaakwaarnemers in een hoerenorganisatie*, Amsterdam: Het Spinhuis

Vickers, Jill, Pauline Rankin and Christine Appelle 1993, *Politics as if Women Mattered: a Political Analysis of the National Action Committee on the Status of Women*, Toronto: University of Toronto Press

Victoria 1985, *Inquiry into Prostitution: Final Report* (Neave Report). Melbourne

Vries, Petra de 1997, *Kuisheid voor mannen, vrijheid voor vrouwen. De reglementering en bestrijding van prostitutie in Nederland, 1850–1911*, Hilversum: Verloren

Walkowitz, Judith 1980a, 'The Politics of Prostitution', *Signs* 6, 1: 123–35

Walkowitz, Judith R. 1980b, *Prostitution and Victorian Society: Women, Class and the State*, Cambridge: Cambridge University Press

Wandling, Therese 1976, 'Decriminalization of Prostitution', *Oregon Law Review* 55: 553–66

Watson, Sophie (ed.) 1990, *Playing the State: Australian Feminist Interventions*, London: Verso

Weitzer, Ronald 1991, 'Prostitutes' Rights in the United States: the Failure of a Movement', *Sociological Quarterly* 32, 1: 23–41

1999, 'Prostitution Control in America: Rethinking Public Policy,' *Crime, Law & Social Change* 32: 83–102

2000, 'The Politics of Prostitution in America', in R. Weitzer (ed.) *Sex for Sale: Prostitution, Pornography, and the Sex Industry*, New York and London: Routledge, pp. 159–80

West, Jackie 2000, 'Prostitution: Collectives and the Politics of Regulation', *Gender, Work and Organization* 7, 2: 106–18

Wijers, M. and Lap-Chew, L. 1997, *Trafficking in Women: Forced Labour and Slavery-like Practices in Marriage, Domestic Labour and Prostitution*, Utrecht: STV

Wijers, Marjan 2001, 'European Union Policies on Trafficking in Women', in Mariagrazia Rossilli (ed.) *Gender Policies in the European Union*, New York: Peter Lang, pp. 209–29

Wolfenden, T. et al. 1957, *Report of the Committee on Homosexual Offences and Prostitution*, London: HMSO

Women and Equality Unit 2001, 'Living Without Fear', available at http://www.cabinet-office.gov.uk/womens-unit/living_without_fear/images/10.htm

Women's Unit 1998, *Delivering for Women: the Progress So Far*, available at http://www.womenandequalityunit.gov.uk

Young, Becki 1998, 'Trafficking of Humans across United States Borders: How United States Laws Can be Used to Punish Traffickers and Protect Victims', *Georgetown Immigration Law Journal* 13, 1: 73–104

Zatz, Noah 1997, 'Sex Work/Sex Act: Law, Labor and Desire in Constructions of Prostitution', *Signs* 20, 2: 227–309

Index

NOTE: page numbers in *italic* type refer to figures, tables and appendices